# HSK 核心词汇天天学

## ONE HOUR PER DAY
## TO A POWERFUL HSK VOCABULARY

# 中册
## VOLUME 2

刘东青 马玉红 王 鑫

编著

华语教学出版社
SINOLINGUA

First Edition    2009

ISBN 978-7-80200-595-2
Copyright 2009 by Sinolingua
Published by Sinolingua
24 Baiwanzhuang Road, Beijing 100037, China
Tel: (86) 10-68320585
Fax: (86) 10-68326333
E-mail: hyjx@sinolingua.com.cn
Printed by Beijing Foreign Languages Printing House

*Printed in the People's Republic of China*

# 致学习者

　　本套书是为海外 HSK 考生及同等水平的学生编写的词汇学习用书。

　　通过使用本书，学生可以在一年内系统掌握 3000 个核心词汇。通过书中的用法示例和丰富习题，可以全面提高汉语词汇的运用能力和 HSK 考试的应试能力。本书有如下特点：

　　系统的学习计划——本书安排了为期一年的学习内容：每天学习 12 个词汇、5天的词汇学习加"周练习"构成 1 周的学习内容；每个月包括 4 周，每册书包括 4 个月，3 册书共一年的学习内容，希望能帮助学习者在一年之内掌握这 3000 个词汇及示例、习题等拓展内容，达到 HSK 中级以上的要求。

　　合理的内容编排——每天学习的词汇由易到难、有难有易。每天的学习内容都包括一定比例的甲级词、乙级词、丙级词和丁级词，随着学习的深入，甲级词和乙级词会越来越少，丙级词和丁级词会越来越多。除词汇的常规项目外，本书还归纳了一些词汇的专项内容，如量词、关联词、尾词等，并配有相应的练习。

　　多样的学习板块——每天的学习项目包括词语、读音、词义、该词的同义词或反义词、常用搭配、用法示例、词义辨析以及多种形式的练习。尽管每个词的内容都十分全面，但经过作者的巧妙编排和多样的学习板块，学生能在 1 小时内轻松掌握 1 天的全部学习内容。

　　经典的语言材料——掌握词汇重在掌握其用法。本书提供了丰富、经典的例句和固定搭配，注重体现词汇的用法和 HSK 考试的重点和难点。

　　详细的英文注释——在词义、常用搭配、用法示例、词义辨析等板块均有详细的英语注释，以确保大家能够准确理解。

# To the Reader

This series of textbooks contains a list of HSK words for foreign students to study and learn in preparation for the HSK.

Through the use of these textbooks, students should be able to master 3,000 words within one year. These textbooks contain many examples and exercises, which will improve students' Chinese, and ability to complete the HSK successfully.

These books have the following features:

Systematic learning program — The one-year study plan consists of three textbooks, with each book containing four months worth of study. A month of study is made up of four weeks, and each week is composed of five days of studying 12 words a day, with added 'weekly practice' sessions. This schedule will help students master the 3,000 words within one year, and will also allow them to fulfill the requirements for the intermediate level of HSK and above.

Methodical arrangement of content — The words to be studied daily range from the simple to the complex, and become more difficult as study progresses. Different levels of HSK words (e.g. A-level words, B-level, C-level, D-level) are included in the study. As students move forward, A-level and B-level words will appear less as they are replaced with more C-level and D-level ones. As well as this efficient method of studying vocabulary, these books also have added classifications and exercises for measure words, conjunctions and suffixes.

Diversity of study materials — Each daily study plan includes words and expressions, pronunciation, word definitions, synonyms and antonyms, commonly used collocations, examples of usage, as well as exercises. Despite the comprehensive coverage of each word, students can easily complete a whole day's content within one hour, due to the author's ingenious arrangement of the diverse study materials.

Typical language materials — This textbook series includes rich and illustrative sentences and allocations, and pays great attention to the usage of words, in order to help the students to learn the words and their practical applications. It also details the key or difficult points of the HSK test.

Detailed English annotations — Detailed annotations in English are given to multiple word definitions, collocations, and examples of usage, to ensure that students will understand the concise and correct meanings and usages.

# 5月 第1周的学习内容

**星期一**

xiǎng
**响** （甲）形／动

① loud ② to make a sound

**常用搭配**

声音太响了。
The sound is too loud.
电话铃响了。
The telephone is ringing.

**用法示例**

爆炸声很响，所以她用手捂着耳朵。
The exploding noise was so loud that she covered her ears with her hands.
她被很响的关门声吵醒了。
She was awakened by a loud bang.
你能听到晨钟响吗？
Can you hear the morning bell ringing?

men
**们** （甲）尾

plural marker for pronouns and a few animate nouns

**常用搭配**

我们 we, us　孩子们 children　朋友们 friends

**用法示例**

女士们，先生们：上午好！
Ladies and Gentlemen: Good morning!

chéngwéi
**成为** （乙）动

become

**常用搭配**

成为朋友 become friends　成为钢琴家 become a pianist

**用法示例**

毕业以后，她成为了一名医生。
She became a doctor after graduation.
他的梦想是将来成为一名工程师。
His dream is to become an engineer.
想外出度假时，宠物会成为累赘。
Pets can be a burden when you want to go away on holiday.

fènnù
**愤怒** 圓 气愤 （乙）形
　　　　　　qìfèn

angry；indignant

**常用搭配**

愤怒的人群 an angry crowd
激起人民的愤怒 provoke the wrath of people
对某事感到愤怒 be indignant at sth.

**用法示例**

母亲因我撒谎而愤怒。
My mother was wrathful with my lying.
我非常愤怒，因为我觉得对我的惩罚是不公平的。
I was indignant because I felt that I had been punished unfairly.
愤怒的乘客们把那个扒手痛打了一顿。
The indignant passengers beat the pickpocket up.

rénzào　　　　　　　　　　tiānrán
**人造** 囻 天然 （乙）形

man-made；artificial

**常用搭配**

人造革 artificial leather　人造材料 man-made material

**用法示例**

他们成功地发射了一颗人造卫星。
They have launched a man-made satellite successfully.
这件衣服是人造纤维的。
This dress is made of artificial fibers.

tōutōu　　　　　　　　　　qiāoqiāo
**偷偷** 圓 悄悄 （乙）副

stealthily；secretly

**常用搭配**

偷偷看一眼 a furtive glance

**用法示例**

窃贼偷偷地进入了那所房子。
The burglars had entered the house by stealth.
这孩子偷偷摸摸地溜出了屋子，向游泳池走去。
The boy slipped out of the room and headed for the swimming pool.
那两个情人偷偷地会面。
The two lovers had met by stealth.

chéngyǔ
**成语** （丙）名

idiom

**常用搭配**

成语故事 stories about idioms

**用法示例**

成语通常不能照字面译成另一种语言。
Idioms usually cannot be translated literally into another language.

据我所知,英文里并没有这样的成语。
To my knowledge, there is no such idiom in English.
我要不时地给你们介绍一些成语。
I'll introduce you to some more idioms from time to time.

## 人为 rénwéi （丁）形

artificial; man-induced

**常用搭配**

人为的障碍 artificial barriers
人为的矛盾 an artificial conflict

**用法示例**

这次事故是人为过失造成的。
The accident was caused by human error.
在男女平等的问题上,我们应尽快消除人为的障碍。
We should get rid of the artificial barriers in the issue of equality between the sexes as soon as possible.

## 响亮 xiǎngliàng 反 低沉 dīchén （丙）形

① loud and clear ② resounding

**常用搭配**

一个响亮的名字 a resounding name

**用法示例**

元音比辅音响亮。
Vowels possess greater sonority than consonants.
他吹了一声响亮的口哨。
He gave a loud whistle.
他回答得十分响亮。
He answered loudly and clearly.

## 悄悄 qiāoqiāo （乙）副

quietly

**常用搭配**

悄悄地离开 leave quietly    悄悄地说 whisper

**用法示例**

豹子悄悄地接近一只鹿。
The leopard quietly stalked the deer.
他悄悄地走进房间。
He came into to room very quietly.
她悄悄告诉了我这个消息。
She whispered the news in my ear.

## 清理 qīnglǐ （丁）动

clear; put in order

**常用搭配**

清理垃圾 clear off the rubbish
清理卫生间 clean up the bathroom

**用法示例**

你应该经常清理卫生间。
You should frequently clean up the bathroom.

他的秘书帮他清理办公桌。
His secretary helps him clear his office desk.
把厨房里所有的垃圾清理掉。
Clear all the rubbish out of the kitchen.

## 暗示 ànshì （丁）动

hint; drop a hint

**常用搭配**

暗示某人 give sb. a hint    用眼神暗示 hint with one's eyes

**用法示例**

当她说她累了时,是暗示她想让我们走。
When she said she was tired, it was a hint that she wanted us to go.
他暗示说他正在找另一份工作。
He hinted that he was looking for another job.
我不停地暗示,但他还是不懂。
I kept dropping hints but he still didn't understand.

 词义辨析

**响、响亮**

1、"响"和"响亮"都可以用作形容词,是声音大的意思。但是"响亮"往往含有褒义,声音高亢而清晰;而"响"是中性词。如:①她唱歌的时候声音非常响亮。②电视声音太响了,把音量调低点儿。

As adjectives, both 响 and 响亮 mean "loud". But 响亮 usually has commendatory sense, meaning the sound is clear, resounding and sonorous; while 响 is neutral. For example: ① Her voice is very sonorous when she sings. ② The television is too loud; turn the volume down.

2、"响"和"响亮"都可以用作谓语和补语,但"响"是单音节词,"响亮"是双音节词,所以很多情况下不能相互替换。"响亮"还可以直接作定语和状语,"响"则不能作状语,作定语也要加"很"等副词。如:①这种鞭炮不太响。②响亮的声音。③响亮地回答。

Both 响 and 响亮 can function as a predicate or a complement, but 响 is monosyllabic and 响亮 is disyllabic, so they are not interchangeable in most cases. And 响亮 can function as an attributive and an adverbial; while 响 can not function as an adverbial, and as an attributive it must take an adverb, such as "很". For example: ① This kind of firework is not very loud. ② sonorous voice ③ answered loudly

 练习

**练习一、根据拼音写汉字，根据汉字写拼音**
fèn（　）（　）liàng（　）lǐ（　）shì chéng（　）
（　）怒　响（　）清（　）暗（　）（　）为

**练习二、搭配连线**
(1) 成为　　　　　　　　　A. 障碍
(2) 成语　　　　　　　　　B. 纤维
(3) 清理　　　　　　　　　C. 故事
(4) 人为　　　　　　　　　D. 朋友
(5) 人造　　　　　　　　　E. 垃圾

**练习三、从今天学习的生词中选择合适的词填空**
1. 怎样才能 _____ 一名优秀的作家？
2. 现在科技很发达，很多东西不是天然的，而是 _____ 的。
3. 服务员把桌子上的东西都 _____ 干净了。
4. 很多事故是 _____ 因素造成的，如果司机加强安全意识，事故是可以避免的。
5. 趁老师不注意，他 _____ 地溜出了教室。
6. 她 _____ 地告诉我，孩子们都睡着了。
7. _____ 让她失去了理智，她冲上去给了他一巴掌。
8. 到现在，我们已经学了很多 _____，比如：画蛇添足、自相矛盾等等。
9. 除夕晚上，炮竹劈劈啪啪地 _____ 了一夜。
10. 我问他怕不怕，他 _____ 地回答，"不怕"。

🔑 **答案**

**练习一：**
略
**练习二：**
(1) D　　　(2) C　　　(3) E　　　(4) A　　　(5) B
**练习三：**
1. 成为　　2. 人造　　3. 清理　　4. 人为　　5. 偷偷
6. 悄悄　　7. 愤怒　　8. 成语　　9. 响　　10. 响亮

 星期二

jiā
**家**　　　　　　　　　　　　　（甲）量／尾
① measure word for families or enterprises. ② a noun suffix, like: -ist, -ian
【常用搭配】
一家公司 a company　　　一家旅馆 a hotel
科学家 scientist　　　　　音乐家 musician
【用法示例】
我们学校附近有一家大型超市。
There is a large supermarket near our school.
他在一家运输公司工作。
He is working in a shipping company.
他想将来要成为一个伟大的艺术家。
He wants to be a great artist in the future.
他是当代最伟大的钢琴家之一。
He is one of the greatest pianists in the contemporary era.

zhèngdàng
**正当**　　🔁 合理　　　　　　（丙）形
reasonable; just
【常用搭配】
正当的要求 a just claim　　正当的理由 a reasonable excuse
【用法示例】
你的意见必须通过正当途径投诉。
Your complaint must be made through proper channels.
那个警察枪击罪犯是正当防卫。
The policeman was justified in shooting the criminal in self-defense.

zhuǎn
**转**　　　　　　　　　　　　　（乙）动
turn; revolve
【常用搭配】
向右转 turn right　　转动的轮子 rotating wheels
【用法示例】
在拐角处向左转。
Turn left at the corner.
发动机转了一圈，但没有起动。
The engine turned over but wouldn't start.
地球绕太阳转。
The earth revolves round the sun.

pèihé
**配合**　　　　　　　　　　　　（乙）动
① coordinate with ② act in concert with
【常用搭配】
互相配合 coordinate with each other

**用法示例**

我们与警方配合进行工作。
We are working in conjunction with the police.
我将会配合他完成任务。
I will coordinate with him to complete the task.

lìzi
**例子** （乙）名

instance; example

**常用搭配**

典型例子 a typical example
举例子 quote an example

**用法示例**

这只是许多例子中的一个。
This is only one instance out of many.
即使绞尽脑汁,他还是连一个例子也想不出来。
Even after racking his brains he couldn't think of a single example.
你能给我举一个例子吗?
Can you quote me an instance?

àn
**暗** （乙）形

dark; secret

**常用搭配**

一条暗道 a secret way
光线太暗。 The light is too dark.

**用法示例**

暴风雨来临时,天空转暗。
The sky turned dark as the storm neared.
这幅画色彩太暗。
There is too much dark in this painting.
他是从一个暗门逃走的。
He escaped through a secret door.

ànàn
**暗暗** （丁）副

secretly; inwardly

**常用搭配**

暗暗思考 think inwardly
暗暗下决心 make up one's mind secretly

**用法示例**

他看报时暗暗发笑。
He chuckled to himself as he read the newspaper.
警察一直在暗暗地跟踪他。
The police have been tailing him secretly.

zhèndòng
**震动** （丙）动

shock; quake

**常用搭配**

大地在他的脚下震动。 The ground quaked under his feet.
减小震动 decrease vibration

**用法示例**

火车一经过,整座房子都震动。
The whole house vibrates when a train passes.
缓冲器使震动减少了许多。
Buffers absorbed most of the shock.
消息传来,引起了震动。
The news came as a jolt.

pèifu                          bǐshì
**佩服**          ⊗ 鄙视          （丙）动

admire

**常用搭配**

我很佩服他。 I admire him greatly.
佩服他的勇气 admire him for his courage

**用法示例**

我佩服他的口才。
I admire him for his eloquence.
有的人对他很佩服,而有的人则认为他是骗子。
Some people admired him greatly while others considered him a cheat.
人人都佩服他的幽默感。
Everybody admires him for his sense of humor.

zhuàn
**赚** （丙）动

earn; make a profit

**常用搭配**

赚钱 earn money

**用法示例**

这个月他已经赚了好多钱了。
He has earned a lot of money this month.
我把赚的钱都花光了。
I've spent all my earnings.
为了赚到更多的钱,他工作到深夜。
In order to earn more money, he worked late into the night.

zhèngcháng                     fǎncháng
**正常**          ⊗ 反常          （乙）形

normal

**常用搭配**

正常状态 normal state    恢复正常 return to normal

**用法示例**

一切都非常正常。
Everything is absolutely normal.
我们现在中断正常节目,播送一则特别新闻。
We now interrupt our normal transmission to bring you a special news bulletin.
我们认为这样的不正常现象不会持续很久。
We do not think such an abnormal phenomenon will last long.

zhènjīng                        jīngyà
**震惊**          ⊜ 惊讶          （丁）动

shock; astonish

**常用搭配**

感到震惊 feel shocked    令人震惊的消息 shocking news

**用法示例**

我们对他的死都感到十分震惊。

His death was a great shock to us all.

总之,他的行为是令人震惊的。

His behavior was, in a word, shocking.

这则消息震惊了每一个人。

The news astonished everybody.

lìwài

# 例外                                           (丁)动

exception

**常用搭配**

毫无例外 without exception

把……作为例外 make an exception of

**用法示例**

这条语法规则有个例外。

There is an exception to this grammatical rule.

富有的人需要爱,贫穷的人也不例外。

The rich need love and the poor are no exception.

所有的学生都要毫无例外地参加考试。

All students without exception must take the examination.

 **词义辨析**

**暗、暗暗**

1、"暗"和"暗暗"都可以表示不动声色,尽量不让别人知道的意思。但"暗"是单音节词,往往修饰单音节动词,"暗暗"是双音节词,往往修饰双音节动词,所以很多情况下不能相互替换。如:暗想,暗暗思考,暗笑,暗暗发笑等。

Both 暗 and 暗暗 mean "in a hidden or confidential manner", "not expressed; inward". But 暗 is a monosyllabic word that modifies a monosyllabic verb, and 暗暗 is a disyllabic word that modifies a disyllabic verb, so they are not interchangeable in most cases. For example: 暗想 (to think inwardly), 暗暗思考 (to think inwardly), 暗笑 (to laugh inwardly), 暗暗发笑 (to laugh inwardly).

2、"暗"是形容词,常作定语或谓语,表示光线弱或颜色浓重等;"暗暗"是副词,用于修饰动词,常常加助词"地",作状语。如:①剧场的灯光很暗。②他暗暗地下决心一定要离开这里。

暗 is an adjective, which functions as an attributive or a predicate, meaning "dark, dim or deep in color";暗暗 is an adverb, which modifies verbs and can take 地 after it, usually functioning as an adverbial. For example: ① The light in the theatre is very dim. ② He inwardly made up his mind to leave here.

 **练习**

**练习一、根据拼音写汉字,根据汉字写拼音**

pèi (  )   pèi (  )   (  )wài   (  )jīng   (  )cháng
(  )合   (  )服   例(  )   震(  )   正(  )

**练习二、搭配连线**

(1) 正当          A. 正常
(2) 互相          B. 例子
(3) 恢复          C. 震惊
(4) 感到          D. 配合
(5) 典型          E. 要求

**练习三、从今天学习的生词中选择合适的词填空**

1. 我的电风扇坏了,插上电,也不_____。

2. 听说公司在这个项目上_____了很多钱。

3. 这个房间在阴面儿,光线不好,有点_____。

4. 他_____地下决心,下次考试一定要超过她。

5. 这件事使他的心灵受到了_____,他开始重新考虑生命的意义。

6. 这个明星自杀了,大家感到很_____。

7. 这个要求很_____,一点也不过分。

8. 他的体温很_____,没有发烧。

9. 警察问凶手一些细节问题,可他很不_____。

10. 我很_____她的毅力和勇气,她简直太优秀了。

 **答案**

**练习一:**

略

**练习二:**

(1)E    (2)D    (3)A    (4)C    (5)B

**练习三:**

1. 转    2. 赚    3. 暗    4. 暗暗    5. 震动
6. 震惊    7. 正当    8. 正常    9. 配合    10. 佩服

**星期三**

yánjiū
## 研究 （甲）动
research

**常用搭配**
科学研究 scientific research　研究人员 researcher
研究历史 make a study of history

**用法示例**
他仔细地研究了这些资料。
He carefully researched this reference data.
会议将研究一些重要事情。
Some important things will be discussed at the meeting.
研究表明,男人比女人更容易戒烟。
Research indicates that men find it easier to give up smoking than women.

zǔguó
## 祖国 （甲）名
motherland; homeland

**常用搭配**
想念祖国 miss one's homeland
热爱祖国 love one's mother-country

**用法示例**
我爱我的祖国。
I love my motherland.
士兵们宣誓效忠于他们的祖国。
The soldiers swore allegiance to their motherland.
他们齐心协力为祖国战斗。
They fought for their motherland shoulder to shoulder.

zuānyán
## 钻研 （乙）动
research; study intensively

**常用搭配**
钻研业务 to study one's work intensively
刻苦钻研 to research assiduously

**用法示例**
他仍然钻研他的生物学。
He still worked at his biology.
他在埋头钻研中国文学史。
He is taking a dive into the history of Chinese literature.

yuán
## 员 （乙）名／尾
① member; person; employee ② suffix (in nouns)

**常用搭配**
运动员 athlete　打字员 typist　演员 actor
服务员 waiter　邮递员 postman　售票员 conductor

**用法示例**
我们的俱乐部是足球联合会的一员。
Our club is a member of the Football League.
几乎所有的成员都同意这项提议。
Virtually all the members were in agreement with the proposal.
他哥哥是国家足球队的队员。
His brother is a member of national football team.

pīnmìng
## 拼命 （乙）副／动
① desperately ② exert the utmost strength; be ready to risk one's life

**常用搭配**
拼命喊 cry desperately　拼命跑 run with all one's efforts

**用法示例**
他拼命地打熊的眼睛。
He exerted the utmost strength to beat the eyes of the bear.
他拼命想得到这个机会。
He was desperate to get the chance.
他拼命在她的书桌里搜寻那封信。
He was rifling through her desk in a desperate search for the letter.

kěài　　　　　　　　　　kěwù
## 可爱　　反 可恶 （乙）形
lovely; cute

**常用搭配**
可爱的孩子 lovely child

**用法示例**
我的小女儿像天使一样可爱。
My little daughter is as lovely as an angel.
我姐姐的小孩儿非常可爱。
My sister's infant is very lovely.
多么可爱的小猫呀!
What a cute kitten!

zhēnxī　　　　　　　　　làngfèi
## 珍惜　　反 浪费 （丙）动
to treasure; to value; to cherish

**常用搭配**
珍惜时间 cherish time　珍惜粮食 treasure food

**用法示例**
我们将珍惜这次宝贵的学习机会。
We will value this precious learning opportunity.
我非常珍惜咱们的友谊。
I treasure our friendship very much.
把好的食物扔掉是浪费。我们要珍惜粮食。
It is a waste to throw away good food. We should treasure food.

pǐn
## 品 （丁）动／尾
① taste ② suffix (in nouns)

**常用搭配**

品茶 taste tea　　样品 sample　　食品 food

日用品 articles of daily use　　贵重物品 valuable article

**用法示例**

品一口酒。

Have a taste of the wine.

我们决定为新产品做广告。

We decided to advertise our new product.

这个妇女买了些小商品。

The woman bought a few small articles.

### 可惜 kěxī　　回 惋惜 wǎnxī　　（丙）形

pity

**常用搭配**

真可惜！ What a pity!　　感到可惜 feel pity

**用法示例**

可惜,他不能来参加聚会。

It's a pity that he can't come to the party.

你今晚不能和我们一起去看戏,真可惜。

What a pity that you can't come to the theatre with us tonight.

真可惜,两个音乐会时间上有冲突,我本来想两个都去。

It's a pity the two concerts clash; I wanted to go to both of them.

### 恰恰 qiàqià　　回 恰巧 qiàqiǎo　　（丙）副

just

**常用搭配**

恰恰相反 exactly contrary

**用法示例**

那恰恰是我想要的。

That is just what I want.

我没有病;恰恰相反,我很健康。

I'm not sick; on the contrary, I'm quiet healthy.

他考试及格了,和他预料的情况恰恰相反。

He passed the exam, contrary to what he had expected.

### 连连 liánlián　　（丁）副

again and again; repeatedly

**常用搭配**

连连点头 nod repeatedly

**用法示例**

她连连点头表示同意我的意见。

She nodded repeatedly to show that she agreed with me.

他连连道谢。

He expressed his thanks again and again.

我们试了很多次,却连连失败。

We have tried many times, but we have failed again and again.

### 租金 zūjīn　　（丁）名

rent

**常用搭配**

交租金 pay rent

**用法示例**

他们把房子租给我,每月租金 500 元。

They let the house to me at a rent of 500 yuan a month.

租金是贵,但是房子很好。

The rent is high, but otherwise the house is fine.

我的房东要把月租金提高 50 块钱。

My landlord wanted to put the rent up by 50 yuan a month.

 词义辨析

**研究、钻研**

　　"研究"和"钻研"是动词,都有思考、探索的意思。"研究"指仔细分析、探索,也有进行商量、讨论的意思,其对象常常是工作、学习中的问题;"钻研"是指更为深入地研究,其对象一般与学术有关,如科学、技术、文化等。例如:①我们将在下周开会研究工作计划。②他一直在钻研物理学。

　　Both 研究 and 钻研 are verbs, meaning "to study or research". 研究 indicates "to analyze carefully or do research on something", "to discuss or talk about something", the objects of it are usually things about work or study in our daily life; while 钻研 means "to study deeply and intensively", the object of study is usually something academic, such as science, technique, culture, and so on. For example: ① We will hold a meeting to discuss a working plan.　② He has been studying physics.

 **练习**

**练习一、根据拼音写汉字，根据汉字写拼音**
( )yán ( )xī pīn( ) ( )jīn ( )guó
钻( ) 珍( ) ( )命 租( ) 祖( )

**练习二、搭配连线**
(1) 钻研　　　　　　　　A. 相反
(2) 珍惜　　　　　　　　B. 业务
(3) 热爱　　　　　　　　C. 研究
(4) 恰恰　　　　　　　　D. 祖国
(5) 科学　　　　　　　　E. 时光

**练习三、从今天学习的生词中选择合适的词填空**
1. 他刻苦 _____，终于成了有名的外科大夫。
2. 科学家正在 _____ 一种治疗艾滋病的新方法。
3. 我的姐姐是公司职 _____，妹妹是饭店的服务 _____，哥哥则是一名运动 _____。
4. 我梦到有一个人拿着刀追我，吓得我 _____ 地跑。
5. 你一定要 _____ 这次出国留学的机会，努力提高自己的外语水平。
6. 因为自己的粗心，错过了一次好机会，真 _____。
7. 领导谈了自己的看法，下边的人 _____ 表示赞成。
8. 我的观点 _____ 与你相反。
9. 我对这套房子很满意，可是 _____ 比较高。
10. 奶奶家有一只 _____ 的小花猫，我特别喜欢逗它玩。

**答案**

练习一：
略
练习二：
(1) B　　(2)E　　(3)D　　(4)A　　(5)C
练习三：
1. 钻研　2. 研究　3. 员　4. 拼命　5. 珍惜
6. 可惜　7. 连连　8. 恰恰　9. 租金　10. 可爱

---

 **星期四**

**yánsè**
**颜色** （甲）名
color

**常用搭配**
什么颜色 What color...　鲜艳的颜色 bright color

**用法示例**
我丈夫有好几件颜色不同的衬衫。
My husband has several shirts of different colors.
你的衣服是什么颜色的？
What color is your dress?
夏天树叶的颜色是绿的。
The color of leaves in summer is green.

**qǐngqiú**
**请求** （乙）动/名
① solicit ② request

**常用搭配**
请求某人帮助 solicit sb. for help
请求她的宽恕 ask her pardon
拒绝他的请求 refuse his request

**用法示例**
我请求她原谅我。
I begged her to forgive me.
他请求我们帮他完成他的计划。
He asked us to assist him in carrying out his plan.
他们请求国际援助。
They've made a request for international aid.

**xīngfèn** **zhènjìng**
**兴奋** 反镇静 （乙）形
excited; exciting

**常用搭配**
令人兴奋的旅行 an exciting trip
他很兴奋。He is very excited.
兴奋剂 stimulant drug

**用法示例**
孩子们兴奋地拆开了他们的礼物。
The excited children opened their presents.
我兴奋得难以入睡。
I am too exited to go to sleep.
浓咖啡使你神经兴奋。
Strong coffee excites your nerves.

**xuǎnzé**
**选择** （乙）名/动
① choice ② choose; select

**常用搭配**
明智的选择 a judicious choice　做出选择 make a choice

精心选择 to select carefully

**用法示例**

她几乎没有选择余地。
She has only a little choice to exercise.
我们每个人都必须做出选择。
We each had to make a choice.
那家商店有各种精美的糕点供我们选择。
That shop has a fine selection of cakes.

huà
# 化 （乙）动/尾

① melt; thaw ② to... -fy ③ -ization

**常用搭配**

现代化 modernization　自动化 automatization
规范化 standardization　净化 purify　丑化 uglify

**用法示例**

当铁烧得很热时就会化成液体。
Iron will melt into liquid when it is made very hot.
山顶上的雪在阳光下化了。
The snow on top of the mountains melted away under the sun.
我们改建园林和公园以美化城市。
We have beautified our city by improving the public gardens and parks.

zhùhè gōnghè
# 祝贺 ◉恭贺 （乙）动/名

① congratulate ② congratulations

**常用搭配**

祝贺你！ Congratulations!
祝贺某人成功 congratulate sb. on his/her success

**用法示例**

我们对她的成功表示祝贺。
We offered our congratulations on her success.
我祝贺你喜获千金。
I congratulate you on the birth of your daughter.
我们祝贺他通过了考核。
We congratulated him on having passed the examination.

jiànjiàn
# 渐渐 （乙）副

gradually

**常用搭配**

伤口渐渐愈合了。 The wound gradually scarred over.
他渐渐老了。 He is growing old.

**用法示例**

渐渐地，我理解了他并爱上了他。
Gradually, I understood him and fell in love with him.
长期患病使她的体力渐渐衰竭。
Her long illness gradually sapped her strength.
这个村庄渐渐发展成了城镇。
The village is growing into a town gradually.

zhùyuàn zhǔfú
# 祝愿 ◉祝福 （丙）动/名

① to wish ② wishes

**常用搭配**

祝愿你们好运 wish you good luck
美好的祝愿 best wishes

**用法示例**

我祝愿你健康愉快。
I wish you well and happy.
请接受我良好的祝愿。
Please accept my best wishes.
我母亲和我一起向你表示美好的祝愿。
Mother joins me in sending you our best wishes.

qǐngshì
# 请示 （丙）动

ask for instructions

**常用搭配**

请示领导 ask for instruction from leader

**用法示例**

花这么点钱也得请示，真烦人。
It's annoying to have to get authorization for spending so little money.
他做任何事都要先请示他老婆。
He never does anything without asking his wife first.
我不能立即做出明确答复，我得向总部请示。
I can't reply definitely at once; I have to ask for instruction from head quarters.

sècǎi
# 色彩 （丙）名

color; tint

**常用搭配**

瑰丽的色彩 resplendent colors
色彩斑斓的 brightly-colored

**用法示例**

我喜欢市场上缤纷的色彩。
I love the bright colors in the market.
旗帜给街道增添了色彩。
The banners lent color to the streets.
这部电影具有独特的地方色彩。
The film has a distinct local flavor.

zhènfèn jǔsàng
# 振奋 ◉沮丧 （丁）动

cheer up

**常用搭配**

令人振奋的消息 a cheering news　感到振奋 feel cheered

**用法示例**

听到这个好消息每个人都很振奋。
Everyone was cheered by the good news.
他的讲话使我们深感振奋。
We were deeply cheered by his speech.

míngmíng
## 明明
（丙）副

obviously

**常用搭配**

这明明是他的笔迹。Obviously it's his handwriting.

**用法示例**

她明明知道真相,可却说对此一无所知。

Obviously she knew the truth, but she said she knew nothing about it.

他否认看到了我,可我明明在公园看到他了。

I surely saw him in the park, but he denied having seen me.

xuǎnqǔ
## 选取
（丁）动

choose; select

**常用搭配**

选取礼物 choose gift

**用法示例**

你可以从这些书中选取三本。

From these books you may choose three.

这是从众多样品当中选取出来的。

It was selected from many samples.

 词义辨析

**颜色、色彩**

"颜色"和"色彩"都是名词,但"颜色"通常指一种具体的颜色,而"色彩"指多种颜色的组合,"色彩"还可以引申为某种情调或思想倾向。比如:①粉红色是她最喜欢的颜色。②图片中的色彩搭配得很好。③她的服装具有民族色彩。

Both 颜色 and 色彩 are nouns. But 颜色 means "a kind of color"; while 色彩 indicates co-ordinated colors, and its extended meaning is "the unique appeal of something, or tendency of one's thought". For example: ① Pink is her favorite color. ② The colors in the picture are a good match. ③ Her garb is quite national in style.

 练习

**练习一、根据拼音写汉字,根据汉字写拼音**

xuǎn（　）（　）fèn　（　）hè　yán（　）（　）qiú
（　）择　振（　）　祝（　）（　）色　请（　）

**练习二、搭配连线**

(1) 鲜艳的　　　　　　A. 样子
(2) 美好的　　　　　　B. 颜色
(3) 明智的　　　　　　C. 祝愿
(4) 兴奋的　　　　　　D. 请求
(5) 急切的　　　　　　E. 选择

**练习三、从今天学习的生词中选择合适的词填空**

1. 这个消息很_____人心,我们一定要抓住这次难得的好机会。
2. _____是他自己说错了,还说别人听错了。
3. 我们_____所有善良、诚实的人们都幸福、平安。
4. 听说他赢得了冠军,大家都来向他表示_____。
5. 这件事我一个人决定不了,我得_____我们老板。
6. 秋天到了,天气_____凉了下来。
7. 在这四个答案当中,你_____的是哪个?
8. 做这道菜要_____优质的深海鳕鱼。
9. 她_____我不要把这件事告诉他。
10. 得了设计大赛一等奖,她_____得一夜没睡。

## 答案

练习一:

略

练习二:

(1) B　　　(2)C　　　(3)E　　　(4)A　　　(5)D

练习三:

1. 振奋　　2. 明明　　3. 祝愿　　4. 祝贺　　5. 请示
6. 渐渐　　7. 选择　　8. 选取　　9. 请求　　10. 兴奋

**星期五**

**yuánliàng**
**原谅** （甲）动
forgive; pardon

〖常用搭配〗
请原谅。I beg your pardon.　原谅他 forgive him

〖用法示例〗
请原谅我来晚了。
Please forgive me for being late.
我希望你能原谅我。
I hope you'll forgive me.
我永远不原谅你。
I'll never forgive you.
如有冒犯之处,请多多原谅。
If I have offended you, I beg your pardon.

**yǒuqù**
**有趣** 反 乏味 （乙）形
interesting; amusing

〖常用搭配〗
有趣的文字游戏 interesting word games
有趣的笑话 an amusing joke

〖用法示例〗
我女儿正在读一本有趣的儿童故事书。
My daughter is reading an interesting story book for children.
我们觉得这个笑话很有趣。
We were amused at the joke.
今天晚上有一个有趣的电视节目。
There is an interesting program on television tonight.

**xué**
**学** （乙）动 / 名 / 尾
① learn; study ② science ③ -ology

〖常用搭配〗
学游泳 learn to swim　上学 go to school
哲学 philosophy　心理学 psychology

〖用法示例〗
我学汉语已经三个月了。
I've been studying Chinese for three months.
他学得很快。
He learns very quickly.
她在大学主修生物学。
She majors in biology at university.

**yǒulì**
**有利** 反 有害 （乙）形
advantageous; favorable

〖常用搭配〗
有利的形势 a favorable situation
有利条件 favorable terms
这对你有利。It's in your favor.

〖用法示例〗
这对我们十分有利。
It is highly advantageous to us.
她丰富的经验使她比其他求职者具有有利条件。
Her rich experience gave her an advantage over the other applicants for the job.
他对他们的候选人发表了一些有利的评论。
He made several favorable comments about their candidate.

**yǒulì**
**有力** （乙）形
powerful

〖常用搭配〗
有力的反击 forceful counter-attack
有力地证明 prove powerfully

〖用法示例〗
我们都觉得她的论据很有力。
We all felt the force of her arguments.
他一记有力的左手拳将对手击倒。
He knocked down his opponent with a powerful left hook.

**biāozhì**
**标志** （丙）动 / 名
① to mark ② sign

〖常用搭配〗
交通标志 traffic sign　停车标志 parking sign

〖用法示例〗
计算机的发明标志着一个新时代的开始。
The invention of the computer marked the beginning of a new era.
这一发现标志着治疗癌症的一大突破
This discovery marks a quantum leap forward in the fight against cancer.
沿途的标志都十分清楚。
The signs along the road are quite clear.

**fànwéi**
**范围** （乙）名
range; scope

〖常用搭配〗
经营范围 scope of business
研究范围 an area of research
在法律范围内 in the reach of the law

〖用法示例〗
你的问题已超出了这本书的范围。
Your question is beyond the scope of this book.
在这个价格范围内,有好几种汽车可供选购。
Several cars are available within this price range.

**huǎnhuǎn**
## 缓缓
同 慢慢 **mànmàn**　　　　　　（丙）副
slowly

常用搭配
缓缓行进 move forward slowly

用法示例
火车在缓缓行进。
The train ran at a very slow speed.
溪水在缓缓流淌。
The stream flows slowly.

**liàngjiě**
## 谅解
同 体谅 **tǐliàng**　　　　　　（丙）动
understand and forgive

常用搭配
达成谅解 reach an understanding

用法示例
请您谅解，我不是有意无礼的。
Please forgive me; I didn't mean to be rude.
他们最后达成了谅解。
They finally reached an understanding.
我们将互相谅解，搞好团结。
We will understand each other and unite well.

**tǒngtǒng**
## 统统
① totally ② all　　　　　　（丙）副

常用搭配
统统卖掉 sell all of them away

用法示例
我把那旧家具统统扔掉了。
I've thrown out all the old furniture.
我把我知道的统统告诉他了。
I told him all that I know.
他把所有的钱统统存进了银行。
He put all of his money in the bank.

**búlì**
## 不利
unfavorable; disadvantageous　　　　（丙）形

常用搭配
对……不利 be disadvantageous to…
不利因素 disadvantageous factor

用法示例
体弱多病对他找工作很不利。
His bad health is very disadvantageous to him to getting a job.
这样的局面对我们不利。
This situation is unfavorable for us.
要是你英语讲得不好，找工作时就会处于不利的地位。
If you can't speak English well, you'll be in a disadvantageous position when trying to get a job.

**bùliáng**
## 不良
① unhealthy ② bad　　　　　　（丁）形

常用搭配
不良行为 bad behavior　　不良影响 bad influence

用法示例
她对自己的不良行为感到羞耻。
She was full of shame at her bad behavior.
抽烟是种不良习惯。
Smoking is a bad habit.
他有开快车的不良嗜好。
He had a bad addiction of driving fast.

 词义辨析

**原谅、谅解**

　　"原谅"和"谅解"是动词。"原谅"强调宽恕、不计较别人的缺点、错误的意思，但是"谅解"有先了解、理解的过程再原谅，有时候表示相互间的理解和宽恕，有达成一致或默契的意思。如：①请原谅我的字写得不好。②我当时很着急，请谅解/原谅我说了激烈的话。③我们意见不一致时，能够互相帮助，互相谅解。

　　Both 原谅 and 谅解 are verbs. But 原谅 means "to forgive or put up with one's fault or mistakes"; while 谅解 means "to know the reason, or to understand before forgiving", sometimes it means "to understand and forgive each other", indicating to reach an agreement or understanding. For example: ① Please excuse my poor handwriting. ② I was very worried at that moment. Pardon my strong words please. ③ We helped and understood each other when we had different ideas about a matter.

 练习

**练习一、根据拼音写汉字,根据汉字写拼音**

( )liáng yǒu ( ) fàn ( ) ( )zhì ( )liàng
不( ) ( )趣 ( )围 标( ) 原( )

**练习二、搭配连线**
(1) 有趣的　　　　　　　A. 反击
(2) 有力的　　　　　　　B. 标志
(3) 有利的　　　　　　　C. 游戏
(4) 不良的　　　　　　　D. 形势
(5) 明显的　　　　　　　E. 影响

**练习三、从今天学习的生词中选择合适的词填空**
1. 形势对我们 _____,恐怕我们要做好应付困难的准备。
2. 警察对那个犯罪集团进行了 _____ 的打击。
3. 这些证据对我们十分 _____,不用担心,我们会赢的。
4. 这次金融危机影响 _____ 很广。
5. 他讲的故事都很 _____,孩子和大人都喜欢听。
6. 计算机的发明和使用 _____ 着人类社会进入了一个新的时代。
7. 火车 _____ 进站,我很快就要看到我的朋友们了。
8. 两国达成 _____,表示要加强双方在经济领域的合作。
9. 他们搬进了新家后,旧家具一件没留, _____ 扔掉了。
10. 政府应该加大力度,打击各种违法犯罪活动和社会 _____ 现象。

**答案**

**练习一:**
略
**练习二:**
(1) C (2)A (3)D (4)E (5)B
**练习三:**
1. 不利 2. 有力 3. 有利 4. 范围 5. 有趣
6. 标志 7. 缓缓 8. 谅解 9. 统统 10. 不良

# 第5月,第1周的练习

**练习一. 根据词语给加点的字注音**
1.( )　2.( )　3.( )　4.( )　5.( )
响　　赚　　佩服　拼命　祝贺
·　　·　　·　　·　　·

**练习二. 根据拼音完成词语**
　fèn　　　fèn　zhèn　zhèn　fàn
1.( )怒 2.兴( )3.( )惊 4.( )奋 5.( )围

**练习三. 辨析并选择合适的词填空**
1. 听,什么在( )? 屋子里好像有老鼠。(响、响亮)
2. 这个收音机很小,但声音却十分( )。(响、响亮)
3. 房间里没开灯,光线有点( ),(暗、暗暗)
4. 他比赛得了第二名,但对自己并不满意,他( )下决心下次一定要拿第一。(暗、暗暗)
5. 这是物理学中的重要课题,科学家们一直在努力( )。(研究、钻研)
6. 现在形势有了变化,我们开会( )一下对策。(研究、钻研)
7. 这套衣服设计简洁、( )明快,适合在正式场合穿。(颜色、色彩)
8. 李莉喜欢粉色,你最喜欢什么( )? (颜色、色彩)
9. 由于维修地下管道,明天上午停水两个小时,请广大市民( )。(原谅、谅解)
10. 如果你再骗我,我一定不会( )你。(原谅、谅解)

**练习四. 选词填空**
偷偷　　悄悄　　暗暗　　恰恰　　连连
渐渐　　缓缓　　统统　　珍惜　　可惜
兴奋　　振奋　　震惊　　有利　　有力
1. 结果( )和人们预料的相反。
2. 她( )对我说:小声点,孩子刚睡着。
3. 博物馆这里不让照相,可我还是( )地照了一张。
4. 这么年轻漂亮的姑娘嫁给了一个老头,真是( )!
5. 这次考试题很难,大家( )没有及格。
6. 领导讲话的时候,她( )点头,一副巴结的模样。
7. 列车( )启动,送行的人们有的流泪,有的挥手。
8. 警方对各种犯罪活动进行了( )的打击。
9. 总统与大集团的交易内幕( )了世界。
10. 前方传来令人( )的消息,人们高兴地欢呼起来。
11. 这个学习机会太难得了,你一定要( )啊!
12. 看到对手在场上发挥得不好,他( )高兴。
13. 这是对国家、对人民都( )的事情,应该做。
14. 打了针,吃了药,孩子的脸色( )好了起来。
15. 咖啡喝太多了,我( )得睡不着觉。

**练习五.选择尾词填空**

家　　　　员　　　　品　　　　化　　　　学

1. 她丈夫是个画（　　），她自己从事音乐创作,是有名的作曲（　　）。
2. 如果形势进一步恶（　　）,很多公司可能会破产。
3. 她学的专业是物理(　　),而她在业余时间喜欢研究哲（　　）。
4. 我喜欢去那家饭馆吃饭,因为服务（　　）态度很好。
5. 现在年轻女孩都喜欢买各种化妆（　　）和装饰(　　)。

**练习六.写出下列词语的同义词**

1. 谅解(　　)　　　　2. 祝愿(　　)
3. 可惜(　　)　　　　4. 震惊(　　)
5. 愤怒(　　)

**练习七.写出下列词语的反义词**

1. 佩服(　　)　　　　2. 振奋(　　)
3. 有趣(　　)　　　　4. 可爱(　　)
5. 响亮(　　)

 **答案**

**练习一.**

| 1.xiǎng | 2.zhuàn | 3.pèi | 4.pīn | 5.hè |
|---|---|---|---|---|

**练习二.**

| 1. 愤 | 2. 奋 | 3. 震 | 4. 振 | 5. 范 |
|---|---|---|---|---|

**练习三.**

| 1. 响 | 2. 响亮 | 3. 暗 | 4. 暗暗 | 5. 钻研 |
|---|---|---|---|---|
| 6. 研究 | 7. 色彩 | 8. 颜色 | 9. 谅解 | 10. 原谅 |

**练习四.**

| 1. 恰恰 | 2. 悄悄 | 3. 偷偷 | 4. 可惜 | 5. 统统 |
|---|---|---|---|---|
| 6. 连连 | 7. 缓缓 | 8. 有力 | 9. 震惊 | 10. 振奋 |
| 11. 珍惜 | 12. 暗暗 | 13. 有利 | 14. 渐渐 | 15. 兴奋 |

**练习五.**

| 1. 家,家 | 2. 化 | 3. 学,学 | 4. 员 | 5. 品,品 |
|---|---|---|---|---|

**练习六.**

| 1. 体谅 | 2. 祝福 | 3. 惋惜 | 4. 惊讶 | 5. 气愤 |
|---|---|---|---|---|

**练习七.**

| 1. 鄙视 | 2. 沮丧 | 3. 乏味 | 4. 可恶 | 5. 低沉 |
|---|---|---|---|---|

# 5月 第2周的学习内容

星期一

**丰富** fēngfù　　反 单调 dāndiào　　（甲）形/动

① plentiful; rich　② enrich

**常用搭配**

经验丰富的老师 an experienced teacher
矿产丰富 rich in ore
丰富某人的经验 enrich one's experience

**用法示例**

这个国家石油和煤炭的资源丰富。
The country is rich in oil and coal.
柠檬含丰富的维生素 C。
Lemons are rich in vitamin C.
艺术欣赏将会丰富你的生活。
An appreciation of art will enrich your life.

**生** shēng　　（乙）动/形

① give birth; produce　② new; unfamiliar

**常用搭配**

生于 1985 年 be born in 1985　生火 make a fire
生肉 raw meat　生面孔 unfamiliar faces　生词 new word

**用法示例**

她已生了两个孩子。
She has borne two children.
汤姆虽然生在中国，但父母是意大利人。
Tom is Italian by birth although he was born in China.
这个西瓜是生的。
This water melon is unripe.
我们每周都要学习很多生字。
We learn many new characters every week.

**剧烈** jùliè　　（丙）形

acute; violent

**常用搭配**

剧烈疼痛 acute pain

**用法示例**

这种药物引起了剧烈的反应。
The medicine produced a violent reaction.
疼痛越来越剧烈了。
The pain increased in intensity.

汽车在山路上行驶时晃动得很剧烈。
The car rocked violently while driving on the mountain road.

**激烈** jīliè　　同 剧烈 jùliè　　（乙）形

keen; fierce

**常用搭配**

激烈的足球赛 keen football match
激烈的战斗 fierce fighting

**用法示例**

竞争很激烈。
Competition is very keen.
这场辩论逐渐变成了激烈的争吵。
The argument developed into a bitter quarrel.

**省** shěng　　（乙）名/动

① province　② save; omit

**常用搭配**

广东省 Guangdong Province　省钱 save money
省时间 save time

**用法示例**

他来自山东省。
He comes from Shandong Province.
我的新车很省油。
My new car is quite economical on fuel.
你去超市购物，省时又省钱。
You can save time and money by shopping at the supermarket.

**升** shēng　　（乙）动

rise; promote

**常用搭配**

升旗 raise a flag　升学 enter a higher school

**用法示例**

太阳六点钟升起。
The sun rose at six o'clock.
我们的老师已升为校长了。
Our teacher has already been promoted to headmaster.

**接受** jiēshòu　　反 拒绝 jùjué　　（乙）动

accept

**常用搭配**

接受邀请 accept an invitation.　接受训练 receive training
接受酬金 accept rewards

**用法示例**

我收到了他送的礼物,但是我不想接受。

I've received a gift from him, but I'm not going to accept it.

你接受他的建议了吗?

Did you take his advice?

他们在教堂接受了洗礼。

They received baptism at the church.

xuéwen

**学问** （乙）名

learning; knowledge

**常用搭配**

有学问的人 a learned man

**用法示例**

因为他有学问,所以我尊敬他。

I respect him because he is knowledgeable.

大部分有学问的人都很谦虚。

Most learned men are modest.

种菜看似简单,其实大有学问。

Growing vegetables looks easy, but actually it takes a lot of knowledge.

gǎn

**感** （丁）尾

sense of

**常用搭配**

羞耻感 sense of shame　荣誉感 sense of honor

正义感 sense of righteousness

**用法示例**

他缺乏幽默感。

He has little sense of humor.

他父亲很有责任感。

His father has a sense of responsibility.

她没有方向感,所以她经常迷路。

She has no sense of direction, so she often loses her way.

xuéwèi

**学位** （丙）名

academic degree

**常用搭配**

博士学位 doctors degree　学位课程 degree course

**用法示例**

要从事这个工作,必须具有英语专业的学位。

To do this job, you must have a degree in English.

他具有经济学专业的硕士学位。

He has a master's degree in economics.

他通过了考试,现在他有了学士学位。

He passed examinations and now he has a bachelors degree.

qíjì

**奇迹** （丙）名

miracle; marvel

**常用搭配**

现代技术的奇迹 a marvel of modern technology

奇迹般的胜利 a miraculous victory

**用法示例**

孩子从三楼摔下来竟没受伤,真是一个奇迹。

It was a real marvel that the baby was unhurt after he fell from the third floor.

这座大教堂被认为是建筑史上的奇迹。

This cathedral was regarded as a miracle in architectural history.

他奇迹般地康复了。

He made a miraculous recovery.

zāoshòu　　　　　　　zāodào

**遭受** 遭到 （乙）动

suffer; sustain (loss, misfortune)

**常用搭配**

遭受水灾 suffer from floods　遭受损失 sustain losses

**用法示例**

他的家庭在战争中遭受了很多苦难。

His family suffered a lot of hardship during the war.

他们在经济危机期间遭受了巨大的损失。

They suffered huge losses in the financial crisis.

hénjì

**痕迹** （丙）名

trace

**常用搭配**

搏斗的痕迹 traces of struggle

**用法示例**

湿杯子在桌面上留下一个痕迹。

The wet glass left a mark on the surface of the table.

岁月在她脸上留下了痕迹。

Age has left its traces on her face.

这房间里有搏斗过的痕迹。

The room has traces of a struggle.

 词义辨析

**激烈、剧烈**

"激烈"和"剧烈"都是形容词,表示十分强烈的意思。但"激烈"通常用于言论、情绪、竞争、比赛;"剧烈"一般用于身体疼痛的感觉,或变化、摇动等。如:①激烈的言辞。②剧烈的疼痛。③现代社会的每个人都面临着激烈的竞争。④他受伤了,但还是忍着剧烈的疼痛站了起来。

Both 激烈 and 剧烈 are adjectives, meaning "to be fierce". But 激烈 is usually applied to speech, sentiments, competition or match; while 剧烈 is usually applied to wound, change or shake. For example: ① a violent language. ② acute pain. ③ Everyone in modern society faces keen competition. ④ He stood up with his acute pain though he was wounded.

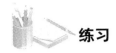 **练习**

**练习一、根据拼音写汉字，根据汉字写拼音**

( ) fù ( ) liè ( )shòu hén ( ) xué ( )
丰( ) 剧( ) 遭( ) ( )迹 ( )问

**练习二、搭配连线**

(1) 经验　　　　　　　A. 疼痛
(2) 遭受　　　　　　　B. 丰富
(3) 博士　　　　　　　C. 辩论
(4) 剧烈　　　　　　　D. 学位
(5) 激烈　　　　　　　E. 损失

**练习三、从今天学习的生词中选择合适的词填空**

1. 出事前，他们发生了 _____ 的争吵。
2. 面条煮的时间不够，吃到嘴里有点 _____。
3. 那位奥运会冠军站在领奖台上，听着国歌，注视着国旗慢慢 _____ 起。
4. 我朋友家的经济条件不太好，所以他花钱很 _____。
5. 这位老人说，只要自己能劳动，就决不 _____ 别人的帮助。
6. 医生对麦克说，这几天要好好休息，不能 _____ 运动。
7. 医生说，这位癌症患者的康复是一个 _____。
8. 王教授特别有 _____，他通晓各个国家的历史和文化。
9. 文件有被修改过的 _____。
10. 这个老师教了二十年汉语，她的经验十分 _____。

**答案**

**练习一：**
略

**练习二：**
(1) B　　(2)E　　(3)D　　(4)A　　(5)C

**练习三：**
1.激烈　　2.生　　3.升　　4.省　　5.接受
6.剧烈　　7.奇迹　　8.学问　　9.痕迹　　10.丰富

---

 **星期二**

zhīshi
**知识** （甲）名
knowledge

**常用搭配**
历史知识 knowledge of history
传授知识 to impart knowledge
保健知识 health knowledge

**用法示例**
我们上学是为了获得各种知识。
We go to school to acquire knowledge about many
different things.
我对他渊博的知识感到惊奇。
I was amazed at the extent of his knowledge.
她对计算机有广博的知识。
She has a broad knowledge of computers.

qīngsōng　　　　　　　fánzhòng
**轻松** 反繁重 （乙）形
relaxed

**常用搭配**
感到轻松 feel relaxed　　轻松的工作 easy work

**用法示例**
听到这条消息，她立刻轻松了。
Her heart lightened at once when she heard the news.
我的心情慢慢轻松下来了。
My mood gradually lightened.
这是件轻松的工作，我们很快就做完了。
It was an easy job and we finished it quickly.

yōngbào
**拥抱** （乙）动
embrace; hug

**常用搭配**
互相拥抱 embrace each other
深情地拥抱 an affectionate hug

**用法示例**
这孩子拥抱了他的父母。
The child embraced his parents.
他以一个深情的拥抱来迎接她。
He greeted her with a loving hug.
她紧紧拥抱着女儿。
She gave her daughter a big hug.

yōnghù　　　　　　　yōngdài
**拥护** 同拥戴 （乙）动
support; stand up for; advocate

**常用搭配**
拥护某个政策 advocate a policy of...

得到拥护 get support
拥护和平的人 an advocate of peace

**用法示例**

这位法官是监狱改革的坚决拥护者。
This judge is a strong advocate of prison reform.
我们拥护自由和正义。
We stand up for the cause of liberty and justice.
我拥护逐步改革的政策。
I advocate a policy of gradual reform.

biāozhǔn
## 标准 （乙）名／形

standard; criterion

**常用搭配**

道德标准 moral standards
达到标准 meet the standard
标准大气压 the standard atmospheric pressure

**用法示例**

只有社会实践才是检验真理的唯一标准。
Only social practice can be the criterion of truth.
该报告建议改进安全标准。
The report advances the suggestion that safety standards should be improved.
他的发音相当标准。
His pronunciation is quite standard.

yóulǎn
## 游览 （乙）动

go sight-seeing; visit

**常用搭配**

游览紫禁城 visit the Forbidden City
在北京游览 go sight-seeing in Beijing

**用法示例**

我把大部分时间都用在观光游览上了。
I spent most of my time sightseeing.
我们已经游览过长城了。
We have already visited the Great Wall.
她在巴黎找到了工作，于是就可以游览法国了。
She has found a job in Paris and so she can visit France.

yōngjǐ
## 拥挤 （丙）动／形

① to crowd ② crowded

**常用搭配**

拥挤的街道 crowded street
拥挤的交通 congestion of traffic

**用法示例**

商店在圣诞节前非常拥挤。
Shops are very crowded before Christmas.
据说东京是一座非常拥挤的城市。
It is said that Tokyo is an overcrowded city.
街道十分拥挤，汽车无法通行。
The street was so crowded that cars were unable to pass.

jiè
## 界 （丁）名／尾

① boundary ② circles (i.e. a group of people)

**常用搭配**

学术界 academic circles　　文化界 cultural circles
政界 political circles　　教育界 educational circles

**用法示例**

这条河是两国的界河。
The river is the boundary between the two countries.
她的第一本书在文学界引起了轰动。
She has caused shockwaves in literary circles with her first book.
他在艺术界很有名。
He is well-known in artistic circles.

lǚyóu
## 旅游 （丙）动

① travel ② journey

**常用搭配**

旅游手册 travel brochure　　去北京旅游 travel to Beijing

**用法示例**

我喜欢在假期的时候旅游。
I like traveling during vacation.
香港是旅游者的乐园。
Hong Kong is a travelers' paradise.
旅游可以使人增长见识。
Travel is an edifying experience.

kěxiào
## 可笑 （丙）形

laughable; ridiculous

**常用搭配**

真可笑！ How ridiculous!
可笑的想法 a ridiculous idea

**用法示例**

他的演讲中有许多可笑的错误。
He made many ludicrous mistakes in his speech.
给狗起这个名字多可笑！
It is so laughable to give this name to the dog.
他们的要求很可笑。
Their request is absurd.

fànchóu
## 范畴 （丁）名

category

**常用搭配**

语法范畴 grammatical category
经济范畴 economic category

**用法示例**

他不喜欢谈论政治范畴的问题。
He doesn't like talking about issues of political category.
他的研究涉及多个范畴。
His research involves many categories.

**kěxǐ**
# 可喜
gratifying

反 可悲 **kěbēi** (丁)形

**常用搭配**
可喜的消息 welcome news
可喜的成绩 gratifying result

**用法示例**
经过努力,他们取得了可喜的成就。
By working hard, they have obtained a gratifying achievement.
在学习汉语方面,他们取得了可喜的进步。
They have made gratifying progress in studying Chinese.

 **词义辨析**

**旅游、游览**

　　1、"旅游"和"游览"都是动词,都有观光游玩的意思。"旅游"是不及物动词,不能直接跟宾语;"游览"是及物动词,可以跟宾语。例如:①我们游览了长城。②我们去长城旅游。

　　Both 旅游 and 游览 are verbs, meaning "to travel or sightsee". 旅游 is an intransitive verb, and can not take a direct object; while 游览 is an transitive verb, and can take a direct object. For example: ① We visited the Great Wall. ② We traveled to the Great Wall.

　　2、有时"旅游"可以用作名词,在句子中充当宾语、定语等。"游览"没有这种用法。如:①我的爱好是旅游。②买一本旅游手册。

　　Sometimes 旅游 can be used as a noun, and function as an object or an attributive; while 游览 does not have this usage. For example: ① My hobby is traveling. ② I want to buy a travel brochure.

 **练习**

**练习一、根据拼音写汉字,根据汉字写拼音**
( )chóu yōng ( )( )lǎn ( )zhǔn qīng ( )
范( ) ( )挤 游( ) 标( ) ( )松

**练习二、搭配连线**
(1) 拥挤的　　　　　　A. 进步
(2) 轻松的　　　　　　B. 想法
(3) 标准的　　　　　　C. 工作
(4) 可笑的　　　　　　D. 发音
(5) 可喜的　　　　　　E. 街道

**练习三、从今天学习的生词中选择合适的词填空**
1. 你的想法真是幼稚_____。
2. 两个月不到,这个项目就有了_____的进展。
3. 我希望退休以后能到世界各地去_____。
4. 在中国的三年里,这位大使_____了很多名胜古迹。
5. 这个问题属于哲学_____。
6. 妻子以为丈夫已经在灾难中死去了,当真的看到他时,两个人紧紧地_____在一起。
7. 上班高峰时,公交车上很_____。
8. 坚决_____党的宗教自由政策。
9. 这个饭店因为不符合卫生_____而被责令停业了。
10. 终于考完试了,不管考得怎么样,他心里都感到_____了许多。

**答案**

练习一:
略
练习二:
(1) E　　(2)C　　(3)D　　(4)B　　(5)A
练习三:
1. 可笑　　2. 可喜　　3. 旅游　　4. 游览　　5. 范畴
6. 拥抱　　7. 拥挤　　8. 拥护　　9. 标准　　10. 轻松

星期三

shuōmíng
## 说明 （甲）动／名

① illustrate; explain ② explanation; direction

**常用搭配**
说明原因 explain the reason
用事实说明 illustrate by facts

**用法示例**
他指着图表来说明他的论点。
He pointed at the diagram to illustrate his point.
我们把计划向委员会做了说明。
We explained our plan to the committee.
在吃药前，你应该仔细阅读说明书。
Before taking medicine you should read the directions carefully.

jiěshì
## 解释 （乙）动／名

① explain; interpret ② explanation

**常用搭配**
解释生词 explain the new words
令人满意的解释 satisfactory explanation

**用法示例**
请让我解释一下。
Let me explain.
请您把这句话给我们再解释一下好吗？
Will you please explain this sentence again for us?
我承认你的解释是合理的。
I grant that your explanation is reasonable.

dānxīn
## 担心 ⊗ 放心 fàngxīn （乙）动

worry; be anxious

**常用搭配**
别担心！ Don't worry!

**用法示例**
孩子们放学后没有回家，我非常担心。
I was anxious about the children when they didn't return home from school.
他担心她的安全。
He was anxious about her safety.
他们担心那条河会发洪水。
They were fearful that the river would flood.
别担心，我会支持你的。
Do not fear; I will support you.

zhòngshì
## 重视 （乙）动

value; attach importance to; emphasize

**常用搭配**
重视教育 attach importance to education

**用法示例**
我们的汉语课程非常重视会话技能。
Our Chinese course places great emphasis on conversational skills.
我一向重视他的意见。
I have always valued his advice.
他的提议得到了委员会的高度重视。
His proposals are highly valued in committee.

zhòngliàng
## 重量 ⊜ 分量 fènliàng （乙）名

weight

**常用搭配**
卡车的重量 the weight of a truck
货物的重量 the weight of goods

**用法示例**
冰太薄，承受不住你们的重量。
The ice is too thin to bear your weight.
这地基不够牢固，无法承受房屋的重量。
The foundations were not strong enough to sustain the weight of the house.
他身体的重量把树枝压弯了。
The branch began to give under his weight.

xuǎnjǔ
## 选举 （乙）动／名

① elect ② election

**常用搭配**
选举新市长 vote for a new mayor
选举的结果 election results

**用法示例**
他被选举为学生会主席。
He was elected as the chairman of the students' union.
下个月将举行选举。
The elections will be held next month.
他在选举中获胜了，因为他得到了大多数的选票。
He won the election because he got the most votes.

qīngshì
## 轻视 ⊜ 藐视 miǎoshì （丙）动

despise; contempt; look down upon

**常用搭配**
轻视他人的意见 disdain other's ideas
轻视女性 despise women

**用法示例**
你不能因为一个人贫穷就轻视他。
You must not despise a man because he is poor.
没有人轻视你。
No one despised you.
她遭人轻视。
She was treated with disdain.

zhě
# 者 (丙)尾
① -ist, -er (person) ② person (who does sth.)

**常用搭配**

读者 reader　旅行者 traveler　竞争者 competitor
胜利者 winner

**用法示例**

人民是历史的创造者。
The people are the makers of history.
小说的作者是一位年轻人。
The writer of the novel is a young man.
他是一位经验丰富的记者。
He is a highly experienced reporter.
护士悉心照顾每一位患者。
The nurse looks after every patient carefully.

yǒngyuè
# 踊跃 (丙)形
eager; active

**常用搭配**

踊跃参与 enthusiastically take part in

**用法示例**

我们班同学踊跃报名参加比赛。
The students in my class actively entered the competition.
孩子们踊跃回答老师的问题。
The children answered their teacher's question actively.

dānyōu
# 担忧 (丁)动
worry

**常用搭配**

为他的安全担忧 worry about his safety

**用法示例**

她为父亲的健康担忧。
She worried about her father's health.
不必为他担忧。
There is no reason to be anxious about him.
（目前的）经济状况令人十分担忧。
The state of the economy is very worrying.
孩子咳嗽得厉害，这使她很担忧。
The child has a bad cough and it rather worries her.

zhěngjié　　　　zāngluàn
# 整洁　反 脏乱 (丁)形
neat; tidy

**常用搭配**

整洁的房间 a neat room
整洁的衬衣 neat shirts

**用法示例**

我们的教室非常整洁。
Our classroom is very tidy.
她总把房间打扫得很整洁。
She always kept her room very neat.

xuǎnbá
# 选拔 (丁)动
select the best

**常用搭配**

选拔赛 selective trials

**用法示例**

有 30 名运动员参加了选拔赛。
30 athletes turned up for the selective trials.
他们是从众多报名者当中选拔出来的。
They were selected from many applicants.

 **词义辨析**

**解释、说明**

1、这两个词都既是动词又是名词，表示使事物明白，易于理解。"解释"多用于讲解词句的意思、难以理解的问题或现象；"说明"多用于指出问题、原因等，还有证明、证实的意思。如：①请解释这个词的含义。②你能向我说明你的意图吗？③他的新书说明他是一位了不起的作家。

The two words can serve both as verbs and nouns, indicating "to make something plain or comprehensible". 解释 mostly indicates to explain the meaning of words or sentences, the problems or phenomena that are hard to understand. 说明 is mostly used to illustrate the problem or the reason of something. For example: ① Please explain what this word means. ② Can you tell me your intention? ③ His new book shows him to be a remarkable writer.

2、"解释"常与"清楚"、"明白"等词搭配，表示"解释"的效果；"说明"没有这种用法，因为"说明"的原意就是说清楚、讲明白的意思。如：他几句话就把问题解释清楚了。

解释 is often used with "清楚" (clearly), "明白" (clearly) and the like, indicating the effect of "解释"; while 说明 has no usage like that, because the original meaning of 说明 is "to tell clearly", "to explain clearly". For example: He made the problem clear with a few words.

3、名词"说明"即指说明书或说明书的内容，"解释"则仍旧保持其动词的意思。如：合理的解释，使用说明。

As a noun, 说明 means direction or instruction; 解释 means explanation. For example: reasonable explanation, directions for use

 练习

**练习一、根据拼音写汉字，根据汉字写拼音**

yǒng（ ）（ ）bá （ ）yōu（ ）shì（ ）shì
（ ）跃 选（ ） 担（ ） 重（ ） 解（ ）

**练习二、搭配连线**

(1) 踊跃        A. 原因
(2) 选举        B. 报名
(3) 说明        C. 人才
(4) 衣着        D. 总统
(5) 选拔        E. 整洁

**练习三、从今天学习的生词中选择合适的词填空**

1. 孩子不好好学习，父母现在就开始为孩子的前程_____。
2. 请你_____一下这是怎么回事。
3. 这台洗衣机的_____书是外文的，我看不懂。
4. 她的房间虽小，可相当_____。
5. 课堂上，学生们发言很_____。
6. 这本书的作_____是谁？
7. 千万不要因为工作繁忙而_____健康，否则一定会付出代价。
8. 现在，大家越来越_____孩子的教育问题了。
9. 空气几乎没有_____。
10. 班长是通过无记名投票_____出来的。

 答案

**练习一：**
略
**练习二：**
(1) B    (2)D    (3)A    (4)E    (5)C
**练习三：**
1. 担忧   2. 解释   3. 说明   4. 整洁   5. 踊跃
6. 者    7. 轻视   8. 重视   9. 重量   10. 选举

---

 星期四

fāngxiàng
**方向** （甲）名

orientation; direction

**常用搭配**
迷失方向 lose one's way
顺时针方向 clockwise direction
逆时针方向 counter-clockwise direction

**用法示例**
我们走的方向对吗？
Are we going in the right direction?
你的房间面向哪个方向？
Which direction does your room face?
他跳上马，朝寺庙方向飞奔而去。
He jumped onto the horse and galloped away in the direction of the temple.

zhúbù       zhújiàn
**逐步** 回 逐渐 （乙）副

① gradually ② step by step

**常用搭配**
逐步改善 improve step by step

**用法示例**
我们将逐步完成这项任务。
We will complete the task step by step.
改革正在逐步实施。
The reform is being carried out gradually.

biǎodá       biǎoshù
**表达** 回 表述 （乙）动

express; convey

**常用搭配**
表达感激之情 express one's gratitude
表达思想 express one's thought

**用法示例**
我们无法用语言表达当时的感受。
No words can express our feelings at that moment.
现在他能用汉语准确地表达自己的意思了。
He can express himself perfectly in Chinese now.

zhújiàn
**逐渐** （乙）副

① gradually ② little by little

**常用搭配**
逐渐变老 get old gradually

**用法示例**
拥有汽车的人在逐渐增多。
There has been a gradual increase in the number of people owning cars.

天气逐渐变冷。
It's gradually getting cold.
他对这门学科的兴趣在逐渐减退。
His interest in this subject is gradually decreasing.
洪水正逐渐退去。
The flood gradually subsided.

### duìhuàn
## 兑换　　　　圓 交换　　　（丙）动
exchange
【常用搭配】
把外币兑换成人民币 exchange foreign currency for Renminbi
【用法示例】
我想把这些美元兑换成英镑。
I would like to change these US dollars to pounds.
你可以在这家银行兑换人民币。
You can exchange Renminbi in this bank.

### kělián
## 可怜　　　　　　　　　　（乙）形/动
① pitiful; pathetic ② take pity on; sympathize
【常用搭配】
可怜的乞丐 pitiful beggar　　可怜的家伙 a poor fellow
可怜穷人 take pity on poor people
【用法示例】
学校的学术水平低得可怜。
The academic standards in the school were pathetic.
她真可怜。
She is so pitiful.
我很可怜这位老人。
I feel a lot of pity for the old man.

### xiǎnde
## 显得　　　　　　　　　　（乙）动
seem; look
【常用搭配】
显得很生气 seem very angry　　显得年轻 look young
【用法示例】
他好像病了，面色显得很苍白。
He seems to be sick, for he looks pale.
她显得很疲劳。
She looks very tired.

### biǎoqíng
## 表情　　　　　　　　　　（丙）名
expression
【常用搭配】
困惑的表情 puzzled expression
冷酷的表情 grim expression
【用法示例】
他表情严肃地望着她。
He looked at her with a solemn expression on his face.
她听到这条消息表情就变了。
Her expression changed when she heard the news.

她毫无表情地讲述她的经历。
She told her story without expression.

### yè
## 业　　　　　　　　　　　（丙）尾
industry
【常用搭配】
商业信函 business letters　　建筑业 building industry
农业 agriculture　　轻工业 light industry
【用法示例】
旅游业已经成为真正的产业。
The tourist trade has become a real industry.
政府决定发展工商业。
The government decided to expand industry and commerce.
去年纺织业发展得很快。
The textile industry developed quickly last year.

### qīngxiàng
## 倾向　　　　圓 趋势　　　（丙）动/名
① trend; incline ② tendency; direction
【常用搭配】
倾向于某事 incline to sth.
倾向于做某事 inclined to do sth.
舆论的倾向 the drift of public opinion
【用法示例】
我倾向于相信他是无辜的。
I'm inclined to believe him to be innocent.
我倾向于另一种观点。
I inclined to take another point of view.
教授介绍了世界教育发展的几种新倾向。
The professor introduced some of the new trends in educational development in the world.

### duìxiàn
## 兑现　　　　　　　　　　（丁）动
to cash; to honor a contract
【常用搭配】
兑现诺言 fulfill one's promise
兑现支票 to cash a check
【用法示例】
这张支票可以凭身分证件兑现。
The check can be cashed upon proof of identity.
他答应帮助我，但不知道什么时候才能兑现承诺。
He has promised to help me, but I don't know when he will fulfill his promise.

### kěwù
## 可恶　　　　　　　　　　（丁）形
hateful
【常用搭配】
可恶的女巫 evil witch　　可恶的罪行 detestable crimes
【用法示例】
他们说那样的话真是可恶。
It's wicked of them to say such things.

我希望那只可恶的狗安静下来。
I wish that cursed dog would be quiet.
凶杀是最可恶的犯罪。
Murder is the most abominable crime.

 **词义辨析**

**逐步、逐渐**

　　"逐步"和"逐渐"都是副词,都指连续地一点一点地发展和进步。但"逐步"表示一步一步地按计划进行,通常修饰动词或动词性短语;"逐渐"表示慢慢地按照事物发展的自然规律发展变化,通常修饰形容词或形容词性短语。如:①我们将逐步解决这些问题。②我的计划逐渐成熟了。③他身体在逐渐好转。

　　Both 逐步 and 逐渐 are adverbs, meaning "to advance or progress by regular or continuous degrees". But 逐步 indicates to develop step by step according to a plan, and usually qualifies a verb or a verb phrase; while 逐渐 indicates to change, or develop slowly and gradually according to the natural processes, and usually qualifies an adjective or adjectival phrase For example: ① We will solve these problems step by step. ② My plan has gradually come to maturity. ③ He is getting better by degrees.

 **练习**

**练习一、根据拼音写汉字,根据汉字写拼音**
(　)lián　(　)qíng　qīng(　)　duì(　)　zhú(　)
可(　)　表(　)　(　)向　(　)换　(　)渐

**练习二、搭配连线**
(1) 兑换　　　　　　　A. 严肃
(2) 兑现　　　　　　　B. 美元
(3) 表情　　　　　　　C. 改善
(4) 表达　　　　　　　D. 诺言
(5) 逐步　　　　　　　E. 思想

**练习三、从今天学习的生词中选择合适的词填空**
1. 这项工作正在 _____ 开展。
2. 随着秋天的临近,天气 _____ 凉快了。
3. 多跟朋友聊天能锻炼你的 _____ 能力。
4. 我刚来北京时,坐公共汽车经常坐错 _____。
5. 三年前她的丈夫离开了她,现在孩子又去世了,她真 _____。
6. 他去银行把手中的美元 _____ 成了人民币。
7. 工作了一天,他 _____ 很疲惫。
8. 他在说这些话时面无 _____,我捉摸不透他的想法。
9. 这两种意见中,我 _____ 于前者。
10. 他当上总统以后,马上 _____ 了选举时的承诺,降低了税金。

**答案**

练习一:
略
练习二:
(1) B　　(2)D　　(3)A　　(4)E　　(5)C
练习三:
1. 逐步　2. 逐渐　3. 表达　4. 方向　5. 可怜
6. 兑换　7. 显得　8. 表情　9. 倾向　10. 兑现

**星期五**

**热情** rèqíng 反 冷漠 lěngmò （甲）名／形
① passion; zeal ② passionate; enthusiastic

常用搭配
热情的支持 warm support　热情的接待 a warm reception
对某事有热情 be enthusiastic for sth.

用法示例
他表现出极大的学习热情。
He shows a great passion for study.
他热情洋溢地对我们说。
He speaks to us with great fervor.
她对我们很热情。
Towards us she is very warmhearted.

**成果** chéngguǒ （乙）名
result; achievement

常用搭配
他的劳动成果 the fruit of his labor
研究成果 results of a research

用法示例
那本书是十年苦心研究的成果。
The book was the result of ten years of dedicatcd research.
她自豪地看着自己的工作成果。
She looked at the result of her work with pride.
这项研究成果能用于开发新技术。
The results of this research can be used in the development of new technologies.

**争取** zhēngqǔ （乙）动
compete for; strive for; try to do

常用搭配
争取自由 struggle for freedom
争取权利 fight for one's rights
争取胜利 strive for victory

用法示例
争取在两天内完成这项工作。
Try to finish the work in two days.
争取早些赶到。
Make an effort to arrive promptly.
我们把他们争取过来了。
We have won them over to our side.

**性** xìng （乙）名／尾
① nature ② sex ③ suffix indicating a property or characteristic

常用搭配
人性 human nature
性教育 sex education
酸性 acidic property
惯性 inertial property
透气性 venting quality

用法示例
这两兄弟仅外表相似,本性却很不一样。
There is a physical likeness between the two brothers, however, their natures are very different.
弹性是橡胶的一种特性。
Resilience is a property of rubber.
这种塑料具有耐热性。
This kind of plastic has heat-resistant qualities.

**热爱** rèài 反 憎恨 zēnghèn （乙）动
ardently love; have deep love for

常用搭配
热爱祖国 love motherland
热爱科学 be fond of science
热爱真理 love truth

用法示例
她热爱网球运动。
She is passionately fond of tennis.
她热爱自己的家庭,但家庭却是她事业的累赘。
She loves her family, but they're a drag on her career.
他们虔诚地热爱上帝。
They love God with godliness.

**奇怪** qíguài （乙）形
odd; strange

常用搭配
奇怪的声音 a strange sound
奇怪的问题 strange questions

用法示例
他有一些很奇怪的想法。
He has some pretty strange ideas.
谁也料不到会有这种奇怪的事情。
No one could have foretold the occurence of such strange events.
很奇怪,我上火车时,竟然没有人查我的车票。
It was strange that nobody checked my ticket before I got on the train.

**争夺** zhēngduó （丙）动
contest; vie over

常用搭配
争夺冠军 contest for the championship
争夺好座位 scramble for good seats

**用法示例**

有多少人在争夺理事会的这个席位?

How many people are campaigning for this seat on the council?

他们是彼此争夺第一名的老对手。

They are old rivals vying with each other for first place.

jiéguǒ

## 结果 （丙）名

① outcome；result ② as a result

**常用搭配**

比赛的结果 result of a match

令人满意的结果 a satisfactory result

**用法示例**

结果并不像他希望的那样。

The outcome was not what he expected.

大选的结果还没有宣布。

The outcome of the election has not been announced.

我相信我们队一定会赢,结果,我们真的赢了。

I bet our team would win the game. In the end, we won .

hòuguǒ

## 后果 （丙）名

consequence

**常用搭配**

承担……后果 take the consequences of…

战争的后果 the aftermath of the war

严重的后果 serious consequences

**用法示例**

你考虑过这个决定的后果吗?

Did you consider the consequences of that decision?

教练将承担失败的后果。

The coach will suffer the consequences of a failure.

他总是随心所欲,不顾后果。

He always does what he wants to do without reflecting on the consequences.

hòudài

## 后代 反 先辈 xiānbèi （丙）名

posterity；future generations

**常用搭配**

国王的后代 posterity of the king

繁殖后代 to produce an offspring

**用法示例**

我们必须为子孙后代保护森林资源。

We must conserve our forests and woodlands for future generations.

据说他是孔子的后代。

It is said that he is the posterity of Confucius.

老人为后代树立了好榜样。

The old man set a good example for future generations.

lüèduó

## 掠夺 （丙）动

pillage；depredate

**常用搭配**

掠夺财物 depreciate property

**用法示例**

敌人掠夺私人财产。

Their enemies depredated the private estates.

该城遭到了入侵军队的掠夺。

The city was pillaged by the invading army.

qítè

## 奇特 反 平常 píngcháng （丁）形

peculiar；strange

**常用搭配**

奇特的声音 a strange sound

奇特的景象 strange sights

**用法示例**

龙是中国人幻想出来的奇特的动物。

Dragons are peculiar creatures of Chinese fancy.

文章的构思十分奇特。

The ideas in the article are quite strange.

这件服装设计得很奇特。

This dress is of a vagarious design.

 **词义辨析**

**结果、成果、后果**

这三个词都是名词,但"结果"是中性词,用来说明事物发展的最终状态,有时候用作连词,引出结局;"成果"含有褒义,多表示研究、改革、工作所取得的成效、成绩;"后果"含有贬义,往往指错误的指示或行为导致的不好的结果。如:①"试验的结果",②"比赛的结果",③"研究的成果",④"学术成果",⑤"马虎的后果",⑥"吸烟的后果",⑦他摔伤了腿,结果他得休学两个月。

The three words are nouns, but 结果 is a neutral word, indicating the consequence or outcome of an action, operation, or course. Sometimes it is used as a conjunction, introducing the clause of a result. 成果 has a commendatory sense, indicating the outcome or achievement of research, reform or work.; while 后果 has a derogatory sense, usually indicating the bad result that was caused by wrong direction or action. For example: ① result of an experiment, ② result of a match, ③ the results of this research, ④ academic achievement, ⑤ result of carelessness, ⑥ result of smoking. ⑦ He slipped and broke his leg, as a result, he will have to be away from school for two months.

 **练习**

**练习一、根据拼音写汉字，根据汉字写拼音**

( )duó ( )guǒ zhēng ( )( )ài ( )tè

掠( ) 结( ) ( )取 热( ) 奇( )

**练习二、搭配连线**

(1) 比赛的 A. 声音

(2) 奇怪的 B. 招待

(3) 严重的 C. 结果

(4) 研究的 D. 后果

(5) 热情的 E. 成果

**练习三、从今天学习的生词中选择合适的词填空**

1. 这座山的形状很 _____，我从没见过类似的山。

2. _____,他是怎么知道这件事的?

3. 这位科学家在这个领域的科研 _____ 很丰硕。

4. 双方商议的 _____ 是什么?

5. 如果你坚持这样,那 _____ 自负。

6. 保护环境是为 _____ 造福的事情。

7. 在历史上,这个国家的财富和土地曾遭到其他强大国家的 _____。

8. 他做好了充分的准备,_____ 一次通过测试。

9. 这三家公司在乳制品行业是竞争对手,都在尽力 _____ 市场。

10. 我的祖国虽然经济不太发达,但我仍然 _____ 她。

**答案**

**练习一：**

略

**练习二：**

(1) C (2)A (3)D (4)E (5)B

**练习三：**

1. 奇特 2. 奇怪 3. 成果 4. 结果 5. 后果

6. 后代 7. 掠夺 8. 争取 9. 争夺 10. 热爱

# 第5月,第2周的练习

**练习一.根据词语给加点的字注音**

1.( )　　2.( )　　3.( )　　4.( )　　5.( )
掠夺　　　可恶　　　范畴　　　踊跃　　　逐渐

**练习二.根据拼音填写词语**

shì　　　shì　　　qīng　　　qīng　　　qíng
1.重( )　2.解( )　3.( )松　4.( )向　5.热( )

**练习三.辨析并选择合适的词填空**

1. 在发生车祸时,头部有( )的疼痛,随即就什么也不知道了。(激烈、剧烈)

2. 场上的比赛进行得很( ),观众看上去似乎比运动员还紧张。(激烈、剧烈)

3. 我最大的爱好是( ),希望能游遍全世界。(旅游、游览)

4. 在中国的一年时间里,我除了学中文以外,还( )了很多名胜古迹。(旅游、游览)

5. 在开始使用新的电器之前,我们应该先认真阅读一下使用( )。(解释、说明)

6. 看到双方都有点生气,他赶忙( )说这是个误会。(解释、说明)

7. 来北京一个月后,我( )适应了这儿的生活。(逐步、逐渐)

8. 政府制定了一个计划,将( )关闭污染环境的工厂。(逐步、逐渐)

9. 昨晚的篮球赛我没看,比赛( )怎么样?谁赢了?(结果、成果、后果)

10. 破坏环境的( )将会十分严重。(结果、成果、后果)

**练习四.选词填空**

可笑　　可怜　　重量　　奇怪　　奇迹
可喜　　可恶　　重视　　奇特　　痕迹

1. 改革开放近30年来,中国取得了( )的成就。

2. 这些桃子真大,平均每个的( )足有半斤。

3. 观众们觉得马戏团的小丑太( )了,一边鼓掌一边笑。

4. ( ),他不是出国了吗?怎么还没走?

5. 警察发现草地上有卡车走过的( )。

6. 医生说他只能活两个星期了,可他却( )般地康复了。

7. 我的护照和钱包都丢了,如果我抓到那个( )的小偷,我一定会教训他一顿。

8. 他的发型很( ),显得很有个性。

9. 校园暴力事件引起了教育部门的( )。

10. 这个小孩真( ),这么小就失去了父母。

**练习五.选择尾词填空**

感　　　界　　　者　　　业　　　性
1. 这种布料有很好的透气( )和吸水( ),所以很适合

运动的时候穿。

2. 这个老师特别有幽默( ),我们都喜欢上他的课。

3. 对这一问题,学术( )存在争议,尚无定论。

4. 这本书的作者在接受采访时说,他希望有更好的作品献给读( )。

5. 今年发生了自然灾害,农( )生产遭受了很大的损失。

**练习六.写出下列词语的同义词**

1. 逐步( )　　　　2. 重量( )
3. 拥护( )　　　　4. 遭受( )
5. 倾向( )

**练习七.写出下列词语的反义词**

1. 整洁( )　　　　2. 热情( )
3. 热爱( )　　　　4. 轻松( )
5. 丰富( )

答案

**练习一.**

1.lüe　　2.wù　　3.chóu　　4.yuè　　5.jiàn

**练习二.**

1. 视　　2. 释　　3. 轻　　4. 倾　　5. 情

**练习三.**

1. 剧烈　　2. 激烈　　3. 旅游　　4. 游览　　5. 说明
6. 解释　　7. 逐渐　　8. 逐步　　9. 结果　　10. 后果

**练习四.**

1. 可喜　　2. 重量　　3. 可笑　　4. 奇怪　　5. 痕迹
6. 奇迹　　7. 可恶　　8. 奇特　　9. 重视　　10. 可怜

**练习五.**

1. 性,性　　2. 感　　3. 界　　4. 者　　5. 业

**练习六.**

1. 逐渐　　2. 分量　　3. 拥戴　　4. 遭到　　5. 趋势

**练习七.**

1. 脏乱　　2. 冷漠　　3. 憎恨　　4. 繁重　　5. 单调

# 5月 第3周的学习内容

**星期一**

**fāngfǎ**
## 方法 圆办法 （甲）名
method; means; way

**常用搭配**
学习方法 learning method
做面包的方法 a way for making bread

**用法示例**
老师在为我们演示一种新的书写方法。
Our teacher is showing us a new method of writing.
要做到这一点的唯一方法就是动手术。
The only way to do this was to operate.
只有用这种方法才能劝得动他。
Only by these means was it possible to persuade him.

**fāngshì**
## 方式 （乙）名
manner; way

**常用搭配**
生活方式 way of life 谈话的方式 way of talking
旅行的方式 ways of traveling

**用法示例**
介绍的方式很重要。
The manner of presentation is highly important.
我觉得你嘲笑他说英语的方式伤害了他的自尊心。
I think you hurt his pride by laughing at the way he speaks English.
我父亲总是对我做事的方式百般挑剔。
My father is always finding fault with the way I do things.

**lǚkè**
## 旅客 （乙）名
passenger; traveler

**常用搭配**
火车上的旅客 passengers on a train

**用法示例**
许多旅客正在候车室里等候。
Many passengers are waiting in the waiting room.
有些旅客坐在这艘轮船的甲板上聊天。
Some passengers are sitting on the deck of the ship.
公共汽车上有 20 名旅客。
There were twenty passengers on the bus.

**xuéshù**
## 学术 （乙）名
academic; learned

**常用搭配**
学术研究 academic research
学术论文 scientific papers
学术团体 an academic society

**用法示例**
这是一个纯学术性的问题。
The question is purely academic.
那是学术方面的事。
It's a matter of academic concern.
他订阅了几本学术刊物，以便了解本领域的发展动向。
He subscribes to several academic journals and magazines to keep abreast of developments in his field.

**lǚtú**
## 旅途 （乙）名
trip; journey

**常用搭配**
愉快的旅途 a pleasant trip

**用法示例**
我们在穿越这个地区的旅途中，看到了不少美丽的景色。
We passed through some beautiful scenic spots on our journey through this district.
在去夏威夷的旅途中，我们都很开心。
On our trip to Hawaii, we were all in high spirits.

**tǐjī**
## 体积 （乙）名
volume; cubage

**常用搭配**
立方体的体积 volume of the cube

**用法示例**
这个箱子的体积是两立方米。
The volume of this box is 2 cubic meters.
你能算出这个立方体的体积吗？
Can you figure out the volume of the cube?
这个集装箱的体积是 20 立方米。
The volume of this container is 20 cubic meters.

**wánshàn** **qiànquē**
## 完善 反 欠缺 （丙）形／动
① perfect; complete ② improve

**常用搭配**
完善的设施 fully equipped installations
使计划更加完善 to make the plan perfect

**【用法示例】**

这个镇的公共交通设施很完善。

The town is well served by public transport.

这还不够好,我要加以完善。

This is not good enough. I want to improve it.

我们的安排还有待完善。

There is still something to be perfected in the arrangement.

kěxíng

**可行** （丙）形

feasible

**【常用搭配】**

可行的计划 a feasible plan  可行性 feasibility

**【用法示例】**

我认为他的建议并不可行。

I don't think his proposal is feasible.

这个部门已经完成了开发该项目的可行性报告。

The department has finished a feasibility report on the project development.

制造电动汽车在技术上是可行的,但成本很高。

Making an electric car is technically feasible, but the cost is very high.

xuéshuō

**学说** （丙）名

theory; doctrine

**【常用搭配】**

孔子的学说 the doctrines of Confucius

社会主义学说 theory of socialism

**【用法示例】**

他们在讨论弗洛伊德的学说。

They are discussing the doctrines of Freud.

该学说已受到质疑。

The theory has been discredited.

suǒ

**锁** （丙）名／动

① lock ② to lock

**【常用搭配】**

锁门 lock the door  双眉紧锁 knit one's brows

**【用法示例】**

他把钥匙插进锁里。

He put the key in the lock.

门锁不上。

The door won't lock.

你走时别忘了锁门。

Don't forget to lock the door when you leave.

他把信锁在抽屉里了。

He locked the letter in a drawer.

fēifǎ

**非法** ⑤ 合法 héfǎ （丁）形

illegal; unlawful

**【常用搭配】**

非法行为 an illegal act  非法交易 an illegal trade

非法活动 illegal activities

**【用法示例】**

他承认他是非法移民。

He admitted that he was an illegal immigrant.

他们非法携带货物入境。

They have brought goods into the country illegally.

他是一个非法组织的成员。

He is a member of an unlawful organization.

kěguì

**可贵** ⑩ 宝贵 bǎoguì （丁）形

valuable; commendable; admirable

**【常用搭配】**

可贵的精神 commendable spirit

可贵的品格 admirable character

**【用法示例】**

失去健康才知道健康的可贵。

We do not know the value of health till we lose it.

时间对每个人来说都是可贵的。

Time is valuable for everybody.

 **词义辨析**

**方法、方式**

　　"方法"和"方式"都是名词,都表示如何做事。"方法"通常强调为达到某种目的而采取的具体的手段和途径;而"方式"则指做事的总的形式、风格和方法。如:①学习方法,②生活方式,③解决这个问题的最好方法是什么? ④你为什么用这种奇怪的方式谈话?

　　Both 方法 and 方式 are nouns, meaning "the way of doing something". 方法 usually indicates the concrete measure or means of accomplishing something; while 方式 indicates the manner or style in doing something or acting. For example: ① learning method, ② way of life, ③ What's the best way to tackle this problem? ④ Why are you talking in such a strange manner?

 **练习**

**练习一、根据拼音写汉字，根据汉字写拼音**
kě（　）（　）shàn　（　）jī（　）tú（　）shì
（　）行　　完（　）　　体（　）　旅（　）　方（　）

**练习二、搭配连线**
(1) 完善的　　　　　　A. 计划
(2) 可行的　　　　　　B. 设施
(3) 非法的　　　　　　C. 精神
(4) 孔子的　　　　　　D. 交易
(5) 可贵的　　　　　　E. 学说

**练习三、从今天学习的生词中选择合适的词填空**
1. 孔子关于教育的 _____ 至今还对中国人有深刻的影响。
2. 他们通过从事 _____ 交易赚钱。
3. 这套方案理论上说很漂亮，但是实际上并不 _____。
4. 这种舍己救人的品质很 _____。
5. 民主法制建设是一个逐步 _____ 健全的过程。
6. 这个作家根据自己的 _____ 见闻写了一本书。
7. _____ 朋友们，列车马上就要进站了，请您收拾好自己的行李，准备下车。
8. 他一心只想做 _____ 研究，不愿意做行政工作。
9. 外国人的生活 _____ 和我们不同。
10. 下面我们请凯特介绍一下她学习汉语的 _____，大家欢迎。

 **答案**

**练习一：**
略
**练习二：**
(1) B　　(2)A　　(3)D　　(4)E　　(5)C
**练习三：**
1. 学说　2. 非法　3. 可行　4. 可贵　5. 完善
6. 旅途　7. 旅客　8. 学术　9. 方式　10. 方法

 星期二

yuànyì
**愿意**　　　圆乐意　　**（甲）助动／动**
① to wish ② willing to do
**常用搭配**
如果你愿意的话……If you like,
**用法示例**
你愿意住在城里还是乡下？
Would you rather live in a town, or in the country?
我愿意这样做。
I am willing to do so.
我宁愿考试不及格，也不愿意作弊。
I would rather fail than cheat in the examination.

bǔchōng
**补充**　　　**（乙）动**
replenish; supplement
**常用搭配**
补充协议 supplementary contract
补充说明 supplementary explanation
**用法示例**
我们需要再次补充煤的储备。
We need to replenish our stocks of coal.
我想补充的是我们非常高兴。
I should add that we are very pleased.
我还要补充一下，我们对测试结果表示满意。
I should like to add that we are pleased with the test result.

xiàolǜ
**效率**　　　**（丙）名**
efficiency
**常用搭配**
提高效率　improve efficiency
**用法示例**
生病降低了他的工作效率。
His illness has impaired his working efficiency.
他们的工作效率很高。
Their labor efficiency is very high.
这台新复印机比那台旧的效率高。
This new copy machine is more efficient than the old one.

guànchè
**贯彻**　　　**（乙）动**
to carry out; to implement
**常用搭配**
贯彻一项政策
implement a policy

**用法示例**

我们将认真贯彻这个教育方针。

We will carefully implemeat the educational guidelines.

他们将立即贯彻委员会的决定。

They will implement the committee's decisions immediately.

你们要认真贯彻会议精神。

You should carefully carry out the spirit of the meeting carefully.

*shēnkè*
## 深刻 　　　　反 肤浅 *fūqiǎn* 　　（乙）形

profound; deep

**常用搭配**

深刻的思想 profound thought

深刻的印象 deep impression

**用法示例**

那位高贵的女士给他留下了深刻的印象。

The regal lady made a deep impression on him.

昨天我们上了一堂深刻的思想教育课。

We had a profound lesson in ideological education yesterday.

*shēnrù*
## 深入 　　　　　　　　　　（乙）动

① thorough ② penetrate deeply

**常用搭配**

深入研究 research sth. deeply

深入领会 to understand deeply

**用法示例**

让我们深入考虑一下这件事。

Let's pore deeply ponder the matter.

她想深入了解他的思想,好知道他在想什么。

She tried to probe his mind to find out what he was thinking.

他喜欢深入研读他所选的每一门课程。

He likes to read deeply on any subject that he chooses to study.

*zhìzuò*
## 制作 　　　　同 制造 *zhìzào* 　　（丙）动

make

**常用搭配**

制作玩具 make a toy 　　制作陶器 make pottery ware

**用法示例**

橡木是制作家具的好材料。

Oak is a good type of wood for making furniture.

他用木头制作了一个飞机模型。

He made a model plane out of wood.

她的结婚礼服是由一位著名的时装设计师制作的。

Her wedding apparel is made by a famous fashion designer.

*wánxiào*
## 玩笑 　　　　　　　　　　（丙）名

joke; jest

**常用搭配**

跟他开玩笑 joke with him

你是在开玩笑吧。You must be joking.

**用法示例**

那句话本来只是个玩笑。

That remark was intended as a joke.

我们跟他开了个玩笑。

We played a joke on him.

我不是那个意思,只不过是开个玩笑。

I didn't mean that seriously — I was only joking.

*běnrén*
## 本人 　　　　反 他人 *tārén* 　　（丙）代

① I (me, myself) ② in person ③ oneself (used for emphasis)

**常用搭配**

作者本人 the author herself 　　我本人 I myself

**用法示例**

我代表我的同事和我本人向你表示感谢。

On behalf of my colleagues and myself I thank you.

我本人对事实确信不疑。

I myself was certain of the facts.

我要见经理本人,而不是他的秘书。

I want the manager himself, not his secretary.

*běnshēn*
## 本身 　　　　　　　　　　（丙）代

① itself ② in itself

**常用搭配**

事件本身 the matter itself

**用法示例**

问题就出在机器本身。

The trouble is in the machine itself.

这件事本身并不太重要。

The thing itself is not so important.

该药本身并无害处,但与酒类同服则有危险。

The drug is not harmful per se, but is dangerous when taken with alcohol.

*bǔcháng*
## 补偿 　　　　　　　　　　（丁）动

compensate; make up

**常用搭配**

补偿某人的损失 make compensation for one's losses

**用法示例**

我将尽力补偿你的损失。

I will try to make up for your loss.

战争给人民带来的痛苦不是用金钱可以补偿的。

The suffering of people caused by the war cannot be compensated for by money.

他的保险单失效了,所以没有得到任何补偿。

He didn't get any compensation because his insurance policy had lapsed.

# 效益 xiàoyì （丁）名

effect and profit; beneficial result

**常用搭配**

提高效益 improve effect and profit

**用法示例**

这项发明会为我们工厂带来丰厚的效益。

The invention will produce great beneficial results for our factory.

政府拒绝补贴效益不佳的企业。

The government refuses to prop up inefficient enterprises.

 **词义辨析**

## 本人、本身

"本人"和"本身"都是代词,都可以用来强调自身。"本人"只用于人,称呼自己时显得严肃而郑重,还有亲自的意思。"本身"可以用于人,也可以用于物,有强调的语气,没有亲自的意思。如:①我想跟医生本人谈谈。②这件事很重要,别人不能代替,必须是他本人来签合同。③这房子本身并不太好,但我喜欢它周围的环境。

Both 本人 and 本身 are pronouns, meaning "oneself". 本人 is used for people, it sounds more formal when one addresses oneself with it, and it also means "by oneself, personally"; while 本身 is used to stress the person himself or the thing itself, and it has no meaning of "by oneself or personally". For example: ① I'd like to speak to the doctor herself. ② It is very important, nobody can replace him, and he must sign the contract by himself. ③ The house itself is not very good, but I like its environment.

 **练习**

**练习一、根据拼音写汉字,根据汉字写拼音**

( )zuò ( )cháng ( )kè ( )chè ( )lǜ

制( ) 补( ) 深( ) 贯( ) 效( )

**练习二、搭配连线**

(1) 补偿　　　　　　　A. 说明

(2) 补充　　　　　　　B. 损失

(3) 印象　　　　　　　C. 领会

(4) 提高　　　　　　　D. 深刻

(5) 深入　　　　　　　E. 效益

**练习三、从今天学习的生词中选择合适的词填空**

1. 这个故事的寓意很 _____ 。

2. 这个报告引用了很多资料,对当前问题作了 _____ 的分析。

3. 她做事 _____ 非常高,是个难得的人才。

4. 现在公司的 _____ 不太好,工资只能发一半。

5. 我没想到的,希望大家多多 _____ 。

6. 在今后的改革工作中要充分 _____ 此次会议的精神。

7. _____ 这样一个玩具的成本是3块钱,可是市场定价是30块。

8. 这个问题你得问他 _____ ,我们作为朋友,不便多说。

9. 这个计划 _____ 没有问题,是在执行的时候出了错。

10. 保险公司 _____ 了农民在自然灾害中遭受的损失。

**答案**

**练习一:**

略

**练习二:**

(1) B　　(2)A　　(3)D　　(4)E　　(5)C

**练习三:**

1. 深刻　2. 深入　3. 效率　4. 效益　5. 补充

6. 贯彻　7. 制作　8. 本人　9. 本身　10. 补偿

**星期三**

**shōushi**
**收拾** 同 整理 （甲）动
to put in order; to tidy up

**常用搭配**
收拾房间 tidy up the room
收拾行李 pack one's belongings
饭后收拾餐具 tidy up after dinner

**用法示例**
他把书架上的书收拾了一下。
He arranged the books on the shelf.
聚会结束后，他们留下来帮助收拾东西。
They stayed behind after the party to help clear-up.
他把东西收拾好就走了。
He packed up his things and left.

**xiūlǐ**
**修理** 同 维修 （乙）动
repair; fix

**常用搭配**
修理玩具 mend a toy　修理收音机 repair a radio

**用法示例**
水龙头在漏水，我们得把它修理一下。
The tap is leaking. We must fix it.
我已把我的表修理好了。
I had my watch repaired.
他把汽车送到修车厂修理了。
He sent his car to the garage for repair.

**xiūgǎi**
**修改** 同 批改 （乙）动
alter; amend

**常用搭配**
修改合同条款 modify the terms of a contract
修改文件 to amend a document

**用法示例**
那项政策经修改后才获得委员会同意。
The policy was agreed by the committee, but only in a modified form.
我们的预算需作重大修改。
Our budget needs drastic revision.
她不断修改完善自己的小说。
She developed her novel through constant revision.

**xíngdòng**
**行动** （乙）名／动
① action ② act

**常用搭配**
采取行动 to take action　果断的行动 prompt action

**用法示例**
我们将马上行动。
We will act immediately.
想到你行动的后果，我就感到害怕。
It terrified me to contemplate the consequences of your action.
你们必须停止你们的危险行动。
You must discontinue your dangerous actions.

**tiáozhěng**
**调整** （乙）动
adjust

**常用搭配**
调整价格 adjust the price
调整演出的顺序 adjust the performance sequence
进行调整 make adjustments

**用法示例**
水压可能需要调整。
The water pressure may need adjustment.
我对座次表做了小小的调整。
I've made a few minor adjustments to the seating plan.
根据目前的价格水平，我们不得不调整报价。
Due to the present price level, we cannot help but adjust our offer.

**xiāochú**
**消除** 同 清除 （丙）动
eliminate; remove

**常用搭配**
消除疑虑 remove doubts
消除分歧 smooth away differences

**用法示例**
医生的报告消除了他们的忧虑。
The doctor's report removed their worries.
我们消除了所有的怀疑与恐惧。
We banished all our doubts and fears.
我试图消除他们之间的误会。
I tried to clear up the misunderstanding between them.

**tiáojié**
**调节** （丙）动
regulate; adjust

**常用搭配**
调节温度 regulate the temperature

**用法示例**
这种书桌的高度是可以调节的。
The height of this kind of desk can be adjusted.
眼睛能自动调节以便观看远近不同的景物。
The eye can adjust to view objects at different distances.
机器的速度可以自动调节。
The speed of the machine may be automatically regulated.

**xiūjiàn**
**修建** ◎ **建造** **jiànzào** （丙）动
to construct; to build

**常用搭配**
修建水库 build a reservoir　修建机场 construct an airport

**用法示例**
他申请资金修建学校。
He applied for funds to build a school.
两个村子合作修建了这座桥。
The two villages cooperated to construct the bridge.

**xíngwéi**
**行为** （丙）名
behavior; action

**常用搭配**
英勇的行为 heroic action　正义的行为 an act of justice
粗鲁的行为 rude action

**用法示例**
他的行为给他的家庭带来了耻辱。
His behavior has brought dishonor upon his family.
帮助盲人过街是友善的行为。
It is an act of kindness to help a blind man across the street.
那位记者被指控有违反职业道德的行为。
The reporter was accused of unprofessional conduct.

**xiāofèi**
**消费** （乙）动
consume

**常用搭配**
消费能力 consuming capacity
消费品 articles of consumption
消费者 consumer

**用法示例**
国内消费水平越来越高。
The level of domestic consumption grows higher and higher.
鼓励消费者对劣质商品进行投诉。
Consumers are encouraged to complain about faulty goods.

**xiūdìng**
**修订** （丁）动
revise

**常用搭配**
修订法规 revise regulations　修订版 a revised edition

**用法示例**
这本书要重新修订。
The book shall be revised.
目录正在修订之中。
The catalogue is under revision.

**tiáojiě**
**调解** （丁）动
mediate; reconcile

**常用搭配**
调解委员会 mediation board
经某人调解 through one's intercession

**用法示例**
他调解了劳资双方的矛盾。
He mediated the conflict between labor and management.
他在两个交战国之间进行调解。
He is mediating between two warring countries.
调解已经取得了很大的进展。
The intercession has made rapid progress.

 **词义辨析**

**修理、修改**

"修理"和"修改"都是动词。"修理"的意思是使损坏的东西恢复原状或作用,其对象多为机器或器具等;而"修改"的意思是使书写的材料正确或完善,其对象通常是文章、计划等。如:①修理汽车,②修理手表,③修改作文,④修改报告。

Both 修理 and 修改 are verbs. 修理 means to "restore to sound condition and functionality after damage", and its object mostly is a machine or a tool; while 修改 means "to correct or improve upon a written material", and its object is usually an article or a plan. For example: ① to repair a car, ② to repair a watch, ③ to modify one's composition, ④ to amend a report.

 **练习**

**练习一、根据拼音写汉字，根据汉字写拼音**

( )shi ( )zhěng xiāo( ) xiū( ) xíng ( )
收( ) 调( ) ( )除 ( )订 ( )为

**练习二、搭配连线**

(1) 收拾      A. 行动
(2) 修理      B. 行李
(3) 调节      C. 分歧
(4) 消除      D. 机器
(5) 采取      E. 温度

**练习三、从今天学习的生词中选择合适的词填空**

1. 请按照专家的意见把这个设计方案 _____ 一下。
2. 师傅，我的自行车坏了，请帮我 _____ 一下。
3. 新 _____ 的机场已经开始启用了。
4. 我的这本书和你的不太一样，我的是最初的版本，你的是 _____ 版。
5. 周末，我一般 _____ 房间、洗衣服。
6. 光认识到自己的错误是没用的，要用 _____ 来证明你的努力。
7. 根据目前的形势，公司 _____ 了销售策略。
8. 现代生活的压力很大，要学会自我 _____。
9. 这种损人利己的 _____ 遭到了大家的批判。
10. 随着收入水平的提高，人们的 _____ 观念有了很大的变化。

**答案**

练习一：
略

练习二：
(1) B    (2)D    (3)E    (4)C    (5)A

练习三：
1. 修改    2. 修理    3. 修建    4. 修订    5. 收拾
6. 行动    7. 调整    8. 调节    9. 行为    10. 消费

---

 **星期四**

**yíyàng**
**一样** （甲）形／助

① like；same ② equal to

**常用搭配**

与……一样 the same as...    像……一样 as if...

**用法示例**

这两个男孩的兴趣不一样。
The two boys are different in their tastes.
我爱她就像爱自己的女儿一样。
I have loved her like a father should.
他能跑得和我一样快。
He can run as fast as I can.

**tóngyàng**
**同样** （乙）形

same；equal

**常用搭配**

同样的事 the same thing
问同样的问题 ask the same question

**用法示例**

每天都做同样的工作是很单调的。
It is very dreary to do the same job every day.
锻炼身体和学习同样重要。
Learning is as important as physical exercise.
使我惊讶的是，他又犯了同样的错误。
To my surprise, he made the same mistake.

**bùjǐn**
**不仅** （乙）连

not only

**常用搭配**

不仅……而且…… not only... but...

**用法示例**

她不仅漂亮，而且善良。
She is not only beautiful, but also kind.
她不仅很会演奏，而且还会作曲。
She not only plays well, but also writes music.
他不仅没有放弃，反而比以前更加努力了。
Instead of giving up, he works harder than before.

**wěndìng**
**稳定** （乙）形

stable；steady

**常用搭配**

社会稳定 social stability
稳定的收入 steady income
稳定增长 increase steadily

**用法示例**

政府采取了措施以确保物价稳定。

The government took measures to maintain the stability of prices.

她情绪十分稳定。

She is mentally very stable.

**shībài**
## 失败 （乙）动／名

① be defeated; fail ② failure

**常用搭配**

失败是成功之母。

Failure is the mother of success.

**用法示例**

他又试了一次，竟然又失败了。

He tried a second time only to fail again.

她失败后感到非常伤心。

She was extremely sad when she failed.

他说自己是一个成功的演员，却是个失败的父亲。

He said he was a successful actor, but a failed father.

**zìrán**
## 自然 ⊗ 做作 **zuòzuo** （乙）名／形

① nature ② natural

**常用搭配**

自然法则 the laws of nature

自然现象 natural phenomenon

自然环境 natural environment

**用法示例**

磁力是一种自然现象。

Magnetism is a natural phenomenon.

学习植物学使我对大自然了解了许多。

Through studying botany, I understand much about nature.

你的成功是很自然的事情。

It's quite natural that you should succeed.

**guòdù**
## 过渡 （丙）动／形

① transit ② interim

**常用搭配**

过渡政府 an interim government

过渡时期 transitional period

**用法示例**

我们希望能够和平过渡到新的制度。

We hope there will be a peaceful transition to the new system.

天气越来越冷了，这个月是从秋季到冬季的过渡。

It is growing colder and colder, as this month marks the transition from autumn to winter.

**bùjīn**
## 不禁 （丙）副

can't help (doing sth.)

**常用搭配**

不禁笑了 cannot help laughing

不禁哭了 cannot help crying

不禁爱上她 cannot help loving her

**用法示例**

当她听到这首民歌的时候不禁流泪了。

She could not help tearing up when she heard the folk song.

听到战争的消息，他不禁为儿子担心。

Hearing the news of the war, he could not help worrying about his son.

看到这张照片，我不禁想家了。

Looking at that picture, I cannot help missing my family.

**shīdiào**
## 失掉 ⊗ 得到 **dédào** （丙）动

lose; miss

**常用搭配**

失掉机会 lose a chance　失掉工作 lose one's job

**用法示例**

这种行为使他失掉了工作。

Such behavior lost him his job.

他抓住了那个机会，却失掉了最亲密的朋友。

He took the opportunity, but he lost his closest friend.

**zìmǎn**
## 自满 ⊚ 自负 **zìfù** （丙）形

complacent; self-satisfied

**常用搭配**

别自满。Don't be complacent.

自满的情绪 the emotions of complacency

**用法示例**

我们不能自满，必须继续改进。

There's no room for complacency; we must continue to improve.

成功多年后他变得自满起来。

He had become complacent after years of success.

自满是进步的障碍。

Complacency is a drawback to progress.

**wěntuǒ**
## 稳妥 ⊚ 妥当 **tuǒdàng** （丁）形

reliable; safe; trustworthy

**常用搭配**

稳妥的计划 a safe plan

**用法示例**

公共汽车可能早到，因此我们得稳妥点，现在就动身。

The bus might be early, so we'd better play safe and leave now.

我认为火车是比较稳妥的交通工具。

I think the train is a safe and reliable means of transportation.

我觉得这个安排不够稳妥。

I don't think the arrangement is safe enough.

## 过度 guòdù (丁)形/副

① excessive ② excessively

**常用搭配**

兴奋过度 excessively excited
过度开采 excessive exploitation

**用法示例**

由于过度劳累,他病了。
He was ill due to excessive weariness.

他过度紧张,昨晚一夜没睡。
He was excessively nervous and couldn't get to sleep last night.

饮酒过度的人常常失去记忆。
Alcoholics often suffer from periods of oblivion.

 词义辨析

**一样、同样**

1、"一样"和"同样"都可以用作形容词,表示相同,没有差别。两个词作定语或状语时可以相互替换。但"同样"还是连词,表示后面的意思与前面的意思相同或相通;"一样"没有这种用法。如:①这个学校的学生都穿着一样/同样的服装。②他不愿被人批评,同样,他也不批评别人。

Both 一样 and 同样 are adjectives, indicating "same, no different". And the two words are interchangeable when they function as an attributive or an adverbial. But 同样 is also a conjunction, indicating the following is the same as what goes before; while 一样 has no usage like this. For example: ① All students in this school dress alike. ② He doesn't like to be criticized by others, and similarly, he never criticizes others.

2、"一样"可以作谓语,可以用否定形式"不一样",可以受程度副词修饰,还经常与"跟","像"等一起使用,表示情况相似或用于比喻;"同样"没有这些用法。例如:①我和你得分一样。②她的性格跟她妈妈不一样。③他们的上衣完全一样。④他像猫一样爬上了树。

一样 can function as a predicate, and can be used in a negative form "不一样" (different), can be modified by adverbs of degree, can be used with "跟", "像", etc. to indicate the same situation or as a metaphor; while 同样 can not be so used. For example: ① I received the same grade as you did. ② Her character is different from her mother's. ③ Their jackets are identical. ④ He climbed the tree like a cat.

 练习

**练习一、根据拼音写汉字,根据汉字写拼音**

wěn ( ) ( )bài guò ( ) ( )mǎn ( )jīn
( )妥 失( ) ( )渡 自( ) 不( )

**练习二、搭配连线**

(1) 失掉      A. 时期
(2) 社会      B. 开采
(3) 自然      C. 稳定
(4) 过渡      D. 机会
(5) 过度      E. 环境

**练习三、从今天学习的生词中选择合适的词填空**

1. 青春期是儿童和成人阶段的 _____ 时期。
2. 他的死跟饮酒 _____ 有直接关系。
3. 我用 _____ 的方法又做了一遍,结果却发现实验结果完全不同 。
4. 我跟他 _____ ,都喜欢吃辣的。
5. 小张 _____ 菜做得好,文章写得也不错。
6. 想到自己犯了一个这么低级的错误,她 _____ 有点儿脸红。
7. 第一次在这么多人面前讲话,她显得有些不 _____ 。
8. 现阶段我们虽然取得了一些成绩,但要克服 _____ 情绪,继续努力。
9. 把钱交给银行保管是个 _____ 的办法。
10. 过了一个月,小女孩的情绪慢慢 _____ 下来了。

## 答案

**练习一:**
略

**练习二:**
(1) D    (2)C    (3)E    (4)A    (5)B

**练习三:**
1. 过渡   2. 过度   3. 同样   4. 一样   5. 不仅
6. 不禁   7. 自然   8. 自满   9. 稳妥   10. 稳定

**星期五**

shuìjiào
**睡觉** （甲）动
go to bed; sleep

（常用搭配）
该睡觉了。It's time to go to bed.

（用法示例）
猫头鹰白天睡觉晚上工作。
Owls sleep by day and work by night.
他睡了两个小时觉。
He slept for two hours.
女儿睡觉之前,我总给她讲故事。
I always tell my daughter a story before she goes to sleep.
昨天晚上你几点上床睡觉的?
What time did you go to bed last night?

shuìmián
**睡眠** （丙）名
slumber; sleep

（常用搭配）
睡眠不足 lack of sleep

（用法示例）
最近我睡眠不足。
I haven't had enough sleep lately.
正发育的孩子必须睡眠充足。
A growing child needs plenty of sleep.
多数人每天需要六至八小时的睡眠。
Most people need six to eight hours of sleep every day.

hánlěng　　　　　　　yánrè
**寒冷** 反 炎热 （乙）形
frigid; very cold

（常用搭配）
寒冷的气候 an arctic climate
寒冷的房间 a frigid room

（用法示例）
寒冷的天气抑制了植物的生长。
Cold weather constrains the plant's growth.
在寒冷的冬天,我们不得不穿皮大衣。
We have to wear fur coats in the cold winter.
挪威人生活在比较寒冷的地区。
The Norwegians live in a comparatively cold zone.

qíngxíng
**情形** （乙）名
situation; case

（常用搭配）
假设的情形 hypothetical situation
在这种情形下 in this case

（用法示例）
根据现在的情形,你必须马上离开这里。
As the case stands, you must leave here at once.
他生气时就大叫,这是常有的情形。
He shouts when he gets angry, as is often the case.
这是该校有史以来未曾出现过的情形。
That is an unprecedented situation in the history of the school.

qiǎomiào
**巧妙** （乙）形
ingenious; clever

（常用搭配）
巧妙的比喻 a felicitous comparison
巧妙的计划 an ingenious scheme

（用法示例）
她以巧妙的手腕处理了这个问题。
She dealt with the problem with consummate skill.
他们用巧妙的提问诱使他招认了。
By clever questioning they trapped him into making a confession.
这件家具是古代风格和仿制品的巧妙结合。
The furniture is an artful blend of antiques and reproductions.

zūnshǒu
**遵守** （乙）动
comply with; obey

（常用搭配）
遵守法律 abide by the law
遵守诺言 keep one's promise

（用法示例）
每个人都必须遵守这条法令。
Everyone should obey this ordinance.
你得遵守图书馆的规则。
You must comply with the library's rules.
每个人都应该遵守纪律,你们军官也不例外。
Everyone should keep the discipline, and you officers are no exception.

yíshì　　　　　　　diǎnlǐ
**仪式** 同 典礼 （丙）名
ceremony; ritual; rite

（常用搭配）
洗礼仪式 the rite of baptism　　签字仪式 signing ceremony

（用法示例）
总统出席了这个仪式。
The president was present at the ceremony.
他们举行了一个宗教仪式。
They hold a religious ceremony.
他们的结婚仪式将在哪里举行?
Where will their wedding ceremony be held?

*dǎozhì*
导致　　　　　*zhāozhì*　圆 招致　　　　（丙）动
lead to; result in
常用搭配
导致失败 lead to failure
导致破产 result in bankruptcy
用法示例
这起事故导致两名乘客死亡。
The accident resulted in the death of two passengers.
他的错误导致了重大损失。
His mistake resulted in severe losses.
他的行为导致我们不信任他。
His actions led us to distrust him.

*qīngxǐng*
清醒　　　　　　　　　　　　（丙）形/动
① sober; clear-minded ② become sober; sober up
常用搭配
头脑清醒 clear-headed
清醒的判断 sober judgment
保持清醒 keep clear-minded
用法示例
你洗个冷水澡,马上就会清醒。
A cold shower will soon wake you up.
给她一杯咖啡,让她清醒清醒。
Give her a cup of coffee; that'll help to sober her up.
他喝酒喝得很多但好像还很清醒。
He drinks a lot but looks sober.

*xǐyuè*
喜悦　　　　　*bēishāng*　圆 悲伤　　　　（丙）形
joyous; happy
常用搭配
丰收的喜悦 happiness of harvest
胜利的喜悦 joy of victory
用法示例
我可以从她的眼睛里看出她的喜悦。
I can see her gladness in her eyes.
她的孩子出生时,她无比喜悦。
When her child was born, her joy was beyond measure.

*lěngdàn*
冷淡　　　　　　　　　　　　（丁）形/动
① cool ② be cold to
常用搭配
冷淡的问候 a cool greeting
态度冷淡 a frigid manner
用法示例
他今天对我们十分冷淡,不知我们是否冒犯了他。
He seemed very cool to us today. I wonder whether we've offended him.
观众对新剧目反应冷淡。
The audience gave a cold response to the new play.

*qíngjié*
情节　　　　　　　　　　　　（丁）名
plot
常用搭配
故事情节 plot of a story
用法示例
这部电影的情节很吸引人。
The plot of the film is very exciting.
随着影片的放映,故事情节展开了。
The story unfolds as the film goes on.
这是一本情节错综复杂的小说。
This is a novel with an intricate plot.

 词义辨析

**睡觉、睡眠**

　　"睡眠"是名词,经常用作书面语,如"睡眠质量","睡眠对健康很重要";"睡觉"是动宾短语,比较口语化,经常用作谓语,如:"他在睡觉呢";还可以用作"去睡觉","我睡一个小时觉","该睡觉了","我睡不着觉"。"睡眠"均不能代替以上例子中的"睡觉"。

　　睡眠 is a noun, and usually used in writing. For example: "睡眠质量" (the quality of sleep), "睡眠对健康很重要" (sleeping is important for health); while 睡觉 is a verb-object phrase which is colloquial, and usually used as a predicate, such as "他在睡觉呢" (he is sleeping) And it can be used as "去睡觉" (go to bed) "我睡一个小时觉" (I slept for an hour), "该睡觉了" (it is time to go to bed), "我睡不着觉" (I can not go to sleep). "睡眠" can not replace 睡觉 in the examples above.

 练习

**练习一、根据拼音写汉字,根据汉字写拼音**
dǎo（　　）　zūn（　　）　（　　）miào　hán（　　）（　　）mián
（　　）致　　　（　　）守　　巧（　　）　（　　）冷　睡（　　）

**练习二、搭配连线**
(1) 清醒的　　　　　　　　A. 仪式
(2) 庄严的　　　　　　　　B. 睡眠
(3) 巧妙的　　　　　　　　C. 头脑
(4) 充足的　　　　　　　　D. 喜悦
(5) 胜利的　　　　　　　　E. 计划

**练习三、从今天学习的生词中选择合适的词填空**
1. 在_____的冬天来临之前,燕子迁徙到了南方。
2. 跟老板吵架后,同事们对她_____起来。
3. 他_____过来后对自己的行为非常后悔,从此不再喝酒了。
4. 他能够_____地处理上下级之间的关系,很快确立了

自己在公司的地位。

5. 从现在的 _____ 看,我们必须进行彻底的改革。

6. 中国有些高收入人群由于长年加班,_____ 严重不足。

7. 学生要 _____ 课堂纪律,上课时不能随便出入教室。

8. 西方的结婚 _____ 大多在教堂举行。

9. 连续一周的暴雨 _____ 河水上涨。

10. 我们怀着 _____ 的心情参加孩子的毕业典礼。

 **答案**

**练习一:**
略
**练习二:**
(1) C     (2)A     (3)E     (4)B     (5)D
**练习三:**

| 1. 寒冷 | 2. 冷淡 | 3. 清醒 | 4. 巧妙 | 5. 情形 |
|---|---|---|---|---|
| 6. 睡眠 | 7. 遵守 | 8. 仪式 | 9. 导致 | 10. 喜悦 |

# 第5月,第3周的练习

**练习一.根据词语给加点的字注音**

| 1.( ) | 2.( ) | 3.( ) | 4.( ) | 5.( ) |
|---|---|---|---|---|
| 睡觉 | 贯彻 | 稳妥 | 遵守 | 喜悦 |

**练习二.根据拼音填写词语**

    shi     shī     shì     yì     yì
1. 收( ) 2.( )败 3. 方( )4.愿( ) 5.效( )

**练习三.辨析并选择合适的词填空**

1. 年轻人的生活( )和老人有所不同,所以住在一起不方便。(方法、方式)

2. 班会上,大家都讲了各自学习汉语的好( )。(方法、方式)

3. 这件事( )是好事,只是大家没有做好而已。(本人、本身)

4. 如果你去邮局取包裹,最好是( )带着有效证件去取。(本人、本身)

5. 师傅,我的车出毛病了,您能不能帮我( )一下?(修理、修改)

6. 这篇文章在发表前( )过几次。(修理、修改)

7. 她跟她妈妈( )温柔,但不像妈妈那么坚强。(一样、同样)

8. 我相信,如果你遇到这样的事情,( ),你也会这么做的。(一样、同样)

9. 研究表明,越来越多的城市白领因( )不足诱发各种疾病。(睡眠、睡觉)

10. 他的生活很有规律,每天六点半起床,晚上十点钟( )。

(睡眠、睡觉)

**练习四.选词填空**

| 过渡 | 调节 | 调整 | 导致 | 方式 |
|---|---|---|---|---|
| 过度 | 调解 | 补偿 | 补充 | 仪式 |

1. 他的病是由睡眠不足( )的,他必须改变生活方式,多休息。

2. 两个人的矛盾无法( ),管理宿舍的老师只好给他们调换了房间。

3. 人们对自然的( )开发破坏了生态平衡。

4. 这个房间的温度是自动( )的,没必要使用空调。

5. 如果有我没想到的地方,请大家( )。

6. 批评人的时候要注意( ),不要伤害别人的自尊心。

7. 他年轻的时候做过对不起妻子的事,现在他想( ),可妻子不接受。

8. 他们的结婚( )是在教堂举行的。

9. 由于教练生病了,训练计划作了相应的( )。

10. 青春期也可以说是一个人从少年到成年的( )时期。

**练习五.写出下列词语的同义词**
1. 仪式( )     2. 自满( )
3. 制作( )     4. 消除( )
5. 收拾( )

**练习六.写出下列词语的反义词**
1. 非法( )     2. 失掉( )
3. 喜悦( )     4. 寒冷( )
5. 深刻( )

 **答案**

**练习一.**

| 1.jiào | 2.chè | 3.tuǒ | 4.zūn | 5.yuè |
|---|---|---|---|---|

**练习二.**

| 1. 拾 | 2. 失 | 3. 式 | 4. 意 | 5. 益 |
|---|---|---|---|---|

**练习三.**

| 1. 方式 | 2. 方法 | 3. 本身 | 4. 本人 | 5. 修理 |
|---|---|---|---|---|
| 6. 修改 | 7. 一样 | 8. 同样 | 9. 睡眠 | 10. 睡觉 |

**练习四.**

| 1. 导致 | 2. 调解 | 3. 过度 | 4. 调节 | 5. 补充 |
|---|---|---|---|---|
| 6. 方式 | 7. 补偿 | 8. 仪式 | 9. 调整 | 10. 过渡 |

**练习五.**

| 1. 典礼 | 2. 自负 | 3. 制造 | 4. 清除 | 5. 整理 |
|---|---|---|---|---|

**练习六.**

| 1. 合法 | 2. 得到 | 3. 悲哀 | 4. 炎热 | 5. 肤浅 |
|---|---|---|---|---|

# 5月 第4周的学习内容

星期一 Monday

### qíngkuàng
## 情况 （甲）名

condition; situation

**常用搭配**

天气情况 weather conditions
实际情况 practical situation

**用法示例**

情况始终都在变化。
Conditions are changing all the time.
我们得研究一下目前的情况。
We must discuss the present situation.
你对当前的情况怎么看？
What do you think of the present situation？

### qíngjǐng
## 情景 （乙）名

scene; sight

**常用搭配**

感人的情景 touching sight
可怕的情景 fearsome sight

**用法示例**

她仍能想起儿时的情景。
She can still recall scenes from her childhood.
这情景使她心寒。
The sight sent a chill through her heart.
那感人的情景铭刻在他的记忆里。
The moving scene was engraved upon his memory.

### lèi
## 类 （乙）名／量

① category; kind ② measure word

**常用搭配**

这类事情 this sort of thing　人类 mankind
两类鱼 two kinds of fishes
几类事物 a few kinds of things

**用法示例**

我们经常做这类练习。
We often do this kind of exercise.
图书馆里有各类书籍。
There are all sorts of books in a library.

### bùzú
## 不足 （丙）形

① short of ② deficient

**常用搭配**

营养不足 a nutritional deficiency　资金不足 short of funds
经验不足 short of experience

**用法示例**

这些商品现在供应不足，价格会上涨。
These goods are in short supply; the price will be high.
他总是抱怨研究经费不足。
He always complains about the shortage of funds for research.
他指出了这项计划的不足之处。
He pointed out some deficiencies in this plan.

### bǐjì
## 笔记 （乙）名

note

**常用搭配**

记笔记 take notes

**用法示例**

我把她的笔记抄在我的笔记本上。
I copied out her notes into my notebook.
小男孩喜欢在书页空白处做笔记。
The little boy likes to make notes on the margin of books.
他停下来看了看笔记，然后继续提问。
He paused to consult his notes, and then proceeded with his questions.

### zhǔnshí
## 准时 　 ànshí 按时 （乙）形

① on time ② punctual

**常用搭配**

准时上课 punctual for the class　准时到达 arrive on time

**用法示例**

雾天我们不能保证火车准时到达。
We cannot guarantee the punctual arrival of trains in foggy weather.
我的猫一到用餐时间就会准时出现。
My cat makes punctual appearance at mealtimes.
他总是准时赴约。
He is always punctual for appointments.

### sīkǎo
## 思考 （丙）动

think

**常用搭配**

认真思考 think carefully

思考问题 think about questions

**用法示例**

我无法思考,脑子里一片混乱。

I couldn't think; my mind was in complete turmoil.

动物能思考吗?

Are animals able to think?

回答之前要仔细思考。

Think carefully before you answer.

qiǎngpò
**强迫**　　圈 **强制**　qiángzhì　　（丙）动

compel; force

**常用搭配**

强迫他投降 compel him to give in

强迫我签合同 force me to sign the contract

**用法示例**

最后我们强迫敌人撤退了。

We forced the enemy to retreat at last.

老板强迫我做那件事。

The boss forced me to do it.

他们强迫我做违背我意愿的事。

They forced me to do things against my will.

bèipò
**被迫**　　反 **自愿**　zìyuàn　　（丙）动

be compelled; be forced

**常用搭配**

被迫同意 be forced to agree

被迫放弃 be forced to give up

**用法示例**

叛乱者被迫投降了。

The rebels were forced to give in.

他被迫改变了想法。

He was forced to change his mind.

我是被迫这样做的。

I was compelled to do so.

lǐngyù
**领域**　　　　　　　　　（丙）名

domain; field

**常用搭配**

政治领域 the field of politics　研究领域 a field of research

文学领域 the field of literature

**用法示例**

他是金融领域的专家。

He is an expert in the financial field.

他在医学领域里广获赞扬。

He has won wide recognition in the field of medicine.

他在自己的领域里已经出名了。

He has become famous in his own field.

bǐjì
**笔迹**　　　　　　　　　（丁）名

handwriting

**常用搭配**

辨认笔迹 identify one's handwriting

**用法示例**

他能够根据笔迹说出你的性格。

He can ascertain your character according to your handwriting.

老师知道是你在黑板上写的,因为他认识你的笔迹。

The teacher knew you wrote it on the blackboard, because he could identify your handwriting.

zhǔnxǔ
**准许**　　反 **禁止**　jìnzhǐ　　（丁）动

allow; permit

**常用搭配**

准许某人做某事 grant sb. permission to do sth.

准许他解释 permit him to explain

**用法示例**

她不准许我们做这件事。

She won't give us permission to do it.

地方法官准许他保释。

The magistrate granted him bail.

准许这个犯人回家跟家人一起过圣诞节。

The prisoner was permitted to go home to spend Christmas with his family.

**词义辨析**

**情况、情景**

"情况"和"情景"都是名词,都可以表示事物呈现的面貌。"情况"强调形势、局势,可以是具体事务,也可以是抽象的事物;"情景"一般是指人们用视觉、听觉能感受到,并能引起感情变化的场景。例如:①病人情况危急。②你无论在什么情况下都不可以告诉他所发生的事。③他们与失散的女儿团聚,快乐的情景是可想而知的。④我永远也不会忘记那感人的情景。

Both 情况 and 情景 are nouns, indicating "the state of affairs". 情况 stresses the condition or situation that may be concrete or abstract; while 情景 usually refers to the scene which one can feel by sight or hearing and which will give rise to changes of one's feelings. For example: ① The patient's condition is critical. ② You must on no condition tell him what has happened. ③ Imagine the joyful scene when they were reunited with their lost daughter. ④ I will never forget that moving sight.

 **练习**

**练习一、根据拼音写汉字，根据汉字写拼音**

( )yù ( )pò ( )jì zhǔn( ) qíng( )
领( ) 强( ) 笔( ) ( )许 ( )况

**练习二、搭配连线**

(1) 营养 A. 放弃
(2) 医学 B. 到达
(3) 被迫 C. 情况
(4) 准时 D. 领域
(5) 实际 E. 不足

**练习三、从今天学习的生词中选择合适的词填空**

1. 这 _____ 商品卖得很快。
2. 小王,你给领导介绍一下具体 _____ 吧。
3. 山田说他永远也忘不了自己在机场与家人告别时的 _____。
4. 大家明天早上七点二十到操场集合,七点半我们 _____ 出发。
5. 孩子不喜欢画画,那你就不要 _____ 他学了。
6. 这起校园暴力事件引发了全社会对教育问题的重新 _____。
7. 她很喜欢这个工作,但是为了孩子教育的问题,她 _____ 辞职了。
8. 近些年,科研 _____ 培养了一大批优秀的人才。
9. 专家鉴定了他的 _____,确认与作案人员的一致。
10. 看到成绩的同时,我们也要看到 _____,千万不能骄傲。

 **答案**

**练习一:**
略

**练习二:**
(1) E (2)D (3)A (4)B (5)C

**练习三:**
1. 类 2. 情况 3. 情景 4. 准时 5. 强迫
6. 思考 7. 被迫 8. 领域 9. 笔迹 10. 不足

---

 **星期二**

shēntǐ
**身体** （甲）名
body; health

**常用搭配**
身体健康 in good health　锻炼身体 take exercise

**用法示例**
身体受烈日曝晒会造成伤害。
Exposure of the body to strong sunlight can be harmful.
青少年时期是身体的成熟期。
Adolescence is the period during which the body reaches maturity.
小孩有柔软的身体。
Little babies have soft bodies.

zhìdìng
**制定** （乙）动
formulate

**常用搭配**
制定规则 constitute a regulation
制定法律 constitute a law

**用法示例**
法律是为维护个人权利和财产而制定的。
Laws are constituted to protect individual rights and properties.
政府制定了新的法案以控制赌博。
The government has made a new bill to regulate gambling.

zhìdìng
**制订** （乙）动
draw up; work out

**常用搭配**
制订计划 draw up a plan　制订合同 draw up a contract

**用法示例**
他专心致志地制订计划。
He was engaged in working out a plan.
我想我们应该制订策略,以应付这种情况。
I think we should work out a strategy to deal with this situation.

jījí
**积极** 反 xiāojí 消极 （乙）形
active; positive

**常用搭配**
积极分子 an active member
积极因素 positive factor
起到积极的作用 play a positive role

**用法示例**
我们应该积极参加课外活动。
We should take an active part in extracurricular activities.

她工作态度非常积极。

She shows a very positive attitude towards her work.

他是俱乐部的积极分子。

He is an active member of the club.

bù

## 部 (乙)名／量

① part; department ② a measure word used for movies, books or machine

**常用搭配**

教育部 Ministry of Education

住院部 in-patient department

北京的北部 the north part of Beijing

两部电影 two movies 一部机器 a machine

**用法示例**

他是一家大公司的营业部经理。

He is manager of the business department of a big company.

我来自中国南部。

I come from the south of China.

他正在写一部关于中国文化的书。

He is writing a new book on Chinese culture.

zhǐshì

## 指示 (乙)名／动

① instructions ② give directives or instructions

**常用搭配**

指示灯 indicating lamp 听候指示 wait for instructions

**用法示例**

他给我们做了非常明确的指示。

He gave us very specific instructions.

必须严格遵从医生的指示。

The doctor's instructions must be followed exactly.

依照你的指示我去了那个地方。

I went to the place in accordance with your instructions.

shēncái

## 身材 (丙)名

stature; figure

**常用搭配**

苗条的身材 slender figure 好身材 fine figure

**用法示例**

她喜欢能充分展示身材的衣服。

She likes the suit that displays her figure to advantage.

我真羡慕她的好身材。

I really admire her fine figure.

xiāojí xiāochén

## 消极 ◎ 消沉 (丙)形

passive; negative

**常用搭配**

消极抵抗 passive resistance

消极的态度 negative attitude

消极的人生观 a negative outlook on life

**用法示例**

他们努力把消极因素化为积极因素。

They tried to turn negative factors into positive ones.

我父母认为我朋友对我有消极影响。

My parents considered my friend to be a negative influence on me.

shēnfèn

## 身份 (丙)名

identity; status

**常用搭配**

身份证 identity card

**用法示例**

那名被害人的身份尚未确定。

The identity of the murdered man has not yet been confirmed.

他在公共场合谦虚礼让,因为他从来没有忘记自己教师的身份。

He looks modest and polite in public because he never forgets his status as a teacher.

zhǐbiāo

## 指标 (丙)名

index; target

**常用搭配**

工作指标 working index 质量指标 quality index

**用法示例**

他们在制定生产指标。

They are setting a target for production.

这位工程师熟悉各种技术指标。

The engineer is familiar with all technique indexes.

xiāoshòu gòumǎi

## 销售 ⊗ 购买 (丁)动

sell

**常用搭配**

销售商品 sell merchandise 销售额 sales amount

销售部 sales department

**用法示例**

超级市场销售各种货物。

The supermarket sells goods of all descriptions.

广告活动对销售额没有起到多大作用。

The advertising campaign didn't have much of an effect on sales.

她的弟弟从事销售工作。

Her brother is in sales.

xiāohào hàofèi

## 消耗 ◎ 耗费 (丙)动

consume; expend

**常用搭配**

消耗精力 consume one's energy

石油消耗 consumption of petroleum

**用法示例**

在中国,酒的消耗量很大。

There's a great consumption of alcohol in China.

敌人的弹药已经消耗殆尽。

The enemy had expended all their ammunition.

 词义辨析

**制订、制定**

"制订"和"制定"都是动词,对象都可以是计划、文件等,但"制订"强调拟定、起草,往往还没有完成或没有经过确认;而"制定"则指制作、完成并确定下来,强调制订妥当的意思,对象多是比较重大的事情,如政策、法规等。例如:①我将制订一份切实可行的方案。②行政制度是依据法律制定的。

Both 制订 and 制定 are verbs, and the object of them can be a plan or a document. 制订 stresses "to draw up something that has not been finished or approved"; while 制定 refers "to make out something that has been finished and approved" or "to have made out well", and the objects of it are usually important things, such as "政策"(policy), "法规"(law or regulation), etc. For example: ① I will draw up a practical scheme for it. ② Institutions of government are established by law.

 练习

**练习一、根据拼音写汉字,根据汉字写拼音**

( )jí ( )biāo xiāo( ) xiāo( ) ( )cái
积( ) 指( ) ( )售 ( )耗 身( )

**练习二、搭配连线**

(1) 锻炼      A.态度
(2) 消极      B.精力
(3) 生产      C.法律
(4) 消耗      D.身体
(5) 制定      E.指标

**练习三、从今天学习的生词中选择合适的词填空**

1. 在领导面前,他表现得很 _____,领导走后什么都不做。

2. 大家不敢多说,但私下里进行了 _____ 抵抗。

3. 公司里,他的 _____ 业绩是最好的。

4. 在比赛前,运动员要适当休息,避免 _____ 体力。

5. 她的 _____ 保持得真好,四十岁了,还这么苗条。

6. 他现在的 _____ 是大使馆的签证官,实际上是一位间谍。

7. 新领导一来,重新 _____ 了一些新的规章制度。

8. 这个学期,我 _____ 了新的学习计划。

9. 这位经理感觉压力很大,因为公司每年一千万的销售 _____ 不好完成。

10. 根据总公司的 _____,所有四十五岁以上的职员都得退休。

🔑 答案

**练习一:**

略

**练习二:**

(1) D      (2)A      (3)E      (4)B      (5)C

**练习三:**

1. 积极    2. 消极    3. 销售    4. 消耗    5. 身材

6. 身份    7. 制定    8. 制订    9. 指标    10. 指示

星期三

jìshù
# 技术 （甲）名
technology; skill

**常用搭配**

科学技术 science and technology
信息技术 information technology
农业技术 agricultural technique
技术员 technician

**用法示例**

这项技术还处于实验阶段。
The technique is still in the experimental stages.
工人们试图将现代技术用于这项传统工业。
The workers are trying to apply modern techniques to this traditional craft.
大工业是随着技术发展而开始出现的。
Large-scale industry emerged as technology evolved.

fēnfù
# 吩咐 （乙）动
tell; command

**常用搭配**

照我吩咐的做！ Do what I tell you.

**用法示例**

如果有什么需求，就请吩咐。
If you need any help, please tell me.
你必须按照吩咐去做。
You must do what you're told.
老板吩咐他到外面去寻找新的顾客。
The manager told him to go out and find new customers.

liè
# 列 （乙）动／量
① to list; line up ② measure word used for row of things.

**常用搭配**

列购物单 make a list of things to buy
一列火车 a train

**用法示例**

我把要买的东西列了个单子。
I made a list of the things I wanted to buy.
士兵们列队接受长官的检阅。
The soldiers lined up for an inspection by their officers.
这列火车半夜出轨了。
The train wreck occurred at midnight.

dānrèn
# 担任 回 担当 （乙）动
dāndāng

occupy a position

**常用搭配**

担任调解人 act as a mediator
担任他的助手 work as his assistant

**用法示例**

他在教育部担任要职。
He occupies an important position in the Ministry of Education.
担任主席的人负责安排会议。
The holder of the Office of Chairman is responsible for arranging meetings.
该大学担任这个会议的东道主。
The conference was hosted by this university.

zhìshǎo
# 至少 反 至多 （乙）副
zhìduō

at least

**常用搭配**

至少六天 not less than six days
至少每天一次 at least once a day
至少 200 元 at least 200 yuan

**用法示例**

他至少去过那儿两次。
He has been there at least twice.
我们每天至少得刷两次牙。
We should brush our teeth at least twice a day.
听众至少也有五千人。
The audience numbered at least five thousand.

rěn
# 忍 （乙）动
bear; tolerate

**常用搭配**

忍着疼痛 to bear pain　　忍一会儿 bear for a while

**用法示例**

最后，我忍不了啦。
In the end, I could not bear it.
他握紧拳头，忍住疼痛。
He clenched his fists tightly to endure the pain.

wānqū
# 弯曲 反 笔直 （丙）形
bǐzhí

winding; curve

**常用搭配**

弯曲的小路 a winding path　　弯曲的线 a curve line

**用法示例**

我沿着弯弯曲曲的山路回家。
I went home along a winding mountain path.
用手够到你的脚趾，膝盖别弯曲。
Touch your toes without bending your knees.

wāiqū
# 歪曲 （丙）动
distort; misrepresent

**常用搭配**

歪曲事实 distort facts

**用法示例**

记者歪曲了事实。

The reporter distorted the facts.

别歪曲我说的话。

Stop distorting what I've said.

报纸歪曲了作家的谈话。

The newspaper misrepresented what the writer had said.

zhízhào

执照 （丁）名

license

**常用搭配**

驾驶执照 a driving license

营业执照 business license

**用法示例**

警察要检查他的驾驶执照。

The policeman wanted to check his driving license.

他们在申请营业执照。

They are applying for a business license.

他撞车后驾驶执照被吊销了。

His driving license was revoked after the crash.

cāixiǎng                    cāicè

猜想            ◉ 猜测        （丙）动／名

① suspect ② conjecture

**常用搭配**

哥德巴赫猜想 Goldbach conjecture

**用法示例**

我猜想他二十岁左右。

I should suppose him to be about twenty.

我猜想他们一定很失望。

I suspect they must be very disappointed.

谣言引起很多猜想。

The rumor raised much conjecture.

dānbǎo

担保 （丁）动

guarantee；vouch for

**常用搭配**

信用担保 credit guarantee    银行担保 bank guarantee

**用法示例**

我们担保这些染料不会褪色。

We guarantee the fastness of these dyes.

我可以为他作担保。

I can vouch for him.

zhìduō

至多 （丁）副

① at most ② upper limit

**常用搭配**

至多一周 a week at the longest

至多 20 元 20 yuan at the most

**用法示例**

我们每周至多工作四十个小时。

We have, at most, 40 hours of work each week.

我想他至多不过 15 岁。

I think he was fifteen at most.

我们至多能呆两天。

We can stay for two days at most.

 词义辨析

**歪曲、弯曲**

"歪曲"是动词，表示片面、虚假地描述事物或曲解原意，含贬义；而"弯曲"是形容词，指形状不直。例如：①记者歪曲了总统的讲话。②那家报纸对国际事件的报道有时是歪曲事实的。③弯弯曲曲的小河。④弯曲的树干。

歪 曲 is a verb, meaning "to give a false or misleading account of something or original meaning, and has a derogatory sense；while 弯曲 is an adjective, which means to be winding or curving in shape or line. For example： ① The reporter misrepresented what the president had said. ② That newspaper's accounts of international affairs are sometimes distorted. ③ a winding river. ④ a bent trunk of a tree

## 练习

**练习一、根据拼音写汉字，根据汉字写拼音**

wāi（　） zhí（　） cāi（　） dān（　）（　）fù
（　）曲 （　）照 （　）想 （　）保 吩（　）

**练习二、搭配连线**

(1) 营业　　　　　　　　A. 事实
(2) 担任　　　　　　　　B. 担保
(3) 信用　　　　　　　　C. 主席
(4) 歪曲　　　　　　　　D. 技术
(5) 科学　　　　　　　　E. 执照

**练习三、从今天学习的生词中选择合适的词填空**

1. 太累了，我昨天_____工作了 10 个小时。
2. 这个试验并不难，我们_____用两个星期就能完成。
3. 主任_____我们赶快搜集市场信息。
4. 他想说什么，可是话到嘴边_____住了。
5. 这条_____的小路通往山里的寺庙。
6. 这则新闻报道_____了事实。
7. 他 18 岁就考取了驾驶_____。
8. 他今天没来上课，我_____他病了。
9. 我拿自己的人格_____，他不会做那样的事情。
10. 从去年开始，他一直_____我们班的班主任。

## 答案

**练习一：**
略

**练习二：**
(1) E　　(2)C　　(3)B　　(4)A　　(5)D

**练习三：**
1. 至少　2. 至多　3. 吩咐　4. 忍　5. 弯曲
6. 歪曲　7. 执照　8. 猜想　9. 担保　10. 担任

---

Thursday
**星期四**

shūfu
**舒服**　　　　　　　　　　（甲）形
comfortable

**常用搭配**
觉得不舒服 feel sick　　感到舒服 feel comfortable

**用法示例**
在药物的作用下我感到舒服些了。
I felt comfortable with the medicine's effect.
踩在松软的海滩上非常舒服。
It's very comfortable to walk on the soft beach.

shūshì
**舒适**　　　　　　　　　　（乙）形
comfortable; cozy

**常用搭配**
舒适的房间 a cozy room　　舒适的椅子 comfortable chair
舒适的生活 a comfortable life

**用法示例**
他住在一个舒适的小屋里。
He lives in a cosy little room.
我们生活在舒适的环境中。
We are living in pleasant surroundings.
他们现在过着比较舒适的生活。
They are now living in relative comfort.

liǎng
**两**　　　　　　　　　　（乙）量／数

① liang, a unit of weight, 50 gram ② two ③ both

**常用搭配**
二两重 100 gram in weight
8 两酒 400 gram of wine
两千二百元 twenty-two hundred yuan

**用法示例**
他比我大两岁。
He is my senior by two years.
把面包切成小片，然后给我两片。
Cut the bread into small pieces and give me two.
他们两人都喜欢流行歌曲。
Both of them like popular music.

dǎban　　　　　　　　zhuāngbàn
**打扮**　　　⑤装扮　　　（乙）动
dress up

**常用搭配**
打扮成……dress up as…

**用法示例**
孩子们都喜欢打扮。
Children love dressing up.

她打扮成了印度公主。
She was dressed up as an Indian princess.
她不喜欢被打扮。
She doesn't like getting dressed up.

## 制造 zhìzào 反 毁灭 huǐmiè （乙）动
manufacture; make

**常用搭配**
制造卫星 make a satellite
中国制造 Made in China

**用法示例**
硫磺可以用来制造火药。
Sulfur can be used to make gunpowder.
我的工作就是在工厂制造产品。
My work is to manufacture goods in a factory.
这台机器是日本制造的。
This machine is made in Japan.

## 以外 yǐwài 反 以内 yǐnèi （乙）名
① beyond ② outside

**常用搭配**
两公里以外 two kilometers away
在长城以外 beyond the Great Wall

**用法示例**
除了他告诉我的以外，别的我什么都不知道。
I know nothing of it beyond what he told me.
我们学校在十公里以外。
Our school is located 10 kilometers away.
你到北京以外的地方旅游过吗？
Did you visit places outside of Beijing?

## 制止 zhìzhǐ 同 阻止 zǔzhǐ （丙）动
to curb; to stop

**常用搭配**
制止孩子打扰别人 stop a child disturbing others
制止了一场争吵 stop a quarrel

**用法示例**
警察制止了一场殴斗。
The police stopped a fight.
母亲制止女儿外出约会。
The mother stopped her daughter from going out on dates.
我要与他们争论，但我爸爸制止了我。
I wanted to argue with them, but my father stopped me.

## 毅力 yìlì （丙）名
perseverance

**常用搭配**
有毅力的人 a perseverant man
缺乏毅力 lack of perseverance

**用法示例**
毅力加上精力是人生成功的要素。
Perseverance combined with energy is necessary to success in life.
靠毅力这位老人学会了俄语。
By perseverance the old man learned to speak Russian.
他学得慢，但是他表现出了不屈不挠的毅力。
He is slow in learning, but shows great perseverance.

## 情报 qíngbào （丙）名
information; intelligence

**常用搭配**
一份情报 a piece of information
情报员 an intelligence agent
向警方提供情报 give information to the police

**用法示例**
这个部门搜集有关政治极端分子的情报。
This department collects information on political extremists.
我们获得了敌方计划的秘密情报。
We have gotten secret intelligence about the enemy's plans.
情报人员报告说敌军正在准备进攻。
Intelligence has reported that the enemy is preparing an attack.

## 义务 yìwù （丙）名
obligation; duty

**常用搭配**
公民的义务 civic duty
对父母应尽的义务 one's duty to his/her parents

**用法示例**
纳税是一种义务。
To pay taxes is an obligation.
为你的国家尽义务。
Do your duty to your country.
她是我妹妹，我有义务照顾她。
She is my sister, and I'm under obligation to care her.

## 化妆 huàzhuāng （丁）名/动
① make-up ② make up

**常用搭配**
化妆品 cosmetics

**用法示例**
对一个这样漂亮的女孩来说，不用化妆。
For such a beautiful girl, there is no need to use make-up.
她每天花几个小时化妆。
She spends hours painting her face every day.
她化妆太浓。
She wears too much paint.

## 制约 zhìyuē　　（丁）动

restrict; condition

**常用搭配**

受法律制约 be restricted by law

相互制约 be conditioned by each other/mutually conditioned

**用法示例**

供应受生产制约。

Supply is restricted by production.

社会的发展受到环境的制约。

The development of society was restricted by environment.

## 辆 liàng　　（甲）量

measure word used for buses, carts, etc.

**常用搭配**

一辆吉普车 a jeep　　两辆自行车 two bikes

**用法示例**

他买了一辆新车。

He bought a new car.

当时他正开着一辆摩托车。

He was driving a motorcycle at that moment.

 **词义辨析**

**舒服、舒适**

　　"舒服"和"舒适"都是形容词,都表示快乐轻松的感觉。"舒服"多指人,强调人的身体或精神上的感受;而"舒适"则多指物,强调外界环境或物品的性能使人产生的感受。例如:①他住在一个舒适的小房间里。②我今天不舒服,不能去上课了。

　　Both 舒服 and 舒适 are adjectives, meaning "comfortable, relaxed". 舒服 mostly refers to people, stressing a physical or spiritual feeling for somebody; while 舒适 mostly refers to something, stressing external environments or something that makes one feel pleasant. For example: ① He stays in a snug little room. ② I am uncomfortable today, and can not go to school.

 **练习**

**练习一、根据拼音写汉字,根据汉字写拼音**

dǎ（　）（　）zhǐ yì（　）（　）zhuāng（　）shì

（　）扮　制（　）（　）力　化（　）　舒（　）

**练习二、搭配连线**

(1) 制约　　　　　A. 舒服

(2) 制止　　　　　B. 生产

(3) 制造　　　　　C. 打架

(4) 缺乏　　　　　D. 机器

(5) 感到　　　　　E. 毅力

**练习三、从今天学习的生词中选择合适的词填空**

1. 昨天晚上我很不 _____,头疼得厉害。

2. 他从小过惯了 _____ 的生活。

3. 这种机器是由我们公司负责设计和 _____ 的。

4. 这两个学生在打架,老师看到了,立即 _____ 了他们。

5. 如果我们现在不保护能源的话,将来有一天能源问题会 _____ 我们发展。

6. 在中国,小学到初中阶段的教育是 _____ 教育,学生不用交学费。

7. 不管天多冷,他都坚持锻炼,我很佩服他的 _____。

8. 除了安娜 _____,所有的同学都通过了考试。

9. 有了男朋友以后,她很注意衣着 _____。

10. 她每年要花很多钱购买 _____ 品。

 **答案**

**练习一:**

略

**练习二:**

(1) B　　(2)C　　(3)D　　(4)E　　(5)A

**练习三:**

1. 舒服　2. 舒适　3. 制造　4. 制止　5. 制约

6. 义务　7. 毅力　8. 以外　9. 打扮　10. 化妆

**星期五** Friday

gānjìng
# 干净 （甲）形
clean
**常用搭配**
把它洗干净 wash it clean
干净的手 clean hands
干净整齐的房间 a neat and tidy room
**用法示例**
她把地板打扫干净了。
She swept the floor clean.
那件衬衣脏了，这里有件干净的。
That shirt is dirty; here is a clean one.
海水好像不干净，不能游泳。
The sea does not look clean enough for swimming.

shǒu
# 首 （乙）量
measure word for poems, songs, etc.
**常用搭配**
一首歌 a song　　三首诗 three poems
**用法示例**
她唱了一首歌。
She sang a song.
他们的生活就是一首诗。
Their lives are like a poem.
他写了一首关于战争的诗。
He wrote a poem about war.

zhěnglǐ
# 整理 （乙）动
arrange; tidy
**常用搭配**
整理房间 tidy the room　　整理行李 pack luggage
**用法示例**
她在整理书架上的书。
She is arranging the books on the shelf.
他把东西整理好就走了。
He packed up his things and left.
她花了整整一个下午整理照片。
She spent a whole afternoon sorting out her photos.

duìbǐ
# 对比 （乙）动 / 名
compare; contrast
**常用搭配**
把 A 和 B 进行对比 compare A with B
鲜明的对比 sharp contrast
**用法示例**
将汉语与英语进行对比。
Compare English with Chinese.
黑和白形成明显的对比。
Black and white have a striking contrast.
有对比才能鉴别。
There can be no differentiation without contrast.

duìdài
# 对待 （乙）动
treat
**常用搭配**
理智地对待问题 deal rationally with the problem
粗暴地对待我们 treat us rudely
**用法示例**
他对待妻子十分蛮横。
His treatment of his wife is outrageous.
他对待这只动物很残忍。
His treatment of the animal was cruel.
这个教师公平地对待他的学生。
The teacher deals fairly with his pupils.

zhǐhuī
# 指挥 （乙）动 / 名
① conduct; command ② conductor
**常用搭配**
指挥军队 command an army
指挥交通 direct traffic
乐队指挥 the conductor of an orchestra
**用法示例**
舰长指挥这艘船。
The captain commands this ship.
乐队都已各就各位，等着指挥。
The orchestra was in position, waiting for the conductor.
他是一名非常有名的指挥家。
He is a very famous conductor.

duìchèn
# 对称 （丁）名 / 形
① symmetry ② symmetrical
**常用搭配**
对称图形 symmetrical figure　　对称轴 axis of symmetry
**用法示例**
这座楼的平面图是对称的。
The plan of the building is symmetrical.
他对花园中对称的布局很感兴趣。
He is interested in the symmetrical arrangement of the garden.

qīngchú　　　　　　qīngsǎo
# 清除 ≡ 清扫 （丙）动
clear; get rid of
**常用搭配**
清除污迹 remove the stain

清除垃圾 clean up the trash

**【用法示例】**

昨天他清除了门前的垃圾。

He cleared away the rubbish by the door yesterday.

他们正在清除路上的积雪。

They are clearing the snow from the road.

### 清洁 qīngjié 反 肮脏 ǎngzàng （丙）形

clean

**【常用搭配】**

清洁的盘子 a clean plate

保持清洁 keep clean

**【用法示例】**

它可以使水保持清洁。

It can keep the water clean.

他的房间不大，但十分清洁。

Her room isn't very big but it is very clean.

### 清晰 qīngxī 反 模糊 móhu （丙）形

clear; distinct

**【常用搭配】**

一张清晰的照片 a clear photograph

思路清晰 clarity of thinking

**【用法示例】**

这位老师讲话很清晰，我们每个字都能听清。

The teacher spoke very clearly so that we could hear every word.

照片上的景色很清晰。

The scenery in the picture is quite clear.

### 整顿 zhěngdùn 同 治理 zhìlǐ （丙）动

rectify

**【常用搭配】**

整顿纪律 rectify discipline

**【用法示例】**

这个新军官的第一项任务是整顿军纪。

The first task of the new officer is to rectify military discipline.

他们将在春节前整顿市场。

They will put the market in order before the Spring Festival.

### 指望 zhǐwàng （丁）动/名

① hope for; depend on ② (n.) hope

**【常用搭配】**

别指望他。Don't rely on him.

**【用法示例】**

别指望他会告诉你真相。

Don't rely on him to tell you the truth.

孩子是她最后能指望的人。

Her child is her last hope.

我指望你帮我安排一切。

I am depending on you to help me with arrangements.

 **词义辨析**

整理、整顿

"整理"和"整顿"都是动词，都有使有秩序的意思。"整理"的行为主体是个人或集体，宾语是具体的事物，如：房间、资料、文件、书籍等。"整顿"的行为主体是行政机关或领导，宾语是抽象的事物，如：纪律、秩序、组织等。例如：①请把这些文件整理一下，用夹子夹在一起。②新经理要整顿公司的工作作风。

Both 整理 and 整顿 are verbs, meaning "to put something in order". But the subject of 整理 is a person or an organization, and its object is something concrete, such as "房间" (room), "资料" (data), "文件" (files), "书籍" (books), etc; while the subject of 整顿 is a government department or leader, and its object is something abstract, such as "纪律" (discipline), "秩序" (order), "组织" (organization), etc. For example: ① Sort out these papers and fasten them together with a clip, please. ② The new manager will rectify the work style of our company.

 **练习**

**练习一、根据拼音写汉字，根据汉字写拼音**

duì（ ）（ ）dùn（ ）huī（ ）jìng（ ）xī（ ）

称 整（ ） 指（ ） 干（ ） 清（ ）

**练习二、搭配连线**

(1) 整顿　　　　　　A. 图形

(2) 整理　　　　　　B. 纪律

(3) 对称　　　　　　C. 清洁

(4) 指挥　　　　　　D. 房间

(5) 保持　　　　　　E. 乐队

**练习三、从今天学习的生词中选择合适的词填空**

1. 下面我们来 _____ 一下这两个词的相同点和不同点。

2. 公司老板 _____ 大家不错，所以大家干活很卖力。

3. 他 _____ 全班同学迅速撤离了危险地带。

4. 他把花园里的杂草都 _____ 干净了。

5. 他们从海水里提取 _____ 的饮用水。

6. 这个相机拍出来的照片非常 _____。

7. 有关部门对音像制品市场进行了 _____。

8. 你要自己努力，别总是 _____ 他人的帮助。

9. 搬家前一天，他把自己的东西都 _____ 好了。

10. 故宫的建筑布局是左右 _____ 的。

答案

练习一：
略
练习二：
(1) B　　(2)D　　(3)A　　(4)E　　(5)C
练习三：
1. 对比　　2. 对待　　3. 指挥　　4. 清除　　5. 清洁
6. 清晰　　7. 整顿　　8. 指望　　9. 整理　　10. 对称

# 第5月,第4周的练习

**练习一.根据词语给加点的字注音**
1.(　) 2.(　)　　3.(　)　　4.(　)　　5.(　)
　强迫　　猜想　　毅力　　吩咐　　打扮

**练习二.根据拼音写词语**
　　zhǐ　　　zhí　　　zhǐ　　xiāo　　　xiāo
1.(　)标 2.(　)照 3.制(　) 4.(　)售 5.(　)耗

**练习三.辨析并选择合适的词填空**
1. 有关部门对失学儿童的家庭(　)进行了调查。(情况、情景)
2. 虽然事情过去几年了,但我现在还清晰地记得当时的(　)。(情况、情景)
3. 中国政府(　)了《义务教育法》,保障孩子们接受教育的权利。(制定、制订)
4. 今天公司开会决定由我们部门(　)新的销售方案。(制定、制订)
5. 记者一定要把事实调查清楚,以免(　)报道。(歪曲、弯曲)
6. 前面是条(　)的小路,我们只好下车步行。(歪曲、弯曲)
7. 我特别想拥有一间(　)的卧室。(舒服、舒适)
8. 运动完以后洗个热水澡,感觉特别(　)。(舒服、舒适)
9. 这是今天的笔记,不过我还没来得及(　)。(整理、整顿)
10. 新领导来后,开始(　)纪律,要求员工必须按时上下班。(整理、整顿)

**练习四.选词填空**
清洁　　清晰　　身材　　制约　　强迫
清除　　身份　　身体　　制造　　被迫
1. 这个间谍公开的(　)是大使馆的工作人员。
2. 环卫工人每天晚上来(　)当天的垃圾。
3. 我父亲的(　)不太好,正在医院疗养呢。
4. 因为急着用钱,他(　)卖掉了以前的房子。
5. 如果我们想保持水源的(　),就必须关闭造成污染的工

厂。
6. 我们不想(　)孩子学习他不喜欢学的专业。
7. 我朋友从美国给我买了一件衬衫,结果发现是中国(　)的。
8. 真羡慕她,都四十多岁了,(　)还保持得那么好。
9. 经济和教育发展的水平是相互(　)的,没有好的教育制度,经济也不会发展得太好。
10. 通过望远镜,我们可以(　)地看到月球表面的情况。

**练习五.量词填空**
　首　　　辆　　　列　　　部　　　类
1. 他买了一(　)自行车,在周末,骑着自行车逛北京城。
2. 晚会上,他唱了一(　)中文歌。
3. 他一年换了三(　)手机。
4. 书店里有各(　)书籍,你想买什么书?
5. 这(　)火车是从北京开往西藏的,沿途停的站很少,所以很快。

**练习六.写出下列词语的同义词**
1. 消极(　　)　　　2. 制止(　　)
3. 整顿(　　)　　　4. 担任(　　)
5. 强迫(　　)

**练习七.写出下列词语的反义词**
1. 制造(　　)　　　2. 积极(　　)
3. 弯曲(　　)　　　4. 准许(　　)
5. 清洁(　　)

答案

练习一.
1.qiǎng　　2.cāi　　3.yì　　4.fù　　5.ban
练习二.
1. 指　　2. 执　　3. 止　　4. 销　　5. 消
练习三.
1. 情况　　2. 情景　　3. 制定　　4. 制订　　5. 歪曲
6. 弯曲　　7. 舒适　　8. 舒服　　9. 整理　　10. 整顿
练习四.
1. 身份　　2. 清除　　3. 身体　　4. 被迫　　5. 清洁
6. 强迫　　7. 制造　　8. 身材　　9. 制约　　10. 清晰
练习五.
1. 辆　　2. 首　　3. 部　　4. 类　　5. 列
练习六.
1. 消沉　　2. 阻止　　3. 治理　　4. 担当　　5. 强制
练习七.
1. 消灭　　2. 消极　　3. 笔直　　4. 禁止　　5. 肮脏

# 6月 第1周的学习内容

星期一 Monday

**fǎngwèn**
## 访问 （甲）动/名

① pay a visit ② visit

**常用搭配**
访问韩国 visit Korea　　私人访问 a private visit

**用法示例**
他们正计划九月份访问日本。
They are planning to visit Japan in September.
总统正在访问欧洲。
The president is paying a visit to Europe.
我们将访问缩短了一周。
We cut our visit short by a week.

**guǎn**
## 管 （乙）动

be in charge of; look after

**常用搭配**
管教学 be in charge of teaching
管学生 administer to students

**用法示例**
李小姐管公司的账目。
Miss Li handles the company's accounts.
我管不了孩子们。
I can't handle children.
他管学生宿舍。
He is in charge of the students' dormitory.

**guǎnlǐ**
## 管理 （乙）动

manage; administer

**常用搭配**
管理公司 manage a company
管理国家 administer a country

**用法示例**
在他父亲生病的时候,他管理公司。
He managed the company when his father was ill.
计划的失败是由于管理不善造成的。
The failure of the scheme was due to bad management.
科学的管理方法已经给我们工厂的生产带来了许多变化。
The scientific management method has brought about many changes in factory production.

**qījiān** 　　　**shíqī**
## 期间 ◎ 时期 （乙）名

① period of time ② during

**常用搭配**
暑假期间 during the summer vacation
她生病期间 during her illness
在战争期间 during the war

**用法示例**
怀孕期间你最好不要吸烟。
You are advised not to smoke during pregnancy.
圣诞节期间生意一向很好。
Trade is always good over the Christmas period.
你在训练期间要尽最大努力。
You'll be on your mettle during the training course.

**dàyuē** 　　　**dàgài**
## 大约 ◎ 大概 （乙）副

approximately; about

**常用搭配**
大约六点半 about 6:30　　大约 10 米 about ten meters

**用法示例**
那个男孩大约十岁。
That boy is about ten years old.
这所中学大约有 300 个学生。
There are 300 students or so in this middle school.
我大约两星期见他们一次。
I meet them about once a fortnight.

**qǐyè**
## 企业 （乙）名

enterprise

**常用搭配**
私营企业 private enterprise
开办企业 open an enterprise

**用法示例**
这家企业很快就会赢利。
This enterprise will soon turn a profit.
越来越多的大学生主修企业管理学。
More and more students are majoring in the science of business management.
他在一家大型企业工作。
He works in a large enterprise.

**qīfu** 　　　**tǎnhù**
## 欺负 ◎ 袒护 （丙）动

to bully

**常用搭配**
欺负别人 bully others　　挨／受欺负 be bullied by

**用法示例**

他总是欺负比他小的男孩子。

He's always bullying smaller boys.

他在学校里受大孩子的欺负。

He was bullied by the older boys at school.

别让他们欺负你,要保护你自己!

Don't allow them to bully you; stick up for yourself!

diǎnlǐ
## 典礼 （丙）名

ceremony

**常用搭配**

结婚典礼 a wedding ceremony

举行典礼 hold a ceremony

**用法示例**

首相出席了典礼。

The prime minister attended the ceremony.

校长将在毕业典礼上讲话。

The headmaster will speak at the graduation ceremony.

diǎnxíng
## 典型 （丙）形

typical

**常用搭配**

典型人物 typical character

典型事例 typical example

**用法示例**

他是典型的美国人。

He is a typical American.

她有典型的金牛座性格。

She has a typically Taurean personality.

qīxiàn
## 期限 （丁）名

time limit; deadline; allotted time

**常用搭配**

延长期限 extend the time limit

设定期限 set a time limit

**用法示例**

这项专利期限为 3 年。

The patent runs out in three years.

现在已经过了申请的最后期限。

It's past the deadline to apply.

他无法在期限内完成任务。

He can't finish the task within the time limit.

dàyú
## 大于 ⑤小于 （丁）动
xiǎoyú

① above or beyond ② greater

**常用搭配**

10 大于 9。10 is greater than 9.

**用法示例**

去年的出生人数大于死亡人数。

Last year there were more births than deaths.

我学过三角形两个边的和大于第三个边。

I was taught that two sides of a triangle were greater than the third.

qīdài
## 期待 （丁）动

expect; look forward to

**常用搭配**

热切地期待着 expect eagerly

期待着毕业 look forward to graduation

期待着假期 look forward to holidays

**用法示例**

我一直期待着和您见面。

I have been looking forward to seeing you.

我们正期待着她的来信。

We are expecting a letter from her.

我们期待着春天的到来。

We look forward to the return of spring.

 词义辨析

**管、管理**

　　"管"和"管理"都是动词,都有"保管、约束、监管"的意思。"管理"比较正式,经常用于书面语;"管"比较口语化。另外,"管"还有一些其它意思,如:管辖、干预、保证、负责提供等,"管理"不具备这些意思。例如:①他在我们系负责管理教学事务 / 他在我们系管教学。②你们公司谁管理账目 / 你们公司谁管账?③总经理管三个部门。④不要管别人的私事。⑤如果你对产品不满意,厂家管换。

　　管 and 管理 are verbs, meaning "to take care of", "to be in charge of" or "to supervise". 管理 is more formal, often used in writing; 管 is colloquial, and 管 has other meanings such as "to administer", "to intervene", "to guarantee", "to supply", etc; while 管理 has no meanings like that. For example: ① He is in charge of teaching affairs in our department. ② Who is in charge of the account in your company? ③ The general manager is in charge of three departments. ④ Don't interfere in other's private affairs. ⑤ If you are not satisfied with the product, the manufacturer is responsible for changing it.

 **练习**

**练习一、根据拼音写汉字，根据汉字写拼音**

( )lǐ ( )lǐ qǐ( ) qī( ) qī( )
管( ) 典( ) ( )业 ( )负 ( )限

**练习二、搭配连线**

(1) 放假 　　　　 A. 企业
(2) 欺负 　　　　 B. 典礼
(3) 私营 　　　　 C. 期间
(4) 结婚 　　　　 D. 期限
(5) 延长 　　　　 E. 小孩

**练习三、从今天学习的生词中选择合适的词填空**

1. 要是全家都出去度假,我们的小狗就没人 _____ 了,能带它一起去吗?
2. 他虽然很年轻,但把公司 _____ 得不错,是一个称职的总经理。
3. 总统今天早上启程去欧洲 _____。
4. 保质期是三个月,在这 _____ 如有问题可以免费维修。
5. 这个项目的 _____ 是一年。
6. 明天上午九点在礼堂举行开学 _____。
7. 黑头发、黄皮肤是亚洲人的 _____ 特征。
8. 这个 _____ 效益不好,员工面临下岗。
9. 哥哥要爱护弟弟,不能 _____ 弟弟。
10. 开车从我们学校到天安门需要 _____ 半小时。

**答案**

**练习一:**
略
**练习二:**
(1) C 　　(2)E 　　(3)A 　　(4)B 　　(5)D
**练习三:**
1. 管 　　2. 管理 　　3. 访问 　　4. 期间 　　5. 期限
6. 典礼 　　7. 典型 　　8. 企业 　　9. 欺负 　　10. 大约

---

 **星期二**

**mǎnyì**
## 满意 　　　　　（甲）形
content; satisfied

**常用搭配**

令人满意 satisfying 　　对……满意 be satisfied with...
对……表示满意 express one's satisfaction at...

**用法示例**

我们的会谈已经取得了令人满意的进展。
We have made pleasing progress in our talks.
我不太满意他对这个句子的翻译。
I'm not satisfied with his interpretation of this sentence.
那位夫人带着满意的微笑看着我。
The lady looked at me with a contented smile.

**mǎnzú**
## 满足 　　　　　（乙）动
satisfy; meet (the needs of)

**常用搭配**

满足人民需要 satisfy the people's needs
满足他的要求 satisfy his requirements

**用法示例**

他的权力欲永远不能得到满足。
His lust for power will never be satisfied.
我只好说明原因来满足他的好奇心。
I had to explain the reasons to him to satisfy his curiosity.
像他这么有才华的人不应满足于现状。
Such a talented person as he shouldn't be satisfied with his position.

**bùgǎndāng**
## 不敢当 　　　　　（乙）
you flatter me

**常用搭配**

噢,不敢当。Oh, you flatter me.

**用法示例**

感谢你的赞扬,不过真是不敢当。
Thank you for your praise. But I really don't deserve it.
李教授说我是教育专家,我不敢当,我只是比大家的经验多一些而已。
Prof. Li said that I was an expert in education. I don't deserve such praise. I just have more experience than you.

**méishénme**
## 没什么 　　　　　（乙）
① (idiom) nothing ② never mind ③ it's nothing

**常用搭配**

没什么可解释的。It's nothing to explain.
这没什么大不了的。It's no big deal. ( Think nothing of it. )

**用法示例**

哦，实际上没什么。
Oh, nothing to it actually.
对这次事件我没什么可说的。
I've nothing to say about the event.
你没什么可抱怨的。
You've got nothing to complain about.

shuōbudìng
**说不定** （丙）副

① maybe ② can't say for sure

**常用搭配**

说不定他现在已经来了。He might have come by now.

**用法示例**

我想我能来，但还说不定。
I think I can come, but don't count on it.
咱们现在就吃，说不定吃完能看场电影。
Let's eat now, and maybe we can catch a movie later.
说不定他已经死了。
He may be dead for all I know.

bú jiàn dé                    bùyídìng
**不见得** 同 **不一定** （丙）

① not likely ② unlikely

**常用搭配**

她不见得去。She is not likely to go.

**用法示例**

他不见得同意。
It is not likely that he will consent.
他不见得会做那种事。
It was very unlikely that he would do that.
他们不见得能来，因为天气这么糟糕。
They are unlikely to come since the weather is so bad.

rìyòngpǐn
**日用品** （乙）名

① daily necessities ② articles of everyday use

**常用搭配**

日用品商店 a shop for daily necessities

**用法示例**

她每周六都去买日用品。
Every Saturday she goes to buy daily necessities.
日用品的价格在上涨。
The prices of daily necessities are rising.

yíxìliè
**一系列** （丙）形

a series of

**常用搭配**

一系列的问题 a series of problems
一系列事件 the sequence of events

**用法示例**

这一理论是以一系列事实为依据的。
The theory is based on a series of facts.

我们在会上讨论了有关新工程的一系列问题。
We discussed a series of topics relating to the new project at the meeting.
他们得解决一系列的问题。
They have to solve a series of problems.

chénzhòng                    qīngsōng
**沉重** 反 **轻松** （丙）形

heavy

**常用搭配**

沉重的箱子 a heavy box
沉重的心情 a heavy heart

**用法示例**

她自己拎不了这个沉重的箱子。
She can not lift the heavy suitcase by herself.
沉重的脚步声说明爷爷已经走近了。
Heavy footsteps signaled grandpa's approach.

chénzhuó                    huāngzhāng
**沉着** 反 **慌张** （丁）形

① calm ② not nervous ③ be composed

**常用搭配**

沉着应对 deal with it calmly
沉着的侦探 a cool-headed detective

**用法示例**

在危险的情况下，他表现得很沉着。
He showed great composure in the face of danger.
她假装沉着。
She affected composure.
她很快就沉着下来了。
She soon composed herself.

chùfàn                    màofàn
**触犯** 同 **冒犯** （丁）动

offend

**常用搭配**

触犯法律 offending the law    触犯他 offend him

**用法示例**

他因被指控触犯选举法而遭逮捕。
He was accused of offending the electoral law and was arrested.
我无意中触犯了他。
I offended him unintentionally.
他的行为是对正义的触犯。
His behavior was an outrage against justice.

xìliè
**系列** （丁）名

series

**常用搭配**

系列教材 a series of textbooks

**用法示例**

安排好了系列讲座。
A series of lectures is scheduled.

将举办系列活动。
A series of activities will be held.

 ## 词义辨析

### 满足、满意

"满足"和"满意"都有符合自己心意或需要的意思。但是"满意"是形容词，一般强调对外在事物的感受，常用作"对……满意"；"满足"是动词，往往强调自身的感受，常用作"满足于……"，"满足"还有"使满足"的意思，宾语常为"要求"、"需要"等。例如：①我对目前的工作很满意。②那个故事的结局令人满意。③我们决不能满足于自己的成绩。④我们必须提高产量满足需求。

满足 and 满意 mean "the gratification of a desire, a need". But 满意 is an adjective, and stresses one's feeling for external affairs, usually used as "对……满意" (be satisfied with…); 满足 is a verb, and stresses one's own feeling, usually used as "满足于……" (be satisfied with…); and 满足 also means "to satisfy or meet (one's requirement or need)". For example: ① I am satisfied with my present job. ② The story had a satisfying ending. ③ We must not be complacent with our achievements. ④ We must increase our output to meet demand.

 ## 练习

**练习一、根据拼音写汉字，根据汉字写拼音**
( )( )qǐ ( )liè chén ( )yòng ( )( )yì
了不( ) 系( ) ( )重 ( )品 满( )

**练习二、搭配连线**
(1) 沉重的　　　　　　　A. 商店
(2) 沉着的　　　　　　　B. 微笑
(3) 一系列　　　　　　　C. 警察
(4) 日用品　　　　　　　D. 事件
(5) 满意的　　　　　　　E. 心情

**练习三、从今天学习的生词中选择合适的词填空**
1. 张经理，您这么夸我，我实在是 _____ 啊。
2. 这个人其实 _____ 真本事，就是嘴巴甜而已。
3. 这个领导因为 _____ 了法律而被捕。
4. 老板对他的新秘书不太 _____。
5. 大家要继续努力，不能 _____ 于现有的成绩。
6. 他得知母亲的病可能治不好了，心情十分 _____。
7. 遇到危险一定要保持 _____，千万不能慌张。
8. 结果怎么样还 _____ 呢，别高兴得太早了。
9. 他最近很忙，今晚他 _____ 能来。
10. 很多学生在那家大超市买生活 _____。

## 答案

**练习一：**
略
**练习二：**
(1) E　　(2)C　　(3)D　　(4)A　　(5)B
**练习三：**
1. 不敢当　2. 没什么　3. 触犯　4. 满意　5. 满足
6. 沉重　7. 沉着　8. 说不定　9. 不见得　10. 日用品

星期三

**fāzhǎn**
## 发展 （甲）动／名
① develop ② development

**常用搭配**
发展工业 develop industry
随着经济的发展 with the development of the economy
病情的发展 the growth of the disease

**用法示例**
中国是发展中国家。
China is a developing country.
在他的管理下，公司发展得很快。
The company developed rapidly under his management.
这个公司已从拥有1个分公司发展到12个了。
The business has expanded from having one branch to having twelve.

**cúnzài**
## 存在 （乙）动
exist

**常用搭配**
存在差别 There is difference…

**用法示例**
我们的观点存在着严重的分歧。
Our views diverged greatly.
这种风俗已不存在了。
The custom has already disappeared.
这设计本身存在弱点。
There is an inherent weakness in the design.
罗马帝国存在了几百年。
The Roman Empire existed for several centuries.

**jǔxíng**
## 举行 〓举办 （乙）动
hold (a meeting, ceremony, etc.)

**常用搭配**
举行会议 hold a meeting　举行辩论会 hold a debate
举行开幕式 perform the opening ceremony

**用法示例**
招待会在草地中的亭子里举行。
The reception was held in a pavilion on the lawn.
下月将在北京举行一场国际比赛。
An international match will be held in Beijing next month.
婚礼是在教堂举行的。
The marriage ceremony took place in the church.

**xīyǐn**
## 吸引 （丙）动
attract

**常用搭配**
吸引顾客 attract customers　互相吸引 attract each other

**用法示例**
今年的花展吸引了大批观众。
The flower show attracted large crowds this year.
他被她的美貌所吸引。
He was attracted by her beauty.
这座大教堂吸引了世界各地的游客。
This cathedral has attracted visitors from all around the world.

**zhuājǐn**
## 抓紧 反放松 （乙）
① grasp firmly ② pay close attention to

**常用搭配**
抓紧时间 make the best use of one's time
抓紧绳子 grasp a rope tightly

**用法示例**
每个学生都在抓紧时间复习，准备期末考试。
Every student is making the best use of his time to revise for a final exam.
抓紧绳子，否则你会摔下来的。
Get a hold of the rope or you will fall.

**xīshōu**
## 吸收 反排放 （乙）动
absorb ; assimilate

**常用搭配**
从空气中吸收水分 absorb moisture from the air
吸收养料 absorb nutrients

**用法示例**
干沙吸收水分。
Dry sand absorbs water.
植物从泥土中吸收养料。
Plants absorb nutrients from the soil.
植物可以吸收二氧化碳并释放氧气。
Plants can absorb carbon dioxide and release oxygen.

**jǔbàn**
## 举办 （丙）动
to hold

**常用搭配**
举办展览 hold an exhibition
举办讲座 hold a lecture

**用法示例**
他们举办了一场音乐会，并把收入捐给了慈善机构。
They gave a concert and donated the proceeds to charity.
我们学校将举办一系列关于中国文化的讲座。
A series of lectures on Chinese culture will be held in our college.

**xīqǔ**
## 吸取 （丙）动
draw

**常用搭配**

吸取教训 draw a lesson

**用法示例**

人们可以从寓言里吸取智慧。

People can draw wisdom from tales.

我们应该从他人的错误中吸取经验。

We should draw experience from others' mistakes .

## zhǐyǐn
## 指引  (乙)动

① guide or direct ② show or indicate the way for

**常用搭配**

指引方向 indicate the direction

**用法示例**

人的思想指引着行动。

One's thinking directs one's actions.

在困难的时候,她祈祷神谕来指引她。

In times of trouble, she prayed for an oracle to guide her.

交通标志指引我们去机场。

The road signs will direct us to the airport.

## yǐndǎo
## 引导  (丙)动

guide; conduct

**常用搭配**

正确引导 proper guidance

**用法示例**

馆长引导着游客们参观博物馆。

The curator showed the visitors round the museum.

这位老师引导学生热爱科学。

The teacher guided students' interests towards science.

## cúnfàng
## 存放  ⊜储存  chǔcún  (丁)动

store; leave in one's care; deposit

**常用搭配**

存放在保险箱里 be deposited in a coffer

**用法示例**

他把食品存放在碗橱里。

He stored foods in his cupboard.

地下室是用来存放各种葡萄酒的。

The basement is used to store all kinds of wine.

他在找新房子时,把家具存放在我的车库里了。

His furniture was stored in my garage while he was looking for a new house.

## kuānkuò
## 宽阔  (丙)形

broad; wide

**常用搭配**

宽阔的道路 a wide road    宽阔的肩膀 broad shoulders

**用法示例**

山脚下曾有一条宽阔的大河。

There was a wide river at the foot of the mountain.

天安门广场非常宽阔。

Tian'anman Square is very broad.

 **词义辨析**

**指引、引导**

"指引"和"引导"都是动词,都有指出前进方向的意思。"指引"强调指点、领导,一般用于"方向"、"路线"、"道路"等;"引导"表示启发、诱导、带领某人做某事的意思。例如:①灯光指引他们返回港口。②律师引导他说出了实情。③秘书引导求职者到相应的部门。

Both 指引 and 引导 are verbs, meaning "to guide, to show the way". 指引 stresses "to instruct and lead", "to give direction", and is usually used for "方向" (direction), "路线" (route), "道路" (way) , and so on; while 引导 indicates "to enlighten or induce somebody to do something", "to show the way by leading, directing, or advising". For example: ① The light guided them back to harbor. ② The lawyer induced him to speak the facts. ③ The secretary steered the applicant to the proper department.

 **练习**

**练习一、根据拼音写汉字，根据汉字写拼音**

( )kuò ( )fàng ( )shōu ( )jǐn ( )zhǎn

宽( ) 存( ) 吸( ) 抓( ) 发( )

**练习二、搭配连线**

(1) 抓紧　　　　　　A. 教训

(2) 吸收　　　　　　B. 讲座

(3) 吸取　　　　　　C. 养料

(4) 举办　　　　　　D. 会议

(5) 举行　　　　　　E. 时间

**练习三、从今天学习的生词中选择合适的词填空**

1. 改建后的马路很 _____，大大改善了以前交通拥堵的情况。

2. 库房里 _____ 了大量的货物。

3. 在热心人的 _____ 下，我们终于找到了这个不愿见记者的老人。

4. 在父亲的 _____ 下，我们慢慢对文学产生了兴趣。

5. 这篇文章的题目很 _____ 读者。

6. 我完全忽略了这些事实，就像它们根本不 _____ 似的。

7. 飞机就要起飞了，我们得 _____ 时间，办理登机手续。

8. 植物的根可以从土壤中 _____ 水分和养料。

9. 由国家教育部 _____ 的全国教育工作者座谈会在北京召开。

10. 我们应该从这次失败中 _____ 教训，避免再犯类似的错误。

**答案**

**练习一：**

略

**练习二：**

(1) E　　(2)C　　(3)A　　(4)B　　(5)D

**练习三：**

1. 宽阔　　2. 存放　　3. 指引　　4. 引导　　5. 吸引

6. 存在　　7. 抓紧　　8. 吸收　　9. 举办　　10. 吸取

---

 **星期四**

jiějué
**解决** 回 处理 　（甲）动

resolve; solve

**常用搭配**

解决问题 solve a problem　　解决矛盾 resolve a conflict

**用法示例**

最后他终于成功地解决了这个问题。

At last, he successfully solved the problem.

会议可能要延长到夜里，因为今晚有太多问题要解决。

The meeting may go on into the evening because so many problems have to be resolved tonight.

他们探索过各种途径，但是没有找到解决的办法。

They explored every option but could not find a solution.

jiāndìng
**坚定** 　（乙）形

steady; staunch; firm

**常用搭配**

坚定的信念 a firm belief　　坚定地说 firmly say

坚定的改革家 a staunch reformer

**用法示例**

困境中，他坚定的信仰支撑着他。

His firmness in his beliefs supported him in times of difficulties.

我知道她意志坚定。

I know she is steady in her purpose.

他是君主制的坚定拥护者。

He's a staunch supporter of the monarchy.

jiānjué
**坚决** 　（乙）形

resolute; firm

**常用搭配**

坚决反对 oppose sth. resolutely

**用法示例**

她坚决不来。

She was quite adamant that she would not come.

我们坚决反对在国与国之间实行强权政治。

We are firmly opposed to the practice of power politics between nations.

他下决心，要坚决惩治那些贪官。

He was adamant in his determination to punish the corrupt officials.

dàxíng
**大型** 回 小型 　（乙）形

large-scale; huge

**常用搭配**

大型企业 large enterprises

大型客机 a large passenger airliner

**用法示例**

西海岸公司是一家大型企业。

West Coast Corps is a large corporation.

这个工厂生产大型机器。

This factory produces big machines.

泰坦尼克号是一艘大型游轮。

The Titanic was a colossal ship.

dǒngdé

## 懂得 （乙）动

understand; comprehend

**常用搭配**

懂得怎样做…… know how to…

**用法示例**

他懂得法律。

He knows the law.

作为军官应懂得怎样统率士兵。

An officer must know how to handle his men.

他懂得怎样与人相处。

He knows how to get along with others.

yíqì

## 仪器 （乙）名

(scientific, etc.) instrument

**常用搭配**

试验仪器 testing instrument

科学仪器 scientific instrument

**用法示例**

这位科学家需要一些精密的仪器。

The scientist needs some delicate instruments.

罗盘是航行仪器。

The compass is an instrument of navigation.

望远镜和显微镜是光学仪器。

Microscopes and telescopes are optical instruments.

dǒngshì

## 懂事 （丙）形

thoughtful; sensible

**常用搭配**

懂事的小女孩 a sensible young girl

**用法示例**

他是个聪明懂事的孩子，我们都喜欢他。

He's a sensible and clever boy, and we all like him.

她很年轻，但特别懂事。

She is very young, but very sensible.

jiàndìng jiànbié

## 鉴定 ⑩鉴别 （丙）动／名

① identify ② identification; appraisal

**常用搭配**

鉴定笔迹 identify one's handwriting

鉴定书 authenticated document

质量鉴定 appraisal of quality

**用法示例**

通过分析原文，鉴定出作者是莎士比亚。

By textual analysis, the author was identified as Shakespeare.

我们将对矿石做实验鉴定。

We will make an assay of the ore.

专家将鉴定油画的真伪。

The experts will identify whether the painting is a authentic or not.

wángù

## 顽固 （丙）形

obstinate; stubborn

**常用搭配**

顽固的人 a stubborn man    思想顽固 obstinate mind

**用法示例**

那个顽固的老头就是不肯进医院。

The obstinate old man refused to go to the hospital.

他的父亲十分顽固，从不接受他的意见。

His father is very stubborn, and never accepts his advice.

wánqiáng cuìruò

## 顽强 ⑫脆弱 （丙）形

tenacious; indomitable

**常用搭配**

顽强抵抗 obstinate resistance

顽强的精神 a tenacious spirit

顽强的意志 an indomitable will

**用法示例**

据说猫的生命力特别顽强。

It is said that cats have a tenacious hold on life.

她不会轻易放弃的，她十分顽强。

She won't give up easily: she's indomitable.

xiǎoxíng

## 小型 （丁）形

① small-scale ② small

**常用搭配**

小型汽车 a compact car    小型企业 minor enterprises

小型农场 a small farm

**用法示例**

他们正在建设一个小型机场。

They are building a small airport.

海星是一种小型海洋动物。

Starfish is a small sea animal.

dǒngshì

## 董事 （丁）名

board member; director

**常用搭配**

董事会 the board of directors

**用法示例**

董事会指定他为新董事。
The board nominated him as the new director.
她一生事业的顶峰是当上董事。
Her career culminated in her appointment as director.
他是这个公司的董事之一。
He is one of the directors of the company.

 词义辨析

**坚定、坚决**

1、"坚定"和"坚决"都是形容词，都表示意志坚强，不动摇的意思。但"坚定"一般用于强调立场、信念不动摇，经常搭配的名词有：意志、信心、信仰等；"坚决"表示态度或行动不犹豫，常与反对、支持、拒绝等动词搭配。如：坚定的声音，坚定的联盟，坚决反对，坚决拥护。

Both 坚定 and 坚决 are adjectives, meaning "firm or steadfast", "unswerving". But 坚定 is often used to stress one's standpoint or faith, and is often used together with nouns, such as "意志"(will), "信心"(confidence), "信仰"(belief), and so on while 坚决 is often used to stress one's attitude and actions, and is often used together with verbs, such as "反对"(oppose), "支持"(support), "拒绝"(refuse), and so on. For example: a firm voice, a firm ally, to oppose firmly, to support firmly.

2、"坚定"作状语时常常加"地"，并含褒义；"坚决"则直接作状语，是中性词。例如：①他坚定地履行自己的职责。②我们将坚决执行这个计划。

When used as an adverbial, 坚定 is usually followed by "地", and has commendatory sense; while 坚决 can function as an adverbial directly, and it is a neutral word. For example: ① He fulfils his duty firmly. ② We will be resolute in carrying out the plan.

 练习

**练习一、根据拼音写汉字，根据汉字写拼音**

wán (　) jiàn (　) yí (　) dǒng (　) (　)jué
(　)强　(　)定　(　)器　(　)得　解(　)

**练习二、搭配连线**

(1) 顽强　　　　　　A. 笔迹
(2) 鉴定　　　　　　B. 矛盾
(3) 坚决　　　　　　C. 抵抗
(4) 解决　　　　　　D. 仪器
(5) 试验　　　　　　E. 反对

**练习三、从今天学习的生词中选择合适的词填空**

1. 考古专家对新出土的文物进行了 _____ 。
2. 他的讲话更加 _____ 了我们克服困难的决心。
3. 姑娘的态度很 _____ ，无论如何也要跟这个小伙子结婚。
4. 他是这家上市公司的 _____ 之一。
5. 孩子很聪明，也很 _____ ，我和他爸爸基本不操心他上学的事。
6. 这孩子太害羞，不 _____ 如何跟别人相处。
7. 这个厂专门生产显微镜、望远镜等精密 _____ 。
8. 老头非常 _____ ，医生让他戒烟，他就是不戒。
9. 我们要同强大的敌人进行 _____ 的斗争，绝不屈服。
10. 吵架不能 _____ 问题，还是坐下来好好谈谈吧。

**答案**

练习一：
略

练习二：
(1) C　　(2)A　　(3)E　　(4)B　　(5)D

练习三：
1. 鉴定　2. 坚定　3. 坚决　4. 董事　5. 懂事
6. 懂得　7. 仪器　8. 顽固　9. 顽强　10. 解决

**mùqián**
## 目前　　　◎现在　　　（甲）名

① at present ② for the moment

**常用搭配**

目前的情况 current situation

**用法示例**

这位教授目前正在写一本书。

The professor is presently writing a book.

目前，他正在度假。

At present, he is on holiday.

到目前为止，有多少人访问了你的主页？

How many people have accessed your homepage by now?

**dāngqián**
## 当前　　　（乙）名

present; current

**常用搭配**

当前的困难 current difficulties

当前的潮流 present trends

**用法示例**

我们未来的规划必须与当前的实际相结合。

Our future plans have to be integrated with our present practices.

当前的贸易赤字表明我们的进出口贸易严重失调。

The current trade deficit indicates a serious imbalance between our import and export trade.

电视观众来信表示对当前节目不满意。

Audiences wrote to express their dissatisfaction with the current programs.

**tuōlí**
## 脱离　　　（乙）动

separate; break away

**常用搭配**

脱离组织 break away from an organization

脱离实际的想法 an idea that is divorced from reality

**用法示例**

病人已经脱离危险了。

The patient was out of danger.

千万不要脱离现实生活。

Never be divorced from reality.

告诫公务员们不要脱离人民群众。

Public servants are warned not to seperate themselves from the masses.

**yèwù**
## 业务　　　（乙）名

business

**常用搭配**

保险业务 insurance business

日常业务 day-to-day business

代理业务 agency business

**用法示例**

他们对办理的各项业务收取一定的费用。

They charge a fixed rate for each transaction.

为发展业务，我们决定开一家分公司。

With a view to developing our business, we decided to establish a branch office.

这家公司已开始减少在亚洲的业务。

The company has begun to scale down its operations in Asia.

**xiàohua**
## 笑话　　　（乙）名/动

① joke; jest ② laugh at

**常用搭配**

讲笑话 tell jokes　　别笑话他。Don't laugh at him.

**用法示例**

那个喜剧演员讲的笑话把人们都逗笑了。

The comedian tickled the crowd with his jokes.

这不过是个笑话而已。

It is nothing but a joke.

他们会笑话我的新领带。

They will laugh at my new tie.

**fēnlí**
## 分离　　　◎团聚　　　（丙）动

to separate

**常用搭配**

与某人分离 separate from sb.

**用法示例**

他们被迫彼此分离。

They were forced to part from one another.

战争使他们母女分离。

She was separated from her mother by the war.

我们可以用一个筛子把石头分离出来。

We can separate and remove the stones with a sieve.

**fēnliè**
## 分裂　　　◎联合　　　（丙）动

split; break up

**常用搭配**

细胞分裂 cell fission　　分裂国家 split the country

**用法示例**

这个政党分裂成两派。

The party was broken in two.

这个州想要从联邦中分裂出去。

The state wanted to break away from the union.

**huìkuǎn**
## 汇款　　　（丙）名/动

① remittance ② remit money

**常用搭配**
收到汇款 receive remittance

**用法示例**
你收到汇款了吗？
Have you received the remittance?
我去银行汇款了。
I went to the bank to remit money.

xiàoróng
## 笑容　　　　　⑩笑脸 xiàoliǎn　（丙）名
① smile ② smiling expression

**常用搭配**
迷人的笑容 attractive smile

**用法示例**
她总是满脸笑容。
She is always all smiles.
她亲切的笑容使每位客人都感到宾至如归。
Her genial smile made every guest feel at home.
她的笑容再一次浮现在他脑海中。
Her smile emerged again from his mind.

tuōluò
## 脱落　　　　　　　　　（丁）动
drop off; shed

**常用搭配**
从……上脱落 drop off from…

**用法示例**
这种树的树皮每年都会脱落。
The bark of the trees peels off every year.
她吃这种药一个月以后,头发开始脱落。
After taking the medicine for one month, her hair began to fall out.
这个平底锅上的搪瓷有些已脱落了。
Some of the enamel on this pan is chipped off.

huìlǜ
## 汇率　　　　　　　　　（丁）名
① exchange rate ② rate of exchange (ROE)

**常用搭配**
固定汇率 fixed exchange rate

**用法示例**
去年,汇率猛跌。
Last year, the exchange rate fell sharply.
我们公司遭受了汇率下跌造成的损失。
Our company suffered from the fall in the exchange rate.
去年汇率降低了百分之十。
The rate of exchange decreased by 10% last year.

fùchū
## 付出　　　　　　　　　（丁）动
① pay ② pay out

**常用搭配**
你必须为此付出代价。You'll have to pay for that.
没有付出,就没有收获。No pain, no gain.

**用法示例**
他为自己的疏忽付出了沉重的代价。
He paid dearly for his careless slip.
许多科学家,在追求知识的过程中付出了生命。
Many scientists have paid the forfeit of their lives in the pursuit of knowledge.
我为那个设计付出了很多心血。
I paid for that design with a lot of my energy.

 **词义辨析**

**当前、目前**
　　1、“当前”和“目前”都是时间名词,都可以表示现在,多用于书面语,有时可以互换使用。例如：①他对自己目前/当前的境遇很满意。②目前/当前的市场相当萧条。
　　Both 目前 and 当前 are time nouns, indicating "now, the present", usually used in writing. Sometimes they can be interchangeable, e.g. ① He is quite content with his present fortune. ② The market is rather depressed at the moment.
　　2、“当前”还有“面临、在前面”的意思,如“大敌当前”、“一事当前”；“目前”没有这个意思。“目前”可以作宾语,如“到目前为止”、“截止目前”；“当前”没有这个用法。
　　当前 has another meaning of "in the face of, in front of", such as “大敌当前” (in the face of powerful enemy), “一事当前” (in the face of a problem); while 目前 does not have this meaning. But 目前 can be used as an object, for example: “到目前为止” (up till now), “截止目前” (so far, by now); while 当前 does not have this usage.

 **练习**

**练习一、根据拼音写汉字,根据汉字写拼音**
( )lǜ　　( )liè　　xiào( )　tuō( )　( )wù
汇( )　　分( )　　( )话　　( )落　业( )

**练习二、搭配连线**
(1) 分裂　　　　　　　　A. 实际
(2) 脱离　　　　　　　　B. 业务
(3) 日常　　　　　　　　C. 汇率
(4) 付出　　　　　　　　D. 国家
(5) 固定　　　　　　　　E. 代价

**练习三、从今天学习的生词中选择合适的词填空**
1. 吃这种药以后,她的头发都脱落了,所以她不愿出门,怕别人 _____ 她。
2. 他为学生 _____ 了很多心血,同时,也获得了学生的爱戴和尊敬。
3. _____ 让他们伤心,只能等一年以后才能再次相见。
4. 那曾经是一个比较大的国家,后来因为政治和宗教的原因，_____ 成了四个小国。

5. 果实成熟以后，包在果实外面的壳就会自然 _____。

6. 昨天我收到了爸爸的 _____，这是我这学期的生活费。

7. 今天美元兑人民币的 _____ 突破了近年来的最低纪录。

8. 公司在 _____ 和今后一段时间的主要任务是开拓海外市场。

9. 到 _____ 为止，我们班已经有十个同学通过了 HSK 6 级考试。

10. 经过抢救，这个可爱的孩子已经 _____ 了危险。

## 答案

**练习一：**
略

**练习二：**
(1) D     (2)A     (3)B     (4)E     (5)C

**练习三：**
1. 笑话   2. 付出   3. 分离   4. 分裂   5. 脱落
6. 汇款   7. 汇率   8. 当前   9. 目前   10. 脱离

# 第 6 月，第 1 周的练习

**练习一 . 根据词语给加点的字注音**

1.( )    2.( )    3.( )    4.( )    5.( )
沉着     分裂     顽强     仪器     汇率

**练习二 . 根据拼音填写词语**

   qī      qī      qǐ      xíng      xíng
1. ( )间   2. ( )负   3. ( )业   4. 大( )   5. 举( )

**练习三 . 辨析并选择合适的词填空**

1. 要想经营好一家公司，( ) 很重要。（管、管理）

2. 父母离婚了，这个孩子没人 ( )，好可怜！（管、管理）

3. 父母对我男朋友的条件不 ( )，他们觉得我应该找个更好的。（满足、满意）

4. 我们不能 ( ) 于已经取得的成绩而是要继续努力。（满足、满意）

5. 在好心人的 ( ) 下，我们终于找到了那个四合院。（指引、引导）

6. 老师应该以正确的方式 ( ) 孩子，使他们对学习感兴趣。（指引、引导）

7. 他无论如何也不肯认错，态度很 ( )。（坚定、坚决）

8. 她的立场很 ( )，敌人根本就拿她没办法。（坚定、坚决）

9. 到 ( ) 为止，群众自发捐款已经超过百万。（当前、目前）

10. 在大敌 ( ) 的时候，我们一定要团结一致。（当前、目前）

**练习四 . 选词填空**

笑容    顽强    典礼    吸收    沉重
笑话    顽固    典型    吸取    沉着

1. 从这件事上我们要（ ）经验教训，以免以后再上当受骗。

2. 最疼爱她的姥姥去世了，她的心情很（ ）。

3. 明天是留学生班的毕业（ ），后天他们就可以回国了。

4. 这个人很幽默，喜欢讲（ ）。

5. 尽管经历了一次又一次的失败，但她表现得非常（ ），从没有向困难低头。

6. 孩子吃得很多，可还是很瘦，医生说她的营养没有被（ ）。

7. 相对于遇事容易紧张的人，人们更喜欢遇事冷静、（ ）的人。

8. 发烧、咳嗽、流鼻涕是感冒的（ ）症状。

9. 不管工作多累多辛苦，只要看见孩子灿烂的（ ），他的烦恼就消失了。

10. 他很（ ），怎么劝都不听。

**练习五 . 写出下列词语的同义词**

1. 大约( )      2. 触犯( )
3. 解决( )      4. 目前( )
5. 举行( )

**练习六 . 写出下列词语的反义词**

1. 抓紧( )      2. 顽强( )
3. 沉着( )      4. 分离( )
5. 欺负( )

## 答案

**练习一 .**
1.zhuó   2.liè   3.wán   4.qì   5.lǜ

**练习二 .**
1. 期   2. 欺   3. 企   4. 型   5. 行

**练习三 .**
1. 管理   2. 管   3. 满意   4. 满足   5. 指引
6. 引导   7. 坚决   8. 坚定   9. 目前   10. 当前

**练习四 .**
1. 吸取   2. 沉重   3. 典礼   4. 笑话   5. 顽强
6. 吸收   7. 沉着   8. 典型   9. 笑容   10. 顽固

**练习五 .**
1. 大概   2. 冒犯   3. 处理   4. 现在   5. 举办

**练习六 .**
1. 放松   2. 脆弱   3. 慌张   4. 团聚   5. 袒护

# 6月 第 2 周的学习内容

星期一

**zuìchū**
## 最初 （甲）名
① at first ② initial ③ originally

**常用搭配**
最初的印象 the first impression
最初的时候 at the very beginning
最初阶段 the initial stage

**用法示例**
现代音乐最初是在意大利发展起来的。
Modern music was first developed in Italy.
现在我住在这儿，但是我想知道最初是谁住在这儿的？
I live here now, but I wonder who lived here originally?
她最初反对这计划，但后来改变了主意。
Initially, she opposed the plan, but later she changed her mind.

**zuìhòu**
## 最后 反首先 （甲）名
last; ultimate; final

**常用搭配**
她是最后到的。She was the last to arrive.
比赛的最后一分钟 the final minute of the game
诗的最后两行 the last two lines of this poem

**用法示例**
她离开房子前做的最后一件事是锁门。
The final thing she did before she left the house was lock the door.
Z 是字母表中最后一个字母。
Z is the final letter in the alphabet.
他是最后一个离开办公室的。
He was the very last person to leave the office.

**gānggāng**
## 刚刚 （乙）副
① just recently ② just a moment ago

**常用搭配**
他们刚刚离开。They've just left.

**用法示例**
比赛刚刚开始就下起雨来。
The game had hardly begun when it started raining.
他刚刚从我身边走过。
Just now he passed by me.

别把镜头弄脏了，我刚刚擦过。
Don't smear the lens; I've just polished it.

**tíngzhǐ**
## 停止 （乙）动
stop; cease

**常用搭配**
停止讨论 stop talking    停止运动 stop moving

**用法示例**
昨晚老人的心脏停止了跳动。
The old man's heart stopped beating last night.
老师走进教室时，我们停止了争论。
We stopped arguing when the teacher came into the classroom.

**chūbù**
## 初步 （乙）形
preliminary; initial

**常用搭配**
初步计划 preliminary plan
初步调查 investigate preliminarily
初步训练 primary training

**用法示例**
经过初步检查，医生告诉他不能再接受训练了。
At the preliminary exam, the doctor told him he should not continue training.
我们初步计划明年去欧洲旅游。
We preliminarily planned to travel in Europe next year.

**chūjí**
## 初级 反高级 （乙）形
elementary; primary

**常用搭配**
初级读物 elementary reading book
初级阶段 elementary stage

**用法示例**
他从初级职员做起，最终成了这家公司的董事。
He joined the firm as a junior clerk, and finished up as a director.
她参加了饭店经理初级课程。
She attended a course to become junior hotel manager.

**zhígōng**
## 职工 同职员 （乙）名
staff; worker

**常用搭配**
下岗职工 laid-off workers
正式职工 regular staff

**用法示例**

这家工厂的所有女职工在妇女节都得到了一份礼物。

All the female workers in this factory got a present on Women's Day.

他是我们公司的老职工。

He is an old company staff member.

### tíngliú
### 停留 （丙）动

① stay somewhere temporarily ② stop over

**常用搭配**

停留一天 stay over for one day

**用法示例**

她去北京以前将在这里停留几日。

She will stay here for a few days before she goes to Beijing.

飞机将在那个机场停留一个小时。

The plane will stop over at that airport for an hour.

### duōkuī
### 多亏 ⓪ 幸亏 （丙）动／副
### xìngkuī

thanks to

**常用搭配**

多亏你的帮助。Thanks to your help.

**用法示例**

多亏王明，我们才打赢了这场比赛。

It was thanks to Wang Ming that we won the game.

多亏许多科学家的工作，我们才能预先知道要发生地震的时间。

Thanks to the work of many scientists, we are able to learn in advance when an earthquake will happen.

### xìngkuī
### 幸亏 （丙）副

luckily; fortunately

**常用搭配**

幸亏我带着雨伞。Luckily, I brought an umbrella with me.

**用法示例**

幸亏我当时系上了安全带。

Luckily I had fastened the safety belt.

幸亏他提醒了我，要不然我就把这件事给忘了。

Luckily, he reminded me of what I should do; otherwise I would have forgotten.

### tíngzhì
### 停滞 （丁）动

① stagnate ② be bogged down

**常用搭配**

经济停滞 economic stagnation

停滞状态 stagnation state

停滞不前 be at a standstill

**用法示例**

改革不能停滞。

The reform shouldn't be at a standstill.

销售现已开始停滞不前了。

Sales have now reached a plateau.

工农业生产停滞不前。

Agriculture and industry are at a standstill.

### zhínéng
### 职能 （丁）名

function; role

**常用搭配**

政府职能 functions of government

委员会的职能 functions of a committee

**用法示例**

法官有权执行某些法律职能。

The judges are authorized to perform certain legal functions.

学校的主要职能是教育学生。

The main function of a school is to educate its students.

 词义辨析

**多亏、幸亏**

"多亏"是动词，也是副词，指因某种有利的情况而使结果更好，可以直接跟单独的词或短语，常与"才"呼应使用；"幸亏"只是副词，指因某种有力的情况而避免了麻烦、困难或危险，常与"不然"、"否则"等呼应使用。例如：①多亏了他，我们才打赢比赛。②多亏您的及时帮助，我们才顺利地完成了工作。③幸亏警察到得及时，否则他就被杀了。

多亏 is a verb and an adverb, indicating that "thanks to some advantageous factors, the result is better than expected", it can be followed by a single word or phrase, and is often used in connection with "才"; while 幸亏 is an adverb, indicating that "some troubles, difficulties or dangers have been avoided because of some favorable conditions", and is often used in connection with "不然" (otherwise), or "否则" (otherwise). For example: ① But for him, we would not have won the game. ② Owing to your timely assistance, we have completed the work smoothly. ③ Luckily, the police came in time, otherwise he would have been killed.

 练习

**练习一、根据拼音写汉字，根据汉字写拼音**
xìng（ ） zuì（ ） （ ）zhì zhí（ ） chū（ ）
（ ）亏 （ ）后 停（ ） （ ）能 （ ）步

**练习二、搭配连线**
(1) 政府　　　　　　　　　A. 职工
(2) 下岗　　　　　　　　　B. 职能
(3) 停滞　　　　　　　　　C. 计划
(4) 初级　　　　　　　　　D. 状态
(5) 初步　　　　　　　　　E. 读物

**练习三、从今天学习的生词中选择合适的词填空**
1. 我对他 _____ 的印象不太好，但是相处了一段时间以后，感觉还不错。
2. 我才学了一个学期的汉语，只具备 _____ 水平。
3. 由于救治不及时，在快到医院时，他的心脏 _____ 了跳动。
4. 我八月到北京，短暂 _____ 后去上海。
5. 当前的经济发展 _____ 不前，经济学家担心会有更多的人失业。
6. 我的 _____ 打算是学好汉语，然后再决定是否留在北京工作。
7. _____ 了我的邻居，是他发现我病了，并给医院打了电话。
8. _____ 老板不在，不然他看到我迟到又要批评我了。
9. 我 _____ 吃了药，不能马上吃冰激凌。
10. 近些年，人们对政府的 _____ 有了新的认识，认为政府既是管理部门还是服务部门。

🔑 答案

**练习一：**
略
**练习二：**
(1) B　　(2)A　　(3)D　　(4)E　　(5)C
**练习三：**
1. 最初　　2. 初级　　3. 停止　　4. 停留　　5. 停滞
6. 初步　　7. 多亏　　8. 幸亏　　9. 刚刚　　10. 职能

---

 星期二

**tèbié**
**特别**　　　　　　　　　　　　　（甲）形／副
① particular ② very
【常用搭配】
特别的服装 a special dress　　特别快 very quickly
特别好的蛋糕 a very good cake
【用法示例】
今天对我来说是个特别的日子。
This is a special day for me.
他们的主要出口货物是纺织品，特别是丝绸和棉布。
Their main exports are textiles, especially silk and cotton.
这个问题特别重要。
This question is of special importance.

**rènzhēn**　　　　　　　zǐxì
**认真**　　🔁 仔细　　　　　　　　（甲）形
① serious ② carefully
【常用搭配】
认真学习 study carefully　　认真研究 research seriously
态度认真 serious attitude
【用法示例】
在服药前，你要认真阅读说明书。
Before taking medicine you should read the instructions carefully.
我看了你的建议并且认真考虑过了。
I've read your proposal and given it some serious thought.

**tèshū**　　　　　　　　yībān
**特殊**　　🔁 一般　　　　　　　　（乙）形
special; extraordinary
【常用搭配】
特殊情况 particular case　　特殊场合 a special case
【用法示例】
这是个特殊的案件，应该予以特殊处理。
This is a special case, deserving special treatment.
我只在特殊场合才打领带。
I only wear a tie on special occasions.

**pǔsù**　　　　　　　　huálì
**朴素**　　🔁 华丽　　　　　　　　（乙）形
simple; plain
【常用搭配】
朴素的衣服 simple dress　　穿着朴素 dress simply
【用法示例】
她穿了一件朴素的棕色衣服。
She wore a plain brown dress.
这间屋子的陈设十分朴素。
The room was furnished in a very simple style.

**céngjīng**

## 曾经　　　　　　　　　（乙）副

① once　② ever（refer to something that happened before）

**常用搭配**

你曾经去过欧洲吗？ Have you ever been to Europe?

他曾经是军人。He was once a soldier.

**用法示例**

我们曾经住在伦敦。

Once we lived in London.

她曾经爱过我,但现在已成往事了。

She loved me once, but that's all ancient history now.

被告否认他曾经遇到过她。

The accused man denies that he has ever met her.

**wéirào**

## 围绕　　　　　　　　　（乙）动

revolve around; center on (an issue)

**常用搭配**

树木围绕着池塘。Trees surround the pond.

**用法示例**

地球围绕着太阳转。

The earth revolves around the sun.

她的全部生活都围绕着丈夫和孩子。

Her whole life revolves around her husband and children.

**xìngqù**

## 兴趣　◎ 兴致 **xìngzhì**　（乙）名

interest

**常用搭配**

对……感兴趣 be interested in...

对体育的兴趣 an interest in sports

**用法示例**

这次争论没有引起公众丝毫的兴趣。

The debate did not arouse a speck of public interest.

他对流行歌曲很感兴趣。

He is very interested in popular music.

我对这种事没兴趣。

I have no interest in such things.

**qùwèi**

## 趣味　　　　　　　　　（丙）名

taste; interest

**常用搭配**

饶有趣味 very interesting　低级趣味 low tastes

**用法示例**

我们在海滩上野餐,趣味无穷。

We had a lot of fun at the picnic on the beach.

英语有着饶有趣味的发展历史。

The English language has an interesting history.

**qìwèi**

## 气味　　　　　　　　　（丙）名

odor; smell

**常用搭配**

医院里的气味 hospital odors　刺鼻的气味 sharp aroma

**用法示例**

这房子有油漆的气味。

The house smells of paint.

干酪散发出强烈的气味。

The cheese was emitting a strong smell.

我能闻到隔壁煎洋葱的气味。

I can smell the aroma of frying onions from next door.

**mèngxiǎng**

## 梦想　　　　　　　　　（丙）动/名

① to dream of ② dream

**常用搭配**

梦想成真 one's dreams come true

**用法示例**

他梦想着成为律师。

He dreams of becoming a lawyer.

我曾梦想在乡间买一所别墅。

I dreamed of buying a villa in the country side.

我的梦想已经破灭了。

My dreams have been shattered.

**shèxiǎng**

## 设想　　　　　　　　　（丙）动/名

① imagine; assume ② assumption; tentative plan

**常用搭配**

后果不堪设想 can't imagine what the result will be

对未来的设想 the conception of the future

**用法示例**

你可以设想那里的情况。

You can imagine the situation there.

很难设想他在那个国家的生活。

It's hard to imagine his life in that country.

**sùzhì**

## 素质　　　　　　　　　（丁）名

quality; making

**常用搭配**

个人素质 personal quality　身体素质 physical quality

**用法示例**

他具有成为一名好医生的素质。

He has the makings of a good doctor.

很难聘请到素质高的教师。

It's difficult to recruit teachers of quality.

我需要一名高素质的秘书。

I need a secretary of high quality.

**wéigōng**

## 围攻　　　　　　　　　（丁）动

besiege

**常用搭配**

遭到围攻 undergo a siege

围攻敌营 besiege the enemy's camp

猛烈围攻 to besiege fiercely

**用法示例**

狼群在围攻一只长颈鹿。

A group of wolves are besieging a giraffe.

我们在沼泽地遭到了蚊子的围攻。

In the swamp we were beset by mosquitoes.

这个城市可能会遭到敌军的围攻。

The city will probably be besieged by enemy troops.

 **词义辨析**

**特殊、特别**

　　"特殊"和"特别"都可以用作形容词,表示不一般,可以作谓语、定语,也可以受程度副词的修饰。但"特别"还是副词,有"非常"和"特地"的意思,可以作状语,修饰动词和形容词;"特殊"一般没有这样的用法。如:①她生日那天收到了一件特别/特殊的礼物。②这封信里没有什么特别重要的事。③他跑得特别快。④我们特别为他准备了一辆三轮车。

　　Both 特殊 and 特别 are adjectives, meaning "special, particular", They can function as a predicate or an attributive, and can be modified with degree adverbs. But 特别 is also an adverb, and indicates "very, extremely" or "especially, for a special purpose", It can function as an adverbial, and modify a verb or an adjective; while 特殊 is rarely used like this. For example: ① She received a special gift on her birthday. ② There was nothing in the letter of particular importance. ③ He runs very fast. ④ We especially arranged a tricycle for him.

 **练习**

**练习一、根据拼音写汉字,根据汉字写拼音**

qù（　　）　shè（　　）　（　　）rào　pǔ（　　）　（　　）shū

（　　）味　（　　）想　围（　　）　（　　）素　特（　　）

**练习二、搭配连线**

(1) 梦想　　　　　　　　A. 认真

(2) 态度　　　　　　　　B. 成真

(3) 特殊　　　　　　　　C. 朴素

(4) 遭到　　　　　　　　D. 情况

(5) 穿着　　　　　　　　E. 围攻

**练习三、从今天学习的生词中选择合适的词填空**

1. 他具备优秀音乐家的一切 _____ 。

2. 这个姑娘从来不化妆,很 _____ 。

3. 除非出现 _____ 情况,所有学生都必须参加毕业典礼。

4. _____ 一下,如果把你一个人留在这座小岛上,你会怎么生活?

5. 大会 _____ 环保问题展开了近一个小时的讨论。

6. 他说他不喜欢这种低级 _____ 的娱乐方式。

7. 动物通过 _____ 来确认自己的领地。

8. 我 _____ 在十年前来过北京。

9. 电视里正在播出一群狮子 _____ 一头野牛的画面。

10. 我 _____ 喜欢爸爸做的炸酱面。

**答案**

**练习一:**

略

**练习二:**

(1) B　　　(2)A　　　(3)D　　　(4)E　　　(5)C

**练习三:**

1. 素质　　2. 朴素　　3. 特殊　　4. 设想　　5. 围绕

6. 趣味　　7. 气味　　8. 曾经　　9. 围攻　　10. 特别

**星期三**

yǐjīng
**已经** （甲）副
already

（常用搭配）
我已经吃午饭了。I have had lunch.
我已经听说了。I've already heard of it.

（用法示例）
我没有注意到他已经走了。
I failed to notice that he had left.
我离开巴黎已经两星期了。
I have been away from Paris for two weeks.
当我们到家时孩子们已经睡着了。
The children were already asleep when we got home.

nénggòu
**能够** （甲）助动
① be capable of ② can

（常用搭配）
能够完成任务 can finish the task
能够用汉语交流 can communicate in Chinese

（用法示例）
今天能够做的事,就不要拖延到明天。
Never put off till tomorrow what you can do today.
这个小男孩能够数到一千。
The little boy can count up to a thousand.
没有人不努力就能够成功。
No one can succeed without working hard.

wéihù
**维护** （乙）动
maintain; safeguard

（常用搭配）
维护权利 to safeguard a right
维护工人的利益 protect workers' interest

（用法示例）
军队的责任之一就是维护民族独立和国家主权。
One of the army's responsibilities is to safeguard national
independence and state sovereignty.
这台旧机器维护得很好,看起来像新的一样。
The old machine is well maintained, and looks as good as
new.

wàngjì
**忘记** 遗忘 yíwàng （乙）动
forget

（常用搭配）
忘记带伞 forget to bring an umbrella
忘记耻辱 forget a disgrace

（用法示例）
我永远不会忘记那一时刻。
That was a moment I shall never forget.
历史学家们告诫我们,我们不应忘记过去。
Historians advise us to never forget the past.
她来的时候忘记带入场券了。
She forgot to bring the tickets with her when she came.

bǎohù
**保护** （乙）动／名
① protect ② protection

（常用搭配）
保护环境 protect the environment
环境保护 environmental protection
在……的保护下 under the protection of…

（用法示例）
他们的职责就是保护野生动物。
Their duty is to protect wild animals.
他伸出手去保护他的孩子。
He raised up his arm to protect his child.
政府决定对进口汽车征收保护税。
The government decided to impose a protective tariff on
foreign cars.

míngshèng
**名胜** （乙）名
① scenic spot ② a place famous for its scenery or
historical relics

（常用搭配）
名胜古迹 place of interest

（用法示例）
他喜欢参观名胜古迹。
He likes to visit places of interest.
来看看北京的名胜。
Come and see the sights of Beijing.

nénglì
**能力** （乙）名
ability; capability

（常用搭配）
支付能力 ability to pay
工作能力 working capability
有能力取胜 capable of winning

（用法示例）
根据各自的能力给这三个人安排了工作。
The three men were given work according to their
respective abilities.
教育应适应儿童的需要和能力。
Education should be geared to the children's needs and
abilities.
他有鉴赏艺术的能力。
He is capable of judging art.

qǐyuán
## 起源 （丙）名/动

① origin ② originate；derive

**常用搭配**

文明的起源 origins of civilization
生命的起源 origins of life
起源于…… originate from…

**用法示例**

这种风俗起源于十九世纪。
The custom originated in the 19th century.
这种建筑风格起源于古希腊。
The style of architecture originated from the ancient Greece.
他们试图解释宇宙的起源。
They tried to explain the origins of life.

qǐchū          zuìchū
## 起初 回 最初 （丙）名

① originally ② at first

**用法示例**

她起初反对这计划,但后来改变了想法。
Initially, she opposed the plan, but later she changed her mind.
起初她觉得这项工作很难。
She found the job difficult at first.
起初谁都没有注意到小孩不见了。
At first nobody noticed the child's disappearance.

mòshēng
## 陌生 （丙）形

unfamiliar；strange

**常用搭配**

陌生的城市 a strange city
陌生的面孔 unfamiliar faces

**用法示例**

我在这座陌生的小镇迷路了。
I got lost in the strange town.
你不应相信任何陌生人。
You shouldn't trust strangers.
在这个陌生的地方,她感到很孤单。
She feels rather lonely in that strange place.

wàngtú          wàngxiǎng
## 妄图 回 妄想 （丁）动

try in vain；vainly attempt

**常用搭配**

不要妄图与对手合作。
To not wish to want to cooperate with your rival in vain.

**用法示例**

敌人妄图把所有铁路都毁掉。
The enemy vainly attempted to destroy all the railways.
不要妄图从这里逃跑。
Don't vainly attempt to escape from here.

他妄图说服她。
He tried to persuade her in vain.

míngshēng          míngwàng
## 名声 回 名望 （丁）名

reputation

**常用搭配**

名声好 of good repute　坏名声 bad reputation

**用法示例**

那家旅馆的名声不好。
That hotel is of bad repute.
他因反复说谎而败坏了自己的名声。
He sullied his reputation by lying repeatedly.
他的所作所为使他的名声变坏了。
What he did put him in bad repute.

 **词义辨析**

**保护、维护**

"维护"和"保护"都是动词,都有尽力使不受损害的意思。"保护"的对象比较具体,可以是人,也可以是物;"维护"的对象一般是抽象的,重大而宽泛的。另外,"保护"还是名词,"维护"不是。比如:①总统宣誓维护宪法的尊严。②我们都在为维护世界和平而努力。③公民的生命和财产受到法律的保护。④他为环境保护事业奉献了一生。

Both 维护 and 保护 are verbs, indicating "to try to keep it undamaged". The object of 保护 is usually concrete, such as people or things; while the object of 维护 is usually abstract, often with great importance and large extension. And 保护 is also a noun, 维护 is not. For example: ① The President swore to uphold the dignity of the constitution. ② We all work to maintain the world peace. ③ The life and property of citizens are protected by law. ④ He devoted his whole life to the environmental protection.

 **练习**

**练习一、根据拼音写汉字，根据汉字写拼音**

wàng（　）（　）hù wàng（　）（　）shēng（　）shēng
（　）图　维（　）　（　）记　名（　）　陌（　）

**练习二、搭配连线**

(1) 保护　　　　　　　A. 能力
(2) 维护　　　　　　　B. 环境
(3) 工作　　　　　　　C. 逃跑
(4) 妄图　　　　　　　D. 古迹
(5) 名胜　　　　　　　E. 利益

**练习三、从今天学习的生词中选择合适的词填空**

1. 最近太忙了,差一点 ＿＿＿＿＿＿＿ 了爸爸的生日。
2. 妈,您别再给我钱了,我挣的钱 ＿＿＿＿＿＿＿ 养活自己。
3. 我们要 ＿＿＿＿＿＿＿ 安定团结的政治局面,不能让敌人有机可乘。
4. ＿＿＿＿＿＿＿,我以为他说的都是真的,后来,我意识到他是在吹牛。
5. 工作了一段时间以后,人们发现虽然她的学历很高,但是她的 ＿＿＿＿＿＿＿ 却一般。
6. 据说这种舞蹈形式 ＿＿＿＿＿＿＿ 于当地的一种宗教仪式。
7. 我们俩是特别好的朋友,谁也别 ＿＿＿＿＿＿＿ 破坏我们的友谊。
8. 这个姑娘以前交过好几个男朋友,所以有的人说她 ＿＿＿＿＿＿＿ 不太好。
9. 十年后再回到家乡,他发现一切都变得 ＿＿＿＿＿＿＿ 了,半天才找到自己原来的家。
10. 孩子在学校时,应该受到校方的 ＿＿＿＿＿＿＿,如果他们发生意外,学校要承担责任。

**答案**

**练习一:**
略
**练习二:**
(1) B　　　(2)E　　　(3)A　　　(4)C　　　(5)D
**练习三:**
1. 忘记　　2. 能够　　3. 维护　　4. 起初　　5. 能力
6. 起源　　7. 妄图　　8. 名声　　9. 陌生　　10. 保护

 **星期四**

fāxiàn
**发现**　　　　　　　　　　　　　　　（甲）动

find; discover

**常用搭配**

发现新油田 discover new oil fields
医学的新发现 a new discovery in medical science
科学发现 scientific discoveries

**用法示例**

据说哥伦布于 1492 年发现了美洲。
Columbus is said to have discovered America in 1492.
如果你发现有错,请改正。
If you find any mistakes, please correct them.
我发现俄语语法很难学。
I find Russian grammar very difficult.

mínzú
**民族**　　　　　　　　　　　　　　　（甲）名

nationality; ethnic group

**常用搭配**

中华民族 the Chinese nation　　民族艺术 ethnic art
民族服装 the national costume

**用法示例**

少数民族音乐会持续了两个小时。
The minority nationality concert lasted two hours.
这些美丽的古老宫殿是我们民族遗产的一部分。
These beautiful old palaces are part of our national heritage.
蒙古族是一个勇敢的民族。
The Mongols are an ethnic warrior group.

gǔlì　　　　　　　jīlì
**鼓励**　　　　◎ 激励　　　　　（乙）动 / 名

① encourage ② encouragement

**常用搭配**

受到……鼓励 be encouraged by…
互相鼓励 encourage each other

**用法示例**

她鼓励我努力学习。
She encouraged me to work hard.
她鼓励我表达内心深处的感情。
She encourages me to express my innermost feelings.
你的鼓励使我对未来更有信心了。
Your encouragement made me more confident in my future.

nàixīn
**耐心**　　　　　　　　　　　　　　（乙）形 / 名

① patient ② patience

## 常用搭配

耐心点儿！ Be patient!

对孩子有耐心 be patient with children

耐心地等待 wait patiently

## 用法示例

我认为他是一个很有耐心的人。

I think he is quite a patient person.

她耐心地教学生。

She teaches her students patiently.

我必须告诉你，我的耐心是有限的。

I must tell you that my patience has its limits.

### gǔwǔ
# 鼓舞 （乙）动/名

① hearten ② encouragement

## 常用搭配

令人鼓舞的消息 heartening news

鼓舞士气 boost one's morale

## 用法示例

最近的发展情况使我们受到很大的鼓舞。

We are much heartened by the latest development.

由衷的称赞可鼓舞一个人的士气。

A sincere compliment boosts one's morale.

艺术家应当创作能教育人民、鼓舞人民的作品。

An artist should create works that will educate and inspire the people.

### fāmíng
# 发明 （乙）动/名

① invent ② invention

## 常用搭配

发明家 inventor　发明传真 invent the fax

一项新发明 a new invention

## 用法示例

电话是 1876 年发明的。

The telephone was invented in 1876.

爱迪生是伟大的发明家。

Edison was a great inventor.

他获得了这项发明的专利权。

He got a patent for this invention.

### mínzhǔ
# 民主 反 专制 （乙）名/形
#### zhuānzhì

① democracy ② democratic

## 常用搭配

社会主义民主 socialist democracy

民主党 the Democratic Party

民主运动 democratic movement

## 用法示例

民主是自由的保障。

Democracy is the bulwark of freedom.

希腊是民主的发祥地。

Greece is the home of democracy.

这场革命把国家引上了通往民主的道路。

The revolution set the country on the road to democracy.

### wéibèi
# 违背 同 违反 （丙）动
#### wéifǎn

violate

## 常用搭配

违背习俗 abandon customs

违背誓言 break an oath

违背诺言 break a promise

## 用法示例

他违背了诺言，没有来看我。

He broke his promise and did not come to see me.

战争迫使我们不得不违背传统习俗。

The war forced us to abandon the traditional customs.

### nàifán
# 耐烦 （丙）形

patient

## 常用搭配

不耐烦 impatient　等得不耐烦 to wait impatiently

## 用法示例

作为幼儿园教师，你不该对孩子不耐烦。

As a nursery teacher, you mustn't be impatient with the children.

他们越来越不耐烦了。

They are growing impatient.

### dùnshí
# 顿时 （丙）副

① at once ② immediately

## 常用搭配

顿时安静了 be quiet at once

## 用法示例

他们听到喜讯，顿时欢呼起来。

People immediately broke into cheers when they heard the good news.

我加上了几块木柴，火顿时旺起来了。

The fire flared up as soon as I put more logs on it.

老师一进来，教室里顿时安静了。

The classroom was quiet as soon as the teacher entered.

### wéifǎ
# 违法 反 守法 （丁）动
#### shǒufǎ

① to break the law ② be illegal

## 常用搭配

违法乱纪 break the law and violate regulations

干违法的事 do something illegal

## 用法示例

如果你再继续违法，你迟早会坐牢的。

If you persist in breaking the law sooner or later you will go to prison.

夜晚行车不亮灯是违法的。

Driving without headlights at night is illegal.

在我们国家,携带枪支是违法的。
It's illegal to carry guns in our country.

nàilì
# 耐力 （丁）名
endurance

**常用搭配**

耐力测验 endurance tests
非凡的耐力 remarkable endurance

**用法示例**

她在行军过程中表现出极大的耐力。
She showed great endurance during the march.
长跑运动员需要有很大的耐力。
Long distance runners need great endurance.
士兵们最终完成了耐力测验。
The soldiers eventually completed their endurance tests.

## 词义辨析

**鼓舞、鼓励**

　　作为动词,"鼓舞"和"鼓励"都表示给人以勇气、希望和信心。"鼓舞"的行为主体是事件,这个事件一般会产生积极的影响;而"鼓励"的行为主体一般是人,这个人可能产生积极的影响,也可能产生消极的影响。例如:①这条好消息使我们很受鼓舞。②教授鼓励他的学生参加竞赛。③你所说的话是在鼓励孩子说谎。

　　As verbs, 鼓励 and 鼓舞 mean "to inspire hope, courage, or confidence". The subject of 鼓舞 is usually an event, the effect of which is usually positive; while the subject of 鼓励 is usually a person, the effect of which may be both positive and negative. For example: ① We were encouraged greatly by the good news. ② The professor encouraged his students to enter the competition. ③ What you said encourages the child to lie.

## 练习

**练习一、根据拼音写汉字,根据汉字写拼音**

wéi（　）gǔ（　）dùn（　）（　）zú（　）fán
（　）法　（　）励　（　）时　民（　）　耐（　）

**练习二、搭配连线**

(1) 违法　　　　　　A. 专利
(2) 违背　　　　　　B. 乱纪
(3) 互相　　　　　　C. 民族
(4) 发明　　　　　　D. 鼓励
(5) 少数　　　　　　E. 诺言

**练习三、从今天学习的生词中选择合适的词填空**

1. 我的老师很有 _____,一遍一遍地纠正我的发音。
2. 科学研究表明,女性比男性更有 _____。
3. 中国有 50 多个 _____,其中汉族的人口最多,分布最广。
4. 我的家庭很 _____,父母都很尊重孩子的意愿。
5. 领导的支持和信任使我们深受 _____,我们一定努力工作,不辜负领导的希望。
6. 老师 _____ 我深入研究中国文化,还借给我一些参考书。
7. 警察在搜查他家的时候,在他的书房 _____ 了一把手枪和十颗子弹。
8. 飞机是莱特兄弟 _____ 的,他们是伟大的 _____ 家。
9. 他缺乏耐心,学生问他问题时,他常常显得很不_____。
10. 我不可能接受他们的贿赂,这 _____ 我的工作原则。

## 答案

练习一:
略
练习二:
(1) B　　　(2)E　　　(3)D　　　(4)A　　　(5)C
练习三:
1. 耐心　　2. 耐力　　3. 民族　　4. 民主　　5. 鼓舞
6. 鼓励　　7. 发现　　8. 发明,发明　　9. 耐烦　　10. 违背

**héshì**
# 合适 （甲）形

suitable；fit

**常用搭配**

合适的工作 suitable job

合适的人选 suitable candidate

**用法示例**

我们什么时候见面合适？

What time is suitable for us to meet?

这对我正合适。

That suits me all right.

这种食物对你的客人来说不合适。

This food is not fit for your guests.

**shèhuì**
# 社会 （甲）名

society

**常用搭配**

社会科学 social science　社会地位 social status

社会调查 social investigations

**用法示例**

在旧社会，贵族们生活奢侈。

In old societies, the nobility lived in luxury.

这些罪犯是社会的渣滓。

These criminals are the dregs of society.

在我们的城市，许多社会服务仍然是由志愿团体提供的。

Many social services are still provided by voluntary

societies in our city.

**shìhé** **shìyí**
# 适合 🔁 适宜 （乙）动

to fit；to suit

**常用搭配**

适合孩子看的书 a book suitable for children

适合你的颜色 a color that suits you

**用法示例**

她不适合做这项工作。

She is not suitable for the job.

她的身高适合打篮球。

Her height made her suitable for basketball.

这个玩具不适合小孩玩。

This toy is not suitable for children.

**wéifǎn** **zūnxún**
# 违反 🔄 遵循 （乙）动

to violate (a law, etc.)

**常用搭配**

违反规定 violate the rules

**用法示例**

如果有人违反了制度，就会受到惩罚。

If someone breaks the rules, he will be punished.

那位记者被控有违反职业道德的行为。

The reporter was accused of unprofessional conduct.

**míngquè** **hánhu**
# 明确 🔄 含糊 （乙）形／动

① definite ② make clear

**常用搭配**

明确的答复 a clear answer

明确告诉他 tell him clearly

**用法示例**

她明确表示反对这个提案。

She made it clear that she objected to the proposal.

观点十分明确，不需要解释。

The proposition is so clear that it needs no explanation.

我希望明确一下儿，这个决定是不可更改的。

I wish to make it clear that the decision is final.

**chūxí**
# 出席 （乙）动

① attend ② be present

**常用搭配**

出席会议 be present at the meeting

出席结婚典礼 attend the wedding ceremony

**用法示例**

请你务必出席会议。

Your presence is requested at the meeting.

当地所有的牧师都出席了这个仪式。

All of the local clergy attended the ceremony.

总理阁下将出席本次论坛。

His Excellency the Premier will be present at the debate.

**míngxiǎn**
# 明显 （乙）形

obvious；clear

**常用搭配**

明显的优势 obvious advantages

明显的差异 obvious difference

明显的目标 obvious target

**用法示例**

很明显，她在说谎。

It is obvious that she is lying.

这项计划的缺陷是很明显的，它不可能成功。

The flaws in this plan are very clear and show that it can't

possibly succeed.

对罪犯的改造有了明显的效果。

The reformation of criminals has produced a clear result.

**zǔài**
# 阻碍 （丙）动／名

① obstruct ② obstacle

**常用搭配**

阻碍交通 obstruct a road　　阻碍进步 obstruct progress

**用法示例**

旧的经济体制阻碍了社会的发展。

The old economic system obstructed social development.

他认为没有什么可以阻碍他的计划。

He thought nothing could obstruct his plan.

她父亲的反对是他们唯一的阻碍。

Her father's opposition remained the only obstacle to them.

### chūxi
### 出息　　　　　　　　　　　　　　（丙）名

prospects

**常用搭配**

有出息 have a good future

**用法示例**

他是个聪明懂事的孩子，将来准会有出息。

He's a sensible and clever boy, and ought to turn out well.

这个学生没什么出息。

There's not much of a prospect for this student.

### shìyí
### 适宜　　　　　　　　　　　　　　（丙）形

suitable; appropriate

**常用搭配**

气候适宜。The climate is suitable.

**用法示例**

这些电影只适宜成人观看。

These films are suitable for adults only.

这件大衣适宜在正式场合穿。

This coat is appropriate for a formal occasion.

这种天气不适宜外出。

The weather is not fit to go out in.

### wéifàn
### 违犯　　　　　　　　　　　　　　（丁）动

violate; break

**常用搭配**

违犯纪律 violate a rule　　违犯禁忌 to break taboos

**用法示例**

他因违犯法律而被捕。

He was arrested for breaking the law.

如果司机违犯交通法规，他将被罚款。

The driver will be fined if he violates traffic rules.

### zǔlán　　　　　　　zǔdǎng
### 阻拦　　　　　🔄 阻挡　　　　　　（丁）动

to stop

**常用搭配**

被……阻拦 be stopped by…

**用法示例**

让她走，别阻拦她。

Let her go. Don't stop her.

老师试图阻拦那个男孩，但他还是跑出了教室。

The teacher tried to stop the boy, but he ran out of the classroom.

 **词义辨析**

**适合、合适**

　　1、"合适"是形容词，表示符合要求或情况，常作谓语和定语。"合适"比较口语化，很常用，可带程度补语。例如：①不说声再见就离开舞会是不合适的。②这个女孩总是抱怨没有合适的衣服。③这件夹克衫合适极了。

　　合适 is an adjective, indicating "suitable or acceptable for a given circumstance or purpose"; it usually functions as a predicate or an attributive. 合适 is more colloquial and very common, and can be followed by a complement of degree. For example: ① It is not right to leave the party without saying goodbye. ② The girl always complains about lacking suitable clothes. ③ The jacket fits very well.

　　2、"适合"是动词，常作谓语，可以直接带宾语。例如：①这件衣服不适合我。②这家商店有很多适合儿童阅读的书籍。

　　适合 is a verb, and usually functions as a predicate followed by an object in a sentence. For example: ① This dress doesn't fit me. ② There are a lot of books suitable for children in this shop.

 **练习**

**练习一、根据拼音写汉字，根据汉字写拼音**

（　　）shì　（　　）què　chū（　　）　shì（　　）　zǔ（　　）
合（　　）　明（　　）　（　　）息　（　　）宜　（　　）碍

**练习二、搭配连线**

(1) 阻碍　　　　　　　A. 规定
(2) 出席　　　　　　　B. 交通
(3) 违反　　　　　　　C. 地位
(4) 违犯　　　　　　　D. 典礼
(5) 社会　　　　　　　E. 纪律

**练习三、从今天学习的生词中选择合适的词填空**

1. 他对这几个应聘者都不太满意，认为他们都不是_____的人选。

2. 这个地方气候温暖湿润，非常_____热带植物生长。

3. 昆明四季如春，气候_____，是休养的好地方。

4. 你的行为_____了法律，你就等着坐牢吧。

5. 父亲对儿子很失望，生气地对母亲说："让他走，不要_____他"。

6._____这次大会的有科学家、教育家和政府部门的领导。

7. 经过一段时间的学习,他的汉语水平有了 _____ 的提高。

8. 他因 _____ 学校的规定而被开除了。

9. 他谦虚、勤奋,而且特别懂礼貌,邻居们都夸他是个有 _____ 的小伙子。

10. 他的态度很 _____,说如果公司不答应他的要求,他就立即辞职。

**🔑 答案**

练习一:
略
练习二:
(1) B　　(2)D　　(3)A　　(4)E　　(5)C
练习三:
1. 合适　2. 适合　3. 适宜　4. 违犯　5. 阻拦
6. 出席　7. 明显　8. 违反　9. 出息　10. 明确

# 6月,第2周的练习

**练习一. 根据词语给加点的字注音**
1.( )　2.( )　3.( )　　4.( )　5.( )
停滞　　朴素　　陌生　　阻碍　　顿时

**练习二. 根据拼音填写词语**
　wàng　　wàng　　wéi　　　wéi　　　wéi
1.( )记　2.( )图　3.( )攻　4.( )护　5.( )反

**练习三. 辨析并选择合适的词填空**
1. ( )公司临时叫他回去了,否则谈判不会这么顺利。(多亏、幸亏)
2. ( )了你的帮助,我们才提前完成了任务。(多亏、幸亏)
3. 公司看重他的能力,他在公司享受( )待遇。(特殊、特别)
4. 她对我( )好,就像我的妈妈一样。(特殊、特别)
5. 军队最主要的任务不是打仗,而是( )和平。(维护、保护)
6. 妈妈说,不要躺着看书,要( )自己的视力。(维护、保护)
7. 读完这个伟人的传记后,小王大受( ),从此干什么活都很努力。(鼓励、鼓舞)
8. 虽然家里很穷,但这位母亲一直( )孩子们要努力学习,不能放弃。(鼓励、鼓舞)
9. 这套西服我穿着很( ),我要买下来。(适合、合适)
10. 这个城市人口少,气候好,( )养老。(适合、合适)

**练习四. 选词填空**
明确　　违背　　能力　　兴趣　　停止

明显　　违法　　耐力　　趣味　　停滞
1. 未成年人开车上路是( )的,所以我现在还不能让儿子开车。
2. 新总统上任后,经济仍然( )不前,人们开始对这届政府表示不满了。
3. 儿童作品要特别注意( )性,否则没有吸引力。
4. 目前,这家工厂还不具备生产大型机械的( ),他们的设备和技术都没有达到要求。
5. 在那种情况下,他被迫说了( )自己意愿的话,事后他很后悔。
6. 人类社会对文明和进步的追求从来没有( )过。
7. 她喜欢跳舞,对唱歌没有( )。
8. 这学期,他的进步很( ),每次考试,都在九十分以上。
9. 她目标很( ),就是要考上北京大学。
10. 科学研究发现,男人比女人力量大,但女人比男人更有( )。

**练习五. 写出下列词语的同义词**
1. 名声( )　　　2. 阻拦( )
3. 违背( )　　　4. 兴趣( )
5. 职工( )

**练习六. 写出下列词语的反义词**
1. 朴素( )　　　2. 违犯( )
3. 违法( )　　　4. 特殊( )
5. 首先( )

**🔑 答案**

练习一.
1.zhì　　2.pǔ　　3.mò　　4.ài　　5.dùn
练习二.
1. 忘　2. 妄　3. 围　4. 维　5. 违
练习三.
1. 幸亏　2. 多亏　3. 特殊　4. 特别　5. 维护
6. 保护　7. 鼓舞　8. 鼓励　9. 合适　10. 适合
练习四.
1. 违法　2. 停滞　3. 趣味　4. 能力　5. 违背
6. 停止　7. 兴趣　8. 明显　9. 明确　10. 耐力
练习五.
1. 名望　2. 阻挠　3. 违反　4. 兴致　5. 职员
练习六.
1. 华丽　2. 遵循　3. 守法　4. 一般　5. 最后

# 6月 第 3 周的学习内容

**星期一 Monday**

## gāi
### 该 （甲）助动 / 动

① should ② It's time to ③ It's one's turn to

**常用搭配**

你不该迟到。You shouldn't be late.
该睡觉了。It's time to go to bed.
该你了。It's your turn.

**用法示例**

你不该骗你爸爸。
You should not lie to your father.
现在该你发言了。
It is your turn to speak.
你早该开始工作了。
It's high time that you started working.

## yīnggāi
### 应该 （甲）助动

should

**常用搭配**

你应该接受忠告。You should accept advice.

**用法示例**

你不应该这样粗心大意。
You shouldn't be so careless.
依我看，我们应该接受他们的道歉。
In my opinion, we should accept their apology.
你应该好好利用这个机会。
You should take advantage of it.

## fādá
### 发达 （乙）形

① developed (country, etc.) ② flourishing

**常用搭配**

发达国家 developed countries
商业发达 flourishing commerce

**用法示例**

法国是发达国家之一。
France is one of the developed countries.
他的公司兴旺发达。
His company is prospering.

## wēijī
### 危机 （乙）名

crisis

**常用搭配**

金融危机 financial crisis　政治危机 political crisis
信任危机 crisis of confidence

**用法示例**

他们在经济危机时遭受了巨大的损失。
They suffered huge losses in the economic crisis.
他们的婚姻面临危机。
Their marriage is facing a crisis.

## luòhòu
### 落后 ⊗先进 （乙）形
*xiānjìn*

① fall behind ② backward

**常用搭配**

落后的经济体制 backward economic system
思想落后 backward thinking

**用法示例**

中国的这个地区仍然很落后。
This part of China is still backward.
那个国家仍然处于落后状态。
The country is still in a backward state.
这个工厂虽然技术先进，但制度比较落后。
The technology of the factory is advanced, but the system is quite backward.

## dāndiào
### 单调 （乙）形

monotonous

**常用搭配**

单调的工作 monotonous work
单调的生活 monotonous life

**用法示例**

每天都做同样的工作，很单调。
It is very dreary to do the same job every day.
他那单调的声音使我要睡着了。
The monotony of his voice sent me to sleep.

## wēihài
### 危害 ⊜损害 （乙）动 / 名
*sǔnhài*

① do harm ② harm

**常用搭配**

危害健康 do harm to one's health
严重危害 seriously harm

**用法示例**

干旱给庄稼带来许多危害。
The drought did a lot of harm to the crops.
如果使用不当，核能会对人的健康和安全造成危害。
Nuclear power will do harm to our health and safety if improperly used.

**zhèngmiàn**
## 正面    ⊗ 反面 **fǎnmiàn**    （丙）名/形
① front ② positive

**常用搭配**
塑像的正面 the obverse side of a statue
明信片的正面 the front of the postcard

**用法示例**
英国硬币的正面有女王的头像。
The head of the Queen appears on the obverse of British coins.
学校主楼的正面朝南。
The front of the main school building faces south.
哪一面是这块布的正面？
Which is the right side of the cloth?

**zǒnggòng**
## 总共    （丙）副
① altogether ② in sum

**常用搭配**
总共 500 个座位 500 seats in all

**用法示例**
吃饭的人总共有二十位。
There were 20 people altogether at the dinner.
你总共要花 750 元。
That will cost you ￥750 in total.
总共来了 23 位客人。
There are 23 guests coming, all told.

**dānchún**
## 单纯    （丙）形
simplistic; naive; mere

**常用搭配**
单纯的女孩 a naive girl    单纯的想法 a naive thought

**用法示例**
她像小孩一样单纯。
She is as simple as a child.
幸福并不在于单纯地占有金钱。
Happiness lies not merely in the possession of money.
他利用了她的无知和单纯。
He took advantage of her ignorance and simplicity.

**wēijí**
## 危急    ⊜ 紧急 **jǐnjí**    （丁）形
critical; desperate

**常用搭配**
危急关头 a critical moment
情况危急 desperate situation

**用法示例**
病人情况危急，需要马上做手术。
The patient's condition was critical and she needed an immediate operation.
国家处于危急状态。
The country is in a desperate state.

**fǎnmiàn**
## 反面    （丁）名
the reverse side of sth.; the other side

**常用搭配**
硬币的反面 reverse side of a coin
衣服的反面 the reverse side of a coat

**用法示例**
我们既要看到事物的正面，也要看到事物的反面。
We must see the reverse as well as the obverse side of things.
这是设计楼房的反面教材。
It is an counter-example of how to design building.

 词义辨析

**该、应该**
　　作为助动词，"该"和"应该"都可以表示可能性、合理性、职责、期望等，通常可以互换使用，但"该"更口语化，语气更加肯定；"应该"的语气比较谨慎，更强调客观的合理性。"该"还是动词，表示轮到、欠的意思；"应该"没有这种用法。例如：①他们这个时候该 / 应该到北京了。②你看我该 / 应该怎么办？③该谁值日了？④他该我 100 块钱。

　　As auxiliary verbs, both 该 and 应该 mean "to express probability, advisability, obligation or expectation", and they are usually interchangeable. But 该 is more colloquial, with more affirmative mood; while 应该 is used with more prudence, stressing the objective advisability. 该 is also a verb, indicating "to be one's turn to do something", "owe (money, things) to"; while 应该 has no usage like that. For example: ① They should have arrived in Beijing by this time. ② What do you think I should do? ③ Whose turn is it to be on duty today? ④ He owes me 100 yuan.

 **练习**

**练习一、根据拼音写汉字，根据汉字写拼音**

dān（　）（　）jí　luò（　）（　）gòng　fǎn（　）
（　）调　危（　）（　）后　总（　）（　）面

**练习二、搭配连线**

(1) 危急　　　　　　A. 健康
(2) 危害　　　　　　B. 危机
(3) 反面　　　　　　C. 关头
(4) 金融　　　　　　D. 国家
(5) 发达　　　　　　E. 教材

**练习三、从今天学习的生词中选择合适的词填空**

1. 在亚洲金融 _____ 期间，多家银行和企业面临破产。
2. 病人情况 _____，医生开始全力抢救。
3. 长期大量吸烟将 _____ 身体健康，甚至导致死亡。
4. 时间过得真快，明天又是星期六了，我们又 _____ 放假了。
5. 前一段时间很辛苦，现在休息一星期是 _____ 的。
6. 这个地区工业很 _____，但是商业发展得不好。
7. 他的工作是检查和维修铁轨，每天都得沿着铁道行走 10 公里，工作辛苦而 _____。
8. 我发现这个工厂的机器设备比较 _____，所以他们的生产效率比较低。
9. 两斤苹果、三斤葡萄，_____ 是 12 块钱。
10. 在这部电影中，他扮演一个 _____ 角色，这是他第一次演坏人。

**答案**

**练习一：**
略

**练习二：**
(1) C　　　(2)A　　　(3)E　　　(4)B　　　(5)D

**练习三：**
1. 危机　　2. 危急　　3. 危害　　4. 该　　5. 应该
6. 发达　　7. 单调　　8. 落后　　9. 总共　　10. 反面

---

 **星期二**

**dàoli**
**道理** （甲）名

principle；sense；reason

**常用搭配**

这没有道理。It makes no sense.
合乎道理 It stands to reason.
有道理 reasonable

**用法示例**

他的忠告很有道理。
There's a great deal of sense in his advice.
你看这有道理吗？
Do you think it makes sense?
按道理他应该到车站去接你。
He should have met you at the station on principle.

**zhèngcè**
**政策** （乙）名

policy

**常用搭配**

经济政策 economic policy
改革开放的政策 reformative policy of openness

**用法示例**

我们需要一个更加灵活的外交政策。
We need a foreign policy that is more flexible.
这项政策不会受到选民的欢迎。
This policy will not appeal to the voters.

**jǐnjǐn**
**仅仅** （乙）副

merely；only (this and nothing more)

**常用搭配**

这仅仅是个开头。
This is merely the beginning.

**用法示例**

他们不满足于仅仅填饱肚子。
They are not content to merely fill the stomach.
别担心，他仅仅是太累了，明天就会好的。
Don't worry. He is just tired, he will be well tomorrow.
屋里仅仅有一把椅子。
There is only a chair in the room.

**zhēnlǐ**
**真理** 反 谬误 **miùwù** （乙）名

truth

**常用搭配**

探求真理 seek after truth
永恒的真理 the eternal truths

他努力追求真理。
He strives for truth.
智者热爱真理,愚者回避真理。
Wise men love truth, whereas fools shun it.

xiāohuà
## 消化 （乙）动

digest

常用搭配
消化不良 bad digestion 消化系统 digestive system
消化器官 digestive apparatus

用法示例
这种油腻的食物不易消化。
This rich food doesn't digest easily.
有些孩子吃肥肉不消化。
Some children can't digest fat.
唾液能帮助咀嚼和消化食物。
Saliva helps one chew and digest food.

qìfēn fēnwéi
## 气氛 回氛围 （丙）名

atmosphere; mood

常用搭配
节日的气氛 a festive atmosphere
友好的气氛 friendly atmosphere

用法示例
会上的气氛有点紧张。
There was tension in the air at the meeting.
那部影片营造出恐怖的气氛。
That film creates a menacing atmosphere.
全国沉浸在节日的气氛中。
The whole country had a festival atmosphere.

qìfèn
## 气愤 （丙）形

indignant; furious

常用搭配
对……感到气愤 be indignant at…

用法示例
他很气愤,因为他觉得对他不公平。
He was indignant because he felt that he had been treated unfairly.
当他撞了我的车时,我很气愤。
I was furious when he crashed my car.

dāndú gòngtóng
## 单独 反共同 （丙）形

① alone ② by oneself

常用搭配
单独旅行 travel by oneself

用法示例
恐怕你不能单独去那儿。
I'm afraid you can't go there alone.

父亲不愿意让我单独出门。
My father doesn't like me going out alone.
他单独去了北京。
He went to Beijing by himself.

gūdān
## 孤单 （丁）形

lonely; lone

常用搭配
孤单的游客 a lone traveler 孤单地生活 live alone

用法示例
他的朋友很少,生活非常孤单。
He has so few friends that his life is lonely.
在只剩下他一人的时候,他并不感到孤单。
He doesn't feel lonely when he is left alone.

gūdú
## 孤独 （丁）形

lonely; solitary

常用搭配
感到孤独 feel lonesome
孤独的老人 lonely old man

用法示例
这个孤独的孩子渴望母亲的爱。
The lonely child is longing for the love of his mother.
他的童年是压抑而孤独的。
His childhood was repressed and solitary.

duìcè
## 对策 （丁）名

countermeasure; solution

常用搭配
制订对策 to work out a countermeasure
有效的对策 an effective solution

用法示例
政府采取对策抑制物价上涨。
The government took countermeasures against rising prices.
我们队要求暂停,以便商讨新的对策。
Our team asked for a timeout to discuss a new plan.
这是唯一可行的对策。
This is the only practicable solution.

cèhuà móuhuà
## 策划 回谋划 （丁）动

to plot; to mastermind

常用搭配
精心策划 to plot carefully
策划一项活动 make a scheme for an activity

用法示例
他们策划了一个推翻政府的阴谋。
They concocted a plot to overthrow the government.
警察知道是谁策划了那次抢劫。
The police know who masterminded the robbery.

经理是营销活动的策划人。
The manager is the mastermind of marketing activities.

 **词义辨析**

**孤独、孤单、单独**

这三个词都是形容词,"孤独"和"孤单"都有寂寞或因为没有人陪伴而感到沮丧的意思,经常作定语、谓语、补语,作状语时常加"地"。但是"孤独"强调内心的感受,"孤单"则强调没有伙伴,而"单独"没有感到寂寞的意思,强调独立地,不与别人结伴或合作,常直接作状语,修饰动词。例如:①妻子和两个孩子离他而去后,他很孤独。②他刚到伦敦时很孤单。③我认为单独去游泳很危险。

The three are adjectives. 孤独 and 孤单 mean "lonely", "to feel dejected by the awareness of being alone", it often functions as an attributive or a predicate or a complement, and is followed by "地" when it functions as an adverbial. But 孤独 stresses "to feel lonely"; 孤单 stresses "without companions"; 单独 has no sense of "loneliness", but stresses "independently", "without others or help", and often functions as an adverbial directly, to modify verbs. For example:① After his wife and two children left him, he was very lonely. ② He was very lonely when he moved to London. ③ I think it is dangerous to go swimming alone.

 **练习**

**练习一、根据拼音写汉字,根据汉字写拼音**
( )fèn ( )huà gū( ) ( )huà ( )li
气( ) 策( ) ( )单 消( ) 道( )

**练习二、搭配连线**
(1) 孤单的      A. 政策
(2) 开放的      B. 对策
(3) 有效的      C. 游客
(4) 友好的      D. 真理
(5) 永恒的      E. 气氛

**练习三、从今天学习的生词中选择合适的词填空**
1. 我觉得他的话很有 _____,就接受了他的建议。
2. 他那么优秀,成功 _____ 是时间问题。
3. 我们去看了昨晚的演唱会,现场 _____ 热烈极了。
4. 男朋友总是做了决定后才告诉她,这让她非常 _____。
5. 春节的时候,同学们都回家与家人团聚了,她一个人在宿舍觉得特别 _____。
6. 我们两个人住一间屋子,她自己 _____ 住一间。
7. 昨天没复习,知识还没有 _____,今天听起课来有点困难。
8. 星期天是他感到最 _____ 的时候,因为他在这里还没有朋友。
9. 这事怎么办?快给我想个 _____。
10. 暗杀总统的事件是他的竞争对手秘密 _____ 的。

**答案**

**练习一:**
略
**练习二:**
(1) C      (2)A      (3)B      (4)E      (5)D
**练习三:**
1. 道理    2. 仅仅    3. 气氛    4. 气愤    5. 孤独
6. 单独    7. 消化    8. 孤单    9. 对策    10. 策划

**yìqǐ**

# 一起 （甲）副

together

**常用搭配**

一起玩儿 play together

一起旅游 travel together

**用法示例**

咱们一起吃顿午餐吧。

Let's get together and have lunch.

我把这两张纸粘在一起了。

I stuck the two pieces of paper together.

工人把沙子和石块混合在一起。

The workers mixed sand with gravel.

**kùnnan**

# 困难 （甲）名／形

① difficulty ② difficult；hard

**常用搭配**

克服困难 overcome difficulty

遇到困难 meet with difficulty

困难时期 difficult times

**用法示例**

尽管有那么多困难，我们仍然及时地到达了这里。

Overcoming all the setbacks, we arrived here in time.

他小的时候，家里生活很困难。

His family had a hard time when he was young.

他遇到困难就容易泄气。

He is easily discouraged by difficulties.

**yìqí**

# 一齐 （乙）副

① at the same time ② simultaneously

**常用搭配**

大家一齐唱。All sing together!

**用法示例**

你们不要一齐说！

Don't all speak at once!

大家一齐跟我读。

You all read after me.

**zhōudào**

# 周到 （乙）形

thoughtful；considerate

**常用搭配**

周到的安排 considerate arrangement

**用法示例**

你送来花，考虑得真周到。

It was very thoughtful of you to send flowers.

你想得真周到呀。

It's very thoughtful of you.

在我工作的时候你不弹钢琴，真是考虑得很周到。

It was considerate of you not to play the piano while I was working.

**jìnbù**　　　　　　　　　　**tuìbù**

# 进步 反退步 （乙）动／形

① progress ② progressive

**常用搭配**

进步人士 progressive elements

取得进步 make progress

**用法示例**

他学习上进步得很快。

He made rapid progress his study.

这学期他的写作有了很大进步。

His writing has improved greatly in this term.

那位著名的进步思想家应邀在大会上演讲。

That famous progressive thinker was asked to deliver a speech at the meeting.

**tǒngyī**

# 统一 （乙）动／形

① unify ② unified

**常用搭配**

语言的统一 unification of language

统一的标准 unified standard

**用法示例**

这个国家统一的结果是成为了一个强大的大国。

The unification of the country led to a big powerful nation.

这个国家于 1871 年统一了。

This country was unified in 1871.

学生要穿统一的校服。

The students should wear a unified school uniform.

**tuìbù**

# 退步 （丙）动／名

① regress；lag behind ② backwards

**常用搭配**

学习退步 fall behind the others in learning

**用法示例**

你的英语退步了。

Your English has regressed.

她似乎好起来了，后来又退步了。

She seemed better until her set back.

**tǒngjì**

# 统计 （丙）动／名

① collect statistics ② statistics

**常用搭配**

统计局 statistic bureau

人口统计 population statistics

统计资料 statistical data

**【用法示例】**

他们出示了一些统计数字来支持他们的论点。

They showed some statistical evidence to support their argument.

她在大学学习统计学。

She's studying statistics at university.

我这里正好有官方的统计数字。

I happen to have the official statistics with me.

jiānnán

## 艰难

⊜ 艰苦 jiānkǔ （丙）形

difficult

**【常用搭配】**

艰难时期 a difficult period

生活艰难 live a hard life

**【用法示例】**

那是一段艰难的岁月。

That was a difficult time.

他的生活变得越来越艰难了。

His life is getting more difficult.

他们经过三个月的艰难行军后到达了营地。

They reached the camp after three-month's hard march.

gōngyìng

## 供应

⊗ 收缴 shōujiǎo （丙）动

supply

**【常用搭配】**

食品供应 supply of food

供应充足 in abundant supply

**【用法示例】**

商人向他们供应货物。

The merchant supplies the goods to them.

这些商品现供应不足,价格会上涨。

These goods are in short supply; the price will be high.

电力供应中断,城市陷于混乱之中。

After the electricity failure the city was in chaos.

zhōumì

## 周密

（丁）形

careful; thorough

**【常用搭配】**

周密的计划 a careful plan

周密地安排 to arrange carefully

周密思考 to think through thoroughly

**【用法示例】**

他们制订了一个非常周密的进攻计划。

They drew up a very careful plan of attack.

要想弄清事实,唯一的办法是做周密的调查。

The only way to get at the facts is to make a thorough investigation.

yánmì

## 严密

⊜ 缜密 zhěnmì （丙）形

tight

**【常用搭配】**

结构严密 compact in construction

严密监视 keep a close watch

**【用法示例】**

警方一直严密监视着可疑分子的活动。

The police have been keeping a close watch on the suspects' movements.

我们严密看守囚犯。

We keep a close eye on the prisoners.

士兵们严密注意着敌人的行动。

The soldiers were keeping close watch over their enemies.

 词义辨析

**困难、艰难**

作为形容词,"困难"和"艰难"都有做事不顺利,境遇穷困的意思,通常"艰难"比"困难"的规模和程度更甚,"困难"更口语化。实际上,"困难"多用作名词,表示遇到的不利和麻烦的情况,也指经济上的不足。例如:①他们小的时候,生活很困难/艰难。②改革教育制度将是一个艰难的过程。③在困难面前我们决不退缩。

As adjectives, both 困难 and 艰难 mean "difficult", "hard to do or hard to endure", but the scale and degree of difficulties denoted by 艰难 usually surpass those of 困难, and 困难 is more colloquial. In fact 困难 is mostly used as a noun, indicating disadvantage, trouble or economic insufficiency. For example: ① Their lives were very hard when they were young. ② Reforming the education system will be a difficult process. ③ We never run away from difficulties.

 **练习**

**练习一、根据拼音写汉字，根据汉字写拼音**

tuì（　　）gōng（　　）tǒng（　　）jiān（　　）（　　）mì
（　　）步　（　　）应　（　　）计　（　　）难　周（　　）

**练习二、搭配连线**

(1) 周密　　　　　　　　A. 资料
(2) 供应　　　　　　　　B. 策划
(3) 取得　　　　　　　　C. 充足
(4) 统计　　　　　　　　D. 困难
(5) 克服　　　　　　　　E. 进步

**练习三、从今天学习的生词中选择合适的词填空**

1. 孩子这次考试成绩提高了，比上次考试有了明显的
_____。

2. 自从他迷上了打游戏，学习就 _____ 了。

3. 遇到 _____，首先要自己想办法克服，尽量不要麻烦
别人。

4. 这个饭店的环境一般，但是服务非常 _____。

5. 这个品牌的服装在全国的价格都是 _____ 的，你在哪
儿买都可以。

6. 最新 _____ 数据表明，6 月份的房价涨了 10%。

7. 他的收入不高，既要照顾生病的妻子，又要供两个孩子上
学，生活很 _____。

8. 由于南方近来水灾，蔬菜 _____ 不足，所以价格上涨
了一些。

9. 为了确保成功，我们得有一个 _____ 的计划。

10. 为了寻找证据，警察正在 _____ 监视犯罪嫌疑人的
行动。

**答案**

**练习一：**
略

**练习二：**
(1) B　　　(2)C　　　(3)E　　　(4)A　　　(5)D

**练习三：**
1. 进步　　2. 退步　　3. 困难　　4. 周到　　5. 统一
6. 统计　　7. 艰难　　8. 供应　　9. 周密　　10. 严密

**星期四**　Thursday

**dàibiǎo**
**代表**　（甲）名/动

① representative; delegate ② to stand for

**常用搭配**
代表团 delegation　工人代表 workers' representative

**用法示例**
他被选为年会代表。
He was elected to attend the annual conference as a delegate.
这张地图上的红线代表铁路。
The red lines on the map represent train lines.
"&" 代表什么？
What does "&" stand for?
TEC 代表技术教育证书。
TEC stands for Technical Education Certificate.

**yīnyuè**
**音乐**　（甲）名

music

**常用搭配**
欣赏音乐 enjoy music　古典音乐 classical music
音乐家 musician　音乐会 concert

**用法示例**
听音乐对她有镇静的作用。
Listening to music has a calming influence on her.
他有音乐天赋。
He has a gift for music.
你喜欢流行音乐吗？
Do you like popular music?

**fǒuzé**
**否则**　（乙）连

① if not ② or else

抓住这个机会，否则你会后悔的。
Seize the chance, otherwise you'll regret it.
他当时很可能知道事情的真相，否则不会这么生气。
He must have known the truth; otherwise he wouldn't be
so angry now.
要准时来，否则你会给人一个不好的印象。
Be here on time, otherwise you'll create a bad impression.

**hǎiguān**
**海关**　（乙）名

customs

**常用搭配**
海关官员 customs officer　海关检查 customs inspection

**用法示例**
在机场，海关人员检查了他的箱子。
At the airport, the customs officers searched his case.

那些走私品是被海关没收的。

The seizure of contraband is done by customs.

我们只花了几分钟就通过了海关检查。

It took us only a few minutes to get through Customs.

### 不然 bùrán （乙）连

① otherwise ② if not

**常用搭配**

快点儿,不然就晚了。Hurry, or else you'll be late.

**用法示例**

把它放下,不然我就揍你。

Put that down or else I'll smack you.

有些人聪明,有些人则不然。

Some are wise, and some are not.

我们得早一点去,不然就没有座位了。

We'll go early, otherwise we may not get seats.

### 信心 xìnxīn 圆 自信 （乙）名

confidence

**常用搭配**

缺乏信心 lack confidence 对……的信心 faith in…

**用法示例**

她充满信心。

She has a lot of confidence.

我们有信心能成功。

We are confident of success.

他对我的能力有信心。

He has faith in my ability.

### 心脏 xīnzàng （乙）名

heart

**常用搭配**

心脏病 heart disease

**用法示例**

心脏是维持生命的关键器官。

The heart is a vital organ.

他的心脏停止了跳动。

His heart stood still.

此人死于心脏病发作。

The man died from a heart attack.

### 灰心 huīxīn 圆 气馁 （丙）动

lose heart; be discouraged

**常用搭配**

别灰心。Don't lose hope.

**用法示例**

不要因为一次失败就灰心,再试试。

Don't let one failure discourage you; try again.

如果你在学习中遇到什么困难,不要灰心。

If you meet with difficulties in your studies, don't be discouraged.

尽管困难在增加,但我们没有灰心。

Difficulties were increasing. However even then we did not lose heart.

### 孤立 gūlì （丙）形／动

① isolated ② isolate

**常用搭配**

感到孤立 feel forsaken

孤立的岛屿 isolated island

孤立敌人 to isolate an enemy

**用法示例**

孤立地看,这些事并不乐观。

Looked at in isolation, these facts are not encouraging.

团结朋友,孤立敌人。

Unite friends, and isolate enemies.

他在班里并不快乐,因为同学们孤立他。

He is unhappy in class, because other students isolate him.

### 野心 yěxīn 圆 雄心 xióngxīn （丁）名

wild ambition

**常用搭配**

野心勃勃 very ambitious

**用法示例**

她的野心没有限度。

Her ambition knows no limit.

他总是野心勃勃。

He is always full of ambition.

### 真相 zhēnxiàng 圆 实情 shíqíng （丁）名

① the truth about sth. ② the actual facts

**常用搭配**

揭示真相 discover the truth

案情的真相 the facts of the case

**用法示例**

无论如何,我必须说出真相。

Anyhow I must speak the truth.

当局终于向新闻界透露了真相。

The authorities finally disclosed the truth to the press.

我们迟早会查明真相。

We shall find out the truth sooner or later.

### 音响 yīnxiǎng （丁）名

① sound field (i.e in a room or theater) ② acoustics

**常用搭配**

音响效果 sound effects 立体声音响 stereo set

**用法示例**

广播剧中那场战斗的音响效果很好。

The sound effects of the fight were very good in that radio play.

这套音响设备非常昂贵。
This set of sound equipment is very expensive.
礼堂的音响效果很好,连最便宜的座位也能听得清清楚楚。
The acoustics in the hall are so good that you can hear everything even from the cheapest seat.

## 词义辨析

**否则、不然**

1、"否则"和"不然"都是连词,都是"如果不这样"的意思,用于后一句话的开头,表示对前一句话做出假设性的否定,并指出可能产生的结果,也可以表示"如果不是这种情况,就是那种情况",通常可以互换。例如:你得去上班了,不然 / 否则就要失去这份工作了。

Both 否则 and 不然 are conjunctions, indicating "otherwise" or "under other circumstances"; they are used at the beginning of the second clause to introduce a supposed negation to the preceding clause or a possible result, and they also mean "either…or…". And they are interchangeable in most cases. For example: You must go to work or else you'll lose your job.

2、不同点是:"不然"比较口语化;"否则"多用于书面语。"不然"可以用作"要不然"、"再不然",还可以不表示假设关系,直接作谓语,意思是"不是这样";"否则"没用这种用法。例如:①快跑,不然 / 要不然 / 再不然你就迟到了。②她沉静而羞涩,她姐姐则不然。

But they are different: 不然 is more colloquial; while 否则 is used more in writing. 不然 can be used as "要不然" (otherwise), "再不然" (or else) or, and it sometimes serves as a predicate, meaning "it is not like that"; while 否则 cannot be used in this way. For example: ① Run or else you'll be late. ② She is quiet and shy, and her elder sister is otherwise.

## 练习

**练习一、根据拼音写汉字,根据汉字写拼音**
( )biǎo ( )guān ( )xiàng ( )xiǎng xīn ( )
代( ) 海( ) 真( ) 音( ) ( )脏

**练习二、搭配连线**
(1) 古典　　　　　　　A. 真相
(2) 海关　　　　　　　B. 音乐
(3) 揭示　　　　　　　C. 检查
(4) 缺乏　　　　　　　D. 效果
(5) 音响　　　　　　　E. 信心

**练习三、从今天学习的生词中选择合适的词填空**
1. 为了打赢这场比赛,我做了充分的准备,所以我们很有_____。
2. 这次试验又失败了,不过他没有_____,准备再试一次。
3. 看问题要全面,不要_____地考虑这些事 。
4. 你新买的那套_____效果真不错,有时间还要来你家听音乐。
5. 记者查明了事情的_____以后,决定将其公布于众。
6. 广州_____近日破获了一批走私要案。
7. 我_____我们全家对你们的热情帮助表示感谢。
8. 申请必须在 24 小时内上交,_____将被罚款。
9. 她谦虚而内向,她的弟弟则_____,总喜欢吹牛。
10. 他住院了,听说是_____病。

## 答案

**练习一:**
略
**练习二:**
(1) B　　　(2)C　　　(3)A　　　(4)E　　　(5)D
**练习三:**
1. 信心　　2. 灰心　　3. 孤立　　4. 音响　　5. 真相
6. 海关　　7. 代表　　8. 否则 / 不然　　9. 不然
10. 心脏

如果要避开市中心,请从这里向右转弯。
To avoid the city center, turn right here.

## gōngsī
## 公司 （乙）名

firm; company

**常用搭配**
一家小公司 a small company
保险公司 insurance company
跨国公司 multinational company

**用法示例**
他在一家广告公司工作。
He is working in an advertising agency.
去年公司生意不好。
The firm did badly last year.
我们的公司成立于 1994 年。
Our corporation was formed in 1994.

## tímù
## 题目 （乙）名

topic; subject

**常用搭配**
作文题目 topic for a composition
讨论的题目 the theme of discussion

**用法示例**
这题目使我很感兴趣。
This subject is very close to my heart.
这位演讲者演讲的题目是 "爱国"。
"Patriotism" was the speaker's theme.

## zhōngxīn
## 衷心 （丙）形

heartfelt

**常用搭配**
衷心的感谢 heartfelt thanks
衷心的祝贺 hearty greetings

**用法示例**
我向各位表示衷心的感谢。
My heartfelt thanks to you all.
我衷心希望他能回来。
It's my devout hope that he will come back.

## mínjiān
## 民间 （丙）名

① folk ② non-governmental

**常用搭配**
民间传说 folklore
民间文化 folk culture

**用法示例**
民间音乐是一代一代地流传下来的。
Folk music has been passed down from one generation to the next.
这是治疗蛇咬伤的民间药物。
It is a folk remedy to cure a snake bite.

**Friday 星期五**

## yǒuyì
## 友谊 ◉友情 yǒuqíng （甲）名

companionship; friendship

**常用搭配**
同学间的友谊 friendship among students

**用法示例**
当他身处困境时,他们向他伸出了友谊之手。
They extended the hand of friendship when he was having difficulties.
让我们为两国间的友谊干杯。
Let's toast to the friendship between these two countries.

## yǒuhǎo
## 友好 ❸敌对 díduì （甲）形

friendly; amicable

**常用搭配**
友好的行为 friendly behavior
对……友好 be friendly to
友好关系 amicable relations

**用法示例**
她对他们很友好。
She is friendly with them.
我们一直就政治问题进行友好的讨论。
We've been having a friendly discussion on politics.

## dānwèi
## 单位 （乙）名

unit

**常用搭配**
长度单位 unit of length　时间单位 time unit

**用法示例**
家庭是最小的社会单位。
The family is the smallest social unit.
镑是英国货币的标准单位。
The pound is the standard unit of money in Britain.

## zhōngxīn
## 中心 （乙）名

center

**常用搭配**
市中心 the city center　医疗中心 a medical center
购物中心 shopping center

**用法示例**
这个中心提供各种娱乐活动设施。
The center provides facilities for a whole range of leisure activities.
北京是中国的政治和文化中心。
Beijing is the political and cultural center of China.

## yǒuqíng
# 友情 （丁）名

① the feeling of friendship ② fellowship

**常用搭配**

深厚的友情 deep feeling of friendship

**用法示例**

我们之间有着牢固的友情。
There were strong ties of friendship between us.
我珍惜我们的友情。
I treasure our friendship.

## jìqiǎo
# 技巧 （丙）名

skill; technique

**常用搭配**

操作技巧 operative skills　　写作的技巧 writing skills

**用法示例**

他的谈判技巧使他赢得了好名声。
His skill in negotiation earned him a good reputation.
在许多体育运动中,体能没有技巧重要。
In many sports physical fitness is not as important as technique.

## chíyí
# 迟疑　⑩犹豫 yóuyù　（丁）动

hesitate

**常用搭配**

毫不迟疑 without hesitation

**用法示例**

他在回答之前迟疑了一下,因为他不知道说什么。.
He hesitated before he answered because he didn't know what to say.
她没有迟疑,痛快地答复了。
She didn't hesitate for a moment, but came straight out with her reply.
她迟疑了一下,然后接着说。
She hesitated for a moment, and then went on.

## chíhuǎn
# 迟缓　⑧敏捷 mǐnjié　（丁）形

slow; sluggish

**常用搭配**

行动迟缓 slow in action
反应迟缓 react sluggishly

**用法示例**

我该退休了,因为我发现脑子越来越迟缓了。
I think I should retire, because I find that my brain is getting slow.
这个老人动作迟缓,这使她很不耐烦。
She gets impatient with the old man for being so slow.
一些队员的动作变得迟缓了。这支队需要一些新鲜血液。
Some of the players are getting sluggish. This team needs some fresh blood.

---

 词义辨析

**友谊、友情、友好**

1、"友谊"和"友情"都是名词,表示朋友之间的感情和关系,一般可以互换,只是"友谊"可以用在人与人之间,也可用于国家和国家之间,而"友情"只能用于人与人之间。例如:①真正的友谊/友情比金钱更有价值。②让我们为两国间的友谊干杯。

Both 友谊 and 友好 are nouns, indicating the relationship and feeling between friends; usually they can be interchanged. But 友谊 can refer to people or countries; while 友情 just refers to people. For example: ① True friendship is worth more than money. ② Let's toast to the friendship between these two countries.

2、"友好"是形容词,可以受程度副词的修饰,可以用作谓语,也可以带补语,"友好"还可以做状语修饰动词;"友谊"和"友情"是名词,没有这样的用法。如:①他们友好地分手了。②我们应该用友好的方式解决问题。③当地人对我们很友好。

友好 is an adjective. It can be modified by adverbs of degree, be used as a predicate, and can have a complement attached. It usually serves as an adverbial to modify verbs. 友谊 and 友情 are nouns and can not be used like that. For example: ① They parted in amity. ② We should settle the question in an amicable way. ③ The local people are friendly to us.

 练习

**练习一、根据拼音写汉字,根据汉字写拼音**

( )xīn　( )yì　( )yí　jì( )　( )jiān
衷( )　友( )　迟( )　( )巧　民( )

**练习二、搭配连线**

(1) 反应　　　　　　　A. 感谢
(2) 毫不　　　　　　　B. 迟缓
(3) 衷心　　　　　　　C. 中心
(4) 跨国　　　　　　　D. 公司
(5) 购物　　　　　　　E. 迟疑

**练习三、从今天学习的生词中选择合适的词填空**

1. 我家在郊区,坐地铁到市_____大约需要半个多小时。
2. 我_____祝愿你们家庭和睦、生活幸福。
3. 中俄两国人民在历史交往中结成了深厚的_____。
4. 第一次来中国时就发现这里的人们对外国人很_____。
5. 我的_____离家很近,工资也比较高,我很喜欢现在的工作。
6. 老师给我们布置了一篇作文,_____是《北京的生活》。

7. 中日两国之间的 _____ 交流很多,政府间的交流也越来越多了。

8. 这个老太太身体不好,行动有点 _____。

9. 她没想到我会直接问她那个问题,所以她 _____ 了一下。

10. 他的写作 _____ 很高,但作品缺乏真情实感。

## 答案

**练习一:**
略

**练习二:**
(1) B      (2)E      (3)A      (4)D      (5)C

**练习三:**
1. 中心    2. 衷心    3. 友谊    4. 友好    5. 单位

6. 题目    7. 民间    8. 迟缓    9. 迟疑    10. 技巧

# 第6月,第3周的练习

**练习一. 根据词语给加点的字注音**
1.( )    2.( )    3.( )    4.( )    5.( )
单调      衷心      迟疑      供应      气氛

**练习二. 根据拼音填写词语**
     jì      jì      jī      huà      huà
1. 统( )    2.( )巧    3. 危( )    4. 策( )    5. 消( )

**练习三. 辨析并选择合适的词填空**
1. 别人帮了你的忙,说声谢谢是( )的。(该、应该)
2. 昨天是我打扫的卫生,今天( )你了。(该、应该)
3. 张奶奶的老伴去世了,虽然儿女常来看她,她还是经常感到( )。(孤独、孤单、单独)
4. 你出来一下,我想( )和你谈谈,可以吗?(孤独、孤单、单独)
5. 刚搬到这儿时,邻居们对我很( )。(友谊、友好、友情)
6. 来,干杯!祝愿我们两个国家的( )天长地久!(友谊、友好、友情)
7. 刚来北京时,日子过得很( ),每天工作很累,还经常吃不饱。(困难、艰难)
8. 如果你有什么( ),请告诉我,我一定会帮助你。(困难、艰难)
9. 电话费必须今天去交,( ),明天就停机了。(否则、不然)
10. 去那个饭店吃饭需要提前预订,要( )很可能没有位子。(否则、不然)

**练习四. 选词填空**
中心      灰心      信心      气愤      危急

衷心      野心      气氛      危机      危害
1. 由于过度开发,人类面临能源( )。
2. 我( )祝福你们幸福美满、白头到老。
3. 长期饮酒会( )肝脏,甚至会导致肝癌。
4. 纽约、伦敦和香港都是世界的金融( )。
5. 医生说,病人情况( ),必须马上抢救。
6. 妈妈说,无论遇到多大的困难,都不要( ),要始终保持积极、乐观的心态。
7. 春节期间,大街上张灯结彩,到处洋溢着节日的( )。
8. 他对赢得比赛显得( )十足。
9. 看了这个关于虐待儿童的节目,观众感到很( ),要求严惩罪犯。
10. 他是个很有( )的家伙,一心想进入公司董事会。

**练习五. 写出下列词语的同义词**
1. 友谊( )      2. 策划( )
3. 灰心( )      4. 紧急( )
5. 严密( )

**练习六. 写出下列词语的反义词**
1. 真理( )      2. 进步( )
3. 迟缓( )      4. 友好( )
5. 落后( )

## 答案

**练习一.**
1.diào    2.zhōng    3.yí    4.yìng    5.fēn

**练习二.**
1. 计    2. 技    3. 机    4. 划    5. 化

**练习三.**
1. 应该    2. 该    3. 孤独／孤单
4. 单独    5. 友好    6. 友谊
7. 艰难    8. 困难    9. 否则／不然
10. 不然

**练习四.**
1. 危机    2. 衷心    3. 危害    4. 中心    5. 危急
6. 灰心    7. 气氛    8. 信心    9. 气愤    10. 野心

**练习五.**
1. 友情    2. 谋划    3. 气馁    4. 危急    5. 缜密

**练习六.**
1. 谬误    2. 退步    3. 敏捷    4. 敌对    5. 先进

# 6月 第4周的学习内容

星期一

**dàshēng**
## 大声 （甲）形

① loudly ② loud

**常用搭配**
大声笑 loud laugh　大声喊叫 to cry aloud
请大点儿声。Speak louder please.

**用法示例**
别那么大声地说话。
Don't talk so loud.
我们大声唱着歌走下山坡。
We walked down the hillside singing loudly.
他们大声地为自己的足球队喊加油。
They cheered loudly for their football team.

**jiāqiáng**
## 加强 反削弱 （乙）动
**xuēruò**

reinforce; strengthen

**常用搭配**
加强团结 strengthen unity

**用法示例**
士兵们加强了防御。
The soldiers strengthened their defense.
社会服务机构和当地医生应该加强协作。
There should be more interaction between the social services and local doctors.

**yídòng**
## 移动 （乙）动

move; shift

**常用搭配**
向右移动 right shift　迅速移动 move rapidly

**用法示例**
我把椅子移动一下好吗?
Shall I move the chairs?
我连移动双脚的力气都几乎没有了。
I have hardly enough strength left to move my feet.
汽车在慢慢移动。
The car is moving slowly.

**zōnghé**
## 综合 （乙）动

integrate; synthesize

**常用搭配**
综合研究 synthetic study　综合疗法 synthetic remedy
综合治理 comprehensive treatment

**用法示例**
北京大学是一所综合性大学。
Peking University is a comprehensive university.
以下是最新新闻的综合报道。
Here is a round-up of the latest news.
他的作品综合了摄影和绘画的技巧。
His works to synthesize photography and painting techniques.

**zǒngjié**
## 总结 （乙）动／名

① summarize; sum...up ② summary

**常用搭配**
总结经验 summarize experience
年度总结 annual summary
做总结 make a summary

**用法示例**
最后一部分总结了双方的全部论点。
The last section sums up all the arguments on either side.
你的总结需要增加一些案例。
Your summary will need more cases.

**péitóng**
## 陪同 （丙）动／名

① accompany ② companion

**常用搭配**
由……陪同 be accompanied by...

**用法示例**
他的妻子陪同他远行。
He was accompanied on the expedition by his wife.
该旅行团将由一名受过专门培训的护士陪同。
The tour will be accompanied by a trained nurse.
秘书陪同部长去考察。
The minister was accompanied to the inspection by his secretary.

**zēngqiáng**
## 增强 反减弱 （丙）动
**jiǎnruò**

strengthen

**常用搭配**
增强竞争力 strengthen competitive ability
增强使命感 deepen one's sense of duty

**用法示例**
他的反对反而增强了我们的决心。
His opposition served only to strengthen our resolve.

体育锻炼可以增强体质。
Physical exercise can improve your health.

**péicháng**
## 赔偿 <sup>cháng huán</sup> 偿还 （丙）动
compensate
**常用搭配**
赔偿损失 compensate for a loss
要求赔偿 claim for compensation
**用法示例**
她受伤后获得了保险公司的赔偿。
The insurance company compensated her for her injuries.
公司赔偿给受伤的工人一大笔钱。
The company compensated injured workers with a large sum of money.

**yímín**
## 移民 （丁）名/动
① immigrant ② immigrate; migrate
**常用搭配**
非法移民 illegal immigrant
移民局 immigration authority
**用法示例**
加拿大有许多欧洲移民。
Canada has many immigrants from Europe.
移民到这个国家有严格的限制。
There are strict controls on immigration into this country.

**zōngzhǐ**
## 宗旨 <sup>zhǔzhǐ</sup> 主旨 （丁）名
tenet; aim
**常用搭配**
党的宗旨 doctrine of the Party
办学宗旨 aim of running the school
**用法示例**
这一慈善团体的宗旨是组织人们互相帮助。
This charity aims to organize people to help each other.
我们教育学会的宗旨是互相学习。
The aim our educational society is to learn from each other.

**fù**
## 副 （乙）量/形
① measure word for a pair ② vice- ③ deputy
**常用搭配**
一副眼镜 a pair of glasses
副主席 vice-chairman
副总统 Vice-President
副校长 deputy headmaster
**用法示例**
她为我织了一副手套。
She knitted a pair of mittens for me.
那个女孩让她的父亲给她买一副滑雪板。
The girl asked her father to buy a pair of skis for her.

他是本市的副市长。
He is the deputy mayor of the city.

**fú**
## 幅 （乙）量
measure word for cloth or picture
**常用搭配**
一幅画 a picture
**用法示例**
上周，他买了一幅中国画。
He bought a traditional Chinese painting last week.
她正在画一幅风景画。
She is painting a landscape.

 **词义辨析**

**加强、增强**

　　"加强"和"增强"都是动词，都有使变得更强的意思，对象多为抽象的事物。"加强"的宾语通常是动词或动词词组，强调增加强度或功效；"增强"的宾语通常是名词或名词性词组，强调内在品质的提高。例如：我需要加强锻炼和改变饮食来增强体质。

　　Both 加强 and 增强 are verbs, meaning "to make strong or increase the strength of", the objects of them are usually something abstract. The object of 加强 is usually a verb or a verb phrase, stressing the increase of strength or effect; while the object of 增强 is usually a noun or a noun phrase, stressing to enhance or strengthen the internal quality of something. For example: I need to tone up with more exercise and a change of diet.

 **练习**

**练习一、根据拼音写汉字，根据汉字写拼音**

yí（　）zōng（　）zōng（　）（　）cháng zǒng（　）

（　）动（　）合　（　）旨　　赔（　）（　）结

**练习二、搭配连线**

(1) 办学　　　　　　A. 经验

(2) 赔偿　　　　　　B. 宗旨

(3) 综合　　　　　　C. 团结

(4) 总结　　　　　　D. 损失

(5) 加强　　　　　　E. 治理

**练习三、从今天学习的生词中选择合适的词填空**

1. 这 ＿＿＿＿ 书法作品是我的一个朋友创作的。

2. 我给我男朋友买了一 ＿＿＿＿ 手套。

3. 政府决定要 ＿＿＿＿ 对市场的管理,防治经济犯罪。

4. 他三岁时,跟随父母 ＿＿＿＿ 去了加拿大了。

5. 感冒时要多喝开水多吃疏菜,这样能 ＿＿＿＿ 免疫力。

6. 学校的领导 ＿＿＿＿ 总理视察了这所大学。

7. 他们没有认真履行合同,不过他们答应 ＿＿＿＿ 咱们的损失。

8. 活动结束以后,我们还要认真 ＿＿＿＿ 举办大型活动的经验和教训。

9. 他身上 ＿＿＿＿ 了父母所有的优点。

10. 我们这个基金会的 ＿＿＿＿ 是为残疾人提供更多的就业机会。

**答案**

**练习一：**

略

**练习二：**

(1) B　　(2)D　　(3)E　　(4)A　　(5)C

**练习三：**

1. 幅　　2. 副　　3. 加强　　4. 移民　　5. 增强

6. 陪同　　7. 赔偿　　8. 总结　　9. 综合　　10. 宗旨

---

 **星期二**

**chūfā**

**出发**　　🔊 启程　　（甲）动

to start out; to set off

**常用搭配**

六点出发 to leave at six

我们出发吧。Let's set out now.

**用法示例**

直到太阳从东方升起,我们才出发。

We did not start until the sun rose in the east.

我们正要出发。

We are just about to start.

也许现在你该出发了。

Perhaps you should start now.

**xiǎnrán**

**显然**　　　　　　　　（乙）形

obvious; evident

**常用搭配**

这显然是敲诈! It's a clear case of blackmail!

**用法示例**

李先生显然是要移民了。

By all appearances, Mr. Li is going to migrate.

显然他在撒谎。

It was obvious that he was lying.

显然,他一封信也没给她写。

Apparently he never wrote a letter to her.

**xiǎnzhù**

**显著**　　🔊 明显　　（乙）形

notable; remarkable

**常用搭配**

显著特征 a notable feature

显著的变化 a remarkable change

**用法示例**

她取得了显著的进步。

She has made remarkable progress.

在编写这本书的过程中,她起到了显著的作用。

She played a notable role in compiling the book.

**zhǔzhāng**

**主张**　　　　　　　（乙）动 / 名

① advocate ② assertion; proposition

**常用搭配**

政治主张 political opinion

坚持主张 stand by one's assertion

**用法示例**

他主张削减军费开支。

He advocates reducing military spending.

他主张多建几所学校。

He advocates building more schools.

我们的总理主张提高教师的工资。

Our premier advocates higher salaries for teachers.

duì
# 对 （乙）量

measure word for a couple or pair

**常用搭配**

一对新婚夫妇 a newly married couple

一对手镯 a pair of bracelets

一对天鹅 a couple of swans

**用法示例**

我弟弟和他的妻子是一对幸福的夫妻。

My brother and his wife are a happy couple.

这对夫妇决定去意大利度假。

The couple decided to spend their vacation in Italy.

zhuānmén
# 专门 （乙）形

① specialized ② special

**常用搭配**

专门的法律 special laws　专门机构 special organs

**用法示例**

他专门研究东方历史。

He specializes in oriental history.

那位医生专门研究儿科疾病。

That doctor specializes in children's illnesses.

这辆汽车是专门为他设计的。

The car is specially designed for him.

zhuānxīn　　　　　fēnxīn
# 专心　　反 分心 （乙）形

attentively

**常用搭配**

专心工作 work attentively

专心学习 pay attention to your study

**用法示例**

上课的时候必须专心听老师讲课。

You must pay attention to your teacher in the class.

他专心于学问。

He is devoted to his studies.

专心工作，不要说话。

Attend to your work and stop talking.

guófáng
# 国防 （丙）名

national defense

**常用搭配**

国防部 the Ministry of Defense

国防建设 build-up of national defense

**用法示例**

空军是国防的重要组成部分。

An air force is an important component of the national defense.

预算中的最大一项照例是国防费用。

As usual, the lion's share of the budget is for defense.

gūfù
# 辜负 （丙）动

① fail to live up to ② disappoint

**常用搭配**

辜负……的好意 fail to live up to one's good intentions

**用法示例**

我们决不能辜负父母对我们的期望。

We will never fail to live up to what our parents expect of us.

不要辜负我们对你的信任。

Don't betray our trust in you.

zhǔquán
# 主权 （丙）名

sovereignty

**常用搭配**

主权国家 sovereign state

**用法示例**

中国的主权不容侵犯。

China's sovereignty must not be infringed upon.

这些岛屿的主权有争执。

The sovereignty of these islands is in dispute.

bānfā
# 颁发 （丁）动

to award; issue

**常用搭配**

颁发证书 award a certificate

颁发奖杯 award a trophy cup

**用法示例**

英国第一项打字机专利证书是 1714 年颁发的。

The first English patent for a typewriter was issued in 1714.

他为获胜者颁发了奖杯。

He awarded the trophy cup to the winners.

chūshòu　　　　　shōugòu
# 出售　　反 收购 （丁）动

sell

**常用搭配**

亏本出售 sell at a loss

半价出售 sell at half price

**用法示例**

他们按八折的价格出售自行车。

They sell bikes at a discount of 20%.

政府将限制出售枪支。

The government will restrict the sale of firearms.

法律禁止向 18 岁以下的人出售含有酒精的饮料。

The law forbids the sale of alcohol to people under 18.

 词义辨析

**显然、显著**

"显然"和"显著"都是形容词,都有明显的意思。但"显然"强调容易看到或感觉到的意思,是中性词,主要用作状语,很少用作定语、补语或谓语;而"显著"则表示很明显,很突出的意思,是褒义词,常作谓语、定语和状语。例如:①显然,他从一开始就十分紧张。②这项政策显然是失败的。③人民的生活水平显著提高了。④一系列的新理论是这本书的显著特点。

Both 显然 and 显著 are adjectives, indicating "obvious". But 显然 stresses "easy to be seen or felt", and is a neutral word, mainly functioning as an adverbial, but rarely as an attributive, a complement or a predicate; while 显著 stresses "noticeable and prominent", and it has commendatory sense, often functioning as a predicate, an attributive or an adverbial. For example: ① His nervousness was obvious right from the start. ② It was evident that the policy was a failure. ③ People's living standards have improved noticeably. ④ A series of new theories is the most prominent feature of the book.

 练习

**练习一、根据拼音写汉字,根据汉字写拼音**

gū (　) bān (　) zhǔ (　)(　) zhù (　) fáng
(　) 负 (　) 发 (　) 张 　显( 　) 国( 　)

**练习二、搭配连线**

(1) 显著　　　　　　　A. 建设
(2) 颁发　　　　　　　B. 机构
(3) 国防　　　　　　　C. 学习
(4) 专心　　　　　　　D. 证书
(5) 专门　　　　　　　E. 特征

**练习三、从今天学习的生词中选择合适的词填空**

1. 我们 _____ 用和平的方式解决国际争端。
2. 他坐在椅子上睡着了, _____ 是太累了。
3. 他们有一 _____ 双胞胎儿子,可爱极了。
4. 经济体制改革已经取得了 _____ 的成效,人民的生活越来越富裕了。
5. 老师讲课的时候,大家都要 _____ 听讲。
6. 为了孩子的未来,有的家长辞去工作 _____ 照顾孩子。
7. 你一定要好好学习,不要 _____ 了父母对你的期望。
8. 维护国家的独立和 _____ ,是军队的基本职责之一。
9. 校长给取得优秀成绩的学生 _____ 了荣誉证书。
10. 这家商店因向未成年人 _____ 香烟而被罚。

🔑 **答案**

**练习一:**
略
**练习二:**
(1) E　　(2)D　　(3)A　　(4)C　　(5)B
**练习三:**
1. 主张　　2. 显然　　3. 对　　4. 显著　　5. 专心
6. 专门　　7. 辜负　　8. 主权　　9. 颁发　　10. 出售

**星期三**

dài
# 带 （甲）动
bring；take

**常用搭配**

把照相机带过来。Bring the camera over here.
带上钱包。Bring the wallet with you.

**用法示例**

我随身带了足够的钱。
I brought enough money with me.
把它带到那里去。
Take it over there.
你为什么不带你女儿一块儿来呢？
Why don't you bring your daughter along?

dài
# 戴 （甲）动
wear；put on

**常用搭配**

戴上眼镜 to wear glasses
戴戒指 to wear a ring

**用法示例**

你能帮我戴上项链吗?
Can you wear the necklace for me？
她戴着一顶漂亮的宽边帽。
She wears a beautiful gypsy hat.

dàitì                                    tìdài
# 代替 回 替代 （乙）动
① instead ② replace

**常用搭配**

用 A 代替 B substitute A for B

**用法示例**

有什么能代替母爱吗？
Can anything replace a mother's love?
机器生产已经代替了手工劳作。
Work done by machines has replaced manual labor.
如果没有煤，可以用石油来代替。
If there is no coal, oil can be used instead.

zhǐdǎo                                zhǐdiǎn
# 指导 回 指点 （乙）动
guide；give directions

**常用搭配**

在……的指导下 under the guidance of…
思想指导行动 One's thinking directs one's actions.

**用法示例**

在他的指导下，我们顺利地完成了工作。
Under his guidance, we finished the work smoothly.

调查是在一位高级警官的指导下进行的。
The investigation was carried out under the direction of a senior police officer.
她指导实习护士练习注射。
She instructed the trainee nurses in giving injections.

gǒnggù
# 巩固 （乙）形／动
consolidate

**常用搭配**

巩固地位 consolidate one's position

**用法示例**

她在任职的第一年内巩固了自己的权力。
She consolidated her power during her first year in office.
我们将进一步巩固和扩大军队。
We will further consolidate and expand our army.
我们一起度假，巩固了我们的友谊。
Our holiday together cemented our friendship.

yìlùn
# 议论 （乙）动
comment；talk about

**常用搭配**

背后议论某人 talk behind one's back

**用法示例**

我知道他们和你在议论我。
I know they have been discussing me with you.
她喜欢议论邻居。
She loves to gossip to her neighbors.
对此我不想发表任何议论。
I don't want to make any comments about it.

shídài
# 时代 （乙）名
epoch；era

**常用搭配**

信息时代 era of information    艰苦时代 hard times

**用法示例**

人类学会制造铁器的时期称为铁器时代。
The period in which man learnt to make tools out of iron is called the Iron Age.
他经常回忆起年轻时代的幸福时光。
He often recalls the happy times during his yonth.
文学是时代的镜子。
Literature is a reflection of its time.

gōngjī                                gōngdǎ
# 攻击 回 攻打 （丙）动／名
① attack ② assail

**常用搭配**

攻击敌人 attack the enemy    发起攻击 launch an attack

**用法示例**

那条船遭到了鱼雷的攻击。
The ship was attacked by a torpedo.

大使馆是恐怖分子攻击的目标。
The embassy is a target for terrorist attacks.
敌机不断攻击我们的阵地。
The enemy plane assailed our defense position.

gōngkè
## 攻克　　　◉ 征服 zhēngfú　　（丙）动
capture; conquer
**常用搭配**
攻克一座小镇 conquer a small town
攻克一道难题 solve a difficult problem
**用法示例**
据报道，军队已经攻克了两座城市。
It is reported that the army has already captured two cities.
科学家正在奋力攻克癌症。
Scientists are battling to overcome the disease of cancer.

yìchéng
## 议程　　　　　　　　　　（丁）名
agenda
**常用搭配**
本次会议的议程是……
The agenda for the meeting is as follows....
根据议程……According to the agenda....
**用法示例**
让我们继续讨论议程中的下一个项目。
Let us go on to the next item on the agenda.
他们试图把这些问题列入议程。
They tried to get these questions put on the agenda.

shíshì
## 时事　　　　　　　　　　（丁）名
current events
**常用搭配**
关心时事 care about current events
**用法示例**
你应该看报以便了解时事。
You should read the newspapers to keep abreast of current affairs.
总统发表时事广播演说。
The president's broadcasts are on current affairs.
他对时事感兴趣。
He is interested in current affairs.

duǒ
## 朵　　　　　　　　　　　（乙）量
measure word for flowers and clouds
**常用搭配**
一朵白云 a white cloud
一朵花 a flower
**用法示例**
她在花园摘了一朵玫瑰花。
She picked a rose in the garden.

这朵花真美。
This flower is very beautiful.

## 词义辨析

**戴、带**

　　"戴"和"带"都是动词，都表示放在身上。"戴"是佩戴的意思，宾语是小饰物、眼镜、手表等；"带"是携带的意思，宾语可以是具体的东西或人，也可以是抽象的祝福等。如：①她戴着一副漂亮的墨镜。②这个护士总戴着个大口罩。③请把书给我带回来。④欢迎你带你的妻子来参加聚会。

　　Both 戴 and 带 are verbs, meaning "to take something along with somebody". 戴 indicates "to wear or put on", and its object is a small ornament, or eyeglasses, a watch, etc.; while 带 indicates "to take or bring", and its object may be either concrete or abstract, such as a thing, people, good wishes. For example: ① She was wearing a pair of beautiful sunglasses. ② The nurse always wears a big antiseptic gauze. ③ Please bring me back the book. ④ You are welcome to bring your wife to the party.

 练习

**练习一、根据拼音写汉字，根据汉字写拼音**

( ) dǎo yì ( ) ( ) shì gōng ( ) gǒng ( )
指( ) ( )程 时( ) ( )克 ( )固

**练习二、搭配连线**

(1) 带着            A. 项链
(2) 戴着            B. 时代
(3) 巩固            C. 难关
(4) 信息            D. 手机
(5) 攻克            E. 地位

**练习三、从今天学习的生词中选择合适的词填空**

1. 老师让山本下次把作业 _____ 来，不要再忘了。
2. 她 _____ 着一副白框的太阳镜，很时髦。
3. 太阳能是一种无污染的能源，将来可能会 _____ 煤和石油。
4. 通过成功地举办宣传活动，他进一步 _____ 了自己在公司的地位。
5. 在此，我要感谢张老师对我论文的 _____。
6. 有什么事当面说，不要在背后 _____ 别人。
7. 他们花了两个星期就 _____ 了这个难关。
8. 在竞选中，他对对手发起了人身 _____。
9. 本次会议有四项 _____。
10. 这份报纸有个专栏叫国际 _____，专门介绍当前国际上正在发生的大事。

答案

**练习一：**
略

**练习二：**

| (1) D | (2) A | (3) E | (4) B | (5) C |
|---|---|---|---|---|

**练习三：**

| 1. 带 | 2. 戴 | 3. 代替 | 4. 巩固 | 5. 指导 |
|---|---|---|---|---|
| 6. 议论 | 7. 攻克 | 8. 攻击 | 9. 议程 | 10. 时事 |

 星期四

chídào
**迟到** （甲）动
to arrive late

**常用搭配**
上学迟到 be late for school     上课迟到 be late for class
别再迟到。Don't be late again.

**用法示例**
如果你再迟到，你将被解雇。
If you are late again, you will be dismissed.
让我解释迟到的原因。
Let me explain why I was late.
他上班迟到了五分钟。
He got to the factory five minutes late.

chéngzhǎng
**成长** （乙）动
mature; grow up

**常用搭配**
青少年的成长 teenagers' growth
快乐地成长 grow happily

**用法示例**
他已成长为一名优秀的青年人了。
He's grown into an excellent young man.
儿童的身体不断发育成长。
Children's bodies grow steadily.

shēngzhǎng
**生长**   反 mièwáng 灭亡 （乙）动
grow

**常用搭配**
植物的生长 plant growth     迅速生长 grow rapidly

**用法示例**
水藻生长在水中。
Algae grow in water.
有些植物能够在阴暗的环境中生长。
Some plants grow in deep shade.

jūnshì
**军事** （乙）名
military

**常用搭配**
军事行动 military operations     军事政变 military coup
军事基地 military base

**用法示例**
他们惧怕敌人强大的军事力量。
They fear the military might of the enemy.
他在学习军事理论。
He is learning military theory.

他们完成了军事训练。

They finished their military training.

**pái**
## 排 （乙）动／名／量

① put in order ② row ③ row of

**常用搭配**

排队 stand in a line    第一排 the first line

一排房子 a row of house    坐成一排 sit in a row

**用法示例**

我们得排几个小时的队才能进去。

We had to queue for hours to get in.

她总是把鞋子排成整齐的一排。

She always arranges shoes in a neat row.

她总坐在教室的最后一排。

She always sits in the last line of the classroom.

我们学校前面有一排新楼房。

There is a row of new buildings in front of our school.

**yīnsù**
## 因素 （乙）名

factor

**常用搭配**

决定性因素 decisive factor    客观因素 impersonal factor

积极因素 positive factor

**用法示例**

委员会的支持是该项目取得成功的一个重要因素。

The committee's support is an important factor in the success of the project.

有很多因素妨碍了我们实现计划。

Many factors worked against the success of our plan.

**shāngxīn**          **kuàilè**
## 伤心 反 快乐 （乙）形

① grieve ② sad

**常用搭配**

感到伤心 feel sad    伤心地哭 cry sadly

伤她的心 hurt her feelings

**用法示例**

她仍在为死去的丈夫伤心。

She is still grieving for her dead husband.

看见他病情严重，我很伤心。

It grieves me to see him in such bad health.

他的话伤透了我的心。

I was very much hurt by his words.

**gǎngkǒu**          **mǎtou**
## 港口 同 码头 （丙）名

port；harbor

**常用搭配**

客运港口 passenger port    货运港口 freight port

**用法示例**

这个港口是天然港。

This harbor is a natural one.

伦敦曾是英国最大的港口城市。

London used to be the largest port in Britain.

船只必须沿航道进入港口。

Ships must follow the channel into the port.

**chōngtū**
## 冲突 （丙）动／名

① conflict ② clash

**常用搭配**

利益冲突 conflict of interest    武装冲突 armed conflicts

与警察的冲突 a clash with the police

**用法示例**

他们的行为与国际法相冲突。

Their actions conflicted with the international laws.

军队在边境附近发生了冲突。

The armies clashed near the border.

我没能去参加她的婚礼，因为和我的考试日期冲突了。

I failed to go to her wedding because it clashed with my examination.

**yuánsù**
## 元素 （丙）名

element

**常用搭配**

化学元素 chemical element

**用法示例**

水是由氢元素和氧元素组成的。

Water is composed of the elements hydrogen and oxygen.

镭是放射性元素。

Radium is a radioactive element.

**jūnyòng**
## 军用 （丁）形

(for) military (use)

**常用搭配**

军用飞机 military aircraft

军用设施 military establishments

**用法示例**

那里将建设一个军用机场。

A new military airport will be built there.

他们正在研制新的军用火箭。

They are developing new rockets for military purposes.

**shānghén**          **shāngbā**
## 伤痕 同 伤疤 （丁）名

bruise；scar

**常用搭配**

伤痕累累 many cuts and bruises

心灵的伤痕 a mental scar

**用法示例**

她手臂上有一处伤痕。

She had a bruise on her arm.

他身上的伤痕证明他曾受到严刑拷打。

His scars bore witness to the torture he had suffered.

 **词义辨析**

**成长、生长**

"成长"和"生长"都是动词,表示人、动物和植物长大的过程。"成长"多用于人,包括人身体的发育和性格、思想的发展成熟,不包括出生;"生长"主要用于动物和植物,包括出生、发育和成熟的过程。如:①他成长为一名坚强的领导人。②稻子生长在温暖的地区。

Both 成长 and 生长 are verbs, meaning "the process of growth for people, animals and plants". 成长 is mostly used for people, indicating the growing and maturing of the human body or one's character and qualities, excluding birth; While 生长 is usually used for animals and plants, indicating the process of birth, growth and maturing. For example: ① He developed into a strong leader. ② Rice grows in warm climates.

 **练习**

**练习一、根据拼音写汉字,根据汉字写拼音**

( )tū ( )hén gǎng ( ) ( )sù chéng ( )
冲( ) 伤( ) ( )口 因( ) ( )长

**练习二、搭配连线**

(1) 化学            A. 因素
(2) 军用            B. 元素
(3) 武装            C. 伤心
(4) 客观            D. 冲突
(5) 感到            E. 设施

**练习三、从今天学习的生词中选择合适的词填空**

1. 这几天的雨水对庄稼的 _____ 非常有利。
2. 他小时候的 _____ 环境不太好。
3. 老师问他为什么 _____ 时,他总说堵车。
4. 学校前边种着一 _____ 松树。
5. 有两艘大轮船停留在 _____。
6. 这两个音乐会时间 _____,本来我两个都会去听的。
7. 勤奋和机遇是他成功的两大 _____。
8. 她一想到刚刚去世的儿子,就 _____ 得想哭。
9. 他在不久前发生了车祸,现在脸上还有两道 _____。
10. 这是一个 _____ 机场,主要用于士兵的飞行训练,普通人不能接近。

**答案**

**练习一:**
略

**练习二:**
(1) B     (2)E     (3)D     (4)A     (5)C

**练习三:**
1. 生长    2. 成长    3. 迟到    4. 排    5. 港口
6. 冲突    7. 因素    8. 伤心    9. 伤痕    10. 军用

**Friday 星期五**

lǐngdǎo
# 领导 (甲)动/名

① lead ② leader

**常用搭配**

领导农民运动 lead the peasants' movement
领导才能 quality of leadership

**用法示例**

我们需要有真知灼见的人来领导这个党。
We need someone with real vision to lead the party.
他被选为工会的领导。
He was elected to the leadership position in the Labor Union.
那位领导负责指挥地铁的建造工程。
The leader was in charge of directing the construction of the subway.

tì
# 替 (乙)动/介

① replace; to substitute for ② for

**常用搭配**

替他请假 ask for leave for him
他替我做。He'll do instead of me.

**用法示例**

如果你不能去,让他替你。
If you cannot go, let him go instead.
他让我替他打开收音机。
He asked me to turn on the radio for him.
经纪人替他人买卖股票。
The broker buys and sells shares for others.

yǎnyuán
# 演员 (乙)名

performer; actor

**常用搭配**

女演员 actress　专业演员 professional actor
歌剧演员 opera performer

**用法示例**

演员们一直在排练这出戏。
The actors have been rehearsing the play.
那个年轻演员扮演哈姆雷特。
The young actor pretended to be Hamlet.
他想当演员的愿望实现了。
His wish to be an actor has come true.

pànduàn
# 判断 (乙)动/名

① to judge ② judgment

**常用搭配**

从外表判断 judge by appearance

据我判断 so far as I can judge
判断错误 a judgmental error

**用法示例**

你判断错了。
You judge incorrectly.
我们相信你的判断。
We are relying on your judgment.
我父亲有很强的判断能力。
My father is a man of good judgment.

shuàilǐng　　　　　　　dàilǐng
# 率领 同 带领 (乙)动

lead; captain

**常用搭配**

率领军队 lead an army　率领一个代表团 lead a delegation

**用法示例**

他率领足球队参加比赛。
He led the football team to participate in the match.
率领主队的是我的哥哥。
The man who captained the home team is my brother.
他率领水手们横跨太平洋。
He captained his sailors to travel across the Pacific Ocean.

gòumǎi　　　　　　　gòuzhì
# 购买 同 购置 (丙)动

purchase; buy

**常用搭配**

购买家具 purchase furniture　购买设备 buy equipment

**用法示例**

他们直接从厂商那里购买了这台机器。
They bought the machine directly from the manufacturer.
他成批地购买原材料。
He purchases the materials wholesale.
我已决定购买那所房子。
I've decided to purchase that house.

dài
# 代 (丙)动/介

① take the place of; replace ② for

**常用搭配**

以茶代酒 to drink tea instead of wine
代课 to have the same lessons with another teacher

**用法示例**

下周,张老师给我代课。
Next week, Mr. Zhang will take my place during my lessons.
老板要出差,经理将代他主持下个月的工作。
The boss is traveling on business, and the manager will take over for him next month.
请代我向你的父母问好。
Please send my best regards to your parents.

guǒduàn　　　　　　　yóuyù
# 果断 反 犹豫 (丁)形

① decisive ② decisively

**常用搭配**

果断的人 a decisive person

他很果断。He is a man of decisiveness.

**用法示例**

果断些，告诉他们你认为应该怎么做。

Be decisive, and tell them what you think should be done.

他一听到这个消息就果断地采取了行动。

He acted decisively as soon as he heard the news.

不果断的人不应当领导。

Anyone who hesitates shouldn't be a leader.

### zhìhuì
### 智慧 ⊠ 愚昧 yúmèi （丙）名

wisdom; intelligence

**常用搭配**

智慧的源泉 the source of wisdom

**用法示例**

那位老人有无穷的智慧。

That old man is a fount of wisdom.

他认为他的智慧来自于书籍。

He adjusted his wisdom to books.

经验是智慧之父。

Experience is the father of wisdom.

### pínlǜ
### 频率 （丁）名

frequency

**常用搭配**

控制频率 control the frequency

频率调节 frequency adjustment

**用法示例**

他变换了无线电传送的频率。

He adjusted the transmission frequency.

近年来死亡事故发生的频率已经下降。

Fatal accidents have decreased in frequency in recent years.

### pínfán
### 频繁 （丁）形

① frequent ② frequently

**常用搭配**

频繁的检查 frequent inspection

频繁地犯错误 to make mistakes frequently

**用法示例**

频繁的停电使工厂停产了。

Production in the factories stopped because of frequent power failures.

那条高速公路上车祸发生得越来越频繁了。

Accidents on that highway are happening with increasing frequency.

公交车频繁地从城市驶往机场。

Buses run frequently from the city to the airport.

### fèn
### 份 （乙）量

① share ② copy (of newspaper, magazine, etc.)

**常用搭配**

一份报纸 a copy of a newspaper

两份杂志 two copies of a magazine

**用法示例**

我们给了这五个孩子每人一份。

We gave each of the five children a share.

随函寄去两份合同副本。

I enclose herewith two copies of the contract.

他叫秘书把文件复制了一份。

He asked his secretary to make a copy of the document.

 **词义辨析**

**代、替**

"代"和"替"都是动词和介词,都有"取代"和"替代"的意思,可以用于人,也可以用于事物。但"代"多用于事物;"替"多用于人。"代"可以直接与动词搭配;"替"不可以这样用。"代"比较正式;而"替"比较口语化。例如:①经理有事,我来替他开会。②必须亲自领工资,不能请他人代领。

Both 代 and 替 are verbs and prepositions, meaning "to take the place of " or "instead of", and they can be used for people or things. But 代 is mostly applied to things; while 替 is usually applied to people. 代 can be used together with verbs to form collocations; while 替 can not be used like that. 代 is formal; 替 is more colloquial. For example: ① The manager has something to do, so I attended the meetings in his place. ② You should take your wages yourself, nobody can do it for you.

 **练习**

**练习一、根据拼音写汉字，根据汉字写拼音**

shuài （ ）（ ）duàn （ ）huì pín （ ） gòu （ ）

（ ）领 判（ ） 智（ ） （ ）繁 （ ）买

**练习二、搭配连线**

(1) 购买     A. 军队

(2) 电影     B. 错误

(3) 率领     C. 频率

(4) 调节     D. 设备

(5) 判断     E. 演员

**练习三、从今天学习的生词中选择合适的词填空**

1. 我让他给我买了 _____ 今天的报纸。

2. 我感冒了,不能去上课,你 _____ 我跟老师请个假吧。

3. 他的妻子是一位著名 _____,我们经常能在电视上看到她。

4. 他 _____ 一个代表团去欧洲考察了。

5. 这个女老板做事特别 _____,从不犹犹豫豫的。

6. 这些古代建筑显示了劳动人民的高度 _____。

7. 这个旅行社可以为游客 _____ 打折机票,当然,也要收取手续费。
8. 据说在日本人们不愿意 _____ 地更换工作。
9. 心脏跳动的正常 _____ 是每分钟60到100次。
10. 根据现场情况来 _____,凶手个子不高。

**答案**

练习一:
略
练习二:
(1) D  (2)E  (3)A  (4)C  (5)B
练习三:
1. 份  2. 替／代  3. 演员  4. 率领  5. 果断
6. 智慧  7. 购买  8. 频繁  9. 频率  10. 判断

# 第6月,第4周的练习

**练习一.根据词语给加点的字注音**
1.( ) 2.( ) 3.( ) 4.( ) 5.( )
　辜负　颁发　频率　率领　巩固

**练习二.根据拼音填写词语**
péi　　péi　　zhǐ　zhǐ　　zhì
1.( )偿 2.( )同 3.宗( ) 4.( )导 5.( )慧

**练习三.辨析并选择合适的词填空**
1. 这次胜利( )了我们继续参加比赛的信心。(加强、增强)
2. 政府的各部门之间要经常沟通情况,( )交流与合作。(加强、增强)
3. ( ),他对我的表现很不满意。(显然、显著)
4. 中国在改革开放以来取得的成就是( )的。(显然、显著)
5. 我的视力很好,所以不用( )眼镜。(戴、带)
6. 老师有点生气,说:"下次来上课时,别忘了( )书"。(戴、带)
7. 气温突然下降,影响了庄稼的( )。(成长、生长)
8. 如果父母整天吵架,就不能给孩子一个温暖的( )环境。(成长、生长)
9. 生病期间,同事( )我做完了工作。(代、替)
10.这个房地产公司可以为客户( )办贷款手续。(代、替)

**练习四.选词填空**
判断　领导　议论　出发　综合
果断　指导　议程　颁发　总结
1. 大会有三项( ),其中第二项是制定下半年的工作计划。
2. 我们在修改这份报告时,( )了各方面专家的意见。
3. 本次大会的主席给获奖者( )了奖牌和荣誉证书。

4. 在草原上迷路的时候可以根据太阳的位置来( )方向。
5. 老师在耐心地( )学生练习中国书法。
6. 请同学们明天早上6:50到操场集合,我们7:00准时( )。
7. 有什么话当面说清楚,背后( )人可不好。
8. 在新的总经理的( )下,公司效益越来越好,职工收入也提高了。
9. 我们完成了任务,但还要认真( )经验和不足。
10. 要不是司机行动( ),很可能会发生一起严重的交通事故。

**练习五.量词填空**
份　排　朵　对　幅
1. 公园的椅子上坐着一男一女,他们可能是一( )恋人。
2. 教室里挂着一( )中国的水墨画。
3. 妻子逛商场时,丈夫总是拿着一( )报纸在走廊的椅子上等她。
4. 请大家站成两( ),按顺序领电影票。
5. 小姑娘获得了比赛的第一名,领奖的时候,她笑得像一( )花似的。

**练习六.写出下列词语的同义词**
1. 显著( )　2. 率领( )
3. 赔偿( )　4. 伤痕( )
5. 指导( )

**练习七.写出下列词语的反义词**
1. 增强( )　2. 果断( )
3. 伤心( )　4. 出售( )
5. 加强( )

**答案**

练习一.
1.gū 2.bān 3.pín 4.shuài 5.gù
练习二.
1. 赔 2. 陪 3. 旨 4. 指 5. 智
练习三.
1. 增强 2. 加强 3. 显然 4. 显著 5. 戴
6. 带 7. 生长 8. 成长 9. 替 10. 代
练习四.
1. 议程 2. 综合 3. 颁发 4. 判断 5. 指导
6. 出发 7. 议论 8. 领导 9. 总结 10. 果断
练习五.
1. 对 2. 幅 3. 份 4. 排 5. 朵
练习六.
1. 明显 2. 带领 3. 偿还 4. 伤疤 5. 指点
练习七.
1. 减弱 2. 犹豫 3. 快乐 4. 收购 5. 削弱

**7月** 第1周的学习内容

**星期一**

cānjiā
**参加** 回 参与 cānyù （甲）动
participate; take part; join

**常用搭配**
参加讨论 participate in a discussion
参加活动 take part in the activity
参加工作 begin one's work

**用法示例**
我们全都受邀参加这次盛典。
We are all invited to take part in the pageant.
他鼓起勇气参加了比赛。
He mustered his courage to take part in the competition.

yìbiān    yìbiān
**一边…一边…** （甲）
① while ② at the same time

**常用搭配**
一边走一边聊 going while chatting
一边说一边笑 laughing while talking

**用法示例**
他们在农场一边干活一边聊天。
They were talking while they were working on the farm.
他一边上大学一边打工。
He does a part-time job while he studies at university.

gǎngwèi
**岗位** （丙）名
post

**常用搭配**
工作岗位 working position
岗位责任 responsibility of a post

**用法示例**
卫兵不能离开岗位。
The guards were ordered not to leave their posts.
这个交警每天在他的岗位上工作。
The traffic policeman works at his post everyday.
他已被调到其他岗位上去了。
He has been transferred to another post.

yíngyǎng
**营养** （乙）名
nutrition

**常用搭配**
营养不良 nutritional deficiency
营养价值 nutritive value

**用法示例**
我们的身体需要充足的营养。
Our bodies need adequate nutrition.
她因缺乏营养而身体虚弱。
She is weak from lack of sustenance.

yíngyè                        tíngyè
**营业** 反 停业 （乙）动
① be open to customers ② ready to transact business

**常用搭配**
营业时间 business hour
商店在营业。 The store is open.

**用法示例**
银行还没开始营业呢。
The banks aren't open yet.
你们营业到几点？
How late are you open?
这家饭店除星期一外，每天都营业。
The restaurant is open every day except Monday.

yùnqì
**运气** （丙）名
luck; fortune

**常用搭配**
好运气 good luck
碰运气 try one's luck

**用法示例**
他的成功主要靠运气。
His successes were largely due to luck.
他们羡慕他的好运气。
They envy him his good fortune.
他想来北京碰碰运气。
He wanted to come to Beijing to try his luck.

rěnnài
**忍耐** （丙）动
restrain; be patient

**常用搭配**
忍耐一下！ Have patience! 忍耐力 tolerance

**用法示例**
最后，我忍耐不了了。
In the end, I could not bear it.
我还得再忍耐一会儿，乏味的演讲快结束了。
I have to have patience for a while longer. The tiring speech will soon be over.

**rěnshòu**
## 忍受 ⊜ 容忍 róngrěn （丙）动
endure; tolerate; suffer

**常用搭配**
忍受痛苦 endure pain

**用法示例**
我忍受不了她没完没了的抱怨。
I can't endure her endless complaints.
治不好的病就必须忍受。
What can't be cured must be endured.
我不能再忍受他那傲慢无礼的行为了。
I could not endure the insolence of his behavior.

**yùnsuàn**
## 运算 （丁）动
calculate; compute

**常用搭配**
加法运算 add operation
精确运算 to calculate precisely

**用法示例**
结果是由计算机运算的。
The result was calculated by a computer.
他在学校已经学习了四则运算。
He has learned the four arithmetic functions at school.

**yùnxíng**
## 运行 （丁）动
move; run

**常用搭配**
运行轨道 orbit of movement
运行速度 speed of movement

**用法示例**
地球环绕太阳运行。
The earth moves around the sun.
这艘船在大连至天津的航线上运行。
The ship operates on the Dalian-Tianjin run.

**tǐzhì**
## 体制 （丁）名
system

**常用搭配**
教育体制 educational system
经济体制 economic system

**用法示例**
你能告诉我英美两国的政府体制有什么不同吗？
Can you tell me the difference between the American and British systems of government?
你认为这种新体制会有什么问题吗？
Do you foresee any problems with the new system?

**dǐzhì**
## 抵制 ⊠ 拥护 yōnghù （丁）动
resist; refuse (to cooperate)

**常用搭配**
抵制改革 resist reform
遭到……的抵制 be resisted by…

**用法示例**
我们应该抵制党内的极端主义。
We must counteract extremism in the party.
很多年轻人不能抵制精神污染。
Many young people could not resist the spiritual pollution.
抵制新政权的某些势力仍然存在。
Pockets of resistance to the new regime still remain.

 词义辨析

**忍耐、忍受**

"忍耐"和"忍受"都是动词,都有克制自己的意思。"忍耐"强调抑制自己不如意的感觉,不表现出来,不能带宾语,经常带补语;"忍受"强调把痛苦、困难和不幸勉强地承受下来,经常带宾语,即使不带宾语也会在上下文中表示出具体的使人产生不如意感情的对象。如:①即使对你的领导不满意,你也要尽量忍耐。②他是一个能忍耐的人,但就连他也没法忍受那种挑衅了。③她无法忍受他的谎言。

Both 忍受 and 忍耐 are verbs, meaning "to bear or endure". 忍耐 stresses "to control or repress one's unhappy feelings", cannot be followed by an object, and often takes a complement; while 忍受 stresses "to bear or endure something with tolerance, such as pain, difficulty or misfortune", It often takes an object, and according to the context, there must be something concrete that makes one unhappy though there is not an object in the sentence. For example: ① Try to restrain yourself though you are dissatisfied with your leader. ② He is a patient man, but not even he could sit still during that kind of provocation. ③ She couldn't bear his lying.

 练习

**练习一、根据拼音写汉字，根据汉字写拼音**
dǐ（　　）　yùn（　　）　（　　）nài　yíng（　　）　（　　）jiā
（　　）制　（　　）行　忍（　　）　（　　）养　参（　　）

**练习二、搭配连线**
(1) 岗位　　　　　　　　A. 痛苦
(2) 忍受　　　　　　　　B. 体制
(3) 营养　　　　　　　　C. 责任
(4) 经济　　　　　　　　D. 抵制
(5) 遭到　　　　　　　　E. 不良

**练习三、从今天学习的生词中选择合适的词填空**
1. 他小时候 _____ 不良，长得又矮又瘦。
2. 这个商场的 _____ 时间是从早上九点到晚上十点。
3. 昨天气温高达 42 度，热得让人难以 _____。
4. 打针时有点疼，医生让我 _____ 一下，说马上就好了。
5. 两国关系恶化，这个国家的人们开始 _____ 对方国家生产的商品。
6. 列车 _____ 时，请不要把头伸到窗外。
7. 这孩子连最简单的加减乘除 _____ 都不会。
8. 中国政府进行经济 _____ 改革以后，经济得到了快速、持续的发展。
9. 他喜欢 _____ 听音乐 _____ 看书。
10. 这个人的 _____ 太好了，买了两张彩票就中了 500 万。

**答案**

**练习一：**
略
**练习二：**
(1) C　　(2)A　　(3)E　　(4)B　　(5)D
**练习三：**
1. 营养　2. 营业　3. 忍受　4. 忍耐
5. 抵制　6. 运行　7. 运算　8. 体制
9. 一边，一边　10. 运气

---

 星期二

**yìbān**
**一般**　　　　　　　　（甲）形
ordinary；general
**常用搭配**
一般而言 generally speaking
一般情况下 in the ordinary way
**用法示例**
这本书是为一般读者写的，不是为专家写的。
This book is intended for the general reader, not for the specialist one.
一般认为出国旅游可以增长见识。
It is generally thought that traveling abroad can enrich one's knowledge.

**kèqi**
**客气**　　　　　　　　（甲）形／动
① polite；courteous ② stand on ceremony
**常用搭配**
不客气。You're welcome.
对生人要客气。Be courteous to strangers.
**用法示例**
别客气，我又不是外人。
Don't stand on ceremony. I'm no stranger.
她在电话中说话不太客气。
She sounded rather out of sorts on the phone.
尽量对她客气些，尽管你不喜欢她。
Try to be civil to her, even if you don't like her.

**pǔtōng**　　　　　　　　**tèbié**
**普通**　⊠ 特别　　　（乙）形
ordinary；common
**常用搭配**
普通人 the common man　　普通话 mandarin
**用法示例**
现在家用电器已经进入普通家庭了。
Now electrical appliances are used by ordinary families.
他是个普普通通的中国男孩。
He is an ordinary Chinese boy.
这个节目给普通观众提供了一个发表意见的机会。
This program gives ordinary viewers a chance to make their voices heard.

**suǒwèi**
**所谓**　　　　　　　　（乙）形
so-called
**常用搭配**
所谓的宫殿 so-called "palace"

**用法示例**

那就是他所谓的"真理",我们意识到不该信任他。

That was his so-called "truth". We realized then that we should not trust him.

他是我们所谓的老板,实际上,所有事都由他的妻子决定。

He's the so-called boss of the company when in fact his wife decides everything.

## xiǎngxiàng
## 想象　　　　　　　　　　　（乙）动

imagine

**常用搭配**

有想象力的作家 an imaginative writer

无法想象的 unimaginable

**用法示例**

你可以想象那里的情况。

You can imagine the situation there.

那是我想象不到的。

That's beyond the reach of my imagination.

你可以想象我是多么惊讶。

You can imagine how surprised I was.

## xiǎngfǎ
## 想法　　　　　　　　　　　（乙）名

idea

**常用搭配**

惊人的想法 a striking idea

**用法示例**

他的想法和我的不一致。

His ideas do not conform to mine.

对那件事她有自己的想法。

She has her own ideas about that matter.

他的想法得到了热烈的响应。

His idea received an enthusiastic response.

## kèchéng
## 课程　　　　　　　　　　　（乙）名

curriculum/course

**常用搭配**

课程表 curriculum schedule

专业课程 professional curriculum

**用法示例**

你们学习什么课程。

What course do you stndy?

你什么时候完成大学课程?

When will you finish your college course?

这是下学期的课程安排。

This is the course arrangement for next term.

## yǔqì
## 语气　　　　　　　　　　　（丙）名

tone

**常用搭配**

愤怒的语气 angry tone

疑问语气 interrogative tone

**用法示例**

他的讲话中带有威胁的语气。

A tone of menace crept into his speech.

他用友好的语气跟我打招呼。

He greeted me in a friendly tone.

## jiāotán
## 交谈　　　　　　 ⊜谈话　　　（丙）动

① talk ② converse

**常用搭配**

和她交谈 talk with her

用电话交谈 talk over the telephone

**用法示例**

她很害羞,不敢和其他同学交谈。

She was too timid to talk with other students.

她和邻居隔着花园篱笆交谈。

She talked with her neighbor across the garden fence.

这是一次亲切友好的交谈。

This is an amicable conversation.

## zhǎnxīn
## 崭新　　　　　　 ⊗陈旧　　　（丙）形

brand new

**常用搭配**

崭新的家具 new furniture

崭新的电脑 new computer

**用法示例**

那男孩给我看他的崭新的运动鞋时得意极了。

The boy was as proud as a peacock when he showed me his new sport shoes.

今天上午他开着一辆崭新的汽车。

He drove a new car this morning.

## wúsuǒwèi
## 无所谓　　　　　　　　　　（丙）动

① to be indifferent ② not to matter

**常用搭配**

这对我来说无所谓。It doesn't matter to me.

**用法示例**

花多少钱都无所谓,只要你喜欢就买。

It doesn't matter about the price; if you like it, buy it.

你愿意告诉谁就告诉谁——对我来说都无所谓。

Tell whomever you like; it makes no difference to me.

## jiāowǎng
## 交往　　　　　　 ⊜来往　　　（丁）动

associate; contact

**常用搭配**

与他交往 associate with him

友好交往 friendly intercourse

**用法示例**

不要和不诚实的孩子交往。

Don't associate with dishonest boys.

英语在国际交往中比法语使用得更为广泛。
English is more widespread, and more used in international discourses than French.
我不想再和他们交往了。
I don't want to associate myself with them any more.

## 词义辨析

**一般、普通**

1、"一般"和"普通"都是形容词,都有平常、不特殊的意思,有时可以互换使用。"一般"往往强调能力、水平、质量不突出,"普通"强调没有特殊的标志、地位或级别。例如:①这个节目给普通/一般观众提供了一个发表意见的机会。②这位著名演员居住在一栋普通的房子里。③这种汽车的质量很一般。

Both 一般 and 普通 are adjectives, indicating ordinary or not special, and are sometimes exchangeable. But 一般 stresses of no exceptional ability, degree, or quality; while 普通 stresses "of no special designation, status, or rank". For example: ① This program gives ordinary viewers a chance to make their voices heard. ② That famous actor lives in an ordinary house. ③ The quality of the car is ordinary.

2、"一般"还有"一样、同样、在多数情况下"的意思,"不"可以修饰"一般",可以说"不一般"。"普通"没有这样的用法。例如:①秋天的红叶像火一般。②他跟哥哥一般高。③他一般骑车去上班。

一般 also means "alike", "the same", "usually outstanding", and it can be modified by "不", as "不一般" meaning "extraordinarily outstanding"; while 普通 has no such meaning or usage. For example: ① The red leaves in autumn are like fire. ② He is as tall as his elder brother. ③ He usually goes to work by bike.

## 练习

**练习一、根据拼音写汉字,根据汉字写拼音**
zhǎn(　) kè(　) kè(　) (　)wèi pǔ(　)
(　)新 (　)程 (　)气 所(　) (　)通

**练习二、搭配连线**
(1) 普通的　　　　　A. 语气
(2) 商量的　　　　　B. 工人
(3) 崭新的　　　　　C. 交谈
(4) 亲切地　　　　　D. 交往
(5) 频繁地　　　　　E. 家具

**练习三、从今天学习的生词中选择合适的词填空**
1. 他原来是一名 _____ 工人,因为工作出色,被选为工厂的副厂长。
2. 她每天 _____ 学习汉语三个小时,有时学习五个小时。
3. _____ "公仆",是指全心全意为人民服务的领导干部。
4. 到这儿就像到自己家一样,别 _____。
5. 他用不满的 _____ 说:"饭怎么还没好?"
6. 这件事跟我没关系,你怎么做,我都 _____。
7. 总理在视察时,与当地群众进行了亲切 _____。
8. 他爷爷跟我爷爷是老朋友,他爸跟我爸是同事,我们两家 _____ 了几十年了。
9. 过生日的时候,父亲给我买了一台 _____ 的电脑,我当时高兴极了。
10. 他独自在那座小岛上呆了三年,那三年的经历真是难以 _____。

## 答案

练习一:
略
练习二:
(1) B　　　(2)A　　　(3)E　　　(4)C　　　(5)D
练习三:
1. 普通　　2. 一般　　3. 所谓　　4. 客气　　5. 语气
6. 无所谓　7. 交谈　　8. 交往　　9. 崭新　　10. 想象

**星期三**

**biǎoyáng**
**表扬** 反 批评 （甲）动

commend; praise

**常用搭配**
得到（受到）表扬 receive acclaim（be praised）
表扬工人 praise a worker

**用法示例**
她父亲很严厉，从来没有表扬过她。
She had a stern father who never praised her.
我们应当表扬好人好事。
We should commend good people and good deeds.
这个学生的表现得到了老师的表扬。
The student's performance was praised by the teacher.

**chāoguò**
**超过** （乙）动

exceed; outstrip

**常用搭配**
超过了 5 分钟 exceed by 5 minutes
超过另一辆车 overtake another car

**用法示例**
费用不会超过 50 美元。
The cost will not exceed $50.
你的演讲超过了规定的时间。
Your speech has overrun the time limit.
后面那辆车想超过我们。
The car behind wants to get ahead of us.

**zāogāo**
**糟糕** （乙）形

① too bad ② terrible

**常用搭配**
糟糕的天气 terrible weather
太糟糕了。 That's too bad.
真是糟糕透了！ What a fearful mess!

**用法示例**
你的字写得很糟糕。
Your writing is terrible.
他是一个糟糕的厨师。
He is terrible cook.
我的英语不好，她的就更糟糕了。
I am bad at English, but she is worse.

**jì ······yòu······**
**既······又······** （乙）

not only… but also…

**常用搭配**
既聪明又可爱 clever and lovely

我的儿子既健康又勇敢。
My son is courageous as well as strong.
他既是我的老师，又是我的好朋友。
He is my teacher and close friend.

**qiángdiào**
**强调** （乙）动

to emphasize; to stress

**常用搭配**
反复强调 repeatedly emphasize
强调……的重要性 emphasize the importance of…

**用法示例**
他强调了小心驾驶的重要性。
He emphasized the importance of careful driving.
我必须强调我们没有多少时间了。
I must stress that we haven't much time.
他强调了一点，就是我们必须准时。
He stressed the point that we should be punctual.

**jì ······yě······**
**既······也······** （乙）

not only… but also…

**常用搭配**
既不赞成也不反对 neither for, nor against

**用法示例**
他既不抽烟也不喝酒。
He doesn't smoke, neither does he drink.
他既不会读也不会写。
He cannot read or write.
我们既没跳舞，也没唱歌。
We did not dance or sing.

**zāoyù**
**遭遇** （乙）动／名

① encounter; befall ② suffering

**常用搭配**
遭遇阻碍 encounter obstacles
遭遇危险 encounter dangers
不幸的遭遇 unfortunate suffering

**用法示例**
我希望我永远不会再遭遇到这种不愉快的经历。
I hope that I shall never again have to undergo such an
unpleasant experience.
得知他的遭遇后，我不禁同情他。
After learning of his sufferings, I couldn't help but
sympathize with him.

**chāochū**
**超出** （丙）动

go beyond; overstep

**常用搭配**
超出权限 overstep one's authority

**用法示例**

新闻节目超出了规定的时间。

The news program overran its allotted time.

结果超出了我们的预期。

The results have exceeded our expectations.

这已经超出了法院的权限。

It has been beyond the competence of the court.

yǎngqì
## 氧气 （丙）名

oxygen

**常用搭配**

氧气瓶 oxygen container

**用法示例**

植物可以吸收二氧化碳释放氧气。

Plants can absorb carbon dioxide and release oxygen.

鱼通过鳃摄取氧气。

Fish take in oxygen through their gills.

飞机上的氧气面具只用于紧急情况。

Oxygen masks are used in aircrafts only in emergencies.

biànlùn            zhēnglùn
## 辩论 同 争论 （丙）动 / 名

① argue over/debate ② argument

**常用搭配**

激烈辩论 a heated argument

辩论比赛 debating competition

**用法示例**

候选人在辩论中唇枪舌箭。

The candidates exchanged barbs in the debate.

经过长时间的辩论，议案才获得通过。

After a long debate the bill was passed.

议会将在下周辩论经济的议题。

Parliament will debate the economic issue next week.

biànbié            fēnbiàn
## 辨别 同 分辨 （丁）动

identify；distinguish

**常用搭配**

辨别是非 distinguish between right and wrong

**用法示例**

标记模糊不清，难以辨别。

The markings are so blurred that it is difficult to identify.

不能辨别颜色的人被称为色盲。

People who cannot distinguish between colors are said to be color blind.

zāota            àixī
## 糟蹋 反 爱惜 （丁）动

waste；spoil

**常用搭配**

糟蹋庄稼 ruin crops

糟蹋钱财 waste money

**用法示例**

糟蹋粮食是不道德的。

wasting food is wicked.

汤里放盐太多了，把汤给糟蹋了。

The soup was spoiled by too much salt.

他把他的财产糟蹋光了。

He has squandered his property.

 词义辨析

**超出、超过**

"超出"和"超过"都是动词。"超出"强调结果或数量超越了一定的范围或预期；"超过"强调在某数量或标准之上，或从某人或事物的后边赶到了前边。例如：①你的演讲超出了规定的时间。②我们学校的学生数超过了800人。③我们很快就超过那些跑得慢的人。

Both 超过 and 超出 are verbs. 超出 indicates "to exceed the quantity specified or to do better than the result anticipated". While 超过 indicates "to surpass (a number or a standard), or to move in front of somebody or something from behind". For example: ① Your speech has overrun the time limit. ② Our school has a student population in excess of 800. ③ We soon outstripped the slower runners.

## 练习

**练习一、根据拼音写汉字，根据汉字写拼音**

zāo（　　）　zāo（　　）　biàn（　　）　biàn（　　）　qiáng（　　）
（　　）塌　（　　）遇　（　　）论　（　　）别　（　　）调

**练习二、搭配连线**

(1) 反复　　　　　　　　A. 是非
(2) 遭遇　　　　　　　　B. 粮食
(3) 辨别　　　　　　　　C. 强调
(4) 糟蹋　　　　　　　　D. 辩论
(5) 激烈　　　　　　　　E. 危险

**练习三、从今天学习的生词中选择合适的词填空**

1. 这孩子 _____ 活泼 _____ 聪明，很招人喜欢。
2. 这东西 _____ 不实用 _____ 不美观，买它干什么？
3. 每个星期，老师在课堂上都要 _____ 作业做得好的孩子。
4. 领导在讲话结束时再次 _____ 了一遍大会的主旨。
5. _____！要下雨了，我没带伞。
6. 水手讲述了他们在海上 _____ 台风的可怕经历。
7. 上个月花销 _____ 了预算，这个月不得不省着点。
8. 委员会的成员就是否支持这个项目进行了激烈的 _____。
9. 这对双胞胎长得太像了，老师也难以 _____ 谁是哥哥谁是弟弟。
10. 不要 _____ 粮食，世界上有的人还在挨饿呢。

## 答案

**练习一：**
略

**练习二：**
(1) C　　　(2)E　　　(3)A　　　(4)B　　　(5)D

**练习三：**
1. 既，又　　2. 既，也　　3. 表扬　　4. 强调
5. 糟糕　　　6. 遭遇　　　7. 超出　　8. 辩论
9. 辨别　　　10. 糟蹋

### 星期四 Thursday

jiāo
## 交　　　　　　　　　　（甲）动

deliver; pay (money)

**常用搭配**

交作业 hand in homework　　交钱 pay money
交货 deliver the goods

**用法示例**

行李将在车站交给你。
The baggage will be delivered to you at the station.
这个百万富翁已把他一半的股票交给了他的长子。
The millionaire handed over 50 percent of his stock to his first son.
通知她交罚款，但她拒不服从。
She was told to pay the fine, but she refused to comply.

fù
## 付　　　　　　　　　　（乙）动

pay

**常用搭配**

预付 pay in advance　　分期付款 pay by installments
付房租 pay a bill for a room　　付账 pay the bill

**用法示例**

买房人下星期付定金。
The purchaser of the house will pay the deposit next week.
我想用支票支付。
I'd like to pay by check.
请付现金。
Pay in cash, please.

fǒudìng
## 否定　　　　　　　　　（乙）动

① negate ② negative

**常用搭配**

否定的回答 a negative answer　　否定句 negative sentence
否定一项建议 oppose a suggestion

**用法示例**

这些事实否定了你的理论。
These facts negate your theory.
你怎么能否定上帝的存在？
How can you deny God?

yìfāngmiàn　　　lìng yì fāng miàn
## 一方面……另一方面……　　　　（乙）

On the one hand...on the other hand...

一方面我是你的经理，另一方面我也是你的朋友。
On the one hand, I am your manager; and on the other hand, I am also your friend.

一方面你不应当拘束,另一方面也不要放肆。

On the one hand, you shouldn't be shy; on the other hand, you mustn't forget your manners.

suíshí
## 随时 ◉ 时时 （乙）副

at any time

【常用搭配】

你随时都可以来。Come whenever you like.

随时准备着 be ready at all times

【用法示例】

欢迎你随时来我们家。

You are always welcome to our house.

活火山随时可能喷发。

An active volcano may erupt at any time.

他可能随时会到。

He is likely to arrive at any time.

suíbiàn
## 随便 ◉ 随意 （乙）形

at random; casual

【常用搭配】

随你的便 as you like　随便聊聊 chat freely

随便选 choose what you like

【用法示例】

他从衣柜里随便挑出一条领带。

He chose a tie at random from the wardrobe.

在正式场合不要随便讲话。

Don't speak so casually at a formal occasion.

对不起,我只是随便说说而已。

Sorry, it's just a casual remark.

suíhòu
## 随后 （乙）动

① soon after ② subsequently

【常用搭配】

他随后就来。He will come soon after.

【用法示例】

他们将先到那里,我们随后就到。

They will get there first. And we shall arrive soon after.

他被指控杀人,但随后被认定是无罪的。

He was charged with murder but later found innocent.

yīnmóu
## 阴谋 （丙）名

conspiracy; intrigue; plot

【常用搭配】

政治阴谋 political intrigues

揭露阴谋 expose a plot

【用法示例】

我看穿了他的阴谋。

I saw through his plot.

两名记者揭露了全部阴谋。

It was the two reporters who uncovered the whole conspiracy.

他泄露了他们推翻政府的阴谋。

He revealed their conspiracy to overthrow the government.

tiāncái
## 天才 （丙）名

genius; talent

【常用搭配】

数学天才 a mathematical genius

天才靠勤奋。Talent depends upon industry.

【用法示例】

爱因斯坦是个伟大的科学天才。

Einstein was a great scientific genius.

她不但是摄影师还是个天才的音乐家。

She is a talented musician as well as a photographer.

fǒurèn
## 否认 ⊠ 承认 （丁）动

to deny

【常用搭配】

否认事实 deny the fact　再三否认 deny repeatedly

【用法示例】

被告否认遇到过她。

The accused man denies that he had met her.

台湾是座美丽的岛屿,这是不可否认的。

There is no denying that Taiwan is a beautiful island.

我说她偷了我的车,可是她否认了。

I said that she had stolen my car, but she denied it.

fǒujué
## 否决 （丁）动

veto; overrule

【常用搭配】

否决一项议案 veto a bill　否决权 veto power

【用法示例】

法官否决了以前的判决。

The judge overruled the previous decision.

昨天总统否决了减税法案。

The president vetoed the tax cut yesterday.

mièshì
## 蔑视 ⊠ 敬重 （丁）动

despise; be defiant of; look down upon

【常用搭配】

蔑视女性 be defiant of women

蔑视年轻人 look down upon young men

【用法示例】

他出示假证据,这就是蔑视法庭。

He gave false evidence, which was in contempt of the court.

他宣称蔑视钱财。

He claims to despise riches.

她用蔑视的态度和我们说话。

She talked to us in a defiant manner.

 **词义辨析**

### 给、付、交

三个词都是动词,都有把某物给某人的意思。在交易行为中往往用"付",它的宾语是钱,如付款、付租金、付账、付费等;"交"的宾语可以是钱也可以是与义务、责任有关的事物,常用于下级对上级,个人对政府机关,如:交作业、交税、交罚金等;"给"指赠予、传递某物,宾语可以是具体的,也可以是抽象的,"给"可以做助动词表示被动,相当于"被",还常作补语,引出动作行为的对象。如:①请把字典给我。②你能给我一些建议吗?③他给了她一个电吹风。④油漆都给他们用光了。

The three verbs all mean "to deliver something to somebody". In business, 付 is often used, and its object is money, such as 付款 (pay money), 付租金 (pay rent), 付账 (pay bill), 付费 (pay fee); the object of 交 can be money or something to do with duty or obligation, mostly from the inferior to the superior, a person to a government department, such as 交作业 (hand in homework), 交税 (pay tax), 交罚金 (pay fine); 给 means "to give or pass something to somebody", and the object can be either concrete or abstract. 给 often serves as an auxiliary verb in the passive voice, equal to the meaning of "by", and often functions as a complement, introducing the object of the action. For example: ① Please pass the dictionary to me. ② Can you give me some feedback? ③ He gave her an electric hair dryer. ④ All the paint was used up by them.

 **练习**

**练习一、根据拼音写汉字,根据汉字写拼音**
miè ( ) ( )móu suí ( ) ( )jué ( )miàn
( )视　阴( )　( )便　否( )　方( )

**练习二、搭配连线**

| | |
|---|---|
| (1) 交 | A. 天才 |
| (2) 付 | B. 挑选 |
| (3) 音乐 | C. 租金 |
| (4) 政治 | D. 作业 |
| (5) 随便 | E. 阴谋 |

**练习三、从今天学习的生词中选择合适的词填空**

1. 因为违章停车,我得去_____罚款。
2. 我的房子是采用分期_____款的方式购买的。
3. 她_____要伺候生病的母亲,_____要照顾孩子,真不容易。
4. 这种花生命力很顽强,_____种哪儿都能活。
5. 你有问题,可以_____来问我,千万别客气。
6. 你先走,我_____就到。
7. 我早就看穿了他们的_____,他们一心想取代我们公司在亚洲市场的地位。
8. 考不好没关系,如果作弊将遭到同学们的_____。
9. 我不_____自己对他有好感,但我确实从来没想过当他的女朋友。
10. 大会_____了关于增加财政拨款的提议。

**答案**

**练习一:**
略

**练习二:**
(1) D　(2)C　(3)A　(4)E　(5)B

**练习三:**
1. 交　2. 付　3. 一方面,另一方面
4. 随便　5. 随时　6. 随后　7. 阴谋
8. 蔑视　9. 否认　10. 否决

星期五

tōngzhī
**通知** （甲）动／名
① inform；notify ② notice

**常用搭配**
接到……的通知 receive notice of（be informed of）
另行通知 further notice
宣读一个通知 announce a notification

**用法示例**
她通知我们开会。
She notified us of the meeting.
地址如有变动，请通知我们。
Please notify us of any change of address.
她把通知贴到公告板上了。
She pinned the notice to the board.

yǒushí   yǒushí
**有时……有时……** （甲）
sometimes

**常用搭配**
有时下雨，有时刮风。
It sometimes rains, sometimes winds.

**用法示例**
他有时努力，有时不努力。
Sometimes he works hard, sometimes he doesn't.
午饭后，这个老太太有时散散步，有时看看电视。
After lunch, the old lady sometimes goes for a walk, sometimes watches TV.

fèndòu                    pīnbó
**奋斗** ◎拼搏 （乙）动
strive

**常用搭配**
为……而奋斗 strive after／for…

**用法示例**
通往成功的唯一途径是奋斗。
The only passport to success is hard work.
他为获得艺术家的声誉而奋斗。
He strove for recognition as an artist.
这些年轻人在为理想奋斗。
These young men are struggling for their ideals.

yuè      yuè
**越……越……** （乙）
the more…the more…

**常用搭配**
越少越好。The less, the better.
越快越好。The sooner, the better.

**用法示例**
他越生气，她就越笑话他。
The more angry he became, the more she laughed at him.
这件事我越想越不明白。
The more I think about it, the more confused I feel.
他得到的越多，想要的也越多。
The more he has, the more he wants.

dòuzhēng
**斗争** （乙）动／名
struggle (with)；fight

**常用搭配**
英勇的斗争 valiant fight
武装斗争 armed struggle
为……而斗争 struggle for...
与……斗争 struggle with...

**用法示例**
人类与环境作斗争。
Mankind struggles with his environment.
他们的长期斗争终于取得了胜利。
Their long struggle finally culminated in success.
他们为维护独立而斗争。
They were fighting in order to preserve their independence.

xiǎngshòu
**享受** （乙）动／名
① enjoy ② enjoyment

**常用搭配**
享受公费医疗 enjoy free medical care
享受美食 enjoy a delicious meal
享受生活 enjoy life

**用法示例**
我坐在庭院里享受明媚的阳光。
I was sitting in the garden enjoying the sunshine.
既然有空，我可以享受一下音乐。
Now that I am free, I can enjoy music for a while.

wēnnuǎn                    nuǎnhuo
**温暖** ◎暖和 （乙）形／动
① warm ② to warm

**常用搭配**
温暖的气候 a warm climate    温暖人心 warm one's heart

**用法示例**
她坐在温暖的阳光下。
She sat in the warm sunshine.
这种花在温暖的环境中长得很茂盛。
This species of flower flourishes in a warm environment.
今天天气很温暖，不冷也不热。
The weather is mild today; it is neither hot nor cold.

wēnhé                    pínghé
**温和** ◎平和 （丙）形
mild；moderate

**（常用搭配）**

温和的气候 moderate climate　　温和地批评 criticize gently

**（用法示例）**

咖啡和茶都是温和的兴奋剂。

Coffee and tea are mild stimulants.

温和的说服往往比强迫更有效。

Gentle persuasion is sometimes more effective than force.

### yìshi
## 意识　　　　　　　　　　　　　（丙）动／名

① realize；be aware ② consciousness

**（常用搭配）**

我没有意识到。I wasn't aware of that.

民族意识 race consciousness

安全意识 consciousness of safety

**（用法示例）**

每个人都意识到了教育的重要性。

Everybody is aware of the importance of education.

当那个人意识到是怎么回事时，便笑了起来。

The man laughed when he realized what had happened.

病人什么时候才能恢复意识？

When will the patient regain consciousness?

### xiǎngyǒu
## 享有　　　　　yōngyǒu
　　　　　　　　⊜拥有　　　　　（丁）动

enjoy (rights, privileges, etc.)

**（常用搭配）**

享有特权 have privileges

享有健康 enjoys good health

**（用法示例）**

退休以后，你可以享有免费医疗。

After retirement you can receive free medical treatment.

他们是大使，因此享有外交豁免权。

They are ambassadors, so they have diplomatic immunity.

从右边驶来的车辆享有优先通行权。

Vehicles coming from the right have right of way.

### qiántí
## 前提　　　　　　　　　　　　　　（丁）名

premise；prerequisite

**（常用搭配）**

在……前提下 on the premise of ( that )...

**（用法示例）**

能力是升职的前提。

Competence is a prerequisite to promotion.

如果你的前提成立，那么就很容易推断出结论。

If your premise is established, your conclusions are easily deduced.

给投资者的建议是以利率将继续下降为前提的。

The advice to investors was based on the premise that interest rates would continue to fall.

### wēnróu
## 温柔　　　　　　　　　　　　　　（丁）形

tender；gentle and soft

---

**（常用搭配）** 温柔的表情 tender expression 温柔的女孩 a gentle girl

**（用法示例）**

他给了她一个温柔的吻。

He gave her a tender kiss.

她像小羊一样温柔。

She is as gentle as a lamb.

 **词义辨析**

**温暖、温和、温柔**

　　三个词都是形容词。"温柔"多用来描写女性的性格温和柔顺。"温和"描写的是态度、性情、气候适中，不强烈。"温暖"主要用来描写温度暖和，有时可以表示人的感受等。例如：①他有一位温柔的妻子。②他的性情太温和了，即使有充分的理由，他也不会发脾气。③冰在温暖的天气中溶化了。

　　The three are adjectives. 温柔 means "soft", mostly referring to the character of a female that is gentle and tender; 温和 means "mild", mostly referring to attitudes, dispositions, and climates that are moderate and not extreme; while 温暖 means "warm", referring to a temperature that is moderately hot, sometimes referring to a feeling or sense of warmth. For example: ① His wife is a very gentle and soft woman. ② He has too mild a nature to get angry, even if he has good cause. ③ Ice dissolves in warm weather.

 **练习**

**练习一、根据拼音写汉字，根据汉字写拼音**

wēn（　）（　）tí　yì（　）　xiǎng（　）　fèn（　）

（　）柔　前（　）　（　）识　（　）受　（　）斗

**练习二、搭配连线**

(1) 温暖的　　　　　　　　A. 斗争

(2) 温和的　　　　　　　　B. 女孩

(3) 紧急的　　　　　　　　C. 通知

(4) 英勇的　　　　　　　　D. 阳光

(5) 温柔的　　　　　　　　E. 态度

**练习三、从今天学习的生词中选择合适的词填空**

1. 她的关怀就像阳光一样 _____ 着我的心。

2. 我国法律规定：女性 _____ 同男性平等的权利。

3. 周末我 _____ 逛街，_____ 在家搞卫生。

4. 安定团结是社会和谐发展的 _____。

5. 送到医院时，他已经没有 _____ 了，三天以后才清醒过来。

6. 他是一个 _____ 的老板，很少见他发脾气。

7. 雨 _____ 下 _____ 大，看来今天的飞机肯定要晚点了。

8. 这些年他一直为成名而 _____,现在梦想终于实现了。

9. 经过了一夜的思想 _____,她决定离家出走。

10. 很多男人喜欢 _____ 的女人,可是我却深深地爱上了这个勇敢而坚强的姑娘。

**答案**

练习一:
略

练习二:
(1) D　　　(2)E　　　(3)C　　　(4)A　　　(5)B

练习三:
1. 温暖　　2. 享有　　3. 有时,有时　　4. 前提
5. 意识　　6. 温和　　7. 越,越　　8. 奋斗
9. 斗争　　10. 温柔

# 第7月,第1周的练习

**练习一.根据词语给加点的字注音**

1.( )　2.( )　　3.( )　　4.( )　5.( )
强调　　蔑视　　阴谋　　运算　　崭新

**练习二.根据拼音完成词语**

　　zāo　　　zāo　　　biàn　　　biàn　　　biàn
1.( )糕　2.( )遇　3.( )别　4.( )论　5.随( )

**练习三.辨析并选择合适的词填空**

1. 他决定搬家了,他实在( )不了这里的噪音污染了。(忍耐、忍受)

2. 经历了人生的种种磨难后他学会了( )和宽容。(忍耐、忍受)

3. 晚上,他( )会呆在家里看电视或者玩电脑。(一般、普通)

4. 跟总统合影的这个人,既不是领导也不是专家,就是一名( )的老工人。(一般、普通)

5. 她生病了,期末考试没考好,别人( )她,成了第一名。(超出、超过)

6. 不是我不答应,的确是你的要求( )了我的承受能力。(超出、超过)

7. ( )你,这是这个月的生活费,电话费自己去邮局( ),我没时间去。(给、付、交)

8. 今天算我请客,账单我来( )。(给、付、交)

9. 外面下大雪,冷极了,可是屋里很( )。(温暖、温柔、温和)

10. 王先生是个性格( )的人,他的太太也很( )漂亮。(温暖、温柔、温和)

**练习四.选词填空**

遭遇　　否认　　运气　　营业　　客气
糟蹋　　否决　　语气　　营养　　氧气

1. 他第一次买彩票就中奖了,( )真好!

2. 你工作那么累,吃点好东西,补充补充( )吧。

3. 联合国大会( )了对那个国家进行制裁的提议。

4. 农民种粮食很辛苦,我们不能( )粮食。

5. 在中国,商店和银行在周末都照常( )。

6. 大家对她的( )都很同情。

7. 我们是老朋友了,您就别跟我( )了。

8. 我不( )你的想法很有道理,但可能很难实施。

9. 海拔高的地方,空气稀薄,有的游客可能会因( )不足而感到头晕、胸闷。

10. 在说自己的悲惨遭遇时,她的( )很平淡,似乎在讲述别人的故事。

**练习五.选择关联词填空**

越……越……　　　　有时……有时……
一方面……一方面　　既……又……
既……也……

1. 这孩子( )漂亮( )活泼,大家别提多喜欢了!

2. 中国( )要大力发展工业,另( )要注意保护环境。

3. 她( )喜欢这件红色的,( )喜欢那件白色的,没办法,只好把两件都买下来了。

4. 他( )睡得很晚,( )睡得很早,生活没有规律。

5. 麻婆豆腐太好吃了,我( )吃( )爱吃。

**练习六.写出下列词语的同义词**

1. 辨别( )　　　　2. 随便( )
3. 享有( )　　　　4. 参加( )
5. 交谈( )

**练习七.写出下列词语的反义词**

1. 抵制( )　　　　2. 崭新( )
3. 糟蹋( )　　　　4. 普通( )
5. 否认( )

**答案**

练习一.
1.diào　　2.miè　　3.móu　　4.suàn　　5.zhǎn
练习二.
1. 糟　　2. 遭　　3. 辨　　4. 辩　　5. 便
练习三.
1. 忍受　　2. 忍耐　　3. 一般　　4. 普通　　5. 超过
6. 超出　　7. 给,交　　8. 付　　9. 温暖
10. 温和,温柔
练习四.
1. 运气　　2. 营养　　3. 否决　　4. 糟蹋　　5. 营业
6. 遭遇　　7. 客气　　8. 否认　　9. 氧气　　10. 语气
练习五.
1. 既,又　　2. 一方面,一方面　　3. 既,也
4. 有时,有时　　　　　　　　5. 越,越
练习六.
1. 分辨　　2. 随意　　3. 拥有　　4. 参与　　5. 谈话
练习七.
1. 拥护　　2. 陈旧　　3. 爱惜　　4. 特别　　5. 承认

# 7月 第2周的学习内容

星期一

## shēnghuó
## 生活 （甲）名/动
① life ② live

**常用搭配**

日常生活 everyday life　靠……生活 live on
生活品质 the quality of living

**用法示例**

他试图改变自己的生活方式。
He tried to change his way of life.
对他来说，生活似乎已失去了乐趣。
Life seems to have lost its flavor for him.
只有懂得如何生活的人们，才会了解自己和人生。
Only those who know how to live can come to know themselves, and life.

## huó
## 活 （甲）动/形
① live ② alive; living

**常用搭配**

他还活着。He is still alive.　一条活鱼 a live fish

**用法示例**

他根本不管我们是死是活。
Little does he care whether we live or die.
这两个人中，前者已死，而后者仍然活着。
Of these two men, the former is dead but the latter is still alive.
猫在戏弄那只活老鼠。
The cat is playing with a live mouse.

## zhǐhǎo
## 只好 （甲）副
① have to ② have no choice but to

**常用搭配**

她只好放弃了。She had to give up.

**用法示例**

要是你不开车送我，那我只好打的去了。
If you won't drive me, I'll have to get there by taxi.
因为缺少一名运动员我们只好叫这个小男孩做我们的队员。
Due to a defaulting player we have to take the little boy as a team member.

我只好随它去了。
I have to leave it as it is.

## lìshǐ
## 历史 （甲）名
history

**常用搭配**

历史剧 a historical play
历史教授 a professor of history
中国历史 history of China

**用法示例**

历史是我最喜爱的学科。
History is my favorite subject.
那是历史上最严重的空难。
That was the worst airline disaster in history.
这一系列历史事件非常有意思。
This series of historical events is very interesting.

## bùdébù
## 不得不 ≈ 只好 zhǐhǎo （乙）
have to

**常用搭配**

不得不离开 have to leave　不得不放弃 have to give up

**用法示例**

我们不得不采取预防措施。
We had to take preventive measures.
他为了养家不得不去拼命工作。
He had to work hard to support his family.
警察不得不使用武力驱散人群。
The police had to employ force to break up the crowd.

## gōngchéng
## 工程 （乙）名
① engineering ② project

**常用搭配**

建筑工程 construction project
生物工程 biological engineering
工程师 engineer

**用法示例**

他的梦想是成为一名工程师。
His dream is to become an engineer.
我的专业是化学工程。
My major is chemical engineering.
这项工程提前完工了。
The project was completed ahead of schedule.

## gōngjù
## 工具 （乙）名
tool; implement

**常用搭配**

园艺工具 gardening tools

绘图工具 drawing implement

**用法示例**

这本字典是非常有用的工具书。

The dictionary is a very useful reference book.

火车是一种安全的交通工具。

The train is a safe means of travel.

语言是重要的交流工具。

Words are important tools of communication.

## 来自 láizì ◉源自 yuánzì （乙）动

to come from; be derived from

**常用搭配**

来自北京 be from Beijing

**用法示例**

我的外籍教师来自澳大利亚。

My foreign teacher came from Australia.

这个国家的财富来自石油。

This country's wealth comes from its oil.

最后,这支来自阿根廷的足球队夺得了冠军。

Finally the football team from Argentina won the championship.

## 不是……就是…… búshì……jiùshì…… （丙）

either... or...

**常用搭配**

不是打篮球就是踢足球

either play basketball or play football

不是今天就是明天 either today or tomorrow

**用法示例**

我不知道把书丢在哪儿了。不是在学校,就是在车里。

I don't know where I left my book – either at school or in the car.

持枪人的外套不是红的,就是绿的——我记不清楚了。

The gunman's coat was either red or green – I can't remember.

## 来源 láiyuán （丙）名

source; origin

**常用搭配**

经济来源 source of income

**用法示例**

工资是我收入的主要来源。

My wages are the principal source of my income.

消息的来源可靠吗?

Does the news come from a reliable source?

## 惊奇 jīngqí ◉惊讶 jīngyà （丙）形

amazed; surprised

**常用搭配**

惊奇地看着 look in surprise

令我惊奇的是…… to my amazement...

**用法示例**

他那愤世嫉俗的态度让我们惊奇。

His cynical attitude gave us a surprise.

我们惊奇地发现房子是空的。

We were surprised at finding the house empty.

这事没什么可惊奇的。

It's nothing to be surprised at.

## 来历 láilì ◉来路 láilù （丁）名

history; origin

**常用搭配**

来历不明 of dubious origin

**用法示例**

这所房子有一段离奇的来历。

This house has a strange history.

他向我讲述了这把古剑的来历。

He told me the history of this ancient sword.

 **词义辨析**

**不得不、只好、得（děi）**

三个词都有必须的意思。"不得不"和"只好"表示被客观条件所迫,别无选择,两个词的意思和用法基本相同,但"不得不"不能用于否定句。"得"有时候带有一定的主观愿望,有应该、需要的意思。例如:①因为起晚了,我们不得不／只好／得打车去。②因为下雨了,我们只好不去公园,而是呆在家里。③我们得更加努力地工作。④孩子得服从他们的父母。

The three words mean "have to", "must". "不得不" and "只好" indicate "to be forced to do something by objective realities", but "不得不" cannot be used in a negative sentence; while "得" has some subjunctive sense, and also means "to need to do", "should". For example: ① We have to go by taxi, because we got up late. ② We have to stay at home instead of playing in the park because it is raining. ③ We need to work harder. ④ Children should obey their parents.

 **练习**

**练习一、根据拼音写汉字，根据汉字写拼音**

jīng（　）（　）yuán（　）jù lì（　）shēng（　）
（　）奇　来（　）　工（　）（　）史（　）活

**练习二、搭配连线**

(1) 日常　　　　　　　　　A. 工程
(2) 经济　　　　　　　　　B. 美国
(3) 生物　　　　　　　　　C. 生活
(4) 来自　　　　　　　　　D. 来源
(5) 交通　　　　　　　　　E. 工具

**练习三、从今天学习的生词中选择合适的词填空**

1. 妈妈出差了,爸爸和我都不会做饭,我们 _____ 煮方便面吃。
2. 这位老人一直 _____ 到了90岁。
3. 丈夫去世后,她一直一个人 _____。
4. 我们学校有五百多名留学生,他们 _____ 世界各地。
5. 这个项目 _____ 浩大,花了五年才完成。
6. 语言是交流的 _____,不会当地语言就不能与当地人交流。
7. 作曲家创作这首歌的灵感 _____ 于当地的一种戏曲。
8. 这钱 _____ 不明,我们不能要。
9. 他对所看到的没表现出一点 _____,这让我们多少有些失望。
10. 这道题的答案 _____ A _____ B,其它答案肯定都不对。

 **答案**

**练习一:**
略

**练习二:**

| (1) C | (2)D | (3)A | (4)B | (5)E |
|---|---|---|---|---|

**练习三:**

| 1.只好 | 2.活 | 3.生活 | 4.来自 |
|---|---|---|---|
| 5.工程 | 6.工具 | 7.来源 | 8.来历 |
| 9.惊奇 | 10.不是,就是 | | |

---

 **星期二**

bǐsài
**比赛**　　　　　　　　　　　　　（甲）动／名

① compete ② match; competition

**常用搭配**
游泳比赛 swimming competition.
足球比赛 a football match

**用法示例**
那位年轻的网球运动员常与著名球员比赛。
That young tennis player has often competed against famous players.
那两个孩子比赛争夺第一名。
The two boys vied with each other for first place.
由于下雨,比赛取消了。
Owing to the rain, the match was cancelled.

bǐjiào　　　　　　　　　　duìbǐ
**比较**　　　　　　　　　　对比　　（甲）副／动

① comparatively ② compare

**常用搭配**
比较容易 relatively easy　　与……相比较 compare with...

**用法示例**
我上星期比较忙。
I was quite busy last week.
人类是地球上出现得比较晚的一种生物。
Man is a comparatively new creature on the surface of the earth.
很难比较。
It is hard to compare.
和别人比较起来,他比较迟钝。
He is rather dull in comparison with others.

yúshì
**于是**　　　　　　　　　　　　　（乙）连

① whereupon ② and then ③ so

**用法示例**
他得罪了上司,于是被解雇了。
He offended his superior and then was fired.
天晚了,于是我们就回家了。
It was late, so we went home.
其中一个男人侮辱了另一个男人,于是他们就打了起来。
One of the men insulted another, whereupon a fight broke out.

qīnqiè
**亲切**　　　　　　　　　　　　　（乙）形

amiable; kind

**常用搭配**
亲切的笑容 genial smile　　亲切的问候 a cordial greeting

**用法示例**

她总是亲切地和孩子们说话。

She always spoke kindly to the children.

他说话的态度很亲切。

He spoke in a friendly way.

**亲戚** qīnqi　◉ 亲属 qīnshǔ　（乙）名

relative

**常用搭配**

看望亲戚 call on one's relatives

**用法示例**

我有些亲戚住在美国，比如我母亲的姑姑和叔叔。

Some of my relations, my mother's aunt and uncle, live in America.

我们邀请了所有的亲戚来参加婚礼。

We invited all our relatives to the wedding.

她是我的亲戚。

She is a connection of mine.

**签订** qiāndìng　◉ 签署 qiānshǔ　（乙）动

sign (contract)

**常用搭配**

签订合同 sign a contract

**用法示例**

有关各国都同意签订这项协定。

The countries concerned all consented to sign the agreement.

签订这项协议将有助于缓和紧张的国际局势。

The signing of this agreement will help to reduce international tension.

为了双方的利益我们签订这项合同。

We entered into this contract in the interests of both parties.

**垃圾** lājī　（乙）名

garbage; rubbish

**常用搭配**

垃圾桶 garbage bin　生活垃圾 household garbage

**用法示例**

清洁工每周来清理一次垃圾。

The dustman comes once a week to remove the rubbish.

请把垃圾放进桶里。

Please put the garbage in the dustbin.

有些人往河里倒垃圾。

Some people throw their rubbish into the river.

**不得了** bùdéliǎo　◉ 了不起 liǎobuqǐ　（乙）形

① very ② exceedingly

**常用搭配**

怕得不得了 exceedingly frightened

累得不得了 only too tired

**用法示例**

外边冷得不得了。

It's too cold outside.

看到混乱的情况，我就气得不得了。

I was extremely angry when I saw the mess.

真是不得了，孩子们自己开车进城了。

It's really terrible. The children drove to town by themselves.

**不是……而是……** búshì……érshì……　（丙）

not... but...

**常用搭配**

不是一，而是二！　Not one, but two!

**用法示例**

他不是我们的新同学，而是新老师。

He is not a new classmate, but our new teacher.

今天不是星期六而是星期日。

Today is not Saturday but Sunday.

我不是不喜欢宠物，而是没有时间照顾它。

It is not that I don't like pet, but I have no time to look after it.

**了不起** liǎobùqǐ　（乙）

remarkable; amazing

**常用搭配**

没什么了不起的 nothing remarkable

**用法示例**

我的老师会讲五种语言，我觉得他很了不起。

My teacher can speak five languages. I think he is very remarkable.

真了不起，他在一周内就圆满地完成了任务。

It is amazing that he has finished the task perfectly within one week.

**亲身** qīnshēn　（丁）形

① personal ② by oneself

**常用搭配**

亲身体会 to experience by oneself

**用法示例**

他给我们讲了一件他亲身经历的事。

He told us a story of his personal experience.

如果不是我亲身经历了此事，我真的不会相信。

I really wouldn't believe it if I hadn't experienced it myself.

**签署** qiānshǔ　（丁）动

to sign (an agreement)

**常用搭配**

签署协议 sign a convention

签署命令 sign an order

**用法示例**

他们拒绝签署这项协定。

They refused to sign the convention.

只有经理有权签署支票。

Only the manager has the authority to sign cheques.

你只需签署这份文件,这辆汽车就是你的了。

Just sign on the dotted line and the car will be yours.

## 词义辨析

**不得了、了不起**

"不得了"和"了不起"都有赞许的意思,表示"非凡的"。但"不得了"还可以用来表示程度很高或情况很严重的意思,"了不起"不能。例如:①看到混乱的情况,我就气得不得了。②他得了三次世界冠军,真不得了 / 了不起。

Both 不得了 and 了不起 have commendatory sense, indicating "extraordinary". But "不得了" also means "extremely, awfully, seriously"; while "了不起" has no meaning like that. For example: ① I was extremely angry when I saw the mess. ② It is so remarkable that he has won the world championship three times.

## 练习

**练习一、根据拼音写汉字,根据汉字写拼音**

qiān ( )　lā ( )　( )qi ( )jiào ( )dìng

( )署　( )圾　亲( )　比( )　签( )

**练习二、搭配连线**

(1) 签署　　　　　　　A. 垃圾

(2) 亲身　　　　　　　B. 命令

(3) 清理　　　　　　　C. 比赛

(4) 签订　　　　　　　D. 体会

(5) 足球　　　　　　　E. 合同

**练习三、从今天学习的生词中选择合适的词填空**

1. 他有 _____ 在国外工作,叔叔在美国,姑姑在加拿大。

2. 我的老师脸上永远挂着微笑,让学生感到很 _____。

3. 上星期我 _____ 了工作合同,下个月我将正式在这家公司上班。

4. 两个国家的领导人已经 _____ 了协议,决定合作开发岛上的石油资源。

5. 昨晚,我的牙疼得 _____,连觉都睡不着。

6. 他没什么 _____ 的,如果不是他父亲,他早被辞退了。

7. 这本书是根据作者的 _____ 经历写成的。

8. 我有些不舒服,_____,我就提前回房间休息了。

9. 年轻人和年轻人 _____ 容易成为朋友。

10. 昨天你看见的 _____ 她,_____ 她姐姐,她俩长得很像。

## 答案

**练习一:**

略

**练习二:**

(1) B　　(2)D　　(3)A　　(4)E　　(5)C

**练习三:**

1. 亲戚　　2. 亲切　　3. 签订　　4. 签署

5. 不得了　6. 了不起　7. 亲身　　8. 于是

9. 比较　　10. 不是,而是

# 星期三

## bìanhuà
### 变化 （甲）名/动
① change ② vary

**常用搭配**
气候变化 climatic change　发生变化 undergo changes

**用法示例**
这座城市发生了巨大的变化。
This city underwent great changes.
这个城镇的面貌变化很大。
The appearance of the town is quite changed.
温度总在变化。
The temperature varies from time to time.

## shòudào
### 受到 （乙）动
receive; suffer

**常用搭配**
受到赞扬 receive acclaim
受到冷遇 receive a cold welcome

**用法示例**
我们受到了热情的接待。
We were received with enthusiasm.
这位医生受到患者的高度赞扬。
This doctor received high praise from his patients.
他们应受到惩罚。
They deserved their punishment.

## hépíng
### 和平 zhànzhēng 反战争 （乙）名
peace

**常用搭配**
世界和平 world peace　和平协定 a peace agreement

**用法示例**
鸽子是和平的象征。
The dove is the symbol of peace.
我们渴望和平。
We are anxious for peace.
人人都想生活在一个和平的世界里。
Everyone wants to live in a world at peace.

## zāodào
### 遭到 （乙）动
① suffer ② meet with (something unfortunate)

**常用搭配**
遭到破坏 suffer damage　遭到谴责 receive censure

**用法示例**
我的要求遭到了断然拒绝。
My request was met with a flat refusal.

他遭到了失败的打击。
He suffered from a failure.
他遭到了上司的斥责。
He received a rebuke from his superior.

## zhèngguī
### 正规 （丁）形
regular; formal

**常用搭配**
正规教育 formal education
正规军 regular army

**用法示例**
做这种工作不需要任何正规训练。
The job does not require any formal training.
正规文件应该存档。
Regular files should be kept in the archives.

## qìwēn
### 气温 （乙）名
temperature

**常用搭配**
气温下降 descent of temperature
气温升高 temperature rises

**用法示例**
在夏天,这里的气温很高。
In summer the temperature here gets very high.
雨后气温下降了。
There was a temperature drop after rain.
今天的气温是 20 摄氏度。
The temperature today is 20 degrees centigrade.

## jǐnggào gàojiè
### 警告 同告诫 （丙）动/名
① warn ② warning

**常用搭配**
发出警告 put out a warning
我警告你…… I warn you that…

**用法示例**
他因粗心而受到警告。
He was admonished for his carelessness.
妻子警告他开车不要太快。
His wife warned him not to drive too fast.
她不把我们的警告放在心上。
She paid no heed to our warnings.

## jīngrén
### 惊人 （丙）形
astonishing; surprising

**常用搭配**
惊人的消息 surprising news
惊人的速度 astonishing speed

**用法示例**
狮子跑起来速度惊人。
The lion can run with astonishing speed.

记者揭露了一个惊人的秘密。
The reporter discovered a surprising secret.

jīngyà
**惊讶** 	@诧异 chàyì 	（丙）形

surprised

**常用搭配**

惊讶的表情 surprised expression
我对此感到惊讶。I am surprised by it.

**用法示例**

见他起得这么早，我十分惊讶。
I was astonished to see he got up so early.
他惊讶地发现他最好的朋友竟成了叛徒。
He was surprised to discover that his best friend had into a traitor.
听说真相后，她感到很惊讶。
She was surprised when she heard the truth.

yǔqí 	bùrú
**与其……不如……** 	（乙）

**用法示例**

与其说她善良不如说她单纯。
She is not kind so much as simple.
与其说成功在于运气不如说在于努力。
Success lies not so much in luck as it does in hard work.

héǎi 	xiōnghěn
**和蔼** 	@凶狠 	（丁）形

kindly; amiable

**常用搭配**

态度和蔼 amiable attitude
和蔼的老人 a kindly old man

**用法示例**

她是一个和蔼可亲的人。
She is a warm and kindly person.
她对学生总是很和蔼。
She is always amiable to her students.

qìxī
**气息** 	（丁）名

breath

**常用搭配**

春天的气息 a breath of spring in the air
东方的气息 a breath of the orient

**用法示例**

今天的天气已露出了一丝秋天的气息。
There is a breath of autumn in the air today.
他的油画里有佛教的某种气息。
There is a breath of Buddhism in his painting.

## 词义辨析

**受到、遭到**

　　"受到"和"遭到"都是动词，都有遇到不如意的事情的意思，都有被动含义。但是"遭到"的宾语只能是坏事或使人不愉快的事，而"受到"还有得到的意思，宾语也可以是好事。例如：①他遭到／受到了上司的斥责。②她受到了老板的表扬。

　　The two verbs mean "to undergo something unpleasant", and both have a passive sense. But the object of 遭受 must be something bad or undesirable; while 受到 also means "to receive, to get", and the object may be something good. For example: ① He received a rebuke from his superior. ② She received praise from her boss.

 练习

**练习一、根据拼音写汉字，根据汉字写拼音**

( )ǎi ( )yà jǐng ( ) ( )guī zāo ( )
和( ) 惊( ) ( )告 正( ) ( )到

**练习二、搭配连线**

(1) 春天的　　　　　　　A. 老师
(2) 和蔼的　　　　　　　B. 表情
(3) 惊讶的　　　　　　　C. 速度
(4) 惊人的　　　　　　　D. 教育
(5) 正规的　　　　　　　E. 气息

**练习三、从今天学习的生词中选择合适的词填空**

1. 他因工作出色而 _____ 公司的奖励。
2. 他们俩的婚事 _____ 了父母的反对。
3. 十年没见，你的 _____ 不大，还是那么漂亮。
4. 医生 _____ 病人：抽烟会使病情加重。
5. 这个东西的尺寸与标准有出入，不是 _____ 货。
6. _____ 坐火车 _____ 坐飞机呢，票价仅相差 200 块钱，可是快多了。
7. 他个子不高，力气却大得 _____ ，能搬动二百多斤重的东西。
8. 令我感到 _____ 的是，他们才结婚两个月就离婚了。
9. 这对老夫妻对我态度非常 _____ 。
10. 他的作品具有浓厚的乡土 _____ 。

**答案**

**练习一：**
略

**练习二：**

(1) E　　　(2)A　　　(3)B　　　(4)C　　　(5)D

**练习三：**

1. 受到　　2. 遭到　　3. 变化　　4. 警告　　5. 正规
6. 与其，不如　　7. 惊人　　8. 惊讶　　9. 和蔼
10. 气息

---

 星期四 Thursday

**tuánjié**
**团结**　　　　　　　　　　　　　（甲）动

① unite ② hold together

**常用搭配**

咱们团结起来。Let's stick together.
团结人民 unite people

**用法示例**

总统号召全国人民团结起来。
The President made a call for national unity.
保守党在紧要关头总是能团结一致。
The Tory party always bands together in times of crisis.
只要我们紧密团结就能克服这些困难。
We can surely overcome these difficulties as long as we are closely united.

**suīrán　　　dànshì**
**虽然……但是……**　　　　　　（乙）

although...but...

**常用搭配**

虽然贵但是好。
It is good though it is expensive.

**用法示例**

虽然他们很穷，但是很快乐。
Although they are poor they are happy.
那篇文章虽然很短，但是很重要。
The article is very important though it is short.

**lìhai**
**厉害**　　　　　　　　　　　　（乙）形

serious; terrible

**常用搭配**

天气冷得厉害。It's terrible cold.
牙疼得厉害 dreadful toothache

**用法示例**

她病得厉害，我们要马上去请医生。
She is seriously ill, we have to send for a doctor at once.
我今天早上头痛得厉害。
I've got a terrible headache this morning.
那头厉害的狮子一下子就挣脱了锁链。
The fierce lion burst free from the chains.

**yǒuxiào　　　　　wúxiào**
**有效**　　反 无效　　　　　　（乙）形

① in effect ② effective

**常用搭配**

有效的方法 an effective method
采取有效措施 take effective measures

**（用法示例）**

这种药治头痛很有效。

The medicine is an effective cure for a headache.

旧制度仍有效。

The old system is still in effect.

这些票的有效期是一个月。

These tickets are available for one month only.

mìngyùn
## 命运 （乙）名

destiny；fate

**（常用搭配）**

不幸的命运 unfortunate fate

民族的命运 destiny of a nation

**（用法示例）**

每个人都是自己命运的创造者。

Everyone is the architect of his own fortune.

有些人相信，命运之神支配人类的命运。

Some people believe that the Fates preside over man's destiny.

命运有时是残酷的。

Destiny is sometimes cruel.

liángshi
## 粮食 （乙）名

foodstuffs；provisions

**（常用搭配）**

粮食短缺 food shortage

粮食生产 food-grain production

**（用法示例）**

他曾是粮食商人。

He was a provisions merchant.

他们又从加拿大订购了一些粮食。

They have ordered more grain from Canada.

这是一家国际粮食贸易公司。

The company is an international trader in grain.

shíshī                  shīxíng
## 实施 ◉ 施行 （丙）动

to implement；to carry out

**（常用搭配）**

实施他的计划 carry out his plan

实施一个设想 implement an idea

**（用法示例）**

这些计划终于得以实施。

The plans were finally put into execution.

政府正要实施一项新政策。

The government is going to implement a new policy.

下个月将实施新法规。

The new law comes into force next month.

lìbì               déshī
## 利弊 ◉ 得失 （丁）名

① advantages and disadvantages ② merits and demerits

**（常用搭配）**

分析利弊 analyze merits and demerits

**（用法示例）**

每种选择都各有利弊。

Each choice has it's own advantages and disadvantages.

咱们考虑一下搬家的利弊吧。

Let's consider the pluses and minuses of moving house.

我希望你们权衡一下利弊。

I want you to consider the pros and cons.

yánlì
## 严厉 （丙）形

strict；stern

**（常用搭配）**

严厉的家长 a strict parent    严厉斥责 a stern rebuke

对我们严厉 be severe on us

**（用法示例）**

他对孩子们太严厉了。

He's much too stern with his children.

他应该受到法律的严厉惩罚。

He deserves to be punished with the full force of the law.

jiāoqū
## 郊区 （乙）名

suburb

**（常用搭配）**

北京郊区 suburb of Beijing

**（用法示例）**

他住在郊区，但在城里工作。

He lives in the suburb and works in the city.

他在郊区有一套别墅。

He has a villa in the suburbs.

wúxiào
## 无效 （丁）形

① in vain ② be of no effect

**（常用搭配）**

无效合同 invalid contracts    无效文件 invalid papers

**（用法示例）**

这张支票是无效的。

This cheque is null and void.

这是无效护照，它已经过期了。

It is a invalid passport because it is out of date.

法官宣布遗嘱无效。

The judge declared the will invalid.

shíyù
## 食欲 （丁）名

appetite

**（常用搭配）**

食欲不振 lack of appetite    促进食欲 whet the appetite

**（用法示例）**

我生病时完全没有食欲。

When I was ill I completely lost my appetite.

长时间的走路使他食欲旺盛。
The long walk gave him a good appetite.
饭前不要吃糖以免影响食欲。
Don't spoil your appetite by eating sweets before meals.

 词义辨析

**厉害、严厉**

　　"厉害"和"严厉"都是形容词,都可以表示人的态度不温和,都可以做定语,但"厉害"经常加"得"作补语,还可以表示程度很深或难以忍受,一般不做状语;"严厉"经常加"地"作状语,表示严肃而厉害,一般不作补语。例如:①他对孩子们太严厉/厉害了。②老师严厉地训斥了他。③我今天早上头痛得厉害。

　　Both 厉害 and 严厉 are adjectives, meaning "to be stern", and can function as an attributive. But 厉害 often takes 得 to function as a complement, indicating "severe, of high degree or hard to deal with", and seldom functions as an adverbial; while 严厉 often takes 地 to function as an adverbial, indicating "serious and stern", and seldom functions as an attributive. For example: ① He's much too stern with his children. ② The teacher rebuked him strongly. ③ I've got a terrible headache this morning.

 练习

**练习一、根据拼音写汉字,根据汉字写拼音**
(　)yù　(　)bì　(　)shī　lì(　)　tuán(　)
食(　)　利(　)　实(　)　(　)害　(　)结

**练习二、搭配连线**
(1) 促进　　　　　　　　A. 计划
(2) 权衡　　　　　　　　B. 短缺
(3) 实施　　　　　　　　C. 措施
(4) 粮食　　　　　　　　D. 食欲
(5) 有效　　　　　　　　E. 利弊

**练习三、从今天学习的生词中选择合适的词填空**
1. 这药非常_____,我吃了三天,血压就恢复正常了。
2. 我们保证这种保健品的疗效,如果您用后_____,我们可以退款。
3. 昨天喝酒太多了,今天早上我觉得头疼得_____。
4. 他的家在_____,离市区有二十公里。
5._____他很努力,_____他的学习方法不太好。
6. 禁烟令将从下周开始_____,以后不能在公共场合吸烟了。
7. 听说多运动可以促进_____,可我做完运动还是不想吃饭。
8. 父亲对我们很_____,以至于孩子们都有点怕他。
9. 这部小说中女主人公的_____十分悲惨。
10. 我现在的工作虽然轻松但是工资很低,而那份工作的工资高却要求经常加班,两份工作各有_____。

**答案**

**练习一:**
略
**练习二:**
(1) D　　　　(2)E　　　　(3)A　　　　(4)B　　　　(5)C
**练习三:**
1. 有效　　2. 无效　　3. 厉害　　4. 郊区
5. 虽然,但是　　6. 实施　　7. 食欲
8. 严厉　　9.命运　　10. 利弊

## 星期五

### fēicháng
### 非常 （甲）副

very; extremely

**常用搭配**

天气非常热。It is terribly hot.
非常感谢您 be extremely grateful to you

**用法示例**

辛苦工作了四个小时后,他觉得非常饿。
He felt very hungry after four-hours' hard work.
我在一家非常富有创新精神的公司工作。
I worked in a very innovative company.
我非常抱歉。
I'm extremely sorry.
她非常喜欢它。
She enjoys it very much.

### búdàn érqiě
### 不但……而且…… （乙）

not only... but also...

**常用搭配**

她不但做了而且做得很好。
She did it, and she did it well.

**用法示例**

他不但会说汉语,而且能写汉字。
He can not only speak in Chinese, but also write Chinese characters.
她不但漂亮,而且聪明。
She is not only beautiful but also clever.
她不但参加了比赛,而且获胜了!
She not only entered the competition, she actually won it!

### yìcháng
### 异常 （乙）形

① exceptional; abnormal ② extremely

**常用搭配**

异常的天气 exceptional weather
异常现象 abnormal phenomenon
异常寒冷 extremely cold

**用法示例**

不知为什么,最近他的行为有些异常。
His behavior is somewhat abnormal recently.
这些天我们异常忙碌。
We are extremely busy these days.

### kànbuqǐ
### 看不起 （乙）

look down upon; despise

**常用搭配**

看不起他人 look down upon others

**用法示例**

我希望你不要看不起这种工作。
I wish you wouldn't look down on this kind of work.
她是专业画家,看不起业余画家。
As a professional painter, she scorns amateurs.
考试不要作弊,否则同学们会看不起你。
Don't cheat on examinations, or your classmates will despise you.

### qiángliè jīliè
### 强烈 回激烈 （乙）形

strong; intense

**常用搭配**

强烈的气味 strong smell
强烈的光线 fierce light
强烈的愿望 fierce attempt

**用法示例**

他对敌人有强烈的仇恨。
He has a fierce hatred of his enemy.
她感到他对她有强烈的吸引力。
She felt a strong attraction to him.
他的计划遭到了强烈的反对。
His plan was opposed with fierceness.

### liàn'ài
### 恋爱 （乙）动/名

① to be in love ② love affair

**常用搭配**

三角恋爱 love triangle
跟她谈恋爱 be in love with her

**用法示例**

他们在恋爱。
They are in love.
班里的每一个人都知道他们在恋爱。
Everyone in the class knows they are in love.
医院禁止医生与病人谈恋爱。
The hospital forbids a doctor to have a love affair with a patient.

### xǐ'ài
### 喜爱 （丙）动

to like; be fond of

**常用搭配**

我最喜爱的老师 my favorite teacher
我喜爱的运动 my favorite sport

**用法示例**

我最喜爱的消遣是读书。
My favorite pastime is reading.
全世界的人都喜爱大熊猫。
Pandas are loved by people all over the world.

老人爱所有的孩子,不过她特别喜爱小儿子。
The old lady likes all her children, but she's especially fond of her youngest son.

jǐngchá
**警察** （乙）名

① policeman ② police

**常用搭配**
警察局 police station　交通警察 traffic police

**用法示例**
他爸爸是一名警察。
His father is a policeman.
警察正在调查这起谋杀案。
The police are investigating the murder.
警察找回了被盗的珠宝。
The police recovered the stolen jewelry.

jǐngtì　　　　　jǐngjué
**警惕** 同 警觉 （丙）动

① guard against ② be vigilant

**常用搭配**
保持警惕 be on guard　放松警惕 relax one's vigilance

**用法示例**
警察说公众应提高警惕。
The police said that the public should be more vigilant.
危险正逼近,我们必须保持警惕。
When danger is imminent we must all be on guard.
警方警告群众警惕恐怖分子。
Police warned the public to be alert for terrorists.

bùyóude
**不由得** （丙）副

cannot help ( doing )

**常用搭配**
不由得想到…… cannot help thinking…

**用法示例**
读这本书的时候,我不由得回忆起自己的童年。
Reading the book, I can not help recalling my childhood.
听说了他的遭遇,我不由得同情起他来。
Hearing of his suffering, I can not help sympathizing with him.
听了这话,他不由得笑了起来。
Hearing the words, he couldn't keep from laughing.

xūwěi　　　　　zhēnchéng
**虚伪** 反 真诚 （丁）形

hypocritical; false

**常用搭配**
虚伪的夸奖 hypocritical praise
虚伪的态度 artificial manners
他很虚伪。He is very hypocritical.

**用法示例**
他是一个很虚伪的人,假装不知道那件事。
He is nothing but a hypocrite, pretending that he knows nothing about it.

她脸上挂着虚伪的笑容来欢迎我们。
She welcomed us with an artificial smile on her face.
她说的话听起来有点儿虚伪。
Her remarks smacked of hypocrisy.

xūruò　　　　　qiángzhuàng
**虚弱** 反 强壮 （丁）形

① weak ② in poor health

**常用搭配**
她身体虚弱。She is weak.

**用法示例**
他虚弱得连手都抬不起来。
He was too weak to even lift his hand.
手术后她仍然很虚弱。
She was still weak after her operation.
我生病的时候感到很虚弱。
I felt feeble when I was ill.

 **词义辨析**

**非常、异常**

1、"非常"和"异常"都可以做副词,都表示程度很高。只是"异常"主要用作书面语,语意比"非常"更重。例如:①我非常高兴。②他异常兴奋。

Both 非常 and 异常 are adverbs, indicating "in a high degree; extremely". But 异常 is mainly used in writing and sounds more serious than "非常". For example: ① I am very glad. ② He is extremely excited.

2、作为形容词,"非常"和"异常"都表示不同寻常。但"非常"只能做定语,修饰几个固定的名词,如:时期、措施、事件等;而"异常"可以作定语和谓语,可以用来表示各种特殊情况。例如:①在非常时期,政府采取了一些非常的措施。②今年春天天气异常。

As adjectives, 非常 and 异常 mean "unusual". But 非常 just functions as an attributive and modifies a few nouns, such as "时期" (period of time), "措施" (measure), "事件" (event), etc.; while 异常 can function as an attributive and a predicate, and it refers to many kinds of unusual things. For example: ① The government took some extraordinary measures during the time of emergency. ② The weather is abnormal this spring.

练习

**练习一、根据拼音写汉字，根据汉字写拼音**

yì ( )　　jǐng ( )　　xū ( )　　liàn ( )　　( )liè
( )常　　( )惕　　( )伪　　( )爱　　强( )

**练习二、搭配连线**

(1) 交通　　　　　　　　A. 现象
(2) 异常　　　　　　　　B. 虚伪
(3) 保持　　　　　　　　C. 虚弱
(4) 态度　　　　　　　　D. 警惕
(5) 身体　　　　　　　　E. 警察

**练习三、从今天学习的生词中选择合适的词填空**

1. 她的同学们说,在她自杀以前,并没有发现她有什么_____行为。

2. 你们不该_____残疾人,更不该嘲笑他们。

3. 我们在公共汽车上抓住了一个小偷,并且把他押送到了_____局。

4. 我最_____的音乐家是贝多芬,他的音乐作品充满了激情和力量。

5. 这个运动员有个_____的愿望:在退役前赢得一块奥运金牌。

6. 我们以为她不敢比赛,结果她_____参赛了,_____夺得了第一名。

7. 看电影的时候,明明知道是编造的故事,还是_____被感动。

8. 自从发生两起盗窃案后,人们都对陌生人提高了_____。

9. 由于流了很多血,这个病人的身体相当_____。

10. 他说他会尽力帮助我们,其实他根本不想帮我们,这个人真_____。

答案

**练习一:**
略

**练习二:**
(1) E　　(2)A　　(3)D　　(4)B　　(5)C

**练习三:**
1. 异常　　2. 看不起　　3. 警察　　4. 喜爱　　5. 强烈
6. 不但,而且　　7. 不由得　　8. 警惕　　9. 虚弱
10. 虚伪

# 第7月,第2周的练习

**练习一 . 根据词语给加点的字注音**
1.( ) 2.( )     3.( )     4.( )     5.( )
有效    郊区    和蔼    签署    虚伪

**练习二 . 根据拼音填写词语**
    shī    shí        lì      lì        lì
1.实( ) 2.( )欲 3.来( ) 4.( )害 5.( )弊

**练习三 . 辨析并选择合适的词填空**
1. 明天下午有课,我( )不去打球了。( 不得不、只好、得 )
2. 我请人帮助的时候( )客气一点,要有礼貌。( 不得不、只好、得 )
3. 他取得了点成绩就自以为( )。( 不得了、了不起 )
4. 这菜辣得( ),我吃不下。( 不得了、了不起 )
5. 他的决定( )家人一致反对。( 受到、遭到 )
6. 学期结束时,全勤生( )了表扬和奖励。( 受到、遭到 )
7. 老师( )地批评了那两名打架的学生。( 厉害、严厉 )
8. 我昨天晚上咳嗽得很( ),几乎一夜没睡。( 厉害、严厉 )
9. 由于环境遭到人为破坏,气候变得( )了。( 非常、异常 )
10. 在这( )时期,政府可以不按照通常的方式处理问题。
( 非常、异常 )

**练习四 . 选词填空**
来自    亲戚    惊讶    惊奇    警察
来源    亲切    惊人    警告    警惕
1. 科学家在那个洞穴里发现了一个( )的秘密。
2. 我的房东是个老太太,待人非常( )。
3. 她男朋友是个( ),长得很帅。
4. 他失业了,没有了经济( )。
5. 最近这条路上经常发生抢劫案,大家一定要提高( )。
6. 第一次参观海洋馆,看到那么多海洋动物,孩子们感到特别( )。
7. 在北京学习的外国留学生( )世界各地。
8. 裁判拿出黄牌,( )犯规的运动员。
9. 我们两家是( ),他爸爸是我舅舅。
10. 她开开门,然后( )地叫了起来,她发现孩子正站在窗台上。

**练习五 . 选择关联词填空**
不但……而且……     虽然……但是……
与其……不如……     不是……而是……
不是……就是……
1. 他一直很自立,他认为( )依靠别人,还( )依靠自己。
2. 你应该感谢的( )我,( )这位医生,是他救了你。
3. 这钱包( )你的( )他的,反正不是我的。
4. ( )大家都想得第一名,( )冠军只能是一个人。
5. 她( )漂亮( )懂事,上哪找这么好的女朋友啊!

**练习六 . 写出下列词语的同义词**
1. 来源( )      2. 警惕( )
3. 实行( )      4. 比较( )
5. 惊讶( )

**练习七 . 写出下列词语的反义词**
1. 虚伪( )      2. 和蔼( )
3. 虚弱( )      4. 和平( )
5. 有效( )

## 答案

**练习一 .**
1.xiào    2.jiāo    3. ǎi    4.shǔ    5.xū

**练习二 .**
1. 施    2. 食    3. 历    4. 厉    5. 利

**练习三 .**
1. 只好    2. 得    3. 了不起    4. 不得了    5. 遭到
6. 受到    7. 严厉    8. 厉害    9. 异常    10. 非常

**练习四 .**
1. 惊人    2. 亲切    3. 警察    4. 来源    5. 警惕
6. 惊奇    7. 来自    8. 警告    9. 亲戚    10. 惊讶

**练习五 .**
1. 与其,不如      2. 不是,而是
3. 不是,就是      4. 虽然,但是
5. 不但,而且

**练习六 .**
1. 起源    2. 警觉    3. 施行    4. 对比
5. 惊奇 / 诧异

**练习七 .**
1. 真诚    2. 粗暴    3. 强壮    4. 战争    5. 无效

# 7月 第3周的学习内容

**星期一**

jiéshù
**结束** 反 开始 kāishǐ　（甲）动

finish; end

**常用搭配**

结束演讲 to conclude a speech
战争结束了。The war was over.

**用法示例**

电影在六点钟前就结束了。
The movie was over before six.
他们决定结束彼此的关系。
They decided to end their relationship.

jīqì
**机器** （甲）名

machine; machinery

**常用搭配**

维修机器 repair a machine　机器零件 the machine parts

**用法示例**

如果机器出故障，就把开关关掉。
Turn off the switch when something goes wrong with the machine.
这台机器是电动的。
The machine is powered by electricity.
他们在安装新机器。
They are installing a new machine.

mùbiāo
**目标** （乙）名

objective; target

**常用搭配**

瞄准目标 aim at the target　生活的目标 life goal

**用法示例**

他的目标是在 10 月前完成任务。
His objective was to finish the task by October.
该公司已经实现了它们的出口目标。
The company has met their export target.
静止的目标是最容易瞄准的。
A stationary target is easiest to aim at.

mùdì
**目的** （乙）名

purpose; aim

**常用搭配**

达到目的 accomplish one's purpose
访问的目的 purpose of visit

**用法示例**

你做那件事的目的是什么？
What is your purpose in doing that?
她学习的目的是为人民服务。
Her purpose in learning is to serve the people.
我们花了一整天才到达目的地。
It took us a day to reach our destination.

búyàojǐn
**不要紧** 同 没关系 méiguānxi　（乙）

① it doesn't matter ② never mind ③ not serious

**常用搭配**

即使……也不要紧 It does not matter if ...

**用法示例**

即使我错过了公共汽车也不要紧，我可以步行。
It doesn't matter if I miss this bus, I can walk.
你没赶上公共汽车吗？不要紧，五分钟就来一辆。
Did you miss the bus? Never mind, there'll be another one in five minutes.
我负伤了，不过不要紧。
I was wounded, but not seriously.

bùyídìng
**不一定** （乙）

① not necessarily ② not always

**常用搭配**

他不一定来。He is not necessarily going to come.

**用法示例**

学习外语不一定很难。
The studying a foreign language is not necessarily difficult.
财富并不一定会带来幸福。
Happiness is not always annexed to wealth.
老师说的也不一定对。
What teacher says is not always correct.

fúcóng
**服从** 反 违抗 wéikàng　（乙）动

obey

**常用搭配**

服从命令 to obey an order
拒绝服从 refuse to obey
服从安排 submit to an arrangement

**用法示例**

军人必须服从命令。
Soldiers must obey orders.

他拒绝服从不公正的决定。
He refused to submit to an unjust decision.

## wànyī
# 万一　　　　　　　　　　　　（丙）名／连

① contingency ② in case

**常用搭配**
以防万一 be prepared for the worst

**用法示例**
你最好随身带把伞,以防万一。
You'd better take along an umbrella, just in case.
万一下雨,他们就不能去了。
In the event of rain they will not be able to go.
万一火车晚点,就不要等我了。
If by any chance the train is late, do not wait for me.

## búzàihu
# 不在乎　　　圓 无所谓 wúsuǒwèi　　（丙）

① not mind ② not care

**常用搭配**
我根本不在乎。I do not mind at all.
我不在乎输赢。I do not care whether I win or lose.

**用法示例**
我不在乎你们会说我什么。
I do not care what you say about me.
无论走多远,我都不在乎。
I don't care how far I'll have to go.
她不在乎你是否喜欢她。
She does not care whether you like her or not.

## qìguān
# 器官　　　　　　　　　　　　（丙）名

organ

**常用搭配**
嗅觉器官 organs of smell　　味觉器官 organs of taste

**用法示例**
肺是呼吸器官。
The lungs are respiratory organs.
眼睛是视觉器官。
The eyes are the organs of sight.
心脏是要害器官。
The heart is a vital organ.

## qìcái
# 器材　　　　　　　　　　　　（丙）名

equipment; apparatus

**常用搭配**
五金器材 hardware materials
电子器材 electronic equipment

**用法示例**
体育馆里有许多体育器材。
There is a lot of sports apparatus in the gym.
仓库保管员负责实验器材。
The store keeper is in charge of the experimental equipment.

## yuèqì
# 乐器　　　　　　　　　　　　（丙）名

musical instrument

**常用搭配**
乐器店 musical instruments' shop

**用法示例**
他会演奏多种乐器。
He can play many kinds of musical instruments.
钢琴是他最喜欢的乐器。
The piano is his favorite musical instrument.
乐队在给乐器调音。
The orchestra tuned their instruments.

 **词义辨析**

**目标、目的**
　　"目标"和"目的"都是名词,表示想要达到的结果或效果。一般情况下,"目标"比较具体、明确,比如:攻击或寻找的对象,想达到的标准等;"目的"比较抽象、广泛,比如:行为的意图,想得到的结果等。例如:①这个猎人的目标是一只野兽。②他的目标是游一英里。③你生活的目的是什么?
　　Both 目标 and 目的 are nouns, indicating "a result or an effect that is intended or desired". Generally, 目标 is more concrete and definite, such as the target of shooting or looking for, the aim toward which one's efforts are directed; 目的 is quite abstract and wide, such as intention or purpose of an endeavor. For example: ① The hunter's target was a wild animal. ② His aim was to swim a mile. ③ What is your aim in life?

 **练习**

**练习一、根据拼音写汉字，根据汉字写拼音**

( )qì （ ）cóng （ ）dì （ ）shù （ ）jǐn
乐( ) 服( ) 目( ) 结( ) 要( )

**练习二、搭配连线**

(1) 维修　　　　　A. 目的
(2) 服从　　　　　B. 机器
(3) 演奏　　　　　C. 器材
(4) 达到　　　　　D. 乐器
(5) 实验　　　　　E. 命令

**练习三、从今天学习的生词中选择合适的词填空**

1. 他是修理工，负责维修生产线上的 _____。
2. 我们这次来你们公司参观考察的 _____ 是要向你们学习管理经验。
3. 他目前的 _____ 是多赚钱，买一套属于自己的房子。
4. 他只想努力完成自己的愿望，至于别人怎么说，他根本 _____。
5. 医生说他就是有点感冒，_____，休息休息就好了。
6. 天气预报说下午会下雨，但我觉得 _____。
7. 自己开车旅游的时候，要带一条备用轮胎和一些药，以防 _____。
8. 因为不 _____ 公司的工作安排，他被公司开除了。
9. 胃是食物的消化 _____，中医认为胃不能受凉。
10. 我们学校又购买了一批新的体育锻炼 _____。

**答案**

**练习一：**
略
**练习二：**
(1) B　　(2)E　　(3)D　　(4)A　　(5)C
**练习三：**
1. 机器　2. 目的　3. 目标　4. 不在乎　5. 不要紧
6. 不一定　7. 万一　8. 服从　9. 器官　10. 器材

---

 **星期二**

yùdào
**遇到**　　　　　　　　　　　　　　（甲）动
to meet; encounter

**常用搭配**
遇到困难 encounter difficulties
碰巧遇到 happen to meet
遇到一位朋友 meet with a friend

**用法示例**
年轻的科学家们在探险期间遇到了许多困难。
The young scientists encountered many difficulties during their exploration.
我在街上遇到了他。
I met him in the street.
我下班回家碰巧遇到了小李。
I happened to meet Xiao Li on my way home from work.

duìxiàng
**对象**　　　　　　　　　　　　　　（乙）名
object

**常用搭配**
嘲笑的对象 an object of derision
打击的对象 an object of attack

**用法示例**
我的研究对象是中国经济。
The Chinese economy is the subject of my research.
他是我们应该帮助的对象。
He is the person whom we should help.
她成了宴会上人们赞美的对象。
She became the object of admiration at the dinner party.

láibùjí
**来不及**　　　　　　　　　　　　　　（乙）
① there's not enough time to do sth. ② it's too late

**常用搭配**
来不及准备 There is little time to prepare.

**用法示例**
快，否则你就来不及了。
Hurry up or you'll be late.
来不及仔细考虑
There is no time to think it over.
我已经来不及做准备了。
I had no time in which to prepare.

láidejí
**来得及**　　　　　　　　　　　　　　（乙）
① there's still time ② be able to do sth. in time

**常用搭配**
时间还来得及。There's still enough time.

**用法示例**

我们十点能到机场,还来得及为他们送行。

We can get to the airport before 10：00. There will still be time to see them off.

今天是星期六,我想我还来得及完成家庭作业。

Today is Saturday. I think I have enough time to finish my homework.

抱歉,我来上海以前没来得及把每件事都安排好。

Sorry, I haven't had time to arrange everything before I leave for Shanghai.

**jùdà**
# 巨大　　　　　　　回 庞大 *pángdà*　　（乙）形

huge; enormous

**常用搭配**

巨大的轮船 a colossal ship

巨大的风险 enormous risk

**用法示例**

这部电视剧取得了巨大的成功。

The TV play was a huge success.

这架新飞机看起来像一只巨大的鸟。

The new airplane looked like a gigantic bird.

**fánróng**
# 繁荣　　　　　　　回 兴旺 *xīngwàng*　　（乙）形／动

① prosperous ② make sth. prosperous

**常用搭配**

经济繁荣 economic boom　　繁荣的城镇 a boom town

**用法示例**

这家商场的生意日趋繁荣。

Business in this shop is booming.

和平带来繁荣。

Peace brings prosperity.

这地方由原来的渔港发展成了一个繁荣的旅游胜地。

The place has developed from a fishing port into a thriving tourist centre.

**tǎngruò**
# 倘若　　　　　　　　　　　　　　（丙）连

if; provided

**常用搭配**

倘若不想去就别去。Don't go if you don't want to.

**用法示例**

倘若那是真的,我们该怎么办呢？

If that is true, what should we do?

倘若没有其他人想借这本书的话,你可以再续借一个礼拜。

You may keep the book for a further week provided (that) no one else requires it.

**fùgài**
# 覆盖　　　　　　　　　　　　　　（丁）动

cover with; overlay

**常用搭配**

冰雪覆盖了道路。Snow covered the roads.

**用法示例**

这座山终年覆盖着积雪。

The mountain is covered with snow all year round.

绿草和鲜花覆盖着田野。

The field is covered with green grass and colorful flowers.

**yǎngài**
# 掩盖　　　　　　　反 揭露 *jiēlù*　　（丙）动

cover up; conceal

**常用搭配**

掩盖实情 cover up reality

**用法示例**

谎言掩盖不住事实。

Lies cannot obscure facts.

不要试图掩盖错误。

Do not try to cover up a mistake.

**bàolù**
# 暴露　　　　　　　反 隐藏 *yǐncáng*　　（丙）动

reveal; expose

**常用搭配**

暴露无遗 be thoroughly exposed

暴露身份 reveal one's identity

**用法示例**

她一时口误暴露了自己的动机。

Through a slip of the tongue she exposed her true motivation.

那时他没暴露他的真实身份。

He didn't reveal his real identity at that time.

炊烟暴露了敌人的位置。

The smoke from their cooking fire betrayed the location of the enemy.

**bàozhà**
# 爆炸　　　　　　　　　　　　　　（丙）动

explode

**常用搭配**

煤气爆炸 gas explosion

爆炸声 explosive sound

人口爆炸 population explosion

**用法示例**

炸弹爆炸了。

The bomb exploded.

爆炸发出巨大的响声。

The explosion gave forth a tremendous sound.

这次爆炸是由于一个爆裂的煤气管引起的。

The explosion was caused by a burst gas pipe.

**duìzhào**
# 对照　　　　　　　　　　　　　　（丁）动

contrast; compare

**常用搭配**

对照两组数据 contrast two sets of data

鲜明的对照 a striking contrast

**用法示例**

作家使美好与邪恶形成对照。
The writer contrasts good with evil.
蓝天和白云形成鲜明的对照。
Blue sky and white clouds show a striking contrast.
警察把伪造的签名与原来的签名进行对照。
The police compared the forged signature with the original.

## 词义辨析

**覆盖、掩盖**

　　"覆盖"和"掩盖"都是动词,都有把某物遮盖起来的意思,"覆盖"一般是用具体的物体遮盖另一个具体的物体;而"掩盖"往往是用某种方法或方式使人不能了解真实的情况或意图。例如:①地板上覆盖着一层尘土。②他表现出很有信心的样子以掩盖内心的紧张。

　　Both 覆盖 and 掩盖 are verbs, meaning "to place something upon or over". 覆盖 usually indicates "to cover a concrete thing with other concrete things; while 掩盖 usually indicates "to conceal a fact or purpose by some way or manner", "to keep a fact or purpose from being found out, or discovered". For example: ① The floor was covered with dust. ② An outward show of confidence concealed his nervousness.

## 练习

**练习一、根据拼音写汉字,根据汉字写拼音**

bào（　　）fù（　　）bào（　　）tǎng（　　）fán（　　）
（　　）露　（　　）盖（　　）炸（　　）若（　　）荣

**练习二、搭配连线**

(1) 碰巧　　　　　　　　A. 对象
(2) 研究　　　　　　　　B. 爆炸
(3) 经济　　　　　　　　C. 实情
(4) 掩盖　　　　　　　　D. 繁荣
(5) 煤气　　　　　　　　E. 遇到

**练习三、从今天学习的生词中选择合适的词填空**

1. 我希望我的国家变得越来越 _____ 富强。
2. 富士山的山顶终年 _____ 着皑皑白雪。
3. 我是她最好的朋友, _____ 我不去参加她的婚礼,她一定会不高兴的。
4. 电影七点半才开始,我们六点四十出发完全 _____ 。
5. 楼下有个女孩约我哥哥去玩儿,哥哥 _____ 吃饭就跑下去了。
6. 记者今天要采访的 _____ 是一位著名的音乐家。
7. 加油站着火了,石油随时可能会 _____ ,情况非常危急。
8. 这本《北京指南》是英汉 _____ 的,外国人使用起来很方便。
9. 短短二十年,我们国家的经济建设取得了 _____ 的成就。
10. 他想 _____ 错误,结果他犯了更大的错误。

## 答案

练习一:
略

练习二:
(1) E　　　(2)A　　　(3)D　　　(4)C　　　(5)B

练习三:
1. 繁荣　　2. 覆盖　　3. 倘若　　4. 来得及　　5. 来不及
6. 对象　　7. 爆炸　　8. 对照　　9. 巨大　　10. 掩盖

**星期三**

**jiànmiàn**
**见面**　　　　　　　　　huìmiàn　圆 会面　　　　　　（甲）动

meet; see (someone)

**常用搭配**
与某人见面 meet somebody
跟某人见过一次面 have met somebody once before

**用法示例**
希望我们很快能再见面。
I hope we meet again soon.
在不久的将来,我们将在北京见面。
We will meet in Beijing in the near future.
下星期我们没有见面的机会了。
We will not have the opportunity to meet with each other a week from now.

**qǐtú**
**企图**　　　　　　　　　　　　　（乙）动／名

① attempt ② in an attempt to do something

**常用搭配**
企图逃跑 attempt to escape

**用法示例**
敌人做那件事的企图是什么?
What is enemy's purpose in doing that?
他企图干涉我的工作。
He attempts to interfere with my work.
他企图欺骗我们,但没有得逞。
His attempt to deceive us was foiled.

**zhǐyǒu**　　**cái**
**只有……才……**　　　　　　　　　（丙）

only that…

**常用搭配**
只有夏天才下雨。Only in summer does it rain.

**用法示例**
只有医生才能这样做。
Only a doctor can do that.
只有在麻醉师给病人施行麻醉以后,手术才能进行。
Only after the anesthetist gave the patient an anesthetic, could the operation be performed.
我们只有乘飞机才能及时到那儿。
Only by air could we get there in time.

**jìngsài**
**竞赛**　　　　　　　　bǐsài　圆 比赛　　　　　（乙）动

contest; compete

**常用搭配**
军备竞赛 competition in arms
生产竞赛 production emulation

**用法示例**
他在竞赛中显示出了精湛的技艺。
He displayed a flawless technique in the competition.
他在竞赛中名列第二十。
He placed twentieth in the competition.
他将参加竞赛。
He will attend the competition.

**zhíjiē**
**直接**　　　　　　　　　　　　（乙）形

direct; immediate

**常用搭配**
直接原因 immediate cause
直接去北京 go straight to Beijing

**用法示例**
放学后直接回家。
Come home straight after school.
他们直接从厂商那里购买了这台机器。
They bought the machine directly from the manufacturer.
发言人从来不直接回答记者提出的问题。
The spokesman never gave a direct answer to any of the reporters questions.

**jìngzhēng**
**竞争**　　　　　　　　　　　　（丙）动／名

① to compete ② competition

**常用搭配**
与他竞争 compete with him　　价格竞争 price competition
不正当竞争 unfair competition

**用法示例**
我们的价格是有竞争力的。
Our prices are competitive.
国际竞争是实现现代化的动力。
International competition is a spur to modernization.
因为失业严重,求职的竞争十分激烈。
Because there is so much unemployment, the competition for jobs is fierce.

**fùdān**　　　　　　　　　　yālì
**负担**　　　　　　　　　圆 压力　　　（丙）动／名

① bear ② burden

**常用搭配**
经济负担 economic burden　　沉重的负担 heavy burdens

**用法示例**
新娘的父母将负担婚礼的费用。
The bride's parents will bear the cost of the wedding.
她认为太多的赞扬是一种负担。
She thinks too much praise is a burden.
他摆脱不了精神负担。
He wasn't rid of his mental burden.

**dānfù**
**担负**　　　　　　　　　　　　（丙）动

undertake; bear

**【常用搭配】**

担负……责任 bear responsibility for…

**【用法示例】**

我们经理将离开我们,并在其他部门担负起新的职责。

Our manager will leave us and undertake fresh responsibilities in another department.

作为教师,我们担负着教育下一代的责任。

Being teachers, we bear the responsibility of educating the young generation.

shènzhì

**甚至** （丙）副/连

even

**【用法示例】**

他很沮丧,甚至想自杀。

He was depressed, even suicidal.

他看上去不难过,甚至可以说很愉快。

He doesn't look sad, he looks pleasant even.

甚至他最好的朋友也不相信他的话。

Even his closest friends didn't believe what he said.

qiánchéng

**前程** （丁）名

future；prospects

**【常用搭配】**

前程远大 have a great future

**【用法示例】**

他们大学毕业后,将有美好的前程。

They will have good prospects after graduating from university.

祝你前程似锦。

I wish you a happy future.

qǐqiú   yāngqiú

**乞求** ◎央求 （丁）动

beg

**【常用搭配】**

乞求他原谅 to beg his pardon

**【用法示例】**

他认为向别人乞求救济是耻辱。

He thinks it's a shame to beg others for alms.

他乞求法官开恩。

He appealed to the judge for clemency.

这不值得我去乞求。

It was beneath me to beg。

jìngxuǎn

**竞选** （丁）动

① elect ② run for (electoral) office

**【常用搭配】**

竞选党主席 run for the chairman of the party

竞选活动 an election campaign

**【用法示例】**

他将参加总统竞选。

He'll run for the Presidency.

谁在竞选中获胜了?

Who won the election?

下周我们就知道竞选的结果了。

Next week, we will know the result of election.

 **词义辨析**

**担负、负担**

1、"担负"和"负担"都可以用作动词,都有承担某项责任的意思。"担负"的宾语多为抽象的事物;"负担"的宾语多为具体的事物,常用作书面语。例如:①他将担负起一项重要的使命。②公司将负担我的学习费用。

Both 负担 and 担负 are verbs, meaning "to bear some responsibility". The object of 担负 is usually something abstract; while the object of 负担 is usually something concrete, and is more literary than 担负. For example: ① He will take on an important mission. ② My company will bear the cost of my studying.

2、"负担"还是名词,表示所承受的内容,如责任、费用、压力等。"担负"没有这种用法。如:政府正在采取措施减轻他们的经济负担。

负担 is also a noun, indicating "all that is being accountable for", such as responsibility, expense, burden, etc.; while 担负 has no usage like that. For example: The government is trying to relieve their economic burden.

 **练习**

**练习一、根据拼音写汉字，根据汉字写拼音**

qǐ（　）　qǐ（　）　shèn（　）　jìng（　）（　）dān
（　）求　（　）图　（　）至　（　）争　负（　）

**练习二、搭配连线**

(1) 竞选　　　　　　　A. 似锦
(2) 前程　　　　　　　B. 总统
(3) 经济　　　　　　　C. 原因
(4) 激烈　　　　　　　D. 竞争
(5) 直接　　　　　　　E. 负担

**练习三、从今天学习的生词中选择合适的词填空**

1. _____ 亲身经历过这种事情，_____ 真正理解当事人的感受。
2. 囚犯们 _____ 逃跑，但是失败了。
3. 现在市场 _____ 越来越激烈，销售人员的工作压力也越来越大。
4. 北京奥运会的 _____ 项目分为28个大项302个小项，你知道吗？
5. 我昨天没去打球，下了班就 _____ 回家了。
6. 他们一家人的生活都靠父亲的收入，所以父亲的 _____ 很重。
7. 公司的领导也不容易，职位越高，_____ 的责任也越大。
8. 他没上过学，不会写信，_____ 连自己的名字都不会写。
9. 他是党主席的候选人，正在为参加 _____ 做准备。
10. 分别时，老师们祝大家 _____ 似锦。

**答案**

**练习一：**
略

**练习二：**
(1) B　　(2) A　　(3) E　　(4) D　　(5) C

**练习三：**
1. 只有,才　2. 企图　3. 竞争　4. 竞赛　5. 直接
6. 负担　7. 担负　8. 甚至　9. 竞选　10. 前程

---

Thursday
**星期四**

chéngjì
**成绩**　　　　　　　　　　（甲）名

grade; result

**常用搭配**
考试成绩 examination results
取得好成绩 to get a high mark

**用法示例**
你的考试成绩十分优异。
Your examination results are excellent.
我希望你们能获得更好的成绩。
I hope you will attain still greater success.
他汉语考试的成绩是 90 分。
He got 90 percent for Chinese.

chéngjiù
**成就**　　　　　　　　　　（乙）名

accomplishment; achievement

**常用搭配**
成就感 sense of achievement
了不起的成就 a great achievement

**用法示例**
她对自己的成就很谦虚。
She is very modest about her success.
她正向大家炫耀她的成就。
She is vaunting her successes to all of us.
那个女人总是贬低我的成就。
That woman always disparages my achievements.

qǐfā
**启发**　　　◎启迪　　　（乙）动／名

① enlighten ② elicitation

**常用搭配**
启发方式 method of elicitation
启发人的言论 illuminating remark
受到启发 be enlightened

**用法示例**
那句话突然启发了她。
That sentence suddenly enlightened her.
他用一个例子启发学生。
He enlightened his students with an example.

mìnglìng
**命令**　　　　　　　　　　（乙）名／动

① order ② command

**常用搭配**
下命令 give orders
违抗命令 defy orders

**〔用法示例〕**

他们命令他停下。

They ordered him to stop.

我命令你去。

I command you to go.

将军命令舰队原地待命。

The general ordered the fleet to remain where they were and wait for the further instructions.

**只要……就……** zhǐyào……jiù…… （丙）

① as long as ② if only

**〔常用搭配〕**

只要你想走，你就走。You can leave if you want.

**〔用法示例〕**

她只要有时间，就练习弹钢琴。

She practices piano as long as she has free time.

只要你努力，你就一定会成功。

You will be successful if you work hard.

只要付给她报酬，她就会告诉你信息。

She will tell you the information only if she is paid to do so.

**进一步** jìnyíbù （乙）

further (onwards)

**〔常用搭配〕**

进一步调查 further investigation

做进一步努力 make further efforts

**〔用法示例〕**

他进一步指出他不愿与委员会合作。

He further stated that he would not cooperate with the committee.

这些情况不利于公司的进一步发展。

The circumstances were not propitious for furthering the expansion of the company.

要进一步了解情况，请与本地代理商联系。

For further information, contact your local agent.

**进修** jìnxiū （乙）动

① advanced studies ② additional studies

**〔常用搭配〕**

进修英语 advanced study of English

**〔用法示例〕**

我得去进修一年。

I've got to go away for a year on a training course.

我想该我去北京进修了。

I think it's my turn to go to Beijing for advanced study.

她正在进修计算机课程。

She is engaged in an advanced study of computer science.

**谨慎** jǐnshèn 反 草率 cǎoshuài （丙）形

prudent; cautious

**〔常用搭配〕**

谦虚谨慎 be modest and prudent

谨慎的外交官 a prudent diplomat

**〔用法示例〕**

他措辞很谨慎。

He is cautious in his choice of words.

择友愈谨慎愈好。

One cannot be too careful in choosing friends.

她很谨慎，不会泄露秘密。

She is cautious of revealing secrets.

**偏偏** piānpiān （丙）副

① just ② (indicates that sth. turns out just the opposite of what one would expect)

**〔常用搭配〕**

要找他时，他偏偏不在。

He would have to go away just when he was wanted.

**〔用法示例〕**

我们正要去度假，他却偏偏摔断了腿。

He would have to break a leg just before we go on holiday.

他和我一起干的，为什么你偏偏批评我呢？

He and I both did it. Why are you only criticizing me?

**启程** qǐchéng 同 动身 dòngshēn （丁）动

set out; start out

**〔常用搭配〕**

启程去北京 set out for Beijing

**〔用法示例〕**

开往上海的轮船星期三启程。

The ships for Shanghai leave on Wednesday.

她要去西藏旅游，明天启程。

She will travel to Tibet, starting out tomorrow.

由于天气不好，我们推迟了启程的时间。

We delayed our departure on account of the bad weather.

**指令** zhǐlìng 同 指示 zhǐshì （丁）名

instruction

**〔常用搭配〕**

发出指令 give instructions

**〔用法示例〕**

为了便于儿童理解，她简化了指令。

She simplified the instructions so that the children could understand them.

每条警犬都严格遵守指令。

Every police dog followed the instructions faithfully.

一收到你的指令我就发货。

On receipt of your instructions I will send the goods.

**进展** jìnzhǎn （丁）动

to make progress

**【常用搭配】**
取得进展 make progress
进展顺利 to progress smoothly
**【用法示例】**
我们的会谈已经取得了令人满意的进展。
We have made pleasing progress in our talks.
他向总部汇报了事情的进展情况。
He reported the progress of events to headquarters.
工作没有进展。
The work has not advanced.

 **词义辨析**

**成绩、成就**

　　"成绩"和"成就"都是名词,都表示已经取得的结果。"成绩"是中性词,指考试、学习、体育比赛等得到的结果和收获;"成就"是褒义词,主要指在科研领域或社会改革中取得的较大的成功或显著的成绩。例如:①她的考试成绩令人失望。②他的杰出成就使他成为本世纪最伟大的人物之一。

　　Both 成绩 and 成就 are nouns, meaning "the results so far". 成绩 is a neutral word, indicating the results or achievements made in exams, studies, and sports matches; while 成就 has a co-mmendatory sense, indicating remarkable achievements or great successes made in the scientific fields and social reforms. For example: ① Her exam result was disappointing. ② His illustrious accomplishments made him one of the greatest men of this century.

 **练习**

**练习一、根据拼音写汉字,根据汉字写拼音**
jǐn (　) jìn (　) (　)jì (　)lìng qǐ (　　)
(　)慎 (　)修 成(　) 指(　) (　)发

**练习二、搭配连线**
(1) 发出 　　　　　　A. 顺利
(2) 考试 　　　　　　B. 谨慎
(3) 受到 　　　　　　C. 成绩
(4) 谦虚 　　　　　　D. 启发
(5) 进展 　　　　　　E. 指令

**练习三、从今天学习的生词中选择合适的词填空**
1. 这个科研项目自开展以来一直没有明显的 _____ ,投资方有些着急了。
2. 你的 _____ 最好,这次考试你又是第一名。
3. 他因物理学方面的 _____ 而被授予诺贝尔奖。
4. 他说他从别人的学习经验中得到了很大 _____ 。
5. 这艘军舰明日 _____ 去日本访问。
6. 这个小孩真淘气,不让他动电脑,他 _____ 要动。
7. 刚参加工作时,我说话很 _____ ,怕不小心得罪了谁。
8. 公司派他来中国 _____ 汉语,一年后再回国继续工作。
9. 我们将要对这一情况作 _____ 的调查,然后才能公布结果。
10. _____ 有问题 _____ 问老师,别不好意思。

**答案**

**练习一:**
略
**练习二:**
(1) E 　　(2)C 　　(3)D 　　(4)B 　　(5)A
**练习三:**
1. 进展 　2. 成绩 　3. 成就 　4. 启发
5. 启程 　6. 偏偏 　7. 谨慎 　8. 进修
9. 进一步 　10. 只要,就

**huódòng**
## 活动 （甲）动／名

① exercise ② activity

**常用搭配**

户外活动 outdoor activity　社会活动 social activity
学术活动 academic activity

**用法示例**

你越来越胖了,应该多活动。
Your weight is increasing, you should exercise more.
他对很多课外活动都不积极。
He doesn't take an active part in many extracurricular activities.

**lùnwén**
## 论文 **wénzhāng** 回 文章 （乙）名

dissertation treatise

**常用搭配**

毕业论文 graduates' dissertation
学术论文 academic dissertation
宣读论文 read a paper

**用法示例**

教授要求我们就这个课题写篇论文。
Our professor asked us to write a treatise on this subject.
请在六月三十日前交论文。
Please hand in your paper before June thirtieth.
拖了那么久,他终于完成了论文。
After much delay, he finished his paper at last.

**lùxiàng**
## 录像 （乙）名

video recording

**常用搭配**

录像带 video tape　录像机 video recorder
看录像 watch video

**用法示例**

好看的录像带总是被借走。
The good video tapes are always rented out.
他们放映了录像片《飘》。
They showed a video of "Gone with the Wind".

**nìngkě** **yěbù**
## 宁可……也不…… （丙）

① prefer ② would rather

**常用搭配**

宁可死也不投降。 prefer to die rather than surrender

**用法示例**

他宁可辞职也不愿意参与这种欺骗的勾当。
He resigned rather than take part in such a dishonest transaction.

他宁可租房子,也不和父母一起住。
He'd rather rent a house than stay with his parents.

**xiǎoxīn**
## 小心 （乙）形／动

① careful ② beware of

**常用搭配**

小心点儿! Be careful!　小心火。 Beware of fire.
小心驾驶 careful driving

**用法示例**

路面结冰了,今晚要格外小心。
Take special care tonight because the roads are icy.
小心别从梯子上掉下来。
Be careful not to fall off the ladder.
小心得肺炎。
Take care not to get pneumonia.

**xiǎngniàn**
## 想念 **sīniàn** 回 思念 （乙）动

① miss ② long to see again

**常用搭配**

我真想念你啊! I do miss you.

**用法示例**

不论你在哪里,我都会想念你的。
Wherever you are, I will miss you.
你想念家人吗?
Do you miss your family?
我会非常想念你的。
I shall miss you very much.

**shìlì**
## 势力 **quánshì** 回 权势 （丙）名

(ability to) influence; force

**常用搭配**

有势力的人 a man of great influence
邪恶势力 the forces of evil
习惯势力 the force of habit

**用法示例**

她是利用她父母的势力谋求的职位。
She used her parents' influence to get the job.
他在政府内有一定的势力。
He is a man of some influence in government circles.

**shèyǐng**
## 摄影 **zhàoxiàng** 回 照相 （丙）名／动

① photography ② to take a photograph

**常用搭配**

摄影师 photographer
摄影技术 skill of photography

**用法示例**

他是个业余摄影爱好者。
He is an amateur photographer.
他特别喜欢摄影。
He has a passion for photography.

huáiniàn
# 怀念 （丙）动
to cherish the memory of; miss

**常用搭配**
怀念战友 miss comrades in arms

**用法示例**
让我们永远怀念为世界和平献身的勇士们。
Let us remember the brave warriors who died for the peace of the world.
他因品质高尚而被人怀念。
He is remembered for the nobility of his character.
我们时常怀念童年时光。
We sometimes reminisce about the memories of our childhood.

lùndiǎn
# 论点 （丁）名
argument; point (of discussion)

**常用搭配**
提出论点 put forward an argument
正确的论点 valid argument

**用法示例**
他们出示了一些统计数字来支持他们的论点。
They showed some statistical evidence to support their argument.
我能驳倒他的论点。
I was able to refute his argument.
最后一部分总结了双方的全部论点。
The last section sums up all the arguments on either side.

shílì
# 实力 （丁）名
strength

**常用搭配**
军事实力 military strength

**用法示例**
两支足球队实力相当。
The two football teams are equal in strength.
中国的经济实力在增强。
The economic strength of China is increasing.

shìlì
# 视力 （丁）名
vision; eyesight

**常用搭配**
视力差 poor eyesight
保护视力 maintain good eyesight

**用法示例**
她的视力非常好。
Her eyesight is very good.
在阳光下看书对视力不好。
It's bad for your vision to read in direct sunlight.

 词义辨析

**怀念、想念**

　　"怀念"和"想念"都是动词,都表示不能忘记或希望再次见到。"怀念"往往强调对久远的过去的回忆,对象一般是已经去世的人或很难再出现的事物或经历;而"想念"强调离开以后还常常想起,其对象一般是健在的人或容易再次见到的人或环境。例如:①他一辈子献身于科学研究事业,我相信每个人都会怀念他。②我非常想念父母。

　　Both 怀念 and 想念 are verbs, meaning "can not forget about and wish to see again". 怀念 usually stresses the recollection of the remote past, and its objects are the dead or something that is unlikely happen again; while 想念 usually stresses "to miss someone who was parted from sometime ago and who you wish to see again", and its object are people or things that can possibly reoccur. For example: ① He devoted his whole life to the study of science. I'm sure that everybody will remember him. ② I miss my parents very much.

 练习

**练习一、根据拼音写汉字,根据汉字写拼音**
( )lì　shè( )( )xiàng　xiǎng ( )　lùn ( )
势( )( )影　录( )　( )念　( )点

**练习二、搭配连线**
(1) 军事　　　　　　　　A. 视力
(2) 邪恶　　　　　　　　B. 实力
(3) 毕业　　　　　　　　C. 势力
(4) 课外　　　　　　　　D. 论文
(5) 保护　　　　　　　　E. 活动

**练习三、从今天学习的生词中选择合适的词填空**
1. 虽然他个子不太高,却是一个非常有 _____ 的篮球运动员,不能小看他。
2. 这两个党派合并以后,在国会的 _____ 进一步扩大了。
3. 雪天开车时,一定要 _____ 驾驶。
4. 他的业余爱好是 _____ ,他拍摄的照片多次被刊登在报纸上。
5. 学校规定所有毕业生在4月15日之前必须上交毕业 _____ 。
6. 除了学习,他还积极参加学校的各种课外 _____ 。
7. 两年没见父母了,我很 _____ 他们,明天我就回家看他们去。
8. 我很 _____ 大学时光,那是我人生中非常重要的一个阶段。
9. 她很害羞, _____ 喜欢你 _____ 不会直接说出来的。

10. 由于经常熬夜上网,他的 _____ 越来越不好了,得去配眼镜了。

**答案**

**练习一:**
略

**练习二:**
(1) B      (2)C      (3)D      (4)E      (5)A

**练习三:**
1. 实力    2. 势力    3. 小心    4. 摄影    5. 论文
6. 活动    7. 想念    8. 怀念    9. 就是,也    10. 视力

# 第7月,第3周的练习

**练习一.根据词语给加点的字注音**
1.( )    2.( )    3.( )    4.( )    5.( )
乐器    竞争    谨慎    启程    摄影

**练习二.根据拼音完成词语**
qǐ    qǐ    qǐ    fú    fù
1.( )图   2.( )发   3.( )求   4.( )从   5.( )盖

**练习三.辨析并选择合适的词填空**
1. 我们这样做的( )是让更多的人了解中国。(目标、目的)
2. 他的( )很明确,就是要在上半年通过 HSK 8 级。(目标、目的)
3. 地上( )着厚厚的积雪,踩上去,发出咯吱咯吱的响声。(掩盖、覆盖)
4. 把这个问题( )起来的做法是愚蠢的,总有一天会暴露的。(掩盖、覆盖)
5. 青少年( )着国家的未来与希望。(负担、担负)
6. 他一个人的工资要养活全家人,所以他的( )很重。(负担、担负)
7. 他这学期的学习( )有了很大的提高。(成绩、成就)
8. 他凭自己的努力奋斗,在事业上取得了辉煌的( )。(成绩、成就)
9. 两年没见面了,我很( )远方的好朋友。(怀念、想念)
10. 现代人活得太累了,闲暇时,人们总喜欢( )以前简单的生活方式。(怀念、想念)

**练习四.选词填空**
不要紧    不在乎    来得及    竞争    实力
不一定    来不及    竞赛    竞选    视力
1. 孩子起床晚了,( )吃早饭就背着书包上学去了。
2. 学得最好的学生( )是最努力的学生,但不努力就一定学不好。

3. 他对别人的议论一点都( ),还是坚持按照自己的想法做。
4. 这个党派的领导人宣布,参加下一届的总统( )。
5. 这几个岗位的( )会很激烈,已经有 200 多个求职者报名了。
6. 她的( )不好,坐在后面根本看不见黑板上的字。
7. 就是普通感冒,( ),明天能坚持上班。
8. 你们足球队准备得很充分,可是对手的( )也很强,所以你们不一定能赢。
9. 安娜在这次的作文( )中获得了第一名。
10. 别慌,还有十分钟,走过去完全( )。

**练习五.选择关联词填空**
宁可……也不……    只要……就……
只有……才……    倘若    甚至
1. ( )农业发展了,工业( )有足够的原料和市场。
2. 我根本不认识她,可她认识我,( )还知道我姐姐的名字。
3. ( )第一套方案不行,我们就马上采取第二套方案。
4. ( )明天不下雪,我们( )按原计划去长城。
5. 他( )挨饿( )向别人乞讨。

**练习六.写出下列词语的同义词**
1. 祈求( )      2. 指令( )
3. 势力( )      4. 竞赛( )
5. 繁荣( )

**练习七.写出下列词语的反义词**
1. 掩盖( )      2. 谨慎( )
3. 服从( )      4. 暴露( )
5. 结束( )

**答案**

**练习一.**
1.yuè    2.zhēng    3.jǐn    4.chéng    5.shè

**练习二.**
1. 企    2. 启    3. 乞    4. 服    5. 覆

**练习三.**
1. 目的    2. 目标    3. 覆盖    4. 掩盖    5. 担负
6. 负担    7. 成绩    8. 成就    9. 想念    10. 怀念

**练习四.**
1. 来不及    2. 不一定    3. 不在乎    4. 竞选    5. 竞争
6. 视力    7. 不要紧    8. 实力    9. 竞赛    10. 来得及

**练习五.**
1. 只有,才   2. 甚至    3. 倘若    4. 只要,就
5. 宁可,也不

**练习六.**
1. 央求    2. 指示    3. 权势    4. 比赛    5. 兴旺

**练习七.**
1. 揭露    2. 草率    3. 违抗    4. 隐瞒    5. 开始

# 7月 第 4 周的学习内容

**星期一**

### wèntí
## 问题 （甲）名

question; problem; issue

**常用搭配**

解决问题 solve a problem　　没问题。No problem.

问问题 ask a question

**用法示例**

你还没有回答我的问题。

You haven't answered my question.

这只是时间问题。

It's only a matter of time.

这是一个极为重要的问题。

This is an issue of the utmost importance.

### gèzhǒng
## 各种 （甲）代

all sorts of

**常用搭配**

各种职业 all kinds of jobs　　各种人 people of all sorts

各种鸟 all kinds of birds

**用法示例**

这个购物中心出售各种商品。

The shopping centre sells a variety of goods.

在学校我们学习各种科目。

At school we learn a variety of subjects.

她喜欢各种运动。

She likes all kinds of sports.

### tàng
## 趟 （乙）量

① measure word for times of coming or going ② one round trip

**常用搭配**

来我办公室一趟。Come to my office please！

**用法示例**

我想明年暑假去一趟欧洲。

I feel like going to Europe during the next summer vacation.

我得去一趟邮局。

I have to go to the post office.

他上个月去了一趟南方。

He made a trip to the South last month

我儿子每周来这儿一趟,并给我买些日用品。

My son comes here once a week to buy me a few daily necessities.

### zhàoyàng
## 照样　　◎ 依旧 yījiù （丙）副

① all the same ② as usual

**常用搭配**

照样进行 proceed in the same way

**用法示例**

老板已经警告过他了,但他照样迟到。

His boss had given him awarning, but he still arrived late as usual.

他已被提升为经理了,但照样对我们很友善。

He has been promoted to manager, but he is friendly to us all the same.

### múyàng
## 模样　　◎ 外表 wàibiǎo （乙）名

appearance

**常用搭配**

好模样不如好心肠。

Good looks are not as good as kindness.

**用法示例**

他的模样像妈妈,性格却跟妈妈不一样。

He looks like his mother, but they have different personalities.

他假扮成士兵的模样。

He disguised himself as a soldier.

### móxíng
## 模型 （丙）名

model

**常用搭配**

飞机模型 model airplane

**用法示例**

他一块一块地装配轮船模型。

He assembled the model ship piece by piece.

他喜欢在业余时间制作火车模型。

He likes building model trains in his spare time.

制作小模型要手巧。

Making small models requires great manual skill.

### cízhí
## 辞职 （丁）动

resign

**常用搭配**

从董事会中辞职

resign from a board of directors

**用法示例**

我上星期交了辞职书。

I sent in my resignation last week.

总经理批准了我的辞职申请。

The general manager accepted my resignation.

他已经从公司辞职了。

He has already resigned from the company.

kuàngqiě

## 况且 （丙）连

moreover; besides

**用法示例**

房价太高，况且房屋的地点也不太合适。

The price is too high, and moreover, the house isn't in a suitable position.

现在去看篮球比赛已经太晚了，况且，又开始下雨了。

It's too late to go to the basketball match now; besides it's beginning to rain.

hékuàng

## 何况 （丙）连

let alone

**用法示例**

老师都解决不了这个问题，何况学生？

The teacher can not solve the problem, let alone the students.

我连小房子的租金都负担不起，何况大房子？

I can not afford the rent of the small house, let alone the big one.

zànshǎng

## 赞赏 （丁）动

admire; appreciate

**常用搭配**

备受赞赏 be highly commended

对……表示赞赏 express admiration for

**用法示例**

我们都赞赏她的勇气。

We all admire her for her bravery.

他的行为应该得到赞赏。

His conduct is deserving of this praise.

他的工作备受赞赏。

His work was highly commended.

zàntóng　　　　fǎnduì

## 赞同 ⑤反对 （丁）动

assent; approve

**常用搭配**

一致赞同 unanimously approve

赞同他的观点 assent to his point of view

**用法示例**

他不赞同你的观点。

He doesn't agree with your view.

我们是不会赞同这种事的。

We can't approve this sort of thing.

他们得到了老师的赞同。

They had their teacher's approval.

jiěgù　　　　　　　　pìnyòng

## 解雇 ⑤聘用 （丁）动

dismiss

**常用搭配**

你被解雇了。You're fired.　解雇工人 dismiss a worker

**用法示例**

他被解雇了。

He was dismissed from his job.

你如果再次迟到，就将被解雇。

If you're late again you'll be dismissed.

根据劳动法，老板不能任意解雇工人。

According the Labor Law, bosses can no longer fire workers at will.

 词义辨析

**况且、何况**

"何况"和"况且"都是连词，表示进一步说明。"何况"经常用在反问句中，可以直接跟短语或名词、代词、数量词等；"况且"只能出现在递进条件的小分句中。例如：①这座房子太小，况且离办公地点也太远。②男孩子都觉得很累，何况女孩子呢？

Both 何况 and 况且 are conjunctions, and can introduce additional causes or further remarks. 何况 is usually used in rh-etorical question sentences, and it can introduce a phrase or a noun, pronoun, numeral or measure word; while 况且 can only be used in progressive clauses. For example: ① The house is too small, and furthermore, it's too far from the office. ② The boys felt very tired, to say nothing of the girls.

## 练习

**练习一、根据拼音写汉字，根据汉字写拼音**

mú（　）mó（　）cí（　）（　）gù（　）shǎng
（　）样　（　）型　（　）职　解（　）赞（　）

**练习二、搭配连线**

(1) 备受　　　　　　　　A. 进行
(2) 飞机　　　　　　　　B. 赞赏
(3) 解决　　　　　　　　C. 申请
(4) 照样　　　　　　　　D. 问题
(5) 辞职　　　　　　　　E. 模型

**练习三、从今天学习的生词中选择合适的词填空**

1. 董事会的所有成员都 _____ 他们对公司进行改革的方案。
2. 领导在会上对他们的工作能力大加 _____。
3. 大人有时也会犯这样的错误，_____ 他还是个孩子？
4. 他不是故意伤害你，_____ 人家已经向你道歉了，你就原谅他吧。
5. 他把我们公司的商业机密泄露给了别的公司，老板决定 _____ 他。
6. 在这个公司工作很辛苦，赚钱又少，于是他 _____ 了。
7. 桌子上摆着一些军舰 _____，可见主人对军事很感兴趣。
8. 你还记得去世的奶奶长得什么 _____ 吗？
9. 已经查出这批货有问题了，但他们还 _____ 出售。
10. 四月份，马经理出差去了 _____ 上海。

## 答案

**练习一：**
略

**练习二：**
(1) B　　(2)E　　(3)D　　(4)A　　(5)C

**练习三：**
1. 赞同　　2. 赞赏　　3. 何况　　4. 况且　　5. 解雇
6. 辞职　　7. 模型　　8. 模样　　9. 照样　　10. 趟

## 星期二

**tǐyù**
### 体育　　　　　　　　（甲）名
sports

**常用搭配**
体育爱好者 sports buff　　体育教师 gym teacher
体育课 PE（physical education）

**用法示例**
足球和跑步是体育运动。
Football and running are sports.
体育运动有益健康。
Athletic sports are good for the body.
每个星期天我们都去体育馆打羽毛球。
We go to play badminton in the gym every Sunday.

**xiàr**
### 下儿　　　　　　　　（甲）量
measure word for the number of time

**常用搭配**
看一下儿 have a look　　试一下儿 have a try

**用法示例**
请等一下儿!Wait a minute. Please!
仔细想一下儿！ Think about it carefully！
请让一下儿，我要过去。Excuse me! Let me pass.

**hé**
### 盒　　　　　　　　　（乙）量
box

**常用搭配**
一盒巧克力 a box of chocolates
两盒粉笔 two boxes of chalk

**用法示例**
我想买一盒烟。
I want to buy a pack of cigarettes.
他给我一盒糖果作为生日礼物。
He gave me a box of candy as a birthday gift.

**chàdiǎnr**
### 差点儿　　　　　　　（乙）副
almost；nearly

**常用搭配**
我差点儿忘了。I almost forgot about it.
他差点儿跌倒。He almost fell.

**用法示例**
他差点儿从梯子上掉下来。
He nearly fell off the ladder.
火车突然停住，我差点儿从座位上摔下来。
The train stopped abruptly, nearly tipping me out of my bunk.

她差点儿死了。She nearly died.

那块石头差点儿砸到男孩。The stone just missed the boy.

## miáoxiě
## 描写　　⊜ miáoshù 描述　　（乙）动

describe

**常用搭配**

生动的描写 a vivid description

描写景色 describe scenery

**用法示例**

她的小说描写的是伦敦现代的生活。

Her novel depicts life in modern London.

他不善于描写。

He is not very good at descriptions.

那位记者发来了一篇描写极地生活的文章。

The reporter sent an article describing life in the poles.

## míxìn
## 迷信　　⊗ kēxué 科学　　（丙）动／名

① be superstitious；have blind faith in

② superstition

**常用搭配**

破除迷信 break down superstitions

**用法示例**

他有一种迷信的想法认为黑猫不吉利。

He has a superstitious belief that black cats are unlucky.

由于无知和迷信，他们无法得到现代医学的好处。

Ignorance and superstition prevent them from benefiting from modern medicine.

## míhu
## 迷糊　　⊗ qīngxǐng 清醒　　（丙）形

muddled；confused

**常用搭配**

把我搞迷糊了 confuses me

**用法示例**

这个老婆婆容易迷糊。

The old lady gets confused easily.

他们问的问题太多了，我都迷糊了。

They asked me so many questions that I got confused.

她迷迷糊糊的，甚至记不起那是哪一天。

She was in a daze; she couldn't even remember what day it was.

## búliào
## 不料　　⊜ jìngrán 竟然　　（丙）副

unexpectedly

**用法示例**

上午的天气还很好，不料，下午的天气又阴又冷。

It's fine in the morning, but it unexpectedly became cloudy and cold in the afternoon.

不料，他改变了主意。

Against all expectations, he changed his mind.

## jìngrán
## 竟然　　（丙）副

unexpectedly；actually

**用法示例**

他竟然指望我给他付票钱。

He actually expected me to pay for his ticket.

我想帮他，可他竟然拒绝了！

I wanted to help him, but he refused!

他不仅请我进屋，竟然还请我喝了一杯。

He not only invited me into his house; he actually offered me a drink!

## miáoshù
## 描述　　（丁）动

describe

**常用搭配**

难以描述 beyond description

描述一起事故 described an accident

**用法示例**

日出的美景难以描述。

The beauty of the sunrise is beyond description.

风景不像你描述的那么好。

The scene is nothing like what you described.

他描述了他所见到的一切。

He gave a description of what he had seen.

## tiánxiě
## 填写　　（丁）动

write；fill in

**常用搭配**

填写表格 fill in a form

**用法示例**

把你的名字填写在括号内。

Write your name in brackets.

请在这份表格上填写你的姓名、年龄和地址。

Please fill in this form, giving your name, age, and address.

申请人得填写几种表格。

The applicants have to fill in several forms.

## tiánbǔ
## 填补　　（丁）动

fill in；fill up

**常用搭配**

填补空白 fill a gap

填补工作空缺 to fill a job vacancy

**用法示例**

我得把墙上的那条裂缝填补好。

I must fill that crack in the wall.

李奇是填补这一工作空缺的最佳人选。

Li Qi is the best person to fill this job vacancy.

 词义辨析

**不料、竟然**

　　"不料"和"竟然"都有没想到和出乎意料的意思。但是"不料"是动词,可以在后边接句子作宾语;"竟然"是副词,放在动词或形容词前作状语。"不料"一般不在主语的后边;"竟然"可以在主语后边。例如:①我惊奇地看着她,她竟然是两个孩子的妈妈了。②我给她邀请信,不料,她拒绝了。

　　Both 不料 and 竟然 mean "beyond expectation". 不料 is a verb, and can take a clause as an object; while 竟然 is an adverb, and usually functions as an adverbial in front of a verb or an adjective. 不料 usually doesn't follow the subject; while 竟然 can follow the subject. For example: ① I looked at her in surprise —she is a mother of two. ② Unexpectedly she refused me when I gave her the letter of invitation.

 练习

**练习一、根据拼音写汉字,根据汉字写拼音**

tián (　)(　)shù　jìng(　)　mí(　)(　)yù
(　)补　描(　)(　)然　(　)糊　体(　)

**练习二、搭配连线**

(1) 填补　　　　　　　　A. 迷信
(2) 填写　　　　　　　　B. 空缺
(3) 破除　　　　　　　　C. 描写
(4) 体育　　　　　　　　D. 表格
(5) 景色　　　　　　　　E. 运动

**练习三、从今天学习的生词中选择合适的词填空**

1. 这篇小说对人物的内心世界 _____ 得很细腻。
2. 你能把旅行中的见闻 _____ 一下吗?
3. 他刚睡醒,还有点 _____。
4. 有些老人认为世界上有鬼魂,年轻人觉得那是 _____。
5. 昨天我去医院看病,医生让我先 _____ 病历。
6. 3号球员受伤下场,6号上场 _____ 了他的空缺。
7. 早上天气好好的, _____,下午突然下起大雪来。
8. 他肯定是太紧张了,这么简单的问题他 _____ 没回答上来。
9. 他去爬山时, _____ 摔下来,把我吓坏了。
10. 他喜欢各种运动,最喜欢上的课当然是 _____ 课。

🔑 **答案**

**练习一:**
略

**练习二:**
(1) B　　　(2)D　　　(3)A　　　(4)E　　　(5)C

**练习三:**
1. 描写　　2. 描述　　3. 迷糊　　4. 迷信　　5. 填写
6. 填补　　7. 不料　　8. 竟然　　9. 差点儿　　10. 体育

星期三

## jì
## 寄 　　　　　　　　　　（甲）动

to mail; to send

**常用搭配**

寄信 send letters
寄包裹 send a parcel

**用法示例**

寄信前,他在信封上写上地址。
He addressed the envelope before mailing the letter.
请给我们公司寄一份详细的简历。
Please send a detailed resume to our company.
请寄给我一张这笔钱的收据。
Please send me a receipt for the money.

## guǎngbō
## 广播 　　　⊜播送　　（甲）动／名

broadcast

**常用搭配**

广播新闻 broadcast news
听广播 listen to the radio
英国广播公司 BBC

**用法示例**

她将发表时事广播演说。
She will be broadcasting on current affairs.
主席的讲话将向全国广播。
The chairman's speech will be broadcast nationwide.

## zāihài
## 灾害 　　　　　　　　（乙）名

disaster

**常用搭配**

自然灾害 natural disasters

**用法示例**

洪水是可怕的灾害。
The floods are a terrifying disaster.
这是我经历过的可怕的灾害。
This was a terrible disaster that I experienced.

## jímáng
## 急忙 　　　⊠缓慢　　（乙）形

hastily; hurriedly

**常用搭配**

急忙回家 hasten home

**用法示例**

他急急忙忙地去了办公室。
He hastened to the office.
他急忙把一大包东西藏到书桌底下了。
He hurriedly hid a large parcel under his desk.

## guǎngdà
## 广大 　　　⊜辽阔　　（乙）形

① vast ② extensive ③ a mass of

**常用搭配**

广大消费者 mass customers
广大观众 mass audience

**用法示例**

这个国家拥有广大的领土。
There is an immense amount territory in this country.
太平洋是一片广大的水域。
The Pacific Ocean is a vast expanse of water.

## shèjī
## 射击 　　　　　　　　（丙）动

to fire; to shoot

**常用搭配**

向敌人射击 fire at the enemy　猛烈射击 shoot fiercely

**用法示例**

她用枪向他们射击。
She fired her gun at them.
士兵对准靶子射击,但又没有打中。
The soldier shot at the target, but missed it again.
他们不停地射击,耗尽了所有的弹药。
They went on firing until they had spent all their ammunition.

## zāinàn
## 灾难 　　　　　　　　（丙）名

disaster; calamity

**常用搭配**

遭受灾难 suffer disasters
可怕的灾难 frightful calamity

**用法示例**

这次地震是一场惨重的灾难。
The earthquake was a terrible catastrophe.
在这次灾难中有五十多人丧生。
More than 50 people were killed in the calamity.
这场灾难过后,许多人既没有食物又没有住处。
After the disaster there were many who wanted food and shelter.

## huì
## 汇 　　　　　　　　　（丙）动

remit

**常用搭配**

给……汇款 remit money to …

**用法示例**

上星期日我去邮局汇款了。
I went to the postoffice to remit money last Sunday.
请把钱汇给我。
Remit me the money, please.
我们能把钱汇到国外吗?
Can we remit money to foreign countries?

shù
# 束 　　　　　　　　　　（丙）量
① bunch ② measure word for flowers

**常用搭配**

一束丁香花 a bunch of lilacs
买束花 buy a bunch of flowers

**用法示例**

他们献给老师一束花。
They presented their teacher with a bunch of flowers.
生日那天,我收到一束红玫瑰。
I received a bunch of roses on my birthday.

shēchǐ
# 奢侈 　　　　　　　　　　（丁）形
① luxurious ② luxury

**常用搭配**

生活奢侈 live in luxury 　奢侈品 luxury

**用法示例**

他们在一所很大的房子里过着奢侈的生活。
They live in luxury in a very big house.
对他们来说,奶油蛋糕是奢侈品。
Cream cakes are a luxury for them.
她很奢侈,买衣服花了很多钱。
She's very extravagant. She spends a lot of money on clothes.

shèjí
# 涉及 　　　　　　　　　　（丁）动
involve; concern

**常用搭配**

涉及到每个家庭 relates to every family
涉及到很多部门 involves many departments

**用法示例**

我们的谈话涉及很多领域。
Our conversation covered a lot of ground.
这件事很严重,因为它涉及到你的声誉。
The matter is serious because it involves your reputation.
这份报告涉及到当前的教育制度。
The report relates to the present educational system.

kāngkǎi　　　　　　lìnsè
# 慷慨 　　　 反 吝啬 　　　（丁）形
generous; vehement

**常用搭配**

慷慨解囊 help sb. generously with money
慷慨陈词 present one's views vehemently

**用法示例**

她一直非常慷慨。
She's been generous in the extreme.
他慷慨地把钱施舍给穷人。
He gives money generously to the poor.
她行善时总是很慷慨。
She was always very generous in her charity.

 **词义辨析**

**汇、寄**

　　"汇"和"寄"都是动词,都可以表示邮寄。"汇"是书面语,它的宾语只能是钱、款,"汇款"是习惯搭配,而"寄"比较口语化,它的宾语可以是信或包裹,也可以是钱。例如:①我去邮局寄信。②她用邮包把礼物寄给了我。

　　Both 汇 and 寄 are verbs, meaning "to post". 汇 is more literary, and the object of it can only be 钱 (money) or 款 (money). "汇款 (means to remit money, or the posted money)" is a set phrase. While 寄 is more colloquial, and the object of it can be a letter, parcel, or money. For example: ① I went to the post office to mail the letters. ② She sent me the present by parcel post.

 练习

**练习一、根据拼音写汉字，根据汉字写拼音**
( )bō zāi( ) shē( ) shè( ) shè( )
广( ) ( )难 ( )侈 ( )及 ( )击

**练习二、搭配连线**
(1) 慷慨　　　　　　　A. 灾害
(2) 生活　　　　　　　B. 解囊
(3) 猛烈　　　　　　　C. 广播
(4) 收听　　　　　　　D. 奢侈
(5) 自然　　　　　　　E. 射击

**练习三、从今天学习的生词中选择合适的词填空**
1. 圣诞节快到了,他去邮局给朋友 _____ 了几张贺卡。
2. 他每天在上班的路上靠听 _____ 打发时间。
3. 一下班,她就 _____ 赶回家,照顾生病的丈夫。
4. 有人认为,是人类对生态环境的破坏导致了自然 _____ 的发生。
5. 最近的地震和南方的暴雨都是场 _____ 。
6. 接到命令以后,我们立刻用机枪向敌人猛烈 _____ 。
7. 她一个月的工资才两千块,花一千多块钱买一双鞋,简直太 _____ 了。
8. 2月14日,他买了一 _____ 红玫瑰送给女朋友。
9. 灾难发生后,国内企业纷纷 _____ 解囊,援助灾区。
10. 这项措施 _____ 到每个人的利益,一定要考虑周到。

🔑 答案

**练习一：**
略
**练习二：**
(1) B　　(2)D　　(3)E　　(4)C　　(5)A
**练习三：**
1. 寄　　2. 广播　　3. 急忙　　4. 灾害　　5. 灾难
6. 射击　　7. 奢侈　　8. 束　　9. 慷慨　　10. 涉及

---

huídá
**回答**　　　🔄 提问　　　　　（甲）动／名
① reply ② answer
**常用搭配**
回答问题 answer questions
**用法示例**
他没有给我回答他问题的机会。
He gave me no opportunity to reply to his question.
如果你同意我的意见,就明白地回答"是"。
Answer with a plain "yes" if you agree with me.
我不知道该怎么回答。
I don't know how to reply.

jiān
**间**　　　　　　　　　　　　（甲）量
measure word for rooms
**常用搭配**
两间屋子 two rooms　　一间办公室 an office
**用法示例**
我们曾在这间教室学习了四年。
We studied for four years in this classroom.
咱们的新公寓里有三间卧室。
There are three bedrooms in our new apartment.

jiàn
**件**　　　　　　　　　　　　（甲）量
measure word for clothes, matter
**常用搭配**
一件急事 an urgent matter　　两件衬衫 two shirts
四件行李 four pieces of luggage
**用法示例**
我有件重要的事要和你谈谈。
I have an important matter to talk to you about.
她给弟弟买了一件毛衣。
She bought a sweater for her brother.

yùnyòng　　　　　　　　shǐyòng
**运用**　　　🔄 使用　　　　　（乙）动
to use; put to use
**常用搭配**
运用权威 exert authority　　熟练运用 apply skillfully
**用法示例**
这样他们就能更好地把理论运用到实践中去。
In this way they can better apply theory to practice.
你们为什么不运用那个新方法呢?
Why didn't you employ the new method?
这个问题需要我们运用智力。
This problem challenges us to use our intellect.

## qīnzì
# 亲自 （乙）副
personally

**常用搭配**

亲自检查 personally check　　亲自做饭 personally cook

**用法示例**

他将亲自过问此事。
He will give the matter his personal attention.
这些计划经部长亲自审阅过。
The plans were personally inspected by the minister.
我得亲自去寄这封信。
I have to mail the letter myself.

## jiélùn
# 结论 （乙）名
conclusion; verdict

**常用搭配**

得出结论 reach a conclusion
公正的结论 a fair conclusion

**用法示例**

不要急于下结论。
Don't jump to conclusions.
你得出了什么结论?
What conclusion did you come to?
你的信息不准确,所以你的结论是错误的。
Your information is inaccurate and your conclusion is therefore wrong.

## zuìxíng
# 罪行 ⊗ gōngjì功绩 （丙）名
crime

**常用搭配**

滔天罪行 towering crimes　　招认罪行 admit a crime

**用法示例**

我饶恕了他的罪行。
I forgave him his crimes.
嫌疑犯供认了罪行。
The suspect confessed to the crime.
他因犯有多种罪行而被捕了。
He was arrested for committing several crimes.

## yùnzhuǎn
# 运转 （丙）动
operate

**常用搭配**

正常运转 operate properly

**用法示例**

这台电梯运转不正常。
The lift doesn't operate properly.
这台机器日夜运转。
This machine operates night and day.
发动机现在运转得很顺畅。
The engine is running smoothly now.

## dáfù
# 答复 （丙）动/名
① reply ② answer

**常用搭配**

答复他 reply to him
一个明确的答复 a definite answer

**用法示例**

他正在想如何答复她。
He is thinking about how to reply to her.
我写了信,但她没有答复。
I wrote to her, but she did not reply.
他给我的答复含糊其辞。
He gave me an indefinite answer.

## qīnyǎn
# 亲眼 （丙）副
① with one's own eyes ② personally

**常用搭配**

那是我亲眼所见。That's what I saw with my own eyes.

**用法示例**

我亲眼看见他拿了钱。
I personally saw him taking money.
她说她亲眼看到了飞碟。
She said she saw a UFO with her own eyes.
他是不会相信的,除非他亲眼看到。
He won't believe it unless he sees it himself.

## yùnsòng
# 运送 ⊜ yùnshū运输 （丁）动
transport; carry

**常用搭配**

免费运送 free delivery
运送食品 deliver groceries

**用法示例**

这艘货轮能够运送五万吨货物。
This freighter can carry 50000 tons of cargo.
将用卡车运送这批货物。
The goods will be transported by truck.
货物是用自行车运送的。
The goods were transported by bike.

## qīnshǒu
# 亲手 （丁）副
① with one's own hands ② personally

**常用搭配**

这是他亲手做的。He did it with his own hands.

**用法示例**

希望你喜欢这件东西,这是我亲手做的。
I hope you'll like this, I've done it all by hand.
女主人亲手为客人煮咖啡。
The hostess made coffee for the guests herself.
她让我亲手把信交给你。
She asked me to give you the letter with personally.

jiéjú
# 结局

（丁）名

ending

**常用搭配**

圆满的结局 a happy ending

**用法示例**

这个故事有一个出人意料的结局。

The story has a surprising ending.

这场战争的结局难以预料。

You can't foretell how the war will end.

结局好就是一切都好。

All is well that ends well.

 **词义辨析**

**答复、回答**

　　"回答"和"答复"可以用作动词,表示对问题的回应。"回答"往往是针对具体问题进行解答,而"答复"往往是针对请示或要求进行回应,"答复"还可以用作名词。例如:①我问她时间,可是她没回答。②老师总是耐心地回答学生的问题。③我把申请书交上去了,学校立即做出了答复。④别支支吾吾,给我一个明确的答复。

　　Both 回答 and 答复 are verbs, indicating "to reply". 回答 usually stresses "to answer a concrete question"; while 答复 stresses "to reply to a report or a request", and it also can be used as a noun. For example: ① I asked her the time but she gave no answer. ② The teacher always answers students' questions patiently. ③ I sent in my application and the university replied immediately. ④ Don't prevaricate, give me a clear answer.

 **练习**

**练习一、根据拼音写汉字,根据汉字写拼音**

（　）jú　（　）sòng　zuì（　）　（　）fù　qīn（　）
结（　）　运（　）　（　）行　答（　）　（　）眼

**练习二、搭配连线**

(1) 正常　　　　　　A. 结论
(2) 明确　　　　　　B. 货物
(3) 得出　　　　　　C. 答复
(4) 运送　　　　　　D. 罪行
(5) 招认　　　　　　E. 运转

**练习三、从今天学习的生词中选择合适的词填空**

1. 这个项目非常重要,老板决定 ＿＿＿＿ 到当地考察。
2. 要不是我 ＿＿＿＿ 看见了,我也无法相信这是真的。
3. 这样,我们就能很好地把理论 ＿＿＿＿ 到实践中去了。
4. 由于电压不稳定,发动机无法正常 ＿＿＿＿ 。
5. 这些国际特快专递邮件都是用飞机 ＿＿＿＿ 的。
6. 这件毛衣是妈妈 ＿＿＿＿ 织的,我一直保留着。
7. 不经过仔细调查就不能随便下 ＿＿＿＿ 。
8. 他犯下了严重的 ＿＿＿＿ ,可能要在监狱里度过余生了。
9. 让我好好考虑考虑,三天后我给你 ＿＿＿＿ 。
10. 我觉得这些电视剧没意思,看到一半就能猜出故事的 ＿＿＿＿ 。

**答案**

**练习一:**
略

**练习二:**
(1) E　　(2)C　　(3)A　　(4)B　　(5)D

**练习三:**
1.亲自　2.亲眼　3.运用　4.运转　5.运送
6.亲手　7.结论　8.罪行　9.答复　10.结局

**次** cì （甲）量

measure word for times

**常用搭配**

下次 next time

一周一次 once a week

第一次 the first time

**用法示例**

他给我们讲的笑话，我们都听过很多次了。

He told us a joke that we'd all heard many times before.

我每周去两次图书馆。

I go to the library twice a week.

我们就下次的选举打个赌吧。

Let's make a bet on the next election.

**一块儿** yíkuàir （甲）副

① together ② at the same location

**常用搭配**

和／跟……一块儿 together with…

跟他坐在一块儿 sit with him

**用法示例**

别都挤在一块儿，分开坐吧。

Don't all sit together, spread yourselves out.

咱们用胶水把它们粘在一块儿。

Let's stick them together with glue.

你是跟她一块儿去的吗？

Did you go with her?

**遍** biàn （乙）量

measure word for times

**常用搭配**

读三遍课文。Read the text three times.

**用法示例**

下课后，我复习了一遍笔记。

I went over the note after class.

你能把这个问题重复一遍吗？

Could you repeat the question?

她用海绵使劲儿擦了一遍地板。

She gave the floor a vigorous once over with the sporge.

**一旁** yìpáng （乙）名

aside

**常用搭配**

站在一旁 stand aside

放在一旁 set it aside

**用法示例**

他把书放在一旁。

He set his book aside.

她把我拉到一旁，悄悄地跟我说话。

She drew me aside and whispered in my ear.

他闪到一旁让她过去。

He stood aside and let her pass by.

**千万** qiānwàn 圓 一定 yídìng （乙）副

be sure to

**常用搭配**

千万别忘了。Be sure not to forget it.

**用法示例**

你过马路千万要当心。

You must be careful when crossing the road.

比赛前千万不要把这个坏消息告诉她。

Make sure not to tell her the bad news before the match.

**一下子** yíxiàzi （乙）副

① in a short while ② all of a sudden

不要一下子全吃光，留一些以后再吃。

Don't eat them all at once; save some for later.

汽油价格一下子上涨了百分之四。

The gasoline price has risen by 4 percent in a short time.

他一下子就猜中了谜底。

He answered the riddle as quick as a flash.

**一再** yízài 圓 反复 fǎnfù （丙）副

① repeatedly ② time and again

**常用搭配**

一再强调 to stress repeatedly

一再解释 to explain again and again

**用法示例**

他一再说他很忙。

He repeated several times that he was busy.

事实一再证明他错了，他最终改变了想法。

Repeatedly proven wrong by reality, he finally changed his mind.

我父亲一再强调学习的重要性。

My father repeatedly stressed the importance of study.

**一向** yíxiàng 圓 向来 xiànglái （丙）副

① always ② all along

**常用搭配**

她一向很友好。She is always friendly.

**用法示例**

他一向来得很晚。

He always comes very late

孩子们的前途一向是我心中最重要的事。

The children's future is always uppermost in my mind.

她一向自负,从来不接受别人的意见。

She has always been conceited and never accepts others' advice.

### 一口气 yìkǒuqì (丙)副

① in one breath ② one breath

**常用搭配**

吸一口气 draw a breath

一口气做完了 finish doing it in one go

**用法示例**

深深地吸一口气,你会感到轻松。

Take a deep breath, then you can relax.

他一口气喝了一大杯牛奶。

He drank a glass of milk in one go.

他一口气吹灭了生日蛋糕上所有的蜡烛。

He blew out all the candles on his birthday cake in a single breath.

### 一心 yìxīn (丙)形

① wholeheartedly ② heart and soul

**常用搭配**

一心学习 learn with one's whole heart

团结一心 be united with one mind

**用法示例**

他一心想工作,所以放弃了大学的学业。

He wanted to work with his whole heart, so he gave up studying at the university.

这孩子一心想要买一匹小马。

The child has set his heart on buying a pony.

他一心想去留学,没有人能阻止他。

He has set his heart on studying abroad and nobody can stop him.

### 一旦 yídàn (丁)名/副

① in a single day ( or in a very short time ) ② once

**常用搭配**

毁于一旦 be destroyed overnight

**用法示例**

一旦下了决心,他就毫不动摇。

Once he's made up his mind, he never budges.

一旦出版,这本书将会非常受欢迎!

Once published, the book will be very popular!

事实一旦公开,他就要受到惩罚。

Once the facts become known, he will be punished.

### 一律 yílù ⊜一概 yígài (丁)形

① all ② without exception

**常用搭配**

一律平等 to all be equal

**用法示例**

所有货物一律八五折。

All goods have been marked down by 15%.

人不分贫富,一律平等。

Whether we are rich or poor, we are all equal.

明天所有学生一律穿校服。

All students should wear school uniform tomorrow.

 **词义辨析**

**次、遍**

"次"和"遍"都是动量词。"次"强调动作重复或事物反复出现的次数,它使用得十分广泛,可以修饰会议、旅行、战争等;而"遍"强调的是动作从开始到结束的整个过程,经常修饰读、写、说、听等突出过程的动作。例如:①我来过两次北京。②对我来说一次就够了。③请注意,我把问题再重复一遍。

Both 次 and 遍 are verbal measure words. 次 stresses the repetition of actions or reoccurrence of events, is used more often, and can modify "会议" (conference), "旅行" (travel), "战争" (war), and so on; while 遍 stresses the course of an action from beginning to end, and often modifies actions like "读" (read), "写" (write), "说" (speak), "听" (listen), etc. which involve a course. For example: ① I have been to Beijing twice. ② Once is enough for me. ③ Attention please, I'll repeat the question once more.

 **练习**

**练习一、根据拼音写汉字，根据汉字写拼音**

| lù | dàn | zài | xiàng | páng |
|---|---|---|---|---|
| —( ) | —( ) | —( ) | —( ) | —( ) |

**练习二、搭配连线**

(1) 毁于　　　　　　A. 平等
(2) 团结　　　　　　B. 强调
(3) 放在　　　　　　C. 一旁
(4) 一律　　　　　　D. 一旦
(5) 一再　　　　　　E. 一心

**练习三、从今天学习的生词中选择合适的词填空**

1. 虽然有十年没见面了,我还是 _____ 就认出了她。

2. 他不但不过来帮助我们,还站在 _____ 看我们的笑话。

3. 国庆节我们跟他们 _____ 去香港玩,好不好?

4. 老师 _____ 强调要遵守纪律,可他还是那么散漫。

5. 他 _____ 主张孩子的童年应该在玩耍中度过,不要给他们太大的学习压力。

6. 他酒量很好, _____ 把一大杯啤酒都喝了。

7. 你一个人去旅行, _____ 要注意安全啊!

8. 他 _____ 想回国创业,所以放弃了在国外的工作机会。

9. 战争 _____ 打响,难民将涌入周边国家。

10. 国家不分大小,应该 _____ 平等。

**答案**

**练习一:**
略

**练习二:**

| (1) D | (2)E | (3)C | (4)A | (5)B |
|---|---|---|---|---|

**练习三:**

| 1. 一下子 | 2. 一旁 | 3. 一块儿 | 4. 一再 | 5. 一向 |
|---|---|---|---|---|
| 6. 一口气 | 7. 千万 | 8. 一心 | 9. 一旦 | 10. 一律 |

# 第7月,第4周的练习

## 练习一.根据词语给加点的字注音
1.（ ）2.（ ）3.（ ）4.（ ）5.（ ）
模样　模型　运转　解雇　灾难

## 练习二.根据拼音完成词语
shè　shè　shē　zuì　kāng
1.（ ）及 2.（ ）击 3.（ ）侈 4.（ ）行 5.（ ）慨

## 练习三.辨析并选择合适的词填空
1. 四个人都很难完成这么多工作,（ ）他们只有两个人?（况且、何况）
2. 现在去看电影已经太晚了,（ ）又下起了雨。（况且、何况）
3. 他们俩（ ）是双胞胎,长得一点都不像。（不料、竟然）
4. 我们早晨就从家里出来了,（ ）,汽车在半路上坏了。（不料、竟然）
5. 这笔钱是从银行直接（ ）到他的账号里的。（汇、寄）
6. 你要是路过邮局,请帮我（ ）封信。（汇、寄）
7. 邀请函发出一个月了,至今没有（ ）。（答复、回答）
8. 老师提出了一个有趣的问题,同学们都争着（ ）。（答复、回答）
9. 这部电影真有意思,我看过一（ ）了,但是还想看。（次、遍）
10. 那个地方我去过很多（ ）了,不想再去了。（次、遍）

## 练习四.选词填空
赞赏　迷信　结局　一块儿　一下子
赞同　迷糊　结论　一口气　一律
1. 校长走了进来,喧闹的教室（ ）变得非常安静。
2. 昨晚,我（ ）把那本小说看完了。
3. 老师要求留学生在上课的时候（ ）用汉语交流。
4. 不要相信那个算命的人的话,他那是（ ）。
5. 我和她做什么事都在（ ）,有人说我们俩像亲姐妹。
6. 领导对他的能力大加（ ）,他可能要被提拔了。
7. 这部电影最后的（ ）是个悲剧。
8. 我很（ ）你的观点。
9. 他虽然睡醒了,可还是有点（ ）,所以他要冲个澡,清醒一下。
10. 在没把事实调查清楚以前,不要随便下（ ）。

## 练习五.量词填空
趟　盒　束　间　件
1. 看望病人的时候,可以带一（ ）鲜花或者拿一些水果。
2. 经理出去了,他说他要去办一（ ）重要的事。
3. 这（ ）房是书房,他每天在这里看书和写作。
4. 前几天,我回了（ ）老家,昨天刚回到北京。
5. 今天是中秋节,我的中国朋友送给我一（ ）月饼。

## 练习六.写出下列词语的同义词
1. 描写（ ）　2. 照样（ ）
3. 一律（ ）　4. 运用（ ）
5. 一再（ ）

## 练习七.写出下列词语的反义词
1. 赞同（ ）　2. 罪行（ ）
3. 慷慨（ ）　4. 迷糊（ ）
5. 解雇（ ）

## 答案

练习一.
1.mú 2.mó 3.yùn 4.gù 5.zāi
练习二.
1. 涉 2. 射 3. 奢 4. 罪 5. 慷
练习三.
1. 何况 2. 况且/何况 3. 竟然 4. 不料
5. 汇 6. 寄 7. 答复 8. 回答
9. 遍 10. 次
练习四.
1. 一下子 2. 一口气 3. 一律 4. 迷信 5. 一块儿
6. 赞赏 7. 结局 8. 赞同 9. 迷糊 10. 结论
练习五.
1. 束 2. 件 3. 间 4. 趟 5. 盒
练习六.
1. 描述 2. 依旧 3. 一概 4. 使用 5. 反复
练习七.
1. 反对 2. 功绩 3. 吝啬 4. 清醒 5. 聘用

# 8月 第1周的学习内容

## 星期一 Monday

**chūxiàn**
**出现** 反 消失 （甲）动
appear; arise; emerge

**常用搭配**
出现了问题 a problem arose

**用法示例**
计算机的出现极大地改变了人们的生活。
The advent of the computer changed people's lives greatly.
太阳出现在地平线上。
The sun appeared above the horizon.
他的突然出现使她很吃惊。
His sudden appearance surprised her.

**guǒrán**
**果然** （乙）副
① as expected ② sure enough

**常用搭配**
他果然通过了考试。 He passed the exam as expected.

**用法示例**
他说他会来的,果然来了。
He said he would come, and sure enough he did.
我说过会发生这样的事,果然如此。
I said it will happen, and sure enough it did.
他说星期日会下雨,果然下雨了。
He said it would rain on Sunday, and it really did rain.

**fèichú**
**废除** 同 废止 （丙）动
repeal; abolish

**常用搭配**
废除一项法令 to repeal a law

**用法示例**
有许多不良的习俗应予以废除。
There are many bad customs that ought to be abolished.
废除农奴制度后,农奴们获得了解放。
The serfs were liberated after the abolishment of serfdom.
不合理的规则被废除了。
The unreasonable rules were revoked.

**hàipà**
**害怕** （乙）动
be afraid; be scared

**常用搭配**
害怕的样子 a frightened look    别害怕 !Never fear!

**用法示例**
他害怕得声音发抖。
His voice shook with fear.
我害怕蛇。
I have a fear of snakes.
他那冷漠的目光让我害怕。
His frigid glance made me afraid.

**hàichu**
**害处** 反 益处 （乙）名
harm

**常用搭配**
噪音的害处 the adverse effects of noise

**用法示例**
努力工作对他没什么害处。
It wouldn't do him any harm to work hard.
你知道吸烟的害处吗?
Do you know the harmful effects of smoking?

**shuōfǎ**
**说法** （丙）名
statement; wording

**常用搭配**
正式的说法 a formal wording
对……说法不一 different versions of…

**用法示例**
两种说法相互矛盾。
The two statements contradict each other.
两家报纸对发生的事说法不同。
The two newspapers gave different versions of what happened.

**mùguāng**
**目光** （丙）名
sight; vision

**常用搭配**
目光远大 have far sight
目光短浅 short sight

**用法示例**
她用怀疑的目光看着我。
She looked at me questioningly.
目光远大的人心胸开阔。
Those who are far sighted in their views are broad-minded.

**kǒngjù**
**恐惧** （丁）动
dread; fear

**常用搭配**

感到恐惧 feel horrified
恐惧感 feeling of fear

**用法示例**

她克服了恐惧,走过了吊桥。
She conquered her fear and crossed the hanging bridge.
他颤抖的双手显示出他内心的恐惧。
His shaking hands showed his inner fear.
谋杀引起了广泛的恐惧。
Murder arouses widespread horror.

shìxiàn
## 视线 （丁）名

line of sight; view line

**常用搭配**

在视线以内 within sight

**用法示例**

火车仍在视线内。
The train is still in sight.
没有人敢把视线离开地面。
Nobody dared lift their eyes from the ground.
沙漠一直伸展到视线的尽头。
The desert continued as far as the eye could see.

shuōhuǎng
## 说谎 （丁）动

to lie; tell lies

**常用搭配**

别对我说谎。 Don't lie to me.

**用法示例**

你为什么对我说谎?
Why did you tell me a lie?
谁对你说这话,谁就在说谎。
Whoever told you that was lying.
他存心说谎。
He told us a deliberate lie.

hàixiū                    xiūqiè
## 害羞    ◎羞怯 （丁）形

shy

**常用搭配**

别害羞! Don't be shy!
害羞的姑娘 a shy girl

**用法示例**

这个小孩很害羞,躲在他妈妈后面。
The child was shy and hid behind his mother.
那个害羞的小男孩遇到陌生人就紧张。
The bashful boy was nervous with strangers.

tuīxuǎn
## 推选 （丁）动

elect; choose

**常用搭配**

推选他当候选人 choose him as a candidate

**用法示例**

你推选谁当咱们足球队的队长?
Whom will you choose for our football team captain?
他被推选为教育委员会委员。
He was elected to be a member of the education committee.
我们都推选他当班长。
We all chose him to be class monitor.

 词义辨析

**害怕、恐惧**

"害怕"和"恐惧"都是动词,都可以表示人或动物惊慌或不安的心理反应,"害怕"多用于口语,是及物动词,后面可以接宾语或宾语从句,但不能用作名词;而"恐惧"多用于书面语,程度比"害怕"深,是不及物动词,不能带宾语,但可以用作名词。例如:①他害怕/恐惧得直发抖。②不要害怕困难,要想办法克服它。③她听到这件事时,心里充满了恐惧。

Both 害怕 and 恐惧 are verbs, indicating "a psychological reaction of fear in a person or an animal". 害怕 is more colloquial, and it is a transitive verb that can take an object or object clause, but can not be used as a noun; while 恐惧 is more literal, and is deeper in fear, it is an intransitive verb, can not take an object, but can be used as a noun. For example: ① He was shaking with fear. ② Don't be afraid of difficulties, try to overcome them. ③ Her heart was filled with fear when she heard of it.

 **练习**

**练习一、根据拼音写汉字，根据汉字写拼音**

( )xiū  tuī( )  ( )huǎng  ( )jù  fèi( )

害( )  ( )选  说( )  恐( )( )除

**练习二、搭配连线**

(1) 害羞的　　　　　　　A. 害处
(2) 害怕的　　　　　　　B. 目光
(3) 吸烟的　　　　　　　C. 说法
(4) 远大的　　　　　　　D. 姑娘
(5) 矛盾的　　　　　　　E. 样子

**练习三、从今天学习的生词中选择合适的词填空**

1. 这个节目介绍了吸烟和酗酒对身体的 _____。
2. 早就听说北京烤鸭好吃，昨天去吃了，味道 _____ 很好。
3. 病人昨天吃药后 _____ 了不良反应。
4. 父母教育孩子说：要诚实，好孩子是不应该 _____ 的。
5. 照你的 _____，你一点错都没有，都是我的错，是吗？
6. 列车开动了起来，我向父母挥手告别，直到他们从我的 _____ 里消失。
7. 孩子看到歹徒凶狠的 _____ 害怕得哭了起来。
8. 一想到刚刚经历的车祸，我的内心就充满了 _____。
9. 老主任退休了，我们都 _____ 小王作为新主任的候选人。
10. 我们决定实施新的规定，同时 _____ 以前的规定。

**答案**

**练习一：**
略

**练习二：**
(1) D　　(2)E　　(3)A　　(4)B　　(5)C

**练习三：**
1. 害处　2. 果然　3. 出现　4. 说谎　5. 说法
6. 视线　7. 目光　8. 恐惧　9. 推选　10. 废除

 **星期二**

liúniàn
**留念**　　　　　　　　　　　　（甲）动

keep as a souvenir

**常用搭配**

与……合影留念

have a photograph taken with sb. as a souvenir

**用法示例**

我的朋友在离别前给我一张照片作为留念。

My friend gave me one of his pictures as a memento before going away.

李叔叔出国时给了我一块手表作为留念。

When Uncle Li went abroad to live, he left me his watch as a souvenir.

jìniàn
**纪念**　　　　　　　　　　　（乙）动 / 名

① commemorate ② commemoration

**常用搭配**

纪念馆 memorial　　　纪念碑 monument
纪念品 souvenir

**用法示例**

为了永远纪念那位领袖，他们决定建一座雕像。

They decided to commemorate the memory of their leader by erecting a statue.

下周一是他们的结婚纪念日。

Next Monday is their wedding anniversary.

我有一枚有纪念意义的奖牌。

I have a commemorative medal.

jiànzhù
**建筑**　　　　　　　　　　　（乙）动 / 名

① build ② construction; architecture

**常用搭配**

古代建筑 ancient architecture
建筑风格 style of architecture

**用法示例**

炸弹把那座建筑夷为平地了。

The bombs razed the building to the ground.

紫禁城是世界上最伟大的建筑之一。

The Forbidden City is one of the world's greatest works of architecture.

这座大教堂被看作是建筑史上的奇迹。

This cathedral was regarded as a miracle in architectural history.

zuòfǎ
**做法**　　　　　　　　　　　　（乙）名

way of doing things

**常用搭配**

饼干的做法 the way of making cookies

**用法示例**

你能给我演示烤鸭的做法吗？

Can you show me how to make roast duck？

处理这类案件的常规做法是请求法院发出指令。

The general practice in such cases is to apply for a court order.

我对陶器的做法很感兴趣。

I am interested in the ways of making pottery.

jiànyì
**建议**　　　　◎ 提议 tíyì　　　（乙）动 / 名

① propose; suggest ② suggestion

**常用搭配**

一项合理的建议 a reasonable proposal

采纳他的建议 take his suggestion

提建议 make a suggestion

**用法示例**

我建议马上动身。

I propose to set off immediately.

科学家建议人们多吃些纤维素。

Scientists are recommending people eat more fiber.

这些建议完全不可行。

These suggestions are entirely impractical.

zuòfēng
**作风**　　　　　　　　　（丙）名

way; style

**常用搭配**

民主作风 a democratic style

工作作风 style of work

**用法示例**

我们很欣赏新领导的工作作风。

Everybody admires the new leader for his style of doing things.

他很专横，我们都讨厌他这种作风。

He was very domineering in company, and the rest of us hated it.

tèsè
**特色**　　　　　　　　　（丁）名

① characteristic ② distinguishing feature or quality

**常用搭配**

地方特色 local color　　特色食品 characteristic food

**用法示例**

这就是中国国画的特色。

This is a characteristic of Chinese traditional painting.

温暖的气候是这个地区的特色。

The mild climate is a feature of this area.

jūrán
**居然**　　　　　　　　　（丙）副

① unexpectedly ② to one's surprise

她不但参加了竞赛,而且居然获胜了！

She not only entered the competition, she actually won it!

你太粗心了,居然连你妈妈的生日也忘了。

It was thoughtless of you to forget your mother's birthday.

令人吃惊的是,她的丈夫居然像他的父亲一样老。

To my surprise, her husband is as old as her father.

jiànzào
**建造**　　　　　　　　　（丙）动

build

**常用搭配**

建造一座桥 build a bridge

建造教堂 build a church

**用法示例**

为了纪念胜利,建造了一座纪念碑。

A monument was built to commemorate the victory.

农舍是用木头建造的。

The farmhouse was built of wood.

他们正在建造一条新的铁路。

They are building a new railway.

tèzhēng
**特征**　　　　◎ 特点 tèdiǎn　　　（丙）名

feature

**常用搭配**

地理特征 geographic features

基本特征 basic features

**用法示例**

教授将要做一个关于青少年心理特征的讲座。

The professor will give a lecture on the psychological features of teenagers.

亚洲人区别于欧洲人的特征是什么？

What are the characteristics that distinguish Asians from Europeans?

zuòfèi
**作废**　　　　⊗ 生效 shēngxiào　　　（丁）动

be invalid

**常用搭配**

作废的支票 invalid cheque

作废的执照 invalid license

**用法示例**

这张票已过了有效期,现在作废了。

This ticket has passed its expiration date, and so it is now invalid.

用过的邮票就作废了。

The used stamps are invalid.

tuīxiāo
**推销**　　　　⊗ 采购 cǎigòu　　　（丁）动

promote sales; to market

**常用搭配**

推销产品 promote the sale pf products

推销的技巧 skills of sales promotion

**用法示例**

我们聘请了一家广告公司来推销我们的产品。

We hired an advertising company for help selling our products.

她负责推销工作。

She is responsible for sales promotion.

我们需要有人为我们向零售商推销产品。

We need somebody to market our products to retailers.

 词义辨析

**纪念、留念**

　　"纪念"和"留念"都可以表示对过去的怀念。"纪念"既可以用于令人愉快的事,也可以用于令人伤心的事,它是名词,也是及物动词,可以接宾语或宾语从句。"留念"多用于愉快的回忆,而且不能带宾语。例如:①这座纪念碑是纪念烈士的。②在毕业前,我们一起合影留念。

　　Both 纪念 and 留念 mean to commemorate somebody or something in the past. 纪念 refers to commemorating occurrences, happy or sorrowful, and can serve as a noun or a transitive verb and can take an object or object clause; while 留念 is mostly used for pleasant memory, and it can not take an object. For example: ① This monument commemorates those who died in the war. ② We took a picture together as a memento before graduation.

 练习

**练习一、根据拼音写汉字,根据汉字写拼音**

zuò (　　) zuò (　　) (　　)zhù (　　)zhēng jì (　　)

(　　)法 (　　)风 建(　　) 特(　　) (　　)念

**练习二、搭配连线**

(1) 推销　　　　　　A. 留念

(2) 建造　　　　　　B. 产品

(3) 工作　　　　　　C. 建议

(4) 提出　　　　　　D. 教堂

(5) 合影　　　　　　E. 作风

**练习三、从今天学习的生词中选择合适的词填空**

1. 医生 _____ 他戒烟戒酒,可是他根本不听。

2. 你知道麻婆豆腐这道菜的 _____ 吗?

3. 毕业离校前,大家都在校园里拍照 _____。

4. 端午节有赛龙舟、吃粽子的风俗,这是为了 _____ 伟大的爱国诗人屈原。

5. 水煮鱼是这家饭馆的 _____ 菜,别的饭馆做得确实不如这一家。

6. 黄头发、蓝眼睛、白皮肤是白种人的 _____。

7. 新学期,我们办理了新的学生证,那个旧的 _____ 了。

8. 出差刚回来,今天他去财务处 _____ 差旅费。

9. 他已经来北京两年了, _____ 没去过长城,真让人难以理解。

10. 为了举行奥运会,这里将 _____ 一个巨大的体育馆。

**答案**

**练习一:**

略

**练习二:**

(1) B　　　(2)D　　　(3)E　　　(4)C　　　(5)A

**练习三:**

1. 建议　　2. 做法　　3. 留念　　4. 纪念　　5. 特色

6. 特征　　7. 作废　　8. 报销　　9. 居然　　10. 建造

星期三

## 基础 jīchǔ （甲）名

foundation；basic

**常用搭配**

在……的基础上 on the basis of...
基础知识 elementary knowledge

**用法示例**

美满的婚姻是建立在互相信任的基础上的。
A good marriage is based on trust.
你必须先弄懂数学的基础知识，我们才能进一步学习。
You must understand the basics of mathematics before we proceed further.
努力学习和努力工作为他的成功打下了基础。
He laid the foundation for his success by studying and working hard.

## 损失 sǔnshī （乙）动/名

① lose ② loss

**常用搭配**

重大损失 heavy loss　赔偿损失 compensate for losses

**用法示例**

保险公司将赔偿他的损失。
The insurance company will recompense his loss.
他们在经济危机时遭受了重大的损失。
They suffered huge losses in the financial crisis.

## 模仿 mófǎng （乙）动

imitate

**常用搭配**

模仿影星 imitate a movie star

**用法示例**

小男孩模仿他的父亲。
The little boy imitated his father.
他模仿老师的声音。
He mimicked the teacher's voice.
猿模仿我们的行为。
The ape imitated our behavior.

## 广泛 guǎngfàn （乙）形

① extensive ② wide range

**常用搭配**

兴趣广泛 wide interests　广泛阅读 read extensively

**用法示例**

广泛的阅读使我受益匪浅。
I have benefited a lot from extensive reading.

这种装置经过了广泛的实验。
The device had undergone extensive testing.
胜利的消息被广泛传播。
The news of victory spread widely.

## 广场 guǎngchǎng （乙）名

square

**常用搭配**

天安门广场 Tiananmen Square

**用法示例**

广场上有成百上千人。
There were hundreds of people in the square.
市民们在广场上集会反对他们的新市长。
The citizens gathered in the square to oppose their new mayor.
在市中心有一个广场。
There was a square in the center of the city.

## 隔阂 géhé ⑩ 隔膜 gémó （丙）名

estrangement

**常用搭配**

产生隔阂 cause an estrangement
消除隔阂 end an estrangement

**用法示例**

我觉得我和女儿之间没有任何隔阂。
I think there is no distance between my daughter and I.
尽管我们一起生活，但我知道我们之间有隔阂。
Although we lived our lives together, I know there was a barrier between us.

## 融洽 róngqià （丁）形

harmonious；compatible

**常用搭配**

融洽的家庭 a harmonious family
融洽地交谈 to talk in harmony

**用法示例**

他们合作得很融洽。
They cooperated in harmony.
这位老师和学生的关系很融洽。
The teacher has a very harmonious relationship with her students.
他俩简直无法融洽地相处，所以就离婚了。
Their marriage came to an end because they were simply not compatible with each other.

## 模范 mófàn ⑩ 楷模 kǎimó （丙）名/形

① model ② fine example

**常用搭配**

模范教师 a model teacher
模范人物 role model

**【用法示例】**

站在他旁边的是一位劳动模范。

Standing by him was a model worker.

她是全班的模范。

She was an example to the rest of the class.

由于他打死了不少狼,他享有 "模范猎手" 的称号。

He holds the title of model hunter for the number of wolves he has killed.

## sǔnhài
# 损害　　反 保护 bǎohù　　（丙）动

do harm

**【常用搭配】**

损害某人的名誉 do harm to one's reputation

**【用法示例】**

这次失败使他的声誉受到了很大损害。

This failure did his reputation a lot of harm.

你不应该损害你们国家的利益。

You shouldn't harm the interests of your country.

## sǔnhuài
# 损坏　　（丙）动

to damage

**【常用搭配】**

损坏机器 damage the machine

损坏庄稼 damage the corn

**【用法示例】**

软木容易损坏。

Soft wood damages easily.

因使用不当造成的损坏,生产厂家不负任何责任。

The manufacturers disclaim all responsibility for the damage caused by misuse.

## gélí
# 隔离　　（丁）动

to separate; to isolate

**【常用搭配】**

隔离病人 keep the patient in quarantine

隔离病房 an isolation sickroom

**【用法示例】**

他接受了一星期的检疫隔离。

He had been kept in quarantine for a week.

这个病人应该被隔离。

This patient should be separated from the others.

她患猩红热后被隔离了三个星期。

She was quarantined for three weeks when she had scarlet fever.

## líbié
# 离别　　反 团聚 tuánjù　　（丁）动

to leave or part (when going on a long journey)

**【常用搭配】**

离别故乡 depart one's hometown

离别一年 be away for one year

**【用法示例】**

他们在离别时都哭了。

They all cried at parting.

他匆匆地离别了家人。

He parted from his family hurriedly.

 词义辨析

**损害、损坏**

　　"损害" 和 "损坏" 都是动词,都是 "使受伤害、损失或破坏" 的意思。但是这两个动词的对象不同,"损害" 往往用于抽象的事物;而 "损坏" 用于具体的事物。如:①他对顾客的态度损害了商店的声誉。②地震使一些建筑受到了损坏。

　　As verbs, 损害 and 损坏 mean "to damage". But the objects of these two verbs are different: 损害 is usually applied to something abstract; while 损坏 is applied to something concrete. For example: ① His attitude to customers did harm to reputation of the shop. ② The earthquake damaged several buildings.

 练习

**练习一、根据拼音写汉字，根据汉字写拼音**

( )fàn　sǔn( )　róng( )( )hé　( )chǔ
模( )　( )失　( )洽　隔( )　基( )

**练习二、搭配连线**

(1) 兴趣　　　　　　　A. 隔阂
(2) 模范　　　　　　　B. 公物
(3) 损坏　　　　　　　C. 损失
(4) 消除　　　　　　　D. 人物
(5) 赔偿　　　　　　　E. 广泛

**练习三、从今天学习的生词中选择合适的词填空**

1. 洪水冲垮了房屋,淹没了庄稼,造成了巨大的_____。
2. 爆炸的强烈震动导致附近的民宅遭到不同程度的_____。
3. 我们认为他们的行为_____了我们公司的名誉,他们应对此负责。
4. 作为演员,要有很强的_____能力,才能演谁像谁。
5. 谈判的双方都很友好,都希望能够长期合作,所以谈判的气氛十分_____。
6. 传染病人一般在医院接受_____治疗,以免相互传染。
7. 他的汉语_____不太好,所以还要经常复习以前的内容。
8. 以前她和姐姐的关系特别好,后来因为遗产的事,姐妹俩有了_____。
9. 他们夫妻俩从来没吵过架,真是对_____夫妻。
10. 经过推广和普及,这项技术已经得到_____应用了。

🔑 **答案**

**练习一:**
略
**练习二:**
(1) E　　(2)D　　(3)B　　(4)A　　(5)C
**练习三:**

1. 损失　2. 损坏　3. 损害　4. 模仿　5. 融洽
6. 隔离　7. 基础　8. 隔阂　9. 模范　10. 广泛

---

 **星期四** Thursday

zhàoxiàng
## 照相　（甲）动
take a photograph

常用搭配
照相机 camera
给……照相 take a picture of

用法示例
照相时照相机不要晃。
Try not to move the camera when taking a photograph.
您能给我们照张相吗?
Can you take a picture of us?
我们给足球队照了张相。
We photographed the football team.

piàoliang　　　　měilì
## 漂亮　回 美丽　（甲）形
beautiful; pretty

常用搭配
漂亮的女孩 a beautiful girl
漂亮的画 a pretty picture

用法示例
她漂亮,但不吸引人。
She is pretty rather than attractive.
这个可爱的小男孩长着漂亮的金色卷发。
The lovely boy has beautiful blonde curls.
等所有的植物都开花时,花园会显得非常漂亮。
The garden will look very beautiful when all the plants are in flower.

nándào
## 难道　（乙）副
Could it be that...?

常用搭配
难道你没听说? Haven't you heard of it?

用法示例
你难道谁也不关心吗?
Don't you care about anybody?
难道你不想夸夸我的新帽子吗?
Aren't you going to admire my new hat?
难道你还不理解你父母吗?
Haven't you understood your parents?

hǎowánr
## 好玩儿　（乙）形
interesting; funny

常用搭配
真好玩儿! How amusing!
好玩儿的游戏 an interesting game

**用法示例**

我们觉得这个游戏很好玩儿。
We think the game is very interesting.
这个玩具很好玩儿。
This toy is very interesting.

### 个别 gèbié 反普遍 pǔbiàn （乙）形

individual; particular

**常用搭配**

个别教学 individual teaching
个别现象 specific phenomenon

**用法示例**

如果班上的学生人数多,老师就不能给予个别辅导了。
A teacher can't give individual attention to each pupil if his class is large.
只有个别学生没有通过考试。
Just a few of the students didn't pass the exam.

### 模糊 móhu （丙）形

vague; indistinct

**常用搭配**

模糊的想法 vague idea    模糊的记忆 indistinct memory

**用法示例**

透过雾,我们看到了轮船模糊的轮廓。
Through the fog we saw the vague outline of a ship.
照片上孩子们的面部非常模糊。
The children's faces were very blurred in the photograph.
这块石头上的字迹很模糊。
The writing on the stone was very faint.

### 个子 gèzi （乙）名

stature; height

**常用搭配**

个子矮小 be of mean stature

**用法示例**

她个子高,能看到墙的那一边。
She can see over the wall because of her height.
他个子很高。
He is very tall.
他个子小但身体很健壮。
He was small but well built.

### 各自 gèzì （丙）代

respective; each

**常用搭配**

他们都有各自的职责。
They all have their respective duties.

**用法示例**

他们在各自的领域都取得了成功。
They are successful in their respective fields.

圣诞节那天他们将各自去看自己的父母。
They will visit their respective parents on Christmas.
聚会之后我们回到各自的房间。
After the party we all went off to our respective rooms.

### 美观 měiguān （丙）形

beautiful; artistic

**常用搭配**

美观的图案 an artistic design
美观大方 artistic and handsome

**用法示例**

这些展品质量优良,设计美观。
These exhibits are fine in quality and beautiful in design.
我觉得这个包装十分美观。
I think the packing is quite beautiful.

### 漫长 màncháng 反短暂 duǎnzàn （丙）形

very long

**常用搭配**

漫长的冬季 long winter

**用法示例**

经过漫长的等待,她的丈夫终于回来了。
There was a very long wait before her husband finally came back.
那一夜对我来说特别漫长。
That night was particularly long for me.
征服癌症的路还相当漫长。
The road to conquering cancer is still rather long.

### 蔓延 mànyán 扩展 kuòzhǎn （丁）动

spread

**常用搭配**

蔓延到全国 spread throughout the country

**用法示例**

火从工厂蔓延到附近的房屋。
The fire spread from the factory to the houses nearby.
这种病在村里蔓延开了。
The illness spread throughout the village.
人们心中的恐惧像瘟疫一样蔓延开来。
Fear spread through the crowd like a contagion.

### 推理 tuīlǐ （丁）名

reasoning; illation

**常用搭配**

正确的推理 sound reasoning    严密的推理 close reasoning

**用法示例**

他的推理无懈可击。
His reasoning can't be flawed.
我觉得律师的推理是令人信服的。
I think the lawyer's reasoning is convincing.

 **词义辨析**

**美观、漂亮**

　　"美观"和"漂亮"都是形容词,都有"好看"的意思。但"美观"往往强调形式美,多用于书面语,用于物,不用于人;"漂亮"多用于口语,可以用于人,也可以用于事物。例如:①窗帘设计得美观大方。②她是我见过的最漂亮的姑娘。

　　Both 美观 and 漂亮 are adjectives, indicating "good-looking". 美观 often stresses the form, is used in writing, and is applied to things; while 漂亮 is mostly used in spoken language, and can be applied to people as well as things. For example: ① The curtain is artistically designed. ② She is the most beautiful girl I've ever seen.

 **练习**

**练习一、根据拼音写汉字,根据汉字写拼音**

màn (　　) màn (　　) gè (　　) mó (　　)(　　) dào

(　　)延 (　　)长 (　　)自 (　　)糊　难(　　)

**练习二、搭配连线**

(1) 漫长的　　　　　　　A. 图案
(2) 模糊的　　　　　　　B. 推理
(3) 高高的　　　　　　　C. 等待
(4) 严密的　　　　　　　D. 个子
(5) 美观的　　　　　　　E. 记忆

**练习三、从今天学习的生词中选择合适的词填空**

1. 暑假的时候,我想去香港散散心,你能告诉我那儿有哪些 _____ 的地方吗?

2. 那个高 _____ 的男生是我们学校篮球队的队长。

3. 他要求每个孩子都要自己打扫 _____ 的房间,谁也不能偷懒。

4. 总的来说,公司的同事是友好的,只有 _____ 人看不起我们外国人。

5. 大火没有被及时扑灭,火势 _____ 到了山的北坡。

6. 晚上,我失眠了,我的内心充满了恐惧和不安,这是我度过的最 _____ 的一夜。

7. 他喜欢看侦探小说,因为里边的 _____ 情节引人入胜。

8. 由于我4岁就离开了那座城市,所以对那里的印象很 _____。

9. 他的技术很熟练,每次干完活,客户都夸他活干得 _____。

10. 你 _____ 甘心在这样的一个小企业里度过一辈子吗?

**答案**

**练习一:**
略

**练习二:**
(1) C　　　　(2)E　　　　(3)D　　　　(4)B　　　　(5)A

**练习三:**
1.好玩儿　2.个子　3.各自　4.个别　5.蔓延
6.漫长　7.推理　8.模糊　9.漂亮　10.难道

**jīhuì**
# 机会 （甲）名
opportunity; chance

**常用搭配**
错过机会 miss the opportunity
抓住机会 seize an opportunity
利用机会 take an opportunity

**用法示例**
别再犹豫了，一有机会就抓住它！
Don't hesitate to seize the first opportunity that comes along!
要是我再有一次机会就好了。
If only I had another chance.
他没有给我回答问题的机会。
He gave me no choice but to reply to the question.

**fādòng**
# 发动 （乙）动
start; mobilize

**常用搭配**
发动引擎 start the engine　发动进攻 launch an attack
发动群众 mobilize the masses

**用法示例**
今天早晨我的汽车发动不起来了。
I couldn't make my car start this morning.
校长发动学校所有的学生帮助那个有困难的同学。
Our headmaster mobilized all the students in our school to help the student who was in difficulty.

**jiūjìng**
# 究竟 **dàodǐ** ⓪ 到底 （乙）副
on earth

**常用搭配**
究竟在哪里 where on earth　究竟是谁 who on earth

**用法示例**
你究竟是什么意思？
What in the world do you mean?
那件事究竟是谁告诉你的？
Who on earth told you that?
你究竟在搞什么？
What the hell are you doing?

**gēnjù**
# 根据 **yījù** ⓪ 依据 （乙）动/介/名
① be based on ② according to ③ foundation; basis

**常用搭配**
根据记录 according to records
毫无根据 without any basis

根据事实 based on facts

**用法示例**
这部影片是根据鲁迅的小说改编的。
This film is based on a novel by Luxun.
根据我们的合同，我们将分期付款。
According to our contract, we will be paying in installments.
这篇新闻报导完全是根据实际情况写成的。
This news report is based entirely on fact.

**jiājǐn**
# 加紧 （丙）动
intensify; speed up; step up

**常用搭配**
加紧工作 intensify one's work
加紧调查 intensify an investigation

**用法示例**
科学家们加紧研究这种新的基因。
The scientists have intensified their study on the new gene.
加紧干吧！ 如果不快点，我们永远也完不成。
Shake a leg there! We'll never finish if you don't hurry up.
天要黑了，加紧搜索。
The search intensified as dusk approached.

**gēnyuán**
# 根源 （丙）名
root

**常用搭配**
问题的根源 root of the problem
烦恼的根源 root of the trouble

**用法示例**
不开心是他生病的根源。
Unhappiness is the root cause of his illness.
问题的根源在于缺乏信任。
The root of the problem is a lack of trust.
她相信一切罪恶的根源是金钱。
She thinks that money is the root of all evil.

**shuōfú**
# 说服 （丙）
persuade; convince

**常用搭配**
说服某人……persuade sb to…

**用法示例**
这个商人说服我买了他的货物。
This trader talked me into buying his goods.
孩子们试图说服妈妈让他们去看马戏。
The children are trying to persuade their mother to allow them to go to the circus.
他说服她在文件上签了字。
He persuaded her to sign the document.

**kāidòng**
# 开动 （丙）动
start

**常用搭配**

开动机器 start a machine

开动脑筋。Use your brain.

**用法示例**

轮船缓缓地开动了。

Slowly the ship began to move.

我一上去,公共汽车就开动了。

The moment that I was on the step, the bus started.

路警吹响了哨子,火车就开动了。

The guard blew his whistle, and the train moved off.

**jīgòu**

## 机构 (丙)名

institution; organization

**常用搭配**

学术机构 academic institution

医疗机构 medical institution

管理机构 administrative organ

**用法示例**

议会是政府的一个机构。

Parliament is an organ of the government.

这个机构得到联合国的资助。

The organization is backed by the UN.

**shuōqíng**

## 说情 (丁)动

intercede; plead for somebody else

**常用搭配**

为他说情 intercede for him

为 B 向 A 说情 make an intercession to A for B

**用法示例**

母亲经常为我向父亲说情。

My mother often intercedes with my father for me.

老师为一名学生向校长说情。

The teacher interceded with the headmaster for a student.

**jiājù**

## 加剧 (丁)动

aggravate; intensify

**常用搭配**

迅速加剧 aggravate quickly

**用法示例**

痛苦加剧了她的病情。

Grief aggravated her illness.

他们的行动没有缓和局势,反而加剧了局势。

Rather than relieving the situation, their actions aggravated it.

**tuīcè** **chuǎicè**

## 推测 ◉揣测 (丁)动

speculate

**常用搭配**

推测竞选的结果

speculate on the result of an election

**用法示例**

他们根据这些事实推测出了结论。

They deduced a conclusion from these facts.

科学家试图推测宇宙的起源。

The scientist tried to speculate on the origins of the universe.

 词义辨析

**开动、发动**

"开动"和"发动"都是动词,都可以表示使机器运转。"开动"还指部队或车辆开始向前进,"发动"没有这个意思。"发动"还指主动开始战争行为或鼓动他人行动,"开动"没有这个意思。例如:①引擎发动 / 开动不起来。②火车开动了。③他发动少先队员清理街道。④去年那个国家发动了一场战争。

Both 开动 and 发动 are verbs, indicating "to set a machine into motion, operation". 开动 also means "to be on the move (of troops or a vehicle)"; while 发动 has no usage like this. 发动 also means "to start a war" or "to mobilize people to engage in a campaign"; while 开动 has no usage like this. For example: ① The engine won't start. ② The train started. ③ He called up young pioneers to clean the street. ④ That country launched a war last year.

 练习

**练习一、根据拼音写汉字,根据汉字写拼音**

( )jìng ( )jù ( )cè ( )gòu ( )jù

究( ) 加( ) 推( ) 机( ) 根( )

**练习二、搭配连线**

(1) 医疗      A. 机器

(2) 抓住      B. 机构

(3) 推测      C. 机会

(4) 开动      D. 调查

(5) 加紧      E. 结果

**练习三、从今天学习的生词中选择合适的词填空**

1. 我们 _____ 工作,如果今天完成了任务,明天我们就可以休息一天了。

2. 我最近经常头疼,昨天吃了医生开的药,不但没减轻,反而 _____ 了。

3. 经理跟我谈话,问了我各种各样的问题,不知道他 _____ 想了解什么。

4. 警察 _____ 笔迹确认他就是诈骗犯。

5. 今天发生的事只是个契机,矛盾的真正 _____ 在于利益的分配不均。

6. 这个社团一直以来积极 _____ 年轻人利用业余时间做志愿者。

7. 大家要 _____ 脑筋,多想办法,争取尽快克服困难。

8. 这个协会是一个民间 _____ ,该组织的成员是一些年轻画家。

9. 妈妈生气地把他赶出家,后来,姐姐为他向妈妈 _____ ,妈妈才原谅了他。

10. 他试图 _____ 主任同意他的意见。

 **答案**

**练习一:**
略
**练习二:**
(1) B　　(2)C　　(3)E　　(4)A　　(5)D
**练习三:**
1. 加紧　2. 加剧　3. 究竟　4. 根据　5. 根源
6. 发动　7. 开动　8. 机构　9. 说情　10. 说服

# 第8月,第1周的练习

**练习一.根据词语给加点的字注音**
1.(　)　2.(　)　3.(　)　4.(　)　5.(　)
隔离　　融洽　　害羞　　作废　　究竟

**练习二.根据拼音完成词语**
màn　　màn　　jù　　jù　　jù
1.(　)长　2.(　)延　3.根(　)　4.加(　)　5.恐(　)

**练习三.辨析并选择合适的词填空**
1. 小女孩非常(　)打雷和闪电。(害怕、恐惧)
2. 事隔十年,孩子们逐渐淡忘了那场大火带给他们的(　)和痛苦。(害怕、恐惧)
3. 很多中外游客在天安门前合影(　)。(纪念、留念)
4. 为了(　)建国60周年,历史博物馆最近展出了革命战争年代的一些物品。(纪念、留念)
5. 开发商的行为严重(　)了周围居民的利益。(损害、损坏)
6. 如果(　)了公共财物,那就得按原价赔偿。(损害、损坏)
7. 这座雕塑外形(　),寓意深刻。(美观、漂亮)
8. 爱美是人的天性,连幼儿园的孩子都喜欢(　)的老师。(美观、漂亮)
9. 我们要广泛地(　)群众,积极参与环保事业。(开动、发动)
10. 早上八点半,工厂里的机器就(　)了,发出轰隆轰隆的声音。(开动、发动)

**练习四.选词填空**
推选　　推理　　建筑　　做法　　作废
推销　　推测　　建造　　作风　　废除

1. 我们要继续发扬实事求是的工作(　)。
2. 从明年1月1日起,这里将试行新修改的法规,同时(　)原来的法规。
3. 近年来,水泥、钢材等(　)材料的价格增长很快。
4. 我们班同学都(　)马克作为学生会主席的候选人。
5. 这座城堡是300年前(　)的。
6. 她找了一份兼职工作,是在大商场里(　)化妆品。
7. 这个人拿着一张已经声明(　)的存折来取钱,这引起了银行工作人员的怀疑。
8. 西红柿炒鸡蛋的(　)其实很简单,一学就会。
9. 在逻辑课上,老师让我们根据已知的条件(　)出结果。
10. 总统没有出席那个重要的仪式,因此,有人(　)总统的病情可能加重了。

**练习五.选择语气副词填空**
果然　　居然　　难道　　究竟
1. 他到现在还没来,(　)他忘了今天要开会吗?
2. 现在医生也还不清楚(　)为什么会得这种病。
3. 这次来北京,我尝了有名的北京烤鸭,(　)非常有特色。
4. 这种谎话你(　)也相信,难怪人家总觉得你像个小孩子。

**练习六.写出下列词语的同义词**
1. 楷模(　)　　2. 根据(　)
3. 建议(　)　　4. 漂亮(　)
5. 废除(　)

**练习七.写出下列词语的反义词**
1. 出现(　)　　2. 损害(　)
3. 漫长(　)　　4. 作废(　)
5. 推销(　)

 **答案**

**练习一.**
1.gé　　2.róng　　3.xiū　　4.fèi　　5.jiū
**练习二.**
1. 漫　2. 蔓　3. 据　4. 剧　5. 惧
**练习三.**
1. 害怕　2. 恐惧　3. 留念　4. 纪念　5. 损害
6. 损坏　7. 美观　8. 漂亮　9. 发动　10. 开动
**练习四.**
1. 作风　2. 废除　3. 建筑　4. 推选　5. 建造
6. 推销　7. 作废　8. 做法　9. 推理　10. 推测
**练习五.**
1. 难道　2. 究竟　3. 果然　4. 居然
**练习六.**
1. 模范　2. 依据　3. 提议　4. 美丽　5. 废止
**练习七.**
1. 消失　2. 保护　3. 短暂　4. 生效　5. 采购

# 8月 第2周的学习内容

**星期一**

---

**yíqiè**
## 一切　　　　　　　　（甲）形/代

① all ② everything

**常用搭配**

一切都好。Everything is OK.
祝您一切顺利。Wishing you every success.

**用法示例**

我会尽一切可能帮助你。
I'll do everything possible to help you.
感谢你所做的一切。
Thank you for everything.
一切商品的价格都有可能调整。
All prices are subject to review.

**wùhuì**　　　　　　　**wùjiě**
## 误会　　　●误解　　（乙）动/名

① to misunderstand ② misunderstanding

**常用搭配**

这只是个误会。It's no more than a misunderstanding.

**用法示例**

别误会，我不是那个意思。
Don't misunderstand me, I don't mean that.
肯定是有误会了！
There must be some misunderstanding!
这一切误会都是他在无意中造成的。
He was the unknowing cause of all the misunderstanding.

**měihǎo**　　　　　　　**chǒuè**
## 美好　　　反丑恶　　（乙）形

happy; fine

**常用搭配**

美好的时光 a happy time
美好的前景 good future

**用法示例**

现实生活并不像人们想象的那样美好。
Real life isn't as happy as people imagine.
她为公司的前景描绘了一幅美好的蓝图。
She painted a rosy picture of the firm's future.

**tèdiǎn**
## 特点　　　　　　　　（乙）名

characteristic feature

**常用搭配**

地形特点 a feature of the landscape
显著的特点 marked traits

**用法示例**

她最为突出的特点是诚实。
Her predominant characteristic is honesty.
骆驼的特点是不喝水也能活很长时间。
A characteristic of the camel is its ability to live for a long time without drinking water.
雄心勃勃是所有成功商人的共同特点。
Ambition is a characteristic of all successful businessmen.

**jiāyǐ**
## 加以　　　　　　　　（乙）动

[before a verb to indicate to deal with the matter mentioned above] handle, deal with

**常用搭配**

加以解释 give an explanation
需要加以改进 need to be improved

**用法示例**

他把我讲的故事加以改进，编了一个更好的故事。
He trumped my story by telling a better one.
夏天的水果可以通过冷藏加以保存。
In the summer, fruits may be preserved by freezing them.
她是相当不错的工人，不过有时需要加以督促。
She is a fairly good worker, but she needs prodding occasionally.

**jiārù**　　　　　　　**tuìchū**
## 加入　　　反退出　　（丙）动

join

**常用搭配**

加入俱乐部 join a club
加入联合国 accede to United Nation

**用法示例**

她脱离自由党，加入了社会党。
She defected from the Liberals and joined the Socialists.
她加入了大学里的艺术协会。
She joined the university art society.
我国政府加入了该条约。
Our government ratified the treaty.

**wùjiě**
## 误解　　　　　　　　（丁）动

to misunderstand

**常用搭配**

你误解了我的意思。
You mistook my meaning.

**(用法示例)**

很抱歉，我们误解了你的好意。

Sorry! We misunderstood your good intentions.

她误解了我说的话。

She misunderstood what I said.

**guòyú**

**过于** （丁）副

① excessively ② too

**(常用搭配)**

过于担心 worry too much　　过于自信 too confident

**(用法示例)**

他对孩子们过于严格了。

He is too strict with his children.

你过于相信你的智力了。

You trust your intelligence too much.

不要过于匆忙地对重要的事作决定。

Don't decide on important matters too quickly.

**měimǎn**

**美满** （丁）形

happy

**(常用搭配)**

美满的婚姻 a happy marriage

美满的家庭 happy family

**(用法示例)**

祝你们俩一生幸福美满。

Here's wishing you both a lifetime of happiness.

这个故事有一个美满的结局。

The story has a happy ending.

**tuìxiū**

**退休** （丙）动

retire

**(常用搭配)**

退休金 retirement pay　　退休工人 retired worker

**(用法示例)**

他 60 岁时退休了。

He retired from the business when he was 60.

我明年退休。

I will retire next year.

我爷爷是一位退休教授。

My grandfather is a retired professor.

**fánnǎo**

**烦恼** （丁）形／名

① worried ② trouble

**(常用搭配)**

自寻烦恼 ask for trouble

**(用法示例)**

什么事使你烦恼？

What is worrying you?

生活的杂事儿使我烦恼。

The complexities of life trouble me.

别为小事烦恼。

Don't bother with trifles.

**fánzào**　　　　　　　　*jiāozào*

**烦躁** ◎ 焦躁 （丁）形

fidgety; agitated

**(用法示例)**

什么事使你烦躁不安？

What's agitating you?

那孩子又疲倦又烦躁。

The child was tired and fretful.

他因担心女儿而烦躁不安。

He was fretting about his daughter.

坏消息使她的心情很烦躁。

She became agitated by the bad news.

 词义辨析

**误会、误解**

"误会"和"误解"都可以作动词和名词,都表示对事物理解得不对。"误会"有时指双方都错误地领会了对方的意思,一般不用于对语言、文字方面的理解错误;而"误解"主要是指一方错误地理解了另一方的言行,也指对语言文字方面的理解错误。例如:①我认为这对夫妇之间发生了误会。②别误解／误会我说的话。③这句话容易使人误解,得改一改。

Both 误会 and 误解 are verbs and nouns, meaning "to misunderstand or to comprehend incorrectly". 误会 sometimes indicates that "both parts misunderstand each other", and is seldom applied to language or writing; while 误解 mainly indicates that "one part misunderstands another", and can be applied to language or writing. For example: ① I think the couple misunderstands each other. ② Don't misunderstand what I said. ③ Make some changes to this sentence, it is apt to be misunderstood.

**练习一、根据拼音写汉字，根据汉字写拼音**

( )zào wù ( ) ( )mǎn ( )xiū ( )rù

烦( ) ( )解 美( ) 退( ) 加( )

**练习二、搭配连线**

(1) 烦躁　　　　　　A. 烦恼

(2) 家庭　　　　　　B. 误会

(3) 发生　　　　　　C. 不安

(4) 退休　　　　　　D. 美满

(5) 自寻　　　　　　E. 工人

**练习三、从今天学习的生词中选择合适的词填空**

1. 导游领着我们参观博物馆时，有两三个外国游客也_____了我们的行列。

2. 有错误要及时_____改正，不能掩盖错误。

3. 我想一定是发生了_____，昨天小张根本没上班，他怎么会弄坏你的电脑呢？

4. 他在报纸上发表的文章遭到_____，认为他是在鼓励婚外恋。

5. 穿西装参加朋友的聚会，是不是_____正式了？

6. 这是一个幸福_____的三口之家，真羡慕他们。

7. 这几天小王在为跟女朋友吵架的事情而_____，我们得想办法帮帮他。

8. 这些天，大家又忙又累，心情都比较_____，所以说话要注意方式，别动不动就吵。

9. 很多老年人_____后在这个沿海小城买了房子安度晚年。

10. 年轻人要注意把握机会，千万不要虚度_____的青春时光。

**答案**

练习一：
略

练习二：

(1) C　　(2)D　　(3)B　　(4)E　　(5)A

练习三：

1. 加入　　2. 加以　　3. 误会　　4. 误解　　5. 过于

6. 美满　　7. 烦恼　　8. 烦躁　　9. 退休　　10. 美好

星期二

**nǔlì**

**努力**　　　　　　（甲）形

strive；try hard

**常用搭配**

努力学习 study hard　　努力工作 work hard

努力完成任务 try hard to complete a task

**用法示例**

请你更努力地学习。

Please put more effort into your school work.

他们为取得成功而努力工作。

They tried hard to succeed.

他的所有努力都白费了。

All his efforts were wasted.

**zhāodài**

**招待**　　　　　　（乙）动

receive (guests)；entertain

**常用搭配**

招待客人 entertain guests

出席招待会 attend a reception

**用法示例**

他剪下一串葡萄招待我们。

He cut off a bunch of grapes to entertain us.

我喜欢在家里用音乐和茶点招待朋友。

I like to entertain friends with music and refreshments at home.

招待会在草地中的亭子里举行。

The reception was held in a pavilion on the lawn.

**zhíwù**

**植物**　　　　　　（乙）名

plant

**常用搭配**

草本植物 herbaceous plant　　植物油 vegetable oil

**用法示例**

树和蔬菜都是植物。

Both trees and vegetables are plants.

他家有很多盆栽植物。

There are a lot of potted plants in his house.

所有的植物都需要水和阳光。

All plants need water and light.

**gōngfèi**

**公费**　　反 **zìfèi** 自费　　（乙）形

at public expense

**常用搭配**

公费旅行 travel at public expense

公费医疗 free medical care

**用法示例**

政府计划严格限制今年的公费开支。

The government plans to set strict limits on public spending this year.

他被派往美国公费留学。

He was sent to America to study at public expense.

### dúzhě
## 读者 （乙）名

reader

**常用搭配**

读者来信 letters from readers

**用法示例**

我的爱人是这部小说的第一个读者。

My wife is the first reader of this novel.

我必须请求读者原谅可能出现的错误。

I must ask the readers' kind indulgence for any inaccuracies that may possibly occur.

图书馆每周一到周六对读者开放。

The library is open to readers every Monday to Saturday.

### guānzhòng
## 观众 （乙）名

spectator; audience

**常用搭配**

电视观众 television viewer

**用法示例**

演出结束时，观众们热烈鼓掌。

Everyone applauded when the play ended.

他那风趣的表演引起了观众的哄堂大笑。

His amusing performance caused a roar of laughter in the audience.

体育场里有很多观众在等着看足球比赛。

There are a lot of spectators who are waiting to watch the football match in the stadium.

### kuǎndài
## 款待 （丙）动

entertain

**常用搭配**

款待朋友 entertain guests

**用法示例**

他们用美味佳肴款待客人。

They plied their guests with delicacies.

谢谢你的盛情款待。

Thank you for your kind hospitality.

### luèwēi
## 略微 ⊜ 稍微 shāowēi （乙）副

① a little bit ② slightly

**常用搭配**

略微超重了点儿。It's a little overweight.

略微高一点儿 be slightly higher

**用法示例**

他今天早晨略微好了一点儿。

He's a little better this morning.

墙上的油画略微有点儿歪。

The painting on the wall is a bit crooked.

她好像比以前略微瘦了点儿。

She looks a little thinner than before.

### dúwù
## 读物 （丙）名

reading material; reading matter

**常用搭配**

儿童读物 books for children

科普读物 reading material on popular science

**用法示例**

这个书店有很多种儿童读物。

There are all kinds of books for children in this bookstore.

我想买一些科普读物。

I want to buy some reading materials on popular science.

### miǎnfèi
## 免费 ⊗ 收费 shōufèi （丁）动

① free (of charge) ② gratis

**常用搭配**

免费参观 visit for free　免费入场。Entrance is gratis.

**用法示例**

这些杂志是免费的。

These magazines are free.

我们提供免费服务。

We provide free service.

市民可以免费使用这个图书馆。

Citizens may have free access to the library.

### zhòngzhí
## 种植 （丁）动

grow; to plant

**常用搭配**

种植果树 plant fruit trees　种植玉米 grow corn

**用法示例**

他善于种植蔬菜。

He is good at growing vegetables.

他计划在花园里种植玫瑰花。

He planned to grow roses in his garden.

### zhíwù
## 职务 ⊜ 职位 zhíwèi （丁）名

position; job

**常用搭配**

担任重要职务 hold an important post

**用法示例**

他希望明年能得到更好的职务。

He hoped he would hold a better post next year.

她在那家大公司谋到了一个好职务。

She got a good position in the large company.

 词义辨析

**款待、招待**

"款待"和"招待"都是动词,表示照顾宾客。"款待"强调用美酒和美食对好朋友或贵宾的热情优厚的照顾,一般不用于祈使句;"招待"指一般的照顾,可能提供茶水、食宿,可以用于祈使句。例如:①他不喜欢招待顾客。②他在本市最有名的饭店款待他的朋友。③我们受到了盛情的款待。

Both 款待 and 招待 are verbs, meaning "to entertain guests". 款待 indicates to royally and warmly entertain close friends or honored guests with good wine and good meals, and can not be applied in an imperative sentence; while 招待 is just entertaining, maybe providing tea, food or lodging, and can be applied in an imperative sentence. For example: ① He doesn't like entertaining his customers. ② He entertained his friends in the most famous restaurant of this city. ③ We were royally entertained.

 练习

**练习一、根据拼音写汉字,根据汉字写拼音**

zhí (　　)(　　) zhí (　　)wù luè (　　) kuǎn (　　)
(　　)务 种(　　) 读(　　)(　　)微 (　　)待

**练习二、搭配连线**

(1) 科普　　　　　　　　A. 客人
(2) 种植　　　　　　　　B. 参观
(3) 免费　　　　　　　　C. 留学
(4) 招待　　　　　　　　D. 读物
(5) 公费　　　　　　　　E. 蔬菜

**练习三、从今天学习的生词中选择合适的词填空**

1. 杂志社每天都能收到_____的来信,其中大部分是谈他们阅读杂志以后的感受。

2. 市场上对儿童_____的需求量非常大,我们要仔细研究儿童的阅读兴趣。

3. 房间里摆几盆绿色_____,既可以净化空气,又可以装饰房间。

4. 听说我们是迷路的游客,女主人热情地接纳并_____了我们。

5. 他们是远道而来的贵客,我们一定要精心准备,好好_____。

6. 退休人员享受_____医疗,他们的住院费由单位承担。

7. 与同龄的孩子相比,我的孩子_____有点胖,不过医生说不要紧。

8. 推销人员说,如果我买一套产品,她就_____送我一个茶杯。

9. 这对夫妇在海南承包了一个农场,准备_____各种果树。

10. 大会宣布:免去他校长的_____。

🔑 **答案**

练习一:
略

练习二:
(1) D　　(2)E　　(3)B　　(4)A　　(5)C

练习三:
1.读者　　2.读物　　3.植物　　4.招待　　5.款待
6.公费　　7.略微　　8.免费　　9.种植　　10.职务

**星期三**

**用法示例**
如果看事情光明的一面,你将活得更快乐。
Look on the bright side of things, and you will live more happily.
作为一个剧作家,他前途光明。
He has a bright future as a dramatist.

## bànfǎ
## 办法　　　　　　　　　　　　　　(甲) 名
method; means; way
**常用搭配**
好办法 good method
没办法 have no idea or have no choice
**用法示例**
治疗背痛的唯一办法是休息。
The only way to cure a backache is to rest.
没办法,我们只好等医生来。
We have no choice but to wait for the doctor to come.
您能告诉我们一个好办法吗?
Can you suggest a good way for us?

## guāngróng
## 光荣　　　　chǐrǔ　　　反 耻辱　　　(乙) 形
honorable; glorious
**常用搭配**
光荣传统 glorious traditions　　光荣榜 honor roll
光荣的使命 a mission of honor
**用法示例**
她是同行的光荣。
She is an honor to her profession.
我们的党是一个伟大、光荣的政党。
Our Party is a great, glorious party.
作为科学家,我感到很光荣。
I am proud to be a scientist.

## cuòshī
## 措施　　　jǔcuò　　回 举措　　　(乙) 名
measure
**常用搭配**
采取措施 take measures　　预防措施 preventive measures
**用法示例**
我们不得不采取预防措施。
We had to take preventive measures.
机场当局已答应重新检查他们的安全措施。
The airport authorities have promised to review their security measures.
政府还没有找出应对失业的有效措施。
The government hasn't worked out effectual measures to combat unemployment.

## dàshǐguǎn
## 大使馆　　　　　　　　　　　　(乙) 名
embassy
**常用搭配**
美国驻华大使馆 American Embassy in China
中国大使馆 Chinese Embassy
**用法示例**
他要去大使馆申请签证。
He will go to the Embassy to apply for a visa.
她哥哥在日本大使馆工作。
Her brother works in the Japanese Embassy.
恐怖分子占领了大使馆。
The terrorists have occupied the Embassy.

## quàngào
## 劝告　　　　　　　　　　　　(丙) 动 / 名
① advise ② advice
**常用搭配**
接受某人劝告 accept one's advice
提出劝告 give advice
**用法示例**
他的朋友劝告他改变生活方式。
His friend advised him to change his way of living.
听从老人的劝告。
Listen to an old man's counsel.
他不接受我的劝告。
He refused to accept my advice.

## géwài
## 格外　　　　　　　　　　　　　(丙) 副
particularly; especially
**常用搭配**
雨后的空气格外新鲜。
The air is particularly fresh after the rain.
**用法示例**
路面结冰了,今晚要格外小心。
Take special care tonight because the road is icy.
那个女孩穿上婚纱格外美丽动人。
The girl is all the more beautiful in her wedding gown.
这星期他格外忙。
He has been especially busy this week.

## guāngmíng
## 光明　　　hēiàn　　反 黑暗　　　(乙) 形
bright (future)
**常用搭配**
光明的前途 bright future

## cuòzhé
## 挫折　　　　　　　　　　　　　(丙) 名
setback; reverse
**常用搭配**
遇到挫折 meet with setbacks

遭受挫折 suffer a defeat

**用法示例**

尽管遇到很多挫折,他仍坚持做实验。

He persisted in carrying out the experiment in spite of all of setbacks.

一遭受挫折,他就容易气馁。

He is easily discouraged when he suffers defeat.

### guānglín
# 光临 （丙）动

be present; to attend

**常用搭配**

欢迎光临 You are welcome to be present.

**用法示例**

如果您能光临,我们将感到很高兴。

We shall be very glad of your presence.

女王光临,我们感到十分荣幸。

We were graced with the presence of the Queen.

你肯光临使我们感到无比荣幸。

You do us a great honor by attending.

### xiézhù
# 协助  ⓘ 辅助 fǔzhù （丙）动

assist; aid

**常用搭配**

大力协助 greatly assist

**用法示例**

我们在调查的过程中得到了警方的协助。

We were aided in our investigation by the cooperation of the police.

一组护士协助医生实施手术。

A team of nurses assisted the doctor in performing the operation.

她所有的朋友都来协助她组织这个活动。

All her friends have come to help her organize the activity.

### quànshuō
# 劝说 （丁）动

persuade; advise

**常用搭配**

劝说某人做某事 persuade sb into doing sth.

**用法示例**

我试图劝说他跟我一起去。

I tried to persuade him to go with me.

经过我多次劝说,她终于同意了。

After a lot of persuading on my part, she at last agreed.

尽管我努力劝说,他还是不同意。

In spite of my efforts at persuasion, he wouldn't agree.

### quànzǔ
# 劝阻 （丁）动

dissuade; advise against doing sth

**常用搭配**

劝阻某人别做某事 dissuade sb. from doing sth.

**用法示例**

我曾设法劝阻她不要投资于股票交易。

I tried to dissuade her from investing her money in stocks and shares.

他的父母劝阻他不要参加空军。

His parents discouraged him from joining the airforce.

他劝阻我不要这样做。

He discouraged me from doing so.

 词义辨析

**措施、办法**

　　"措施"和"办法"都是名词,都指处理问题的方法。"措施"比较正式,多用在书面语中,一般用于比较大的事情,常和"采取"、"制定"搭配,受量词"项"修饰;"办法"运用得比较广泛,书面语、口语、大事、小事都可以用"办法",常和"采用"、"想"搭配,受量词"个"修饰。例如:①他们对危害公众的司机采取了一项强硬的措施。②我想出了一个解决问题的好办法。

　　Both 措施 and 办法 are nouns, meaning "method for dealing with something". 措施 is more formal, mostly applied in writing and used for important matters, in collocation with 采取 (adopt), 制定 (draw up), and can be modified by measure word 项; while 办法 can be used in written or colloquial forms, can be used for important or ordinary matters, in collocation with 采用 (adopt), 想 (think out), and can be modified by the measure word 个. For example: ① They took strong measures against those dangerous drivers. ② I have a good idea about how to solve the problem.

 **练习**

**练习一、根据拼音写汉字，根据汉字写拼音**

cuò（　　）　cuò（　　）　（　　）zǔ（　　）zhù（　　）róng
（　　）施　（　　）折　劝（　　）　协（　　）　光（　　）

**练习二、搭配连线**

(1) 前途　　　　　　　　A. 传统
(2) 遇到　　　　　　　　B. 光临
(3) 欢迎　　　　　　　　C. 挫折
(4) 光荣　　　　　　　　D. 措施
(5) 采取　　　　　　　　E. 光明

**练习三、从今天学习的生词中选择合适的词填空**

1. 我早就提醒他，要按时上班，努力工作，可他就是不接受我的 _____。
2. 父母 _____ 他把大学读完，他说他现在只想工作，不想学习。
3. 警察试图 _____ 她，让她别做傻事，但她最终还是开枪自杀了。
4. 这是一个新兴行业，有着巨大的发展空间和 _____ 的前景。
5. 这个小镇出了一名战斗英雄，当地人觉得很 _____。
6. 政府应该采取积极、有效的 _____ 抑制通货膨胀。
7. 高大的篮球运动员姚明走在人群中，显得 _____ 引人注意。
8. 在成功的路上，难免会遇到 _____，别灰心，坚持就是胜利。
9. 据说这个餐厅常常有明星 _____。
10. 他的助手 _____ 他调查市场前景。

 **答案**

**练习一：**
略

**练习二：**

| (1) E | (2)C | (3)B | (4)A | (5)D |

**练习三：**

| 1. 劝告 | 2. 劝说 | 3. 劝阻 | 4. 光明 | 5. 光荣 |
| 6. 措施 | 7. 格外 | 8. 挫折 | 9. 光临 | 10. 协助 |

---

 **星期四**

bùtóng
**不同**　　　反 相同　　　xiāngtóng　　　（甲）形

① different ② not the same ③ not alike

**常用搭配**
不同的材料 different materials
与……不同 be different from

**用法示例**
那些苹果大小不同。
The size of the apples varied.
和他弟弟不同，他很有幽默感。
Unlike his brother, he has a good sense of humor.
他的人生观跟你的不同。
His view of life is different from yours.

jīhū
**几乎**　　　（乙）副

nearly; almost

**常用搭配**
几乎每天 nearly everyday

**用法示例**
海洋几乎占地球表面的四分之三。
The sea covers nearly three-fourths of the world's surface.
路太滑了，我几乎要摔倒了。
The road was slippery, and I nearly fell over.
几乎每个人都在谈论这件事。
Almost everybody talks about it.

guànjūn
**冠军**　　　（乙）名

champion

**常用搭配**
拳击冠军 the boxing champion
世界冠军 world champion
夺得冠军 win the championship

**用法示例**
他曾是世界网球冠军。
He was the world tennis champion.
小女孩给冠军献上了花环。
The little girl presented the champion with a garland.
我们队夺得了游泳冠军。
Our team won the swimming championships.

fāchū
**发出**　　　反 收回　　　shōuhuí　　　（乙）动

emit; send out; issue

**常用搭配**
发出警告 sound a warning　　发出命令 issue orders
发出声音 give forth a sound

**用法示例**

太阳发出光和热。
The sun emits light and heat.
她发出痛苦的呼叫。
She emitted a cry of pain.
那些烂香蕉发出了难闻的气味。
Those rotting bananas gave off a bad smell.

dàduōshù
# 大多数 （乙）名
majority

**常用搭配**

绝大多数 great majority　大多数人 majority of people

**用法示例**

绝大多数人同意。
The great majority approved.
我们班大多数学生来自亚洲。
The majority of students in our class are from Asia.
大多数孩子都喜欢吃糖。
Most children like sweets.

sīniàn
# 思念 （丙）动
miss; think of

**常用搭配**

思念故乡 yearn for the homeland
对孩子的思念 thought of children

**用法示例**

我多么思念我的祖国呀!
I miss my motherland terribly!
在坐牢期间,她日夜思念她的孩子。
She missed her child day and night when she was in prison.
她给你礼物足以表达出她对你的思念。
The present she gave you spoke volumes about what she thinks of you.

fāchóu
# 发愁 （丁）动
worry

**用法示例**

你发什么愁呢?
What do you worry about?
别发愁,一切都会好的。
Don't worry! Everything will be all right.
你为什么事发愁呢?
What are you worried about?

dǐkàng
# 抵抗 （丙）动
resist

**常用搭配**

抵抗侵略 resist aggression
顽强地抵抗 resist tenaciously

**用法示例**

他们英勇地抵抗敌人的进攻。
They withstood bravely the attacks from the enemy.
他无法抵抗漂亮女人的引诱。
He can't resist the allure of a pretty woman.
他再也抵抗不住了。
He could resist no longer.

chàbuduō
# 差不多 （乙）形
similar

**常用搭配**

长得差不多 look similarly　重量差不多 similar weight

**用法示例**

这座桥差不多有两公里长。
The bridge is almost 2 kilometers long.
近来,差不多每样东西都涨价了。
In recent times the price of just about everything has gone up.
那辆车跟新的差不多。
The car is nearly new.

diànjì　　　　diànniàn
# 惦记　　◎惦念 （丙）动
remember with concern; think about

**常用搭配**

惦记孩子 worry about children
总惦记着…… keep on thinking about …

**用法示例**

我一直惦记着那件事。
I've constantly kept thinking about that.
她总惦记着期末考试,玩得并不开心。
She kept thinking about the final exam; she couldn't enjoy herself.

dǐdá　　　　dàodá
# 抵达　　◎到达 （丁）动
arrive; reach (a destination)

**常用搭配**

抵达北京 arrive in Beijing
顺利抵达 to successfully arrive

**用法示例**

他刚抵达就病倒了。
No sooner had he arrived than he fell sick.
我告诉母亲我已安全抵达。
I told my mother that I had arrived safely.
我们将在日落时抵达港口。
We will reach the harbor at sunset.

fāqǐ
# 发起 （丁）动
initiate; launch

**常用搭配**

发起攻击 launch an attack

发起一项运动 launch a movement

**用法示例**

今晚他们将向敌人发起攻击。
They will launch an offensive against the enemy tonight.
是谁发起的禁酒运动?
Who launched the temperance movement?

 **词义辨析**

**差不多、几乎**

1、"差不多"和"几乎"都可以表示相近的意思,都可以做状语。"差不多"是形容词,还可以作定语、谓语;"几乎"是副词,不能作定语或谓语。例如:①差不多/几乎每个人都参加了比赛。②这两个男孩的身高差不多。

Both 差不多 and 几乎 mean "almost", and can function as an adverbial. 差不多 is an adjective, and can also function as an attributive or a predicate; while 几乎 is an adverb, and can not function as an attributive or a predicate. For example: ① Nearly everybody entered the Competition. ② The two boys are about the same height.

2、"几乎"还可以表示接近于某种状况而实际上并没有达到;"差不多"没有这种用法。例如:她的儿子去世时,她悲伤得几乎疯了。

几乎 also indicates some state of affairs which seems to almost reach but actually does not; while 差不多 can not be used like this. For example: She was almost mad with grief when her son died.

 **练习**

**练习一、根据拼音写汉字,根据汉字写拼音**

dǐ ( ) guàn ( )( ) chóu diàn ( )( ) hū
( )抗 ( )军 发( ) ( )记 几( )

**练习二、搭配连线**

(1) 抵抗            A. 抵达
(2) 世界            B. 攻击
(3) 发出            C. 侵略
(4) 安全            D. 警告
(5) 发起            E. 冠军

**练习三、从今天学习的生词中选择合适的词填空**

1. 这位母亲显得很苍老,她一直在为没钱给孩子治病而_____。

2. 这种花不仅好看,还能 _____ 淡淡的香味。

3. 常喝含有酒精的饮料会削弱身体对疾病的 _____ 能力。

4. 那个歌星 _____ 了为灾区捐款的义演活动,很多名人都应邀参加了。

5. 他们俩是同时来北京留学的,汉语水平 _____。

6. _____ 居民都不希望自己小区附近再建购物中心,他们担心会破坏环境。

7. 他出国后,很 _____ 年迈的父母,想把他们也接到国外和他一起生活。

8. 那座城市变化太大了,_____ 找不到我原来住的地方了。

9. 他是上届奥运会的长跑亚军,他这次的目标是夺得奥运会长跑 _____。

10. 参加会议的各国代表团陆续 _____ 北京。

**答案**

**练习一:**
略

**练习二:**

(1) C      (2)E      (3)D      (4)A      (5)B

**练习三:**

1. 发愁    2. 发出    3. 抵抗    4. 发起    5. 差不多
6. 大多数    7. 惦记    8. 几乎    9. 冠军    10. 抵达

**星期五**

**tǎoyàn**
## 讨厌　⑩ 厌恶　（乙）动／形
① dislike ② troublesome
**常用搭配**
讨厌的人 an obnoxious man
讨厌刷盘子 dislike washing dishes
令人讨厌的味道 an obnoxious smell
**用法示例**
我讨厌自私的人。
I dislike selfish people.
我讨厌参加这些会议。
I loathe going to these conferences.
我顶讨厌这个学生。
I dislike this student very much.

**jíqí**
## 极其　（乙）副
extremely；exceedingly
**常用搭配**
极其重要的事 highly important matter
极其严重的后果 terribly serious result
**用法示例**
这项任务极其艰巨。
This task is extremely difficult.
军队是极其复杂的组织。
The army is an extremely complex organism.
我对会议的结果感到极其满意。
I was extremely pleased with the outcome of the meeting.

**hàomǎ**
## 号码　（乙）名
number
**常用搭配**
电话号码 telephone number
**用法示例**
你拨错号码了。
You've dialled the wrong number.
你能告诉我你的电话号码吗？
Can you tell me your phone number?
你们公司的海关注册号码是多少？
What's your company's registration number in customs?

**hàozhào**
## 号召　（乙）动／名
① call ② appeal
**常用搭配**
号召某人做某事 call on sb. to do sth.
发出号召 make a call

**用法示例**
政府号召青年人义务献血。
The government is calling on the youth to voluntarily donate their blood.
总统号召全国人民团结起来。
The President made a call for national unity.
政府号召大家要节约用水。
The government is appealing to everyone to save water.

**gùkè**
## 顾客　（乙）名
customer
**常用搭配**
吸引顾客 attract customers
**用法示例**
价格低得令顾客难以相信。
The customers were in disbelief at the low prices.
这家新开的商店里挤满了顾客。
The new store is crowded with customers.

**yǒudeshì**
## 有的是　（乙）动
① have plenty of ② there's no lack of
**常用搭配**
有的是时间。There's plenty of time.
**用法示例**
用不着这样匆忙，我们有的是时间。
There's no need to be in such a tearing hurry; we've got plenty of time.
里面有的是地方，大家都可以进来。
There's plenty of room for everyone inside.
他应该主动提出付款，他有的是钱。
He should have offered to pay, he has plenty of money.

**gāoshàng**
## 高尚　⑫ 卑鄙　（丙）形
noble
**常用搭配**
高尚的心灵 a noble soul　高尚的品质 noble character
**用法示例**
她的高尚品格令人钦佩。
Her nobility of character made people admire her.
他解救溺水儿童的行为很高尚。
It was a noble act that he performed, saving a child from drowning.

**gāojí**
## 高级　（丙）形
① advanced ② high quality
**常用搭配**
高级军官 a senior officer　高级服装 high quality clothing
高级工程师 senior engineer
**用法示例**
她丈夫是政府的高级官员。
Her husband is a senior official in the government.

这个学生学得很快,我们现在可以让她升到高级班去。
The student learns so fast that we can now move her up to the advanced class.
高级化妆品对她来说太昂贵了。
Highend cosmetics are too expensive for her.

### gùwèn
## 顾问 （丙）名
consultant; adviser

**常用搭配**
顾问委员会 consultant committee
法律顾问 consultant-law

**用法示例**
李教授曾做过总统的特别顾问。
Professor Li once served as special adviser to the President.
请来了专家担任政府的顾问。
Experts were brought in to advise the Government.
在宣布决定前,她先跟顾问商量了一下。
She talked with her advisers before announcing her decision.

### yànwù
## 厌恶 （丙）动
detest; disgust

**常用搭配**
真令人厌恶。It's very disgusting！

**用法示例**
我厌恶他说话的腔调。
His accent repels me.
他厌恶一切虚伪的行为。
He detests all affectations.
我厌恶这种说谎的人。
I detest people who tell lies.

### gùlǜ
## 顾虑 ◎顾忌 gùjì （丁）动/名
① misgive ② misgivings

**常用搭配**
顾虑重重 have many misgivings

**用法示例**
我对是否接受那项工作有些顾虑。
I have some misgivings about taking the job.
你有什么顾虑吗？
What misgivings do you have？
那一番谈话打消了他的顾虑。
Talking eased his anxiety.

### gāomíng
## 高明 ⑧拙劣 zhuōliè （丁）形
wise; brilliant

**常用搭配**
高明的领导 brilliant leader  高明的建议 wise advice

**用法示例**
我们需要一位高明的设计师。

We need a brilliant designer.
这位医生因医术高明而闻名。
The doctor is famous for his brilliant medical skill.

 词义辨析

**讨厌、厌恶**

"讨厌"和"厌恶"都是动词,都有不喜欢、让人心烦的意思。"讨厌"比较口语化,有时候用作形容词;"厌恶"是书面语,语气比"讨厌"重,表示十分反感,不能用作形容词。例如：①他喜欢猫但讨厌狗。②真讨厌,我忘记带票了。③不要成为讨厌的人。④他的行为令我们厌恶。

Both 讨厌 and 厌恶 are verbs, meaning "to dislike, to be disturbed". 讨厌 is very colloquial, and sometimes can be used as an adjective; while 厌恶 is quite literary, and more serious than "讨厌", It indicates "to disgust", and can not be used as an adjective. For example: ① He likes cats but dislikes dogs. ② What a nuisance! I've forgotten my ticket. ③ Don't make yourself a nuisance to others. ④ His behavior disgusted us very much.

 练习

**练习一、根据拼音写汉字,根据汉字写拼音**
(  )shàng  yàn (  )  (  )lǜ  (  )mǎ  (  )qí
高(  )  (  )恶  顾(  )  号(  )  极(  )

**练习二、搭配连线**
(1) 高明的　　　　　　　A. 设备
(2) 高尚的　　　　　　　B. 医术
(3) 高级的　　　　　　　C. 号码
(4) 讨厌的　　　　　　　D. 品质
(5) 手机的　　　　　　　E. 苍蝇

**练习三、从今天学习的生词中选择合适的词填空**
1. 在北京学习了三年,他通过了 HSK 11 级,汉语已经达到_____水平。
2. 我觉得他的设计非常_____,既美观,又实用,还可以节约能源。
3. 这个捡垃圾为生的老人品质_____,一直在默默资助山区的失学儿童。
4. 这个富翁_____钱,但他不赞成他的孩子过奢侈的生活。
5. 随地吐痰的行为令人_____。
6. 来北京以前,我还有些_____,后来发现汉语并不难学,中国人也很友好。
7. 这位老专家已经退休了,现在在一家公司担任技术_____。
8. 这个明星虽然有的是钱,但婚礼却_____简单,只是邀请了双方家人。

9. 总理 _____ 人们节约能源,共同应对金融危机。

10. 虽然都说 _____ 是上帝,但这个上帝是临时的,买东西的时候是,退换货的时候不是。

**答案**

练习一:
略
练习二:
(1) B　　　(2) D　　　(3)A　　　(4)E　　　(5)C
练习三:
1. 高级　　2. 高明　　3. 高尚　　4. 有的是
5. 厌恶／讨厌　　6. 顾虑　　7. 顾问
8. 极其　　9. 号召　　10. 顾客

# 第8月,第2周的练习

**练习一 . 根据词语给加点的字注音**

1.(　)　2.(　)　3.(　)　4.(　)　5.(　)
抵达　措施　烦躁　发愁　免费

**练习二 . 根据拼音完成词语**

cuò　　　wù　　　wù　　　wù　　　wù
1. (　)折　2. 厌(　)　3. 错(　)　4. 职(　)　5. 读(　)

**练习三 . 辨析并选择合适的词填空**

1. 法律条文中不能出现让人产生(　)的句子。(误会、误解)
2. 我想是你(　)了,我不是那个意思。(误会、误解)
3. 我现在没时间,你去帮我(　)一下那两位客人吧。(招待、款待)
4. 代表团在这个国家受到了盛情(　)。(招待、款待)
5. 别光在那儿抽烟、叹气,快想想(　)啊!(措施、办法)
6. 为了治理环境污染,政府将采取一系列的(　)。(措施、办法)
7. 北京冬天的风特别厉害,把我的脸吹得(　)没有知觉了。(差不多、几乎)
8. 我觉得这两件衣服的样子(　),买哪件都可以。(差不多、几乎)
9. 邻居家的狗真(　),越到晚上叫得越凶,吵得我们睡不着觉。(讨厌、厌恶)
10. 在公共场所,大声喧哗、随地吐痰等行为令人(　)。(讨厌、厌恶)

**练习四 . 选词填空**

烦恼　读者　光明　抵达　有的是
烦躁　观众　高明　抵抗　大多数

1. 据说,当时侵略军进攻这座城市时,所有市民都参与了(　)运动。

2. 相比于他,他的竞争对手的手段更(　)。
3. 孩子们是马戏团最忠实的(　),他们往往会在父母的陪同下来看马戏。
4. (　)市民都拥护政府的倡议,只有很少的人表示反对。
5. 不要为一点小事(　),生活还是很美好的。
6. 飞机将在下午2:00(　)北京首都机场。
7. 他们家(　)钱,他从小就过着奢侈的生活。
8. 炎热的天气和没完没了的噪音使他的心情很(　)。
9. 他是个盲人,小时候的一次医疗事故使他永远地失去了(　)。
10. 这本杂志每月出两期,拥有大批忠实的(　)。

**练习五 . 选择程度副词填空**

过于　　略微　　格外　　极其
1. 雨后的空气(　)新鲜,我们出去散散步吧。
2. 很多家长对这个老师(　)不满意,纷纷要求学校辞退这种不负责任的人。
3. 医生让他多休息,不能(　)劳累。
4. 这双鞋好像(　)有点大,有小一点儿的吗?

**练习六 . 写出下列词语的同义词**

1. 误会(　)　　　2. 略微(　)
3. 顾虑(　)　　　4. 抵达(　)
5. 措施(　)

**练习七 . 写出下列词语的反义词**

1. 高尚(　)　　　2. 发出(　)
3. 光荣(　)　　　4. 美好(　)
5. 加入(　)

**答案**

练习一 .
1.dǐ　2.shī　3.zào　4.chóu　5.fèi
练习二 .
1. 挫　2. 恶　3. 误　4. 务　5. 物
练习三 .
1. 误解　2. 误会　3. 招待　4. 款待
5. 办法　6. 措施　7. 几乎　8. 差不多
9. 讨厌　10. 厌恶／讨厌
练习四 .
1. 抵抗　2. 高明　3. 观众　4. 大多数　5. 烦恼
6. 抵达　7. 有的是　8. 烦躁　9. 光明　10. 读者
练习五 .
1. 格外　2. 极其　3. 过于　4. 略微
练习六 .
1. 误解　2. 稍微　3. 顾忌　4. 到达　5. 举措
练习七 .
1. 卑鄙　2. 收回　3. 耻辱　4. 丑恶　5. 退出

# 8月 第3周的学习内容

**星期一**

### xīnkǔ
## 辛苦 回 辛劳 xīnláo （甲）形／动

① hardworking；exhausting ② work hard

**常用搭配**

辛苦的工作 hard work

辛苦地工作 work hard

**用法示例**

马车夫的工作非常辛苦。

Wagoner's work is very hard.

为了养家我父亲辛辛苦苦地工作。

My father works hard in order to support us.

辛苦一天之后，看电视是很好的消遣。

TV can be a welcome distraction after a hard day's work.

### xiànmù
## 羡慕 反 鄙视 bǐshì （乙）动

admire；envy

**常用搭配**

我真羡慕你！How I envy you!

**用法示例**

他们羡慕他的好运气。

They envy him his good fortune.

真羡慕刘飞，他的车子真漂亮。

I envy Liu Fei, whose car is fancy.

他对我的成功满怀羡慕。

He was filled with envy at my success.

### xiànxiàng
## 现象 （乙）名

phenomenon

**常用搭配**

自然现象 a natural phenomenon

社会现象 a social phenomenon

**用法示例**

磁力是一种自然现象。

Magnetism is a natural phenomenon.

国际恐怖主义并不是近年才有的现象。

International terrorism is not just a recent phenomenon.

### xiànshí
## 现实 （乙）名

reality

**常用搭配**

现实生活 real life 逃避现实 to escape from reality

**用法示例**

我们必须面对现实。

We must face reality.

现实生活并不像人们想象的那样美好。

Real life isn't as happy as people imagine.

### xíngli
## 行李 （乙）名

luggage；baggage

**常用搭配**

寄存行李 left luggage 四件行李 four pieces of luggage

**用法示例**

我有一些随身携带的行李。

I have some accompanying baggage.

我刚接到通知说我的行李已经运到了。

I've just been informed that my luggage has already arrived.

他把箱子放在行李寄存处了。

He deposited the case in the left luggage office.

### pǐndé
## 品德 （丙）名

moral character

**常用搭配**

高尚的品德 noble moral character

**用法示例**

至于他的品德，也是值得称赞的。

As for his moral character, that is also praiseworthy.

他是一个品德高尚的人，人人都敬佩他。

He is a man of moral integrity, everybody admires him.

### fāxíng
## 发行 （丙）动

issue；publish

**常用搭配**

发行报纸 issue paper 发行债券 issue bonds

新发行的邮票 newly-issued stamp

**用法示例**

总统宣布将发行新货币。

The President proclaimed that a new currency would be issued.

这部电影将在下个月发行。

The film will be released next month.

### fùyù
## 富裕 反 贫困 pínkùn （丙）形

prosperous；well-off

**常用搭配**

富裕的家庭 a well-off family

**用法示例**

即使我们富裕了也应厉行节约。

We should practice economy even if we are rich.

由于有了新工作,我们现在很富裕。

We are very well-off now with the new job.

他们过着富裕的生活。

They lead a very comfortable life

zàisān
## 再三　　　　　　　　　　（丙）副

① over and over ② again and again

**常用搭配**

再三考虑 think over and over

**用法示例**

我再三肯求,他才答应帮忙。

He made a promise to help, as I pleaded with him again and again.

我在做出决定之前不得不再三考虑此事。

I have to think the matter over and over before I make a decision.

他再三强调,我们必须守时。

He stressed again and again that we should be punctual.

fùyǒu
## 富有　　　　　　　　　（丙）形／动

① rich ② be full of

**常用搭配**

富有的人 rich man

**用法示例**

他年轻英俊,而且还很富有。

He is young and good-looking, and also very rich.

他富有经验。

He is full of experience.

虽然他严格,却富有同情心。

Stern as he is, he is full of sympathy.

fābù　　　　gōngbù
## 发布　　ⓖ公布　　　　（丁）动

issue；distribute

**常用搭配**

发布命令 issue an order

新闻发布会 a press conference

**用法示例**

最近发布了禁止进口葡萄酒的法令。

A ban on the importation of wines was issued recently.

这份政府公告是今天早晨发布的。

The government statement was issued this morning.

xiànzhuàng
## 现状　　　　　　　　　　（丁）名

current situation

**常用搭配**

维持现状 to maintain the status quo

经济的现状 current state of the economy

**用法示例**

她总是对现状不满意。

She is always dissatisfied with existing conditions.

公司的现状很困难。

At present the company's situation is very difficult.

我们一定要努力改善现状。

We must do our best to improve upon the current situation.

 词义辨析

**富有、富裕**

1、"富有"和"富裕"都可以用作形容词。"富有"表示拥有很多财富,"富裕"表示生活宽裕。例如:①她并不像人们想象的那么富有。②改革开放的政策给我们中国人民带来了富裕的生活。

Both 富有 and 富裕 are adjectives. 富有 means "rich", "possessing great wealth"; while 富裕 means "well-off", "having enough money to live well". For example: She's not as rich as people think. ② The policy of reform and opening-up has brought the Chinese people a more comfortable life.

2、"富有"还可以用作动词,表示大量拥有或具有很多的意思,宾语往往是抽象意义的多音节词语;"富裕"没有这种用法。例如:①年轻人富有热情。②诗人富有想象力。

富有 is also a verb, indicating "to have a lot of", "to be rich in"; the object of 富有 is usually a polysyllabic word or phrase with an abstract meaning. For example: ① The youths are full of passion. ② Poets are full of imagination.

**练习**

**练习一、根据拼音写汉字,根据汉字写拼音**

xiàn (　) xiàn (　)(　) yù xīn (　)(　) dé
(　) 慕 (　) 象 富(　)(　) 苦 品(　)

**练习二、搭配连线**

(1) 维持　　　　　　　A. 富裕
(2) 发布　　　　　　　B. 高尚
(3) 发行　　　　　　　C. 现状
(4) 品德　　　　　　　D. 公告
(5) 生活　　　　　　　E. 报纸

**练习三、从今天学习的生词中选择合适的词填空**

1. 随着社会的发展,这里的不排队、随地吐痰及大声喧哗等不文明 _____ 越来越少了。
2. 因为对公司的 _____ 不满意,所以领导决定进行改革。
3. 经过多年的努力,他的梦想终于变成了 _____。
4. 这个女孩长得漂亮,人又聪明能干,别的女孩很 _____ 她。
5. 他善于写科幻小说,是一名非常 _____ 想象力的作家。
6. 今天气象台 _____ 了恶劣天气的预报,明天早晨可能有暴雨和台风。
7. 这本杂志的 _____ 量非常大,拥有世界各地的读者。
8. 改革开放以后,越来越多的普通百姓过上了 _____ 的生活。
9. 这个企业在招聘人才时,非常注重个人的 _____,德才兼备是最主要的标准。
10. 我很忙,可朋友 _____ 邀请我去她家做客,我不好意思拒绝她。

 **答案**

**练习一:**
略
**练习二:**
(1) C　　(2) D　　(3) E　　(4) B　　(5) A
**练习三:**
1. 现象　2. 现状　3. 现实　4. 羡慕　5. 富有
6. 发布　7. 发行　8. 富裕　9. 品德　10. 再三

**星期二**

jiānglái
**将来** ⚡过去 guòqù **（甲）名**
future
【常用搭配】
在不久的将来 in the near future　　将来的家 future home
学生的将来 the future of students
【用法示例】
这个男孩想将来成为一名哲学家。
The boy wants to become a philosopher in the future.
将来我会尽力做得更好些。
I will try to do better in the future.
你真的一点也不关心你的将来吗?
Do you really care nothing about your future?

qūbié
**区别** **（乙）名/动**
① difference ② distinguish; to make a distinction
【常用搭配】
两个词的区别 difference between the two words
【用法示例】
我看不出他们有什么大的区别。
I can't see much difference in them.
我们应具有区别好书和坏书的能力。
We should have the ability to discriminate good books from bad ones.
这两位政治家的态度有着根本的区别。
There is a fundamental difference in attitude between these two politicians.

fēnbié
**分别** **（乙）动/副**
① separate; part ② separately; respectively
【常用搭配】
与她分别 part from her
【用法示例】
你能分别这两种树吗?
Can you tell me the difference between the two species of trees.
他们分别写了报告。
They wrote their respective reports.
孩子们分别睡在各自的床上。
The children sleep in separate beds.
妈妈不愿意与她的孩子分别。
Mother is unwilling to be separated from her children.

yāpò
**压迫** **（乙）动**
oppress

**常用搭配**

被压迫 be oppressed

压迫穷人 oppress the poor

在……的压迫下 under the oppression of...

**用法示例**

那时候女人受男人压迫。

Women were oppressed by men at that time.

这个老板经常压迫工人。

The boss often oppresses his workers.

在政府的压迫下他们没有屈服。

They did not cave under the oppression of the government.

## dàochù
# 到处 （乙）名

① everywhere ② in all places

**常用搭配**

到处找 to look for everywhere

**用法示例**

我们到处找你。

We have looked everywhere for you.

到处都是垃圾。

There is litter everywhere.

春天蝴蝶到处飞。

Butterflies flit hither and thither in spring.

## dàolái
# 到来 （丁）动

① arrive ② arrival

**常用搭配**

等候他的到来 wait for his arrival

春天的到来 the advent of spring

**用法示例**

强盗们在警察到来之前逃走了。

The robbers escaped before the police arrived.

我期待着他的到来。

I am expecting his arrival.

随着冬天的到来，天气越来越冷了。

With the advent of winter, it's growing colder and colder.

## yālì
# 压力 （丙）名

pressure

**常用搭配**

生活的压力 pressures of life

社会压力 social pressure

**用法示例**

我的压力很大。

I'm under a lot of pressure.

我们应对他施加压力。

We must put pressure on him.

她无法承受现代生活的压力。

She can't bear the pressures of modern life.

## ànqī
# 按期 ⑩按时 ànshí （丙）副

on schedule

**常用搭配**

按期归还 return on time

**用法示例**

他们按期完成工程项目。

They finished the project on schedule.

他们将按期偿还借款。

They will pay you back the money according to the schedule.

## lǚcì
# 屡次 ⑩多次 duōcì （丁）副

① repeatedly ② time and again

**常用搭配**

屡次迟到 be late repeatedly

屡次遭到批评 be criticized time and again

**用法示例**

比分屡次出现平局。

The score was tied several times.

最近他屡次犯错误。

Recently he has been making mistakes constantly.

屡次失败都没有使他泄气。

Frequent failures did not affect his morale.

## dàotuì
# 倒退 ⑰前进 qiánjìn （丁）动

fall back; go in reverse

**常用搭配**

倒退着走 walking backwards

**用法示例**

车子倒退着开出大门。

The car backed through the gate.

"别开枪！"他边说边倒退。

'Don't shoot!' he said as he backed away.

我希望时光能够倒退，我可以重新生活。

I wish I could turn the clock back and relive my life.

## dàoqī
# 到期 （丁）动

expire; become due

**常用搭配**

合同到期 the expiration of a contract

**用法示例**

合同快到期了。

The expiration date of the contract is coming up.

我的护照再过两个月就到期了。

My passport is due to expire in two months.

这张票据要到期了。

This bill will become due.

## zhuǎnjiāo
# 转交 （丁）动

pass on; deliver to

**常用搭配**
转交给……deliver to...
**用法示例**
她把信转交给玛丽了。
She passed the letter to Mary.
你写给我的信可由律师转交。
Your letter for me might be in the care of the lawyer.
请把这件礼物转交给你妈妈。
Please deliver the gift to your mother.

 **词义辨析**

**区别、分别**

1、"区别"和"分别"都可以用作动词,都表示对两个或两个以上的事物进行辨别,很多时候可以互换使用,只是"区别"的对象和过程往往比"分别"复杂。另外"分别"还有别离、与某人分开的意思。例如:①不能分别颜色的人被称为色盲。②和她分别后,我感到很寂寞。③我们在学习外国文化时,一定要区别精华与糟粕。

Both 区别 and 分别 can be used as verbs, indicating "to try to find the difference between two or more things", and can be interchangeable in most cases. But the object and process of 区别 is usually more complicated than 分别. And as a verb 分别 also means "to separate from", "to leave each other". For example: ① People who cannot distinguish between colors are said to be color-blind. ② Having parted from her, I feel lonely. ③ We must distinguish between the best and worst of foreign cultures when we study them.

2、"区别"还是名词,表示不同点,不同之处的意思;"分别"不能这样用。"分别"可以作副词,表示分开进行或各自的意思;"区别"没有这样的用法。如:请注意这两个词之间的区别。他们俩分别去了欧洲和亚洲。

区别 is also a noun, and means "the difference," "the points or elements that distinguish one thing from another"; while 分别 has no such usage. 分别 is also an adverb, meaning "respectively"; while 区别 has no such usage. For example: ① Please pay attention to the difference between the two words. ② Those two went to Europe and Asia respectively.

 **练习**

**练习一、根据拼音写汉字,根据汉字写拼音**
qū（　）dào（　）dào（　）（　）cì　yā（　）
（　）别　（　）退　（　）期　屡（　）（　）迫

**练习二、搭配连线**
(1) 屡次　　　　　　A. 寻找
(2) 社会　　　　　　B. 失败
(3) 到处　　　　　　C. 压迫
(4) 按期　　　　　　D. 压力
(5) 受到　　　　　　E. 完成

**练习三、从今天学习的生词中选择合适的词填空**
1. 春节的_____为这座城市增添了更多的生机和活力。
2. 这个化工厂里_____弥漫着一股刺鼻的味道,躲都没处躲。
3. 我租房子的合同快_____了,这几天我在忙着找新的房子。
4. 在北京过了一个暑假,我发现他的汉语水平不但没有进步,反而_____了。
5. 麻烦您把这个信封_____给小王,我没时间等他回来了。
6. 尽管时间紧,任务重,他还是_____完成了领导交待的工作。
7. 他_____找相关单位投诉,但至今没有得到答复。
8. 工会领导工人抵抗管理层的_____。
9. 对于朋友和敌人我们要_____对待。
10. 老师让我们_____完成各自的论文。

**答案**

**练习一:**
略
**练习二:**
(1) B　　　(2)D　　　(3)A　　　(4)E　　　(5)C
**练习三:**
1. 到来　　2. 到处　　3. 到期　　4. 倒退　　5. 转交
6. 按期　　7. 屡次　　8. 压迫　　9. 区别　　10. 分别

星期三
Wednesday

## yǐngxiǎng
## 影响 （甲）动／名

① influence ② effect

**常用搭配**

对……有影响 have an effect on...
在……的影响下 under the influence of...
电视的影响 the influence of television

**用法示例**

不要让他影响你的决定。
Don't let him influence your decision.
这件事情对社会造成了有害的影响。
This event had a pernicious influence on society.
她是个很有影响力的人。
She wields a lot of influence.

## měishù
## 美术 （乙）名

① art ② the fine arts

**常用搭配**

工艺美术 crafts and arts
美术馆 art gallery

**用法示例**

她在美术学校学习油画。
She studied painting at art school.
你看美术展览了吗?
Did you see the art exhibition?

## gǔdài
## 古代 （乙）名

① ancient times ② olden times

**常用搭配**

古代建筑 ancient buildings
古代的服装 clothes in ancient times

**用法示例**

他正在研究中国古代历史。
He is studying the ancient history of China.
孔子被认为是中国古代最伟大的教育家。
Confucius is considered the greatest educator of ancient China.
有许多关于古代英雄的传说。
There are many legends about the ancient heroes.

## dùguò
## 度过 （乙）动

spend; pass

**常用搭配**

度过艰难的岁月 pass through difficult years
度过暑假 spend the summer holidays

**用法示例**

他计划在乡村度过余生。
He planned to spend the rest of his life in the country.
他在家里度过了一个寂寞的夜晚。
He spent a lonely evening at home.
我在家乡度过了幸福的童年。
I spent a happy childhood in my hometown.

## wēixiào
## 微笑　　反 kūqì 哭泣　　（乙）动

smile

**常用搭配**

迷人的微笑 attractive smile　　对我微笑 to smile at me

**用法示例**

老太太微笑着开了门。
The old lady opened the door with a beaming smile.
她有着天使般的微笑。
She has an angelic smile.
她的微笑使她更美丽了。
Her smile makes her even more beautiful.

## lùguò
## 路过 （丙）动

pass by; pass through

**常用搭配**

路过银行 pass by the bank
碰巧路过 happen to pass by

**用法示例**

他那时碰巧路过那里。
He happened to pass by at that time.
我每天都会路过那家邮局。
I go past the post office every day.
我从公司回家时,会路过我儿子的学校。
When I go home from my company, I pass by the school my son studies in.

## gǔdiǎn
## 古典 （丙）形

classical

**常用搭配**

古典音乐 classic music
中国古典诗歌 Chinese classical poetry

**用法示例**

我喜欢古典音乐,不太喜欢流行音乐。
I prefer classical music to pop music.
她对古典文学感兴趣。
She is interested in classical literature.

## zǎowǎn
## 早晚　　近 chízǎo 迟早　　（丙）名／副

① sooner or later ② morning and evening

**常用搭配**

他们早晚会分手。They will part sooner or later.
人早晚会死。People will die sooner or later.

**用法示例**

我早晚会报复他！

I'll find a way of getting back at him!

她早晚会知道事情的真相。

She will know the truth of the matter sooner or later.

医生告诉你早晚吃两次药。

The doctor told you to take the medicine twice a day—in the morning and in the evening.

---

zànměi

赞美　　　　反 耻笑　　　　（丙）动

praise

**常用搭配**

赞美上帝 to give praise to God

**用法示例**

他写了一首诗赞美她的品德。

He wrote a poem praising her moral character.

赞美会让人感到振奋。

Praise can be a good boost to morale.

---

zànyáng

赞扬　　　　　　　　　　（丙）动

praise

**常用搭配**

赞扬他的行为 praise his performance

得到赞扬 receive praise

**用法示例**

我们应当赞扬好人好事。

We should commend good people and good deeds.

老师赞扬了她的勇气。

The teacher praised her for her courage.

他因谦虚而赢得人们的赞扬。

He won praise for his modesty.

---

lùchéng

路程　　　　同 路途　　　　（丁）名

lùtú

distance; journey

**常用搭配**

一天的路程

one day's journey

**用法示例**

你到学校要走多远的路程？

How far do you have to walk to get to school?

从家到学校的路程要花一个小时。

The journey from home to school takes about an hour.

这段路程一小时足够了。

An hour should suffice for the journey.

---

gǔguài

古怪　　　　　　　　　　（丁）形

queer; eccentric

**常用搭配**

行为古怪 act in a queer way 　 古怪的人 an odd fellow

脾气古怪 peculiar in temper

---

**用法示例**

她是个古怪的老太太。

She is an eccentric old lady.

他有点儿古怪。

There is something peculiar about him.

他经常有些古怪的想法。

He often has some queer ideas

 词义辨析

**赞美、赞扬**

　　"赞美"和"赞扬"都是动词，都表示称赞。"赞美"的对象通常是事物或人的某些方面，如品德、精神等，强调欣赏其美好；而"赞扬"的对象通常是人，强调表示认同和钦佩。例如：①这位医生受到病人的高度赞扬。②他写了很多赞美祖国的诗。

　　Both 赞美 and 赞扬 are verbs, meaning "to praise". 赞美 stresses "to appreciate the beauty or good quality of ", and its object is usually a thing, or something about a person, such as moral character, spirit, and so on; while 赞扬 stresses "to approve or admire", and its object is usually a person. For example: ① This doctor received high praise from his patients. ② He wrote a lot of poems to eulogize his country.

**练习**

**练习一、根据拼音写汉字，根据汉字写拼音**
( )yáng ( )diǎn wēi ( )( )xiǎng ( )shù
赞( ) 古( ) ( )笑 影( ) 美( )

**练习二、搭配连线**
(1) 古典        A. 赞扬
(2) 得到        B. 古怪
(3) 脾气        C. 传说
(4) 工艺        D. 音乐
(5) 古代        E. 美术

**练习三、从今天学习的生词中选择合适的词填空**
1. 我出差时 _____ 家乡，于是回老家看望了一下父母。
2. 从北京到我的家乡 _____ 遥远，所以我每年只回一次家。
3. 这个人的 _____ 行为引起了邻居的注意，于是他们给公安局打了电话。
4. 他写了一首诗来 _____ 大自然的神奇。
5. 在颁奖大会上，领导热情地 _____ 了他的无私奉献的精神。
6. 他有才华，又这么努力，相信他 _____ 会成功。
7. 他受父亲 _____，从小喜爱音乐，22岁时就成了世界著名的钢琴家。
8. 这位作家的青春岁月都是在草原上 _____ 的。
9. 那个姑娘看见他，没有说话，只是对他 _____ 了一下。
10. 他喜欢听 _____ 音乐，不喜欢现代流行音乐。

**答案**

**练习一：**
略

**练习二：**
(1) D     (2)A     (3)B     (4)E     (5)C

**练习三：**
1. 路过    2.路程    3.古怪    4.赞美    5.赞扬
6. 早晚    7.影响    8.度过    9.微笑    10.古典

星期四 Thursday

bùfen
**部分**       （甲）名
part; portion
**常用搭配**
大部分 for the most part
整体的一部分 a portion of the whole
划线的部分 the underlined part
**用法示例**
一部分肉已经坏了。
Part of the meat was spoilt.
剑桥商务英语考试一部分是笔试，一部分是口试。
The BEC exams are part written, part oral.
她一生的大部分时间都和丈夫住在纽约。
She lived in New York with her husband for the greater part of her life.

shǐzhōng
**始终**       （乙）副
① always ② from beginning to end
**用法示例**
她始终很友好。
She is always friendly.
情况始终都在变化。
Conditions are changing all the time.
旅行中她始终兴致勃勃。
She remained cheerful throughout the trip.

guāngxiàn
**光线**       （乙）名
light; optical line
**常用搭配**
光线暗。The light is dim.
**用法示例**
别在光线不好的地方看书。
Don't read in poor light.
当百叶窗打开时，房间里光线很充足。
The room is light when the shutters are open.
在森林幽暗的光线下，他们看不清道路。
They couldn't see the path clearly in the dusky light of the forest.

duōshù      shǎoshù
**多数**   反 少数   （乙）名
① majority ② most
**常用搭配**
少数服从多数。
The minority is subordinate to the majority.

**用法示例**

多数孩子都喜欢吃巧克力。

Most children like chocolate.

多数学生通过了考试。

Most students passed the examination.

多数人都知道了这件事。

Most of the people are aware of it.

shǎoshù
## 少数 （乙）名

① minority ② few

**常用搭配**

少数民族 a minority nationality　占少数 be in the minority

**用法示例**

我国有 55 个少数民族。

There are 55 different minorities in our country.

英国只有少数家庭没有汽车。

Only a small minority of British households do not have a car.

只有少数亲戚参加了他的葬礼。

Only a few of his kindred were present at his funeral.

qiànyì
## 歉意 ⑩歉疚 qiànjiù （丙）名

regret; apology

**常用搭配**

表示歉意 express regret

**用法示例**

我是来向您表示歉意的。

I have come to apologize to you.

我得首先表示歉意。

I have to begin with an apology.

guāngcǎi
## 光彩 （丙）名／形

luster; brilliance ② honorable

**常用搭配**

放出光彩 shine with splendor

光彩夺目 dazzlingly brilliant

**用法示例**

她两眼露出幸福的光彩。

Her eyes were sparkling with happiness.

欺骗他们是不光彩的。

It's not honorable to deceive them.

ǒuěr
## 偶尔 （丙）副

occasionally; once in a while

**常用搭配**

偶尔出现 appear occasionally

偶尔发生 happen occasionally

**用法示例**

我们偶尔去饭店,但一般都在家吃饭。

Once in a while we go to a restaurant but usually we eat at home.

我们晚上在家看电视,偶尔出去看场电影。

In the evening we watch TV at home; once in a while we go to cinema.

我只是偶尔抽一支雪茄。

I only smoke an occasional cigar.

ǒurán
## 偶然 （丙）形

accidental; by chance

**常用搭配**

偶然相遇 meet accidentally

偶然事件 accidental event

**用法示例**

他偶然发现了这幅画。

Perchance he discovered the painting.

他们的结合是偶然的。

Their marriage was quite accidental.

一次偶然的机会使我找到了这本书。

I found the book by a fortuitous accident.

qiǎnzé
## 谴责 ⑩指责 zhǐzé （丁）动

condemn; denounce

**常用搭配**

受到谴责 be condemned

强烈谴责 condemned severely

**用法示例**

我们立即谴责了那种暴行。

We condemned the violence with swiftness.

他的无耻行为遭到了所有人的谴责。

His base conduct was condemned by everyone.

她强烈谴责政府的虚伪。

She strongly denounced the government's hypocrisy.

shǎoliàng
## 少量 ⑫大量 dàliàng （丁）形

a little bit

**常用搭配**

放少量的糖 put a little sugar

**用法示例**

在死者胃中检测到了少量的毒药。

Small quantities of poison were detected in the dead man's stomach.

在汤里放少量胡椒。

Put a little pepper in the soup.

饮用少量的葡萄酒有益于健康。

Drinking a little wine is good for your health.

zhuǎnràng
## 转让 （丁）动

transfer; make over

**常用搭配**

转让所有权 transfer ownership

转让财产 make over property

**用法示例**

他打算把财产转让给儿子。

He intends to transfer the property to his son.

他已把房子转让给了妻子。

He had made over the house to his wife.

她已签字把农场转让给女儿了。

She has signed her farm over to her daughter.

## 词义辨析

**偶尔、偶然**

"偶尔"和"偶然"都可以表示很少发生的意思。"偶尔"是副词,只能作状语,不受其它词的修饰;而"偶然"是形容词,可以作状语、定语、谓语和补语,还可以受程度副词的修饰。例如:①李教授对我们很好,但偶尔也会发脾气。②我偶然在街上遇到了她。③我认为那是偶然现象。

Both 偶尔 and 偶然 indicate "occasionally or rarely occurring". 偶尔 is an adverb, functions as adverbial, and is not modified by other words; while 偶然 is an adjective, can function as an adverbial, an attributive, a predicate and a complement, and can be modified by adverbs of degree. For example: ① Professor Li is very kind to us, but he loses his temper occasionally. ② I met her by chance in the street. ③ I think it is just a fortuitous phenomenon.

### 练习

**练习一、根据拼音写汉字,根据汉字写拼音**

qiǎn( )qiàn( )( )xiàn( )zhōng ǒu( )

( )责 ( )意 光( ) 始( )( )尔

**练习二、搭配连线**

(1) 少数　　　　　　　　A. 谴责

(2) 表示　　　　　　　　B. 财产

(3) 偶然　　　　　　　　C. 民族

(4) 受到　　　　　　　　D. 事件

(5) 转让　　　　　　　　E. 歉意

**练习三、从今天学习的生词中选择合适的词填空**

1. 会上,_____人同意第一个方案,这些人数超过了70%。

2. 既然多数人都同意,那我们就遵循_____服从多数的原则,选用第一个方案。

3. 这种饮料中含有_____酒精,喝一点儿没关系,喝太多也会醉。

4. 这件古董是我在一个旧家具市场_____发现的。

5. 我最喜欢踢足球,_____也打打乒乓球。

6. 我们见面时,我对于没能参加她的婚礼表达了_____,希望能得到她的谅解。

7. 他急于用钱,想在一个月内_____这套房子的所有权。

8. 对于这起恐怖分子杀害平民的事件,总理进行了强烈的_____。

9. 父母觉得女儿做了件不_____的事,从此不许她回家。

10. 不管遇到多大的困难,我的妻子都_____坚定地支持我,我非常感激她。

### 答案

**练习一:**

略

**练习二:**

(1) C　　　(2)E　　　(3)D　　　(4)A　　　(5)B

**练习三:**

1. 多数　　2. 少数　　3. 少量　　4. 偶然　　5. 偶尔

6. 歉意　　7. 转让　　8. 谴责　　9. 光彩　　10. 始终

他没有就此事发表任何意见。
He didn't express any opinions on it.

## 答案 dáàn (乙)名

answer

**常用搭配**

正确答案 correct answer

练习的答案 keys to the exercises

**用法示例**

你知道这道题的答案吗？

Do you know the solution to the problem?

他的答案是错误的。

He gave an incorrect answer.

他的答案不令人满意。

His answer is unsatisfactory.

## 游戏 yóuxì (丙)名

game

**常用搭配**

电脑游戏 computer game

文字游戏 word games

**用法示例**

孩子们在玩儿游戏。

The children are playing games.

我们来玩纸牌游戏吧。

Let's have a game of cards.

## 游行 yóuxíng (丙)动

parade; demonstrate

**常用搭配**

参加游行 take part in a parade

**用法示例**

人们穿着古代服装游行。

People wore historical costumes for the parade.

在两座大城市同时举行示威游行。

The simultaneous demonstrations are held in two big

cities.

## 发觉 fājué ◉觉察 juéchá (丙)动

discover; detect

**用法示例**

我发觉她变了。

I found her changed.

我发觉这本书非常有意思。

I found the book to be very interesting.

他发觉有人在跟踪他。

He realized that someone was following him.

她发觉丈夫在跟一个女人约会。

She discovered that her husband was seeing another

woman.

Friday
星期五

## 永远 yǒngyuǎn (甲)副

forever; eternally

**常用搭配**

永远怀念他 embalm him

永远幸福 be happy forever

**用法示例**

我将永远记住那个快乐的日子。

I shall remember that happy day forever.

如果你一直呆在家里，就永远不会懂得生活的真谛。

You'll never experience life if you stay at home forever.

他发誓永远爱她。

He swore to love her for evermore.

## 具备 jùbèi ◉具有 jùyǒu (乙)动

possess; have

**常用搭配**

具备高素质 have a high quality

**用法示例**

那个人具备领导民众的才能。

The man had the qualities needed for leading the people.

你已经具备了参军的条件。

You have been qualified to join the army.

## 具有 jùyǒu (乙)动

possess; have

**常用搭配**

具有博士学位 have a Doctorate

**用法示例**

许多植物具有药性。

Many plants have medicinal properties.

他具有丰富的教学经验。

He possesses much experience in teaching.

从事这个工作的人必须具有英语专业的大学学历。

To do this job, you must have a degree in English.

## 发表 fābiǎo (乙)动

to state; publish

**常用搭配**

发表声明 issue a statement　发表文章 publish an essay

**用法示例**

那位教师在这些杂志上发表了许多文章。

That teacher published many articles in these magazines.

他的文章在省级报纸上发表了。

His articles are published in the provincial newspaper.

## měidé
# 美德 (丁)名

virtue

**常用搭配**

传统美德 traditional virtue

**用法示例**

信守诺言是一种美德。

To stand by an to engagement is a virtue.

美德远远胜于美貌。

Virtue is fairer than beauty.

这姑娘具有谦恭和善良的美德。

The girl possesses the great virtues of humility and kindness.

## xìjù
# 戏剧 (丙)名

drama; play

**常用搭配**

戏剧评论 theatrical review

戏剧效果 dramatic effect

**用法示例**

我对戏剧不感兴趣。

I have no interest in drama.

他正把她的一生改编成戏剧。

He is dramatizing the story of her life.

她正在戏剧研讨班学习。

She is studying in a theatre workshop.

## fāshì
# 发誓    qǐshì
         回 起誓    (丁)动

swear

**常用搭配**

对天发誓 swear by Heaven

发誓讲实话 swear to speak the truth

**用法示例**

他发誓要戒烟。

He swore to abstain from smoking.

我发誓不把你的秘密告诉别人。

I swear I won't tell anyone your secret.

## zhuǎnhuà
# 转化    zhuǎnhuàn
         回 转换    (丙)动

transform; change

**常用搭配**

转化能量 transform the energy

**用法示例**

蒸汽机将热能转化成动力。

A steam engine transforms heat into power.

我们能将水力转化为电力。

We can transmute water power into electrical power.

## 词义辨析

**具备、具有**

"具备"和"具有"都是动词,都表示"有"的意思。"具备"的宾语往往比较具体并有齐全的意味,如:条件、资格、素质等;"具有"的宾语多为抽象的事物,如:信心、意义、价值、作用等。"具备"可以用于句末,不带宾语;"具有"不可以。例如:①他还不具备做医生的资格。②这次事件具有重要的历史意义。③这方面的技能我不具备。

Both 具备 and 具有 are verbs, indicating "to have or to process". The object of 具备 is usually something concrete and with the sense of completeness, such as "条件" (condition), "资格" (qualification), "素质" (quality), etc.; while the object of 具有 is usually something abstract, such as "信心" (confidence), "意义" (significance, meaning), "价值" (value), "作用" (function). 具备 can be used at the end of a sentence and without an object; while 具有 can not. For example: ① He is not qualified to be a doctor yet. ② The event is of great historical significance. ③ I have no skill in this area.

## 练习

**练习一、根据拼音写汉字,根据汉字写拼音**

fā ( )  ( )xì  ( )huà  ( )àn  ( )bèi

( )誓  游( )  转( )  答( )  具( )

**练习二、搭配连线**

(1) 转化          A. 美德

(2) 对天          B. 游行

(3) 传统          C. 声明

(4) 示威          D. 发誓

(5) 发表          E. 能量

**练习三、从今天学习的生词中选择合适的词填空**

1. 他 _____ 女朋友对他的态度变了,果然,不久以后女朋友提出要跟他分手。

2. 他的第一篇小说 _____ 在《中学生文艺报》上。

3. 他的演讲 _____ 很强的感染力,听众的情绪变得很激动。

4. 他不 _____ 法官应有的素质,所以被撤职了。

5. 我们要继承祖先勤劳、勇敢的 _____。

6. 结婚时,他们 _____ 一辈子在一起,可是没过两年就离婚了。

7. 这个结局出乎大家意料,很有 _____ 性。

8. 液体在高温加热下 _____ 成了气体。

9. 学生聚集到政府门前,准备举行 _____,抗议增加学费。

10. 离开那个地方时,他暗暗发誓 _____ 不再回来。

6. 事情在向好的方面（　　），你要耐心一点。

7. 病人已经（　　）了危险期,好好休息,加强营养,慢慢就会康复。

8. 这条消息属于国家机密,没有对外（　　）。

9. 朋友急需用钱,想低价（　　）一套房子。

10. 他在权威杂志上（　　）了一篇学术论文。

## 答案

**练习一:**
略

**练习二:**
(1) E　　(2)D　　(3)A　　(4)B　　(5)C

**练习三:**
1. 发觉　2. 发表　3. 具有　4. 具备　5. 美德
6. 发誓　7. 戏剧　8. 转化　9. 游行　10. 永远

# 第8月,第3周的练习

## 练习一.根据词语给加点的字注音

1.(　) 2.(　)　　3.(　) 4.(　)　5.(　)
富裕　　屡次　　发觉　　谴责　　歉意

## 练习二.根据拼音完成词语

xiàn　　xiàn　　xiàn　dào　　dào
1.(　)慕 2.(　)状 3.光(　) 4.(　)处 5.(　)退

## 练习三.辨析并选择合适的词填空

1. 两个孩子都工作了,他们的生活逐渐（　　）起来了。（富有、富裕）

2. 孩子的心灵纯真美好,（　　）想象力与创造力。（富有、富裕）

3. 这两个词有相同点,也有（　　）。（区别、分别）

4. （　　）的时候,他与我们一一握手道别。（区别、分别）

5. 记者写了一篇报道,（　　）这个勇敢、果断的警察。（赞美、赞扬）

6. 这个作家写了一首诗,（　　）这里迷人的风景。（赞美、赞扬）

7. 他坚持写作,（　　）也能发表几篇。（偶尔、偶然）

8. 出现这种问题,我想绝不是（　　）的,一定要把原因调查清楚。（偶尔、偶然）

9. 中国（　　）悠久的历史和灿烂的文化。（具备、具有）

10. 经过长期的学习和锻炼,他已经（　　）了优秀企业家的素质。（具备、具有）

## 练习四.选词填空

发行　　发表　　转让　　转交　　度过
发布　　发觉　　发誓　　转化　　路过

1. 孩子从这件事上吸取了教训,（　　）以后再也不撒谎了。

2. 麻烦你把这份文件（　　）给张秘书。

3. 这件衣服是我昨天（　　）一家小店时买的。

4. 这位歌星新专辑的（　　）量超过八百万张,创下了亚洲新纪录。

5. 小偷偷她的钱包时,她只顾打电话,完全没有（　　）。

## 练习五.写出下列词语的同义词

1. 发誓(　　)　　2. 谴责(　　)
3. 按期(　　)　　4. 辛苦(　　)
5. 早晚(　　)

## 练习六.写出下列词语的反义词

1. 倒退(　　)　　2. 赞美(　　)
3. 将来(　　)　　4. 多数(　　)
5. 富裕(　　)

## 答案

**练习一.**
1.yù　　2.lǚ　　3.jué　　4.qiǎn　　5.qiàn

**练习二.**
1. 羡　2. 现　3. 线　4. 到　5. 倒

**练习三.**
1. 富裕　2. 富有　3. 区别　4. 分别　5. 赞扬
6. 赞美　7. 偶尔　8. 偶然　9. 具有　10. 具备

**练习四.**
1. 发誓　2. 转交　3. 路过　4. 发行　5. 发觉
6. 转化　7. 度过　8. 发布　9. 转让　10. 发表

**练习五.**
1. 起誓　2. 指责　3. 按时　4. 辛劳　5. 迟早

**练习六.**
1. 前进　2. 耻笑　3. 过去　4. 少数　5. 贫穷

# 8月 第4周的学习内容

**星期一**

## 掌握 zhǎngwò （甲）动

grasp

**常用搭配**

掌握一门语言 to master a language

**用法示例**

她已全面掌握了这一学科。

She has a comprehensive grasp of the subject.

我们完全掌握了形势。

We have the situation well in hand.

谁掌握国家的最高权力？

Who holds sovereign power in the state?

## 用处 yòngchu ◉用途 yòngtú （乙）名

use

**常用搭配**

有很大用处 be of great use

**用法示例**

这本参考书对我有什么用处吗？

Is this reference book of any use to me?

这个机器对我们没有多大用处。

This machine is not of much use to us.

## 行 háng （乙）量

row; line

**常用搭配**

一行汉字 a line of Chinese characters

第一行 the first row

**用法示例**

这一页有多少行字？

How many lines of text are there on this page?

军官让士兵们站成两行。

The officer ordered soldiers to stand in two lines.

## 勉强 miǎnqiǎng （丙）形／动

① reluctant ② force sb. to; do with difficulty

**常用搭配**

勉强同意 agree reluctantly

勉强的微笑 a reluctant smile

勉强通过测验 complete the test with difficulty

**用法示例**

他勉强答应了。

He gave a reluctant promise.

我们的钱只能勉强维持到周末。

We had barely enough money to last us through the weekend.

如果他不愿意去，不要勉强他。

If he doesn't wish to go, do not force him.

## 预告 yùgào ◉预报 yùbào （丙）动／名

① herald ② advance notice

**常用搭配**

预告节目 an advance program

新书预告 advance notice of new books

**用法示例**

嫩枝预告春天的到来。

The first buds herald the coming ofspring.

我有一份电影预告。

I have an advance notice of the coming movies.

## 预防 yùfáng ◉防止 fángzhǐ （丙）动

prevent; take precautions against

**常用搭配**

预防疾病 prevent a disease

预防措施 preventive measures

**用法示例**

预防胜于治疗。

Prevention is better than cure.

我们不得不采取预防措施。

We had to take preventive measures.

这种疫苗是用来预防传染病的。

The vaccine was used to take precautions against infection.

## 攻读 gōngdú （丁）动

major in a field; study assiduously

**常用搭配**

攻读博士学位 proceed to a doctorate

刻苦攻读 study diligently

**用法示例**

我在那所大学攻读物理学。

I am studying physics at that university.

他想攻读文学硕士学位。

He wanted to go on to an M.A.

他哥哥正刻苦攻读相对论。
His brother is assiduous in the study of relativity.

yòngtú
**用途** （丙）名

use

**常用搭配**
多用途工具 a tool with several uses

**用法示例**
这台机器有多种用途。
The uses of this machine are manifold.
这笔钱有专门用途：建造新剧院。
The money is to be used for one specific purpose: the building of the new theatre.

gōngguān
**攻关** （丁）动

tackle a key problem

**常用搭配**
攻关小组 a group that researches critical problems.
科研攻关 tackle a scientific research project

**用法示例**
专家组正在对这个项目进行攻关。
A group of experts are trying to tackling the critical problems of the project.
他是该项目攻关小组的成员。
He is a member of the group that researches the critical problems of the project.

gōngguān
**公关** （丁）名

public relations

**常用搭配**
公关公司 a company in PR
公关小姐 PR lady

**用法示例**
她在公关部工作。
She works in the PR department.
他是一名公关专家。
He is an expert in public relations.

miǎnlì　　　　gǔlì
**勉励** 圖 鼓励 （丁）动

encourage

**常用搭配**
勉励他刻苦学习 encourage him to study hard

**用法示例**
他经常勉励我要努力工作。
He often exhorts me to work hard.
校长勉励学生参加竞赛。
The headmaster encouraged us to enter the competition.

xiá'ài
**狭隘** （丁）形

narrow；parochial

**常用搭配**
狭隘的眼界 parochial outlook　　心胸狭隘 narrow-minded

**用法示例**
她对宗教的见解很狭隘。
She has very narrow ideas about religion.
他很狭隘，所以没几个朋友。
He is narrow-minded so he has few friends.

 词义辨析

**用途、用处**

　　"用途"和"用处"都是名词，表示使用的目的和应用的范围。"用途"是书面语，只用于物；"用处"多用于口语，可以用于物，也可以用于人，用于人时表示人所发挥的作用。例如：①这件工具有什么用途？②这个报告对我没什么用处。

　　Both 用途 and 用处 are nouns, indicating "the purpose and scope of use". 用途 is often used in writing and is applied to things only; while 用处 is more colloquial and is applied to both things and people. 用处 usually stresses the function of somebody when it is applied to a person. For example: ① What use does this tool have? ② The report is not of any use to me.

 练习

**练习一、根据拼音写汉字，根据汉字写拼音**

( )ài ( )tú gōng ( ) miǎn ( ) zhǎng ( )
狭( ) 用( )( )读 ( )强 ( )握

**练习二、搭配连线**

(1) 预防        A. 狭隘
(2) 科研        B. 外语
(3) 掌握        C. 同意
(4) 勉强        D. 攻关
(5) 心胸        E. 疾病

**练习三、从今天学习的生词中选择合适的词填空**

1. 他刚好考了 60 分，_____通过了考试。
2. 总统给这位小学生回了信，_____他好好学习。
3. 我看了电视节目_____，今天晚上没什么值得看的节目。
4. 我们要定期消毒，保持室内干净整洁，_____疾病传播。
5. 他申请到奖学金，去哈佛大学_____硕士学位了。
6. 根据他的特长，领导把他调到了公司的_____部，负责对外联络。
7. 工程现在已经进入_____阶段，大家注意不要在这个关键时刻出问题。
8. 竹子的_____十分广泛，可以做工艺品、家具、厨房用具等等。
9. 这个人又自私又_____，他只关心自己的利益和感受。
10. 经过一年的学习，他已基本_____电脑技术，现在已经可以熟练地操作电脑了。

**答案**

**练习一：**
略

**练习二：**
(1) E    (2)D    (3)B    (4)C    (5)A

**练习三：**
1. 勉强    2. 勉励    3. 预告    4. 预防    5. 攻读
6. 公关    7. 攻关    8. 用途    9. 狭隘    10. 掌握

---

 星期二

jièshào
**介绍** （甲）动

① introduction ② introduce

**常用搭配**

自我介绍 introduce oneself
把某人介绍给…… introduced somebody to…
介绍信 a letter of introduction

**用法示例**

他向我们简要地介绍了他的公司。
He gave us a brief introduction to his company.
她把我介绍给她的朋友。
She introduced me to her friend.
这本杂志里有一篇介绍中国的文章。
There is an introduction to China in this magazine.

gōngkāi
**公开** （乙）形/动

① public；open ② make public

**常用搭配**

公开赛 an open competition    公开信 an open letter

**用法示例**

我不喜欢在公开场合演说，太难为情了。
I don't like making speeches in public, it's so embarrassing.
他第一次就此事件发表公开表态。
He made his first public statement about the affair.
他不爱他的妻子，这是一个公开的秘密。
It is an open secret that he doesn't love his wife.

tái
**台** （乙）名/量

① platform；station ② measure word for some machines or performances

**常用搭配**

广播电台 radio station    站台／讲台 platform
一台电视机 a TV set    一台电脑 a computer
一台话剧 a stage play

**用法示例**

舞台上有很多聚光灯。
There are many spotlights on the stage.
他把球踢到看台上了。
He kicked the ball to the stand.
他在电视台工作，而他的爱人在气象台工作。
He works in a TV station and his wife works in a weather station.
昨天我们去欣赏了一台歌剧。
Yesterday we went to enjoy an opera.

**gòngxiàn**
# 贡献 （丁）动／名
① contribution ② contribute

**常用搭配**

为……贡献力量 dedicate one's life to…
为……作出贡献 make a contribution to…

**用法示例**

他为祖国作出了重要的贡献。
He has made an important contribution to his country.
她对国家的贡献极大。
Her service to the state has been immense.
他决心为祖国的教育事业贡献力量。
He decided to dedicate his life to the educational cause of his country.

**fùqiáng**
# 富强 （丁）形
rich and powerful

**常用搭配**

繁荣富强 prosperous and strong

**用法示例**

中国日益富强。
China is prospering with each passing day.
希望我的祖国更加富强。
I hope my country becomes more wealthy and powerful.

**chíjiǔ**
# 持久 （丙）形
lasting; enduring

**常用搭配**

持久的和平 lasting peace

**用法示例**

这个协议将为持久和平铺路。
This agreement will pave the way for lasting peace.
他怀疑这场婚姻能否持久。
He wondered if the marriage would last long.

**tuījiàn**
# 推荐 ◎引荐 （丙）动
recommend

**常用搭配**

推荐他做那项工作 recommend him for the job

**用法示例**

你能为我推荐一本好字典吗？
Can you recommend to me a good dictionary?
我推荐她代表我们出席会议。
I nominate her to represent us at the meeting.
我将给你推荐一家新旅馆。
I will recommend a new hotel for you.

**yáoyuǎn**
# 遥远 （丙）形
distant; remote

**常用搭配**

遥远的地方 distant places
遥远的未来 the remote future

**用法示例**

他想，那些日子现在显得多么遥远啊。
How distant that time seems now, he reflected.
宇宙飞船向一颗遥远的行星飞去。
The spaceship flys to a distant planet.

**fèngxiàn**
# 奉献 （丁）动
devote; dedicate

**常用搭配**

为……奉献生命 devote one's life to…
无私奉献 selfless devotion

**用法示例**

他的一生都奉献给了科学研究事业。
He devoted his whole life to scientific research.
他的奉献精神值得我们大家学习。
His dedication should be studied by us all.

**juānxiàn**      **juānzèng**
# 捐献 ◎捐赠 （丁）动
to donate; to contribute

**常用搭配**

捐献图书 donate books    无私地捐献 donate selflessly

**用法示例**

我们每个人都向红十字会捐献了十元钱。
Each of us contributed ￥10 to the Red Cross.
这个商人捐献给医院很多钱。
The businessman donated a lot of money to the hospital.
我们要为贫民捐献食品和衣服。
We will contribute food and clothing for the poor.

**chíxù**      **zhōngduàn**
# 持续 ◎中断 （丁）动
last

**常用搭配**

持续了多久？ How long did it last?

**用法示例**

这场战争持续了四年。
The war lasted for four years.
罢工持续了三天。
The strike lasted for three days.
这雨不会持续很久。
The rain will not last long.
炎热的天气将持续到九月。
The hot weather will last till September.

**xiázhǎi**      **kuānkuò**
# 狭窄 ◎宽阔 （丁）形
narrow

**常用搭配**

狭窄的街道 narrow street

狭窄的走廊 narrow corridor

**用法示例**

狭窄的山路崎岖不平。

The mountain path is narrow and rugged.

他们得钻过狭窄的隧道。

They had to worm their way through the narrow tunnel.

他在狭窄的窗台上很难保持平衡。

He balanced precariously on the narrow window-ledge.

 词义辨析

**奉献、捐献**

　　"奉献"和"捐献"都是动词,都有献出某物的意思。"奉献"的宾语一般是抽象名词,比如奉献青春、奉献爱心等;而"捐献"的宾语一般是钱或物,如捐献衣物。他把全部积蓄都捐献给了祖国。

　　Both 奉献 and 捐献 are verbs, indicating "to offer as a tribute", "to make a contribution". The object of 奉献 is usually an abstract noun, e.g. "奉献青春" (devote one's youthful time), "奉献爱心" (devote one's love), etc.; while the object of 捐献 is usually things or money, e.g. "捐献衣物" (to contribute clothing). He gave all of his savings to his country.

 练习

**练习一、根据拼音写汉字,根据汉字写拼音**

( )jiàn ( )xù juān ( ) yáo ( )( )shào
推( ) 持( )( )献 ( )远 介( )

**练习二、搭配连线**

(1) 自我　　　　　　　　A. 力量
(2) 贡献　　　　　　　　B. 奉献
(3) 繁荣　　　　　　　　C. 介绍
(4) 无私　　　　　　　　D. 图书
(5) 捐献　　　　　　　　E. 富强

**练习三、从今天学习的生词中选择合适的词填空**

1. 科学家为人类的发展进步做出了巨大的_____。
2. 他把自己的一生都_____给了环境保护事业。
3. 他把自己收藏的文物都无偿_____给了国家。
4. 这位总统在自传中_____了他处理国家危机时的一些细节。
5. 我们只能通过电视和电影了解生活在_____的北极的动物。
6. 摆脱战争的威胁以后,人们希望国家和平发展的形势能够_____。
7. 祝愿我们亲爱的祖国繁荣_____,人民生活幸福!
8. 这位教授_____他的学生去研究所工作。
9. 战争_____了五年,这个国家的基础设施全被破坏了。
10. 前面是一条_____的通道,大家通过时要小心。

**答案**

**练习一:**
略

**练习二:**
(1) C　　　(2)A　　　(3)E　　　(4)B　　　(5)D

**练习三:**

1. 贡献　　2. 奉献　　3. 捐献　　4. 公开　　5. 遥远
6. 持久　　7. 富强　　8. 推荐　　9. 持续　　10. 狭窄

**星期三**

liánxì
## 联系 （甲）动／名
① contact；be in touch with ② relation；connection

**常用搭配**
保持联系 keep in touch
和……失去联系 lose contact with somebody
联系人 linkman

**用法示例**
她一到就和我联系了。
She contacted me as soon as she arrived.
这两个概念之间有什么联系？
What is the connection between the two ideas?
他们和我保持着密切的联系。
They keep in close touch with me.

pòhuài
## 破坏 （乙）动
destroy；damage；ruin

**常用搭配**
破坏房屋 damage houses    破坏庄稼 damage crops

**用法示例**
据报道，珊瑚礁正在遭受破坏。
It is reported that the coral reefs are being destroyed.
污染破坏了臭氧层。
The pollution had destroyed ozone layer.
敌人曾试图破坏这座城市。
The enemy tried to destroy the city.

cè
## 册 （乙）量
① measure word for books ② volume

**常用搭配**
课本的第一册 the first volume of textbooks
一千册书 one thousand copies of a book

**用法示例**
这本书出版社已印了 10000 册。
The publisher has printed10000 copies of the book.
这本参考书非常有用，我们人手一册。
This reference book is very useful. Each of us has one.

chījīng
## 吃惊 （乙）动
surprise；amaze

**常用搭配**
令人吃惊的消息 surprising news

**用法示例**
我很吃惊。
I was amazed.

他的粗鲁使我大吃一惊。
I was astonished by his rudeness.
结果非常令人吃惊。
The result is quite startling.
我吃惊地看着他，没想到又见到他了。
I looked at him in surprise. I didn't expect to see him again.

shìfēi
## 是非 （丙）名
right and wrong

**常用搭配**
分辨是非 discriminate right from wrong
是非观念 sense of what is right and wrong

**用法示例**
我们应该分清是非。
We should make a distinction between right and wrong.
他不辨是非。
He doesn't know the difference between right and wrong.
他们正在争论这个事件的是非曲直。
They are disputing about the rights and wrongs of the case.

shìfǒu
## 是否 （丙）副
whether

**用法示例**
问他是否明白了。
Ask him whether he has understood.
警察问我是否有枪。
The police asked me if I owned a gun.
只有时间才能证明你是否正确。
Only time will tell if you are right.
问题是他是否同意。
The question is whether or not he agrees.

chīlì
## 吃力 ◎ 费劲 fèijìn （丙）形
with strenuous effort

**常用搭配**
学得很吃力 to have difficulty in learning
吃力地走 walk with effort

**用法示例**
老人很吃力地坐了起来。
The old man sat up with great effort.
"我嗓子疼"，他吃力地说。
"I've got a sore throat," he wheezed.
他感到学法语很吃力。
He thought French was difficult to learn.

liánluò
## 联络 （丙）动
get in touch；contact

**常用搭配**

跟他联络 make contact with him

与他保持联络 keep in touch with him

**用法示例**

警察通过无线电互相联络。

The police communicate with each other by radio.

他们用电话跟总部联络。

They make contact with headquarters by telephone.

我一到那里,就会跟你联络。

Once arriving there, I'll make contact with you.

**yāzhì**

## 压制 　　　　　 ⏎扶植　　　　（丙）动

**fúzhí**

suppress; inhibit

**常用搭配**

压制邪念 inhibit wrong desires

压制他人 suppress others

**用法示例**

我们应该鼓励年轻人,而不是压制他们。

We should encourage young men instead of suppressing them.

谁也无法压制人民的自由意愿。

No one can suppress the free will of the people.

**kàngyì**

## 抗议　　　　　　　　　（丙）动/名

protest

**常用搭配**

抗议者 protester

**用法示例**

他们向市长提出抗议说税款过高。

They protested to the mayor that the taxes were too high.

他们表示强烈抗议。

They expressed their vehement protest.

我对他的粗暴提出抗议。

I made an objection to his rudeness.

**yāyì**

## 压抑　　　　　 ⏎宣泄　　　　（丁）动

**xuānxiè**

constrain; oppress

**常用搭配**

觉得压抑 feel constrained

**用法示例**

在这个窄狭的房间里面我感到压抑。

I am stifled in this close room.

他的童年是压抑而孤独的。

His childhood was repressed and solitary.

**táoqì**

## 淘气　　　　　 ⏎调皮　　　　（丁）形

**tiáopí**

naughty

**常用搭配**

淘气的男孩 naughty boy

**用法示例**

他是班里最淘气的学生。

He is the naughtiest student in the class.

老师要惩罚那些淘气的孩子。

The teacher will punish the mischievous boys.

他小的时候非常淘气。

He was very naughty in his boyhood.

 **词义辨析**

**压抑、压制**

　　"压抑"和"压制"都是动词,都有抑制的意思。"压抑"指精神或心理上受到限制,强调感受,往往是被动的;"压制"是利用职权或舆论进行限制,强调行为,往往是主动的。例如:①与他们一起工作的时候,我有一种压抑的感觉。②政府不能压制人民的自由意愿。

　　Both 压抑 and 压制 are verbs, meaning "to oppress". 压抑 indicates to hold back in spirit or mind, stresses feeling, and is usually used in the passive voice; while 压制 indicates "to hold back by authority or public voice", stresses action, and is usually used in the active voice. For example: ① I have a feeling of oppression when I work with them. ② The government should not suppress the free will of the people.

 **练习**

**练习一、根据拼音写汉字，根据汉字写拼音**

( )luò  ( )yì  ( )yì  táo( )  pò( )

联( )  压( )  抗( )  ( )气  ( )坏

**练习二、搭配连线**

(1) 是非            A. 压抑

(2) 感到            B. 环境

(3) 受到            C. 压制

(4) 保持            D. 观念

(5) 破坏            E. 联系

**练习三、从今天学习的生词中选择合适的词填空**

1. 这个年轻人的 _____ 观念很强,他决不会做损人利己的事。

2. 他问你这个周末 _____ 有时间? 他想请你看电影。

3. 过度的放牧和砍伐森林,严重 _____ 了生态平衡。

4. 这套教材分为三 _____,我已经学完其中的两 _____ 了。

5. 他年纪大了,学习语言比较 _____。

6. 现在群众有怨气,我们不能过分 _____,要尽量疏导这种情绪。

7. 很多市民坐在市政府门前,对提高税率表示 _____。

8. 他 _____ 着心中的怒气,尽量平静地听她抱怨。

9. 他没在家,手机也关了,我 _____ 不到他。

10. 中国人觉得 _____ 的孩子比较聪明,真的是这样吗?

**答案**

**练习一:**

略

**练习二:**

(1) D      (2)A      (3)C      (4)E      (5)B

**练习三:**

1. 是非    2. 是否    3. 破坏    4. 册,册    5. 吃力

6. 压制    7. 抗议    8. 压抑    9. 联络／联系

10. 淘气

---

 **星期四**

**fāshēng**

**发生**  （甲）动

happen; take place

**常用搭配**

发生事故 an accident happens

发生变化 to have changed

**用法示例**

这种事可能发生在任何人身上。

It can happen to anyone.

我知道发生了什么事。

I know what has happened.

我决不对发生的事情负责。

In no way am I responsible for what has happened.

**xúnzhǎo**

**寻找**  （乙）动

search for; look for

**常用搭配**

寻找线索 search for clues

寻找走失的孩子 looking for a lost child

**用法示例**

他打开了手电筒,寻找钥匙。

He turned on the torch to look for his keys.

我在人群中寻找她,但没看到。

I looked for her in the crowd but couldn't find her.

他们计划去岛上寻找财宝。

They were going to search for treasure on the island.

**xùnsù**

**迅速**  圓**快速** kuàisù  （乙）形

speedy; quick

**常用搭配**

迅速的变化 a speedy change

反应迅速 react rapidly

迅速采取措施 to take steps swiftly

**用法示例**

她迅速开车向小偷撞去。

She quickly drove the car towards the thief.

他迅速的反应让我们吃了一惊。

His swift reaction surprised us.

她去世的消息迅速传开了。

The news of her death circulated quickly.

**xiāngdāng**

**相当**  （乙）形

① equivalent to ② considerably ③ quite

**常用搭配**

能力相当 equal in ability

相当便宜 very cheap
相当好 quite good

**用法示例**

一华里相当于半公里。
One li is equal to half a kilometer.
他与你棋艺相当吗？
Is he your equal in chess?
对我们来说这个问题相当难。
The problem is of considerable difficultly to us.

xiāngsì
**相似** 类似 （乙）形

① similar ② resemble

**常用搭配**

与／跟……相似 be similar to...
相似的习惯 similar habit
相似的发型 similar hairstyle

**用法示例**

她和她姐姐外貌相似，但性格不同。
She resembles her sister in appearance, but not in character.
这儿的气候和北京非常相似。
The climate here is like that of Beijing.
这两个男孩有某些相似之处。
There is a degree of resemblance between the two boys.

dàzhòng
**大众** （丙）名

① the masses ② general public

**常用搭配**

大众教育 mass education
大众媒介 mass media

**用法示例**

公园对大众开放。
The gardens are open to the public.
他被大众视为英雄。
He was regarded as a hero by the common people.

dàzhì
**大致** （丙）形

roughly; approximately

**常用搭配**

大致的分析 an approximate analysis
大致了解 know sth roughly

**用法示例**

我很高兴地发现我的意见与你大致相同。
I am glad to find myself in general accord with your opinions.
大致有 50 人。
There were roughly 50 people.
美国国会大致相当于英国议会。
The American Congress corresponds roughly to the British Parliament.

bàofā
**爆发** （丙）动

break out; erupt

**常用搭配**

火山爆发 eruption of a volcano
爆发出一阵欢呼声 burst into cheers

**用法示例**

两国之间爆发了战争。
The war broke out between the two countries.
他们爆发出阵阵笑声。
They burst into peals of laughter.
那儿正爆发禽流感。
There has been an outbreak of bird flu.

chuàn
**串** （丙）动／量

① to string ② bunch

**常用搭配**

串珠子 string the beads
一串葡萄 a bunch of grapes
一串钥匙 a bunch of keys
一串珠子 a string of beads

**用法示例**

她用尼龙线把扣子串了起来。
She strung the buttons with nylon line.
这个项链是用一串珍珠做成的。
The necklace is made of a string of pearls.

xiāngděng
**相等** （丁）动

equal; be equivalent

**常用搭配**

大小相等 equal in size

**用法示例**

他和我力气相等，但智力不同。
He equals me in strength but not in intelligence.
他们俩体重相等。
They two are equal in weight.

xúnqiú
**寻求** 谋求 （丁）动
móuqiú

to seek; quest for

**常用搭配**

寻求真理 seek truth
寻求成功的方法／途径 seek a key to success

**用法示例**

科学家仍在寻求治疗流感的方法。
Scientists are still searching for a cure to the flu.
他们正在寻求改进的方法。
They are searching for a way to improve.
科学家们正在研究火星的照片，寻求生命的迹象。
Scientists are studying the photographs of Mars for signs of life.

táopǎo
# 逃跑
táotuō
⊜ 逃脱　　　（丁）动

escape; run away

**常用搭配**

企图逃跑 try to escape　　偷偷地逃跑 to escape secretly

**用法示例**

他带着赃物逃跑了。

He escaped with his plunder.

据报道，三名犯人从监狱逃跑了。

It is reported that three prisoners escaped from prison.

警察到这里的时候，小偷已逃跑了。

The thief had run off by the time the police arrived here.

 **词义辨析**

**发生、暴发**

"发生"和"暴发"都是动词。"发生"表示一般事物的产生或出现；"暴发"强调重大事件的突然来临及情绪、力量的突然发作。例如：①这个事故发生在我家房子的外面。②昨天地铁里发生了一件有趣的事。③那座火山在沉睡多年后爆发了。④两个朋友相互猜疑，后来便暴发了一场争吵。

Both 发生 and 暴发 are verbs. 发生 usually means "something happens or occurs"; while 暴发 indicates "an important thing or event takes place suddenly or emerges violently". For example: ① The accident happened outside my house. ② A funny thing happened in the subway yesterday. ③ The volcano erupted after years of dormancy. ④ The two friends didn't believe each other and a quarrel broke out between them.

 **练习**

**练习一、根据拼音写汉字，根据汉字写拼音**

（　）sì　　bào（　）　（　）qiú　　táo（　）　xùn（　）
相（　）　（　）发　寻（　）　（　）跑　（　）速

**练习二、搭配连线**

(1) 企图　　　　　　　A. 爆发
(2) 火山　　　　　　　B. 媒介
(3) 大众　　　　　　　C. 事故
(4) 发生　　　　　　　D. 迅速
(5) 反应　　　　　　　E. 逃跑

**练习三、从今天学习的生词中选择合适的词填空**

1. 随着中国经济的快速发展，越来越多的外国人到中国来_____发展机会。

2. 母亲_____了三年，终于找到了丢失的孩子。

3. 趁警察不注意，那个小偷_____了。

4. 这两个选手实力_____，很难预测谁会获胜。

5. 两种方法算下来，结果_____，都是7。

6. 主持人刚说出歌星的名字，观众席中就_____出一阵欢呼声。

7. 我同意他的意见，我对这个问题的看法和他的_____相同。

8. 这座房子的主人自杀以后，这里曾_____过一些奇怪的事，有人说这是"鬼屋"。

9. 他和哥哥的长相十分_____，可他们的性格却完全不同。

10. 车祸发生后，医生_____赶到，抢救受伤的人员。

# 答案

**练习一：**
略

**练习二：**
(1) E　　　(2)A　　　(3)B　　　(4)C　　　(5)D

**练习三：**
1. 寻求　　2. 寻找　　3. 逃跑　　4. 相当　　5. 相等
6. 爆发　　7. 大致　　8. 发生　　9. 相似　　10. 迅速

**星期五**

bǐaoxiàn
**表现** （甲）动／名

① show ② manifestation; performance

**常用搭配**

表现得好 behave well

表现得差 behave badly

**用法示例**

他在面对危险的时候表现得很镇静。

He was very calm in the face of the danger.

他的慷慨在困境中表现了出来。

His generosity manifests itself in times of need.

那孩子在聚会上的表现很差。

The child behaved badly at the party.

máobìng
**毛病** ⑤优点 （乙）名

shortcoming; fault

**常用搭配**

坏毛病 bad habit

……出毛病了 There is something wrong with...

**用法示例**

不要动不动就挑毛病。

Don't be so ready to find fault.

这台机器出毛病了。

There is something wrong with the machine.

你惟一的毛病是马虎。

Your only fault is carelessness.

yàng
**样** （乙）量

kind; sort

**常用搭配**

各种各样 all kinds of

几样水果 some kinds of fruits

**用法示例**

这个商店卖各种各样的工具。

The shop sells tools of all sorts.

市场里的每样商品都很便宜。

Every article in the market is very cheap.

我不喜欢这样的衣服。

I don't like this sorf of clothing.

xiàngmù
**项目** （乙）名

item; project

**常用搭配**

研究项目 research project

规划项目 planned project

**用法示例**

我想感谢每一个为这个项目辛勤工作的人。

I'd like to thank everyone for their hard work on the project.

你知道那个新的合作项目吗?

Did you hear about the new cooperative project?

政府已经批准了这个项目。

The government has ratified the project.

máodùn
**矛盾** ⑥统一 （乙）名／形

① contradiction ② contradictory

**常用搭配**

矛盾的观点 conflicting views

不可调和的矛盾 irreconcilable conflict

与……相矛盾 in contradiction with...

**用法示例**

他的叙述跟事实是矛盾的。

His remark was contradictory to the truth.

这个报道与我们昨天听到的有矛盾。

The report contradicts what we heard yesterday.

他对那些事情的说法前后矛盾。

His account of the events was inconsistent.

tǔdàng
**妥当** ⑥恰当 （丙）形

appropriate; proper

**常用搭配**

准备妥当 be well prepared

**用法示例**

他的计划似乎不够妥当。

His scheme doesn't seem sound enough.

他们正试图寻求妥当的方式来处理这些问题。

They are trying to seek a proper way to deal with these issues.

táobì
**逃避** （丙）动

evade

**常用搭配**

逃避追捕 evade arrest    逃避责任 evade responsibility

**用法示例**

逃避兵役是可耻的。

It is dishonorable to shirk military service.

他说他从没想过要逃避责任。

He said he had never wanted to evade his duty

振作起来! 不要逃避现实。

Cheer up! Do not turn a blind eye to reality.

tǐxiàn
**体现** （丙）动

embody; reflect

**常用搭配**

体现了他的品格 embody his moral character

体现出她的智慧 reflect her intelligence

**用法示例**

这个国家的宪法体现了自由和平等的理想。

The country's constitution embodies the ideals of freedom and equality.

这篇文章体现了他对这一事件的全部看法。

The article embodied all his opinions on the incident.

这封信体现了他的真实想法。

The letter reflects how he really thinks?

## 奴隶 *núlì* （丙）名

slave

**常用搭配**

奴隶主 slave owner　　废除奴隶制 the abolition of slavery

**用法示例**

很久以前,许多黑人作为奴隶被掠到美洲。

A long time ago, many black people were taken to America as slaves.

他把妻子当作奴隶看待。

He treats his wife as a slave.

这个奴隶梦想着成为一个自由人。

This slave dreamed of becoming a free man.

## 妥善 *tuǒshàn* （丁）形

proper; appropriate

**常用搭配**

妥善安排 arrange properly

**用法示例**

问题已得到妥善解决。

The problem has been solved well.

我们必须妥善处理这些政治问题。

We must deal with these political issues carefully and skillfully.

## 妥协 *tuǒxié* ◎让步 *ràngbù* （丁）动

compromise

**常用搭配**

与……妥协 make a compromise with

达成妥协 strike a compromise

**用法示例**

我宁死不妥协。

I would rather die than compromise.

政府不会在工资制度方面与工人妥协。

The government won't compromise with workers on the wage system.

## 淘汰 *táotài* （丁）动

to eliminate (in a competition)

**常用搭配**

淘汰赛 elimination series

---

**用法示例**

他们队在第一轮就被淘汰了。

Their team was eliminated in the first round.

上次的考核淘汰了多少应聘者?

How many applicants were washed out in the last examination?

 **词义辨析**

**妥善、妥当**

"妥善"和"妥当"都是形容词,都有适当和恰当的意思,都可以做状语和补语。但是"妥当"还常常作谓语和定语,"妥善"很少作谓语和定语。例如:①他妥当／妥善地解决了这些问题。②我有一个妥当的办法来解决问题。③我觉得这个主意不太妥当。

Both 妥善 and 妥当 are adjectives, meaning "proper, fitting", and both can serve as an adverbial or a complement. 妥当 usually functions as a predicate or an attributive; while 妥善 seldom functions as a predicate or attributive. For example: ① He solved these problems properly. ② I have a proper way to solve the problem. ③ I don't think this idea is very proper.

 **练习**

**练习一、根据拼音写汉字,根据汉字写拼音**

( )lì ( )tài ( )dùn tuǒ ( ) xiàng ( )

奴( ) 淘( ) 矛( ) ( ) 当 ( )目

**练习二、搭配连线**

(1) 达成　　　　　　A. 责任

(2) 妥善　　　　　　B. 妥协

(3) 逃避　　　　　　C. 妥当

(4) 科研　　　　　　D. 安排

(5) 准备　　　　　　E. 项目

**练习三、从今天学习的生词中选择合适的词填空**

1. 我的电脑突然出 _____ 了,我能用用你的吗?

2. 顾客和商家总是存在 _____ ,顾客总想少花钱,商家总想多赚钱。

3. 由于事前做了 _____ 安排,活动进展得非常顺利。

4. 谈判双方态度强硬,都不愿 _____ ,所以最终没能达成一致意见。

5. 以前的老板把我们当成了 _____ ,总想方设法地让我们多干活,而且还不尊重我们。

6. 新颁布的法规 _____ 了政府对残疾人的关怀。

7. 强者生存,弱者被 _____ 是自然的生存法则。

8. 这件事你认为怎么 _____ 就怎么办吧。

9. 工作中出现问题的时候,我们首先要考虑如何改进,而不

是 _____ 责任。

10. 这段音乐 _____ 了人们在丰收时的喜悦心情。

答案

**练习一：**

略

**练习二：**

| (1) B | (2)D | (3)A | (4)E | (5)C |

**练习三：**

| 1. 毛病 | 2. 矛盾 | 3. 妥善 | 4. 妥协 | 5. 奴隶 |
| 6. 体现 | 7. 淘汰 | 8. 妥当 | 9. 逃避 | 10. 表现 |

## 第8月,第4周的练习

**练习一.根据词语给加点的字注音**

1.( )  2.( )  3.( )  4.( )  5.( )

勉强　富强　妥当　相当　推荐

**练习二.根据拼音完成词语**

táo　　táo　　yì　　yì　　yáo

1.( )跑 2.( )气 3.抗( )4.压( )5.( )远

**练习三.辨析并选择合适的词填空**

1. 这东西先别扔,迟早会有( )的。（用途、用处）

2. 这是新研发的具有多种( )的新型电子仪器。（用途、用处）

3. 家属按照他生前的愿望把眼角膜( )给了那个失明的孩子。（奉献、捐献）

4. 战士们把青春( )给了祖国的边防事业。（奉献、捐献）

5. 最近,他工作不太顺利,心情比较( )。（压制、压抑）

6. 院长利用自己的职位( )年轻有为的副院长,唯恐他取代自己的职位。（压制、压抑）

7. 跟十年前相比,北京( )了巨大的变化。（发生、爆发）

8. 洪水过后,紧接着( )了一场可怕的瘟疫。（发生、爆发）

9. 虽然这样做比较麻烦,但这是最( )的办法。（妥善、妥当）

10. 事故发生后,警察和医生马上对现场进行了( )处理。（妥善、妥当）

**练习四.选词填空**

是非　持久　狭隘　勉强　相当
是否　持续　狭窄　勉励　相似

1. 越往上走,山路越( ),有的地方还不到一米宽。

2. 两天以后我们才能确认试验( )成功。

3. 这场辩论已经( )一个上午了,估计快结束了。

4. 如果不开发新的产品,公司的繁荣将不会( )。

5. 这些人热情而正直,有很强的( )观念,相信他们会支持你从事这项正义的事业。

6. 我们俩对很多事都有相同或( )的看法,所以很谈得来。

7. 本来父亲希望我在他的公司工作,经过再三劝说,他才( )同意我来北京留学。

8. 她思想( ),个人利益至上,从不考虑集体利益。

9. 他在北京学习了四年,现在的汉语水平已经( )高了。

10. 在艰难的岁月里,他们俩互相( ),互相支持,终于取得了今天的成就。

**练习五.量词填空**

行　　台　　册　　串　　样

1. 老板,苹果、香蕉、葡萄,给我一( )来三斤。

2. 这套书分上、中、下三( )。

3. 我家的冰箱不能用了,我想再买一( )新的。

4. 刚学写汉字时,安娜一小时写不了几( )字,几个月之后,就好多了。

5. 我在桌子上发现了一( )钥匙,不知道是谁丢的。

**练习六.写出下列词语的同义词**

| 1. 妥协( ) | 2. 淘气( ) |
| 3. 捐献( ) | 4. 迅速( ) |
| 5. 预告( ) | |

**练习七.写出下列词语的反义词**

| 1. 毛病( ) | 2. 压制( ) |
| 3. 持续( ) | 4. 狭窄( ) |
| 5. 压抑( ) | |

答案

**练习一.**

| 1.qiǎng | 2.qiáng | 3.dàng | 4.dāng | 5.jiàn |

**练习二.**

| 1. 逃 | 2. 淘 | 3. 议 | 4. 抑 | 5. 遥 |

**练习三.**

| 1. 用处 | 2. 用途 | 3. 捐献 | 4. 奉献 | 5. 压抑 |
| 6. 压制 | 7. 发生 | 8. 爆发 | 9. 妥当 | 10. 妥善 |

**练习四.**

| 1. 狭窄 | 2. 是否 | 3. 持续 | 4. 持久 | 5. 是非 |
| 6. 相似 | 7. 勉强 | 8. 狭隘 | 9. 相当 | 10. 勉励 |

**练习五.**

| 1. 样 | 2. 册 | 3. 台 | 4. 行 | 5. 串 |

**练习六.**

| 1. 让步 | 2. 调皮 | 3. 捐赠 | 4. 快速 | 5. 预报 |

**练习七.**

| 1. 优点 | 2. 扶植 | 3. 中断 | 4. 宽阔 | 5. 宣泄 |

# 附录

## 全书词义辨析包含词汇和页码

## 八月

责任编辑：韩芙芸
封面设计：王　薇
印刷监制：佟汉冬

**图书在版编目（CIP）数据**

HSK 核心词汇天天学 . 中 / 刘东青，马玉红，王鑫编著 . —北京：华语教学出版社，2009
ISBN 978-7-80200-595-2

Ⅰ.H… Ⅱ. 刘… Ⅲ. 汉语—词汇—对外汉语教学—水平考试—自学参考资料
Ⅳ. H195.4

中国版本图书馆 CIP 数据核字（2009）第 089351 号

**HSK 核心词汇天天学·中**

刘东青　马玉红　王鑫　编著
＊
© 华语教学出版社
华语教学出版社出版
（中国北京百万庄大街 24 号　邮政编码 100037）
电话：(86)10-68320585
传真：(86)10-68326333
网址：www.sinolingua.com.cn
电子信箱：hyjx@ sinolingua.com.cn
北京外文印刷厂印刷
2009 年（16 开）第一版
2009 年第一次印刷
（汉英）
ISBN 978-7-80200-595-2
定价：49.00 元